Nurturing Success

NURTURING SUCCESS

Successful Women of Color and Their Daughters

Essie E. Lee

PRAEGER

Westport, Connecticut
London

Library of Congress Cataloging-in-Publication Data

Lee, Essie E.
 Nurturing success : successful women of color and their daughters / Essie E. Lee.
  p. cm.
 Includes bibliographical references and index.
 ISBN 0–275–96033–1 (alk. paper)
  1. Mothers and daughters—United States—Case studies. 2. Minority women—United
States—Case studies. 3. Minority teenagers—United States—Case studies. 4. Successful
people—United States—Case studies. I. Title.
 HQ755.85.L43 2000
 306.874'3—dc21   99–037530

British Library Cataloguing in Publication Data is available.

Library of Congress Catalog Card Number: 99–037530
ISBN: 0–275–96033–1

First published in 2000

Praeger Publishers, 88 Post Road West, Westport, CT 06881
An imprint of Greenwood Publishing Group, Inc.
www.praeger.com

Printed in the United States of America

(∞)™

The paper used in this book complies with the
Permanent Paper Standard issued by the National
Information Standards Organization (Z39.48–1984).

10 9 8 7 6 5 4 3 2 1

Contents

Preface

In 1857 Susan Anthony, in a letter to Elizabeth C. Stanton, wrote that reproduction is the "highest and holiest function." To be a mother, to be a father is the last and highest wish of any human being . . . to reproduce himself and herself, she observed.

How different are daughters' lives today from their mothers' lives? Changes in these relationships over the past decades may be the result of changes in attitudes toward sex and chastity. Young women cohabit in increasing numbers before they marry, and they marry at a later age. Not only do they anticipate working after marriage and motherhood, but their wage-earner role has become increasingly essential to maintain their standard of living. They are having fewer children, and they are divorcing in record numbers (Fischer, 1991).

Some researchers feel that these changes undermine the special mother–daughter bond. These trends may widen the "generation gap" so that mothers' experience may have little relevance to their daughters' actual and future experiences. With all of these changes, is there still a "mother link"—a special bond between mother and daughter?

Interest in the mother–daughter relationship has resulted in a plethora of books on the subject. Most of these books deal with the problems mothers and daughters face in adolescence or in adulthood, and most focus on the negative aspects of these interactions. All address situations found in the main culture population. Future research needs to look beyond prevailing stereotypes and discover a deeper understanding of how ethnicity affects contemporary relationships between mothers and their daughters.

The purpose of this book is to help the general public become aware, become interested in, and understand the positive aspect of the mother–daughter relationship in other cultures. Unlike most books, this one examines 17 mother–daughter relationships within 13 cultures in families across the nation, in preteen to adult age groups of working-class to middle-class and diverse socioeconomic status. These mother–daughter relationships are evaluated by the distance needed to travel from the margins of achievement toward the mainstream, including examination of values, impact of intergenerational kin, and potential role models. The reader will discover different family expectations and behavior associated with ethnicity in this multicultural sample, but the relationships are basically positive and mutually satisfying.

My desire and interest in writing this book stem from years of working with women, including women of color who were often poor, abandoned, abused, neglected, and humiliated but continued to strive for excellence, recognition, self-improvement, and a productive environment. Across the country, thousands of such women can be found. With the help of colleagues and other professionals working in social and community agencies, educational and health facilities, government and private organizations, I have identified this sample of 17 women of color with survivor characteristics and membership in 13 different, specific ethnic groups and have attempted to trace these characteristics in the women they produced—their daughters and their granddaughters. The participants' enthusiasm and willingness to share personal experiences that offer encouragement and hope to the sisterhood are admirable and greatly appreciated.

REFERENCE

Fischer, L. "Between Mothers and Daughters." *Marriage and Family Review* 16 (3/4), 1991.

Introduction

WOMEN OF COLOR

Who Are They?

In 1996 the U.S. Bureau of the Census estimated that 25,654,000 women of color were living in the United States. This total number included 12,327,000 African Americans; 757,000 Native Americans; 3,650,000 Asian Americans; and 8,920,000 Hispanics. The ages of the women were 18 years and older.

What Do They Do?

They care for the frail elderly; they care for the babies and children of working mothers; they tend to the needs of Alzheimer victims; they assist the disabled with self-care; they flip burgers at McDonald's; they clean offices at night; they teach second graders; they are college professors; they are flower and fruit vendors; they bag groceries at checkout counters; they are journalists; they are members of Congress; they are computer experts; one was an astronaut on the *Endeavor* space shuttle in 1992; and recently, they supervised the prenatal care of the mother of the Iowa septuplets. In fact, they do almost everything that many women do, except, at times, the choices are limited.

Many have struggled to adjust to a foreign language and a new culture in a strange environment. There are other adjustments, too, like single parenthood, the decline of public education, inferior housing, neighborhood and social disorganization, fear of local crime and violence, limited health care, unstable and unpredictable income levels due to unemployment and underemployment, preoccupation with the well-being of children in an unsafe environment, lack of child care; a growing feeling of lack of opportunity; and a sense of continuing demoralization, isolation, and racial animosity from the nonminority population daily.

Minority families are considerably more vulnerable to economic hardships as a result of structural conditions and change in their condition over time. Among all groups, families headed by women have lower income levels and are much poorer than families in general.

Despite the provocative and dismal array of hardships confronting women of color and their families, they are not defenseless. Their cultural behaviors are strongly familistic, with high-quality social support provided by family networks offering powerful protective effects on health and emotional well-being. Complex demographic trends are under way as both the low-income and middle-income families of color rapidly increase in number, the former as the result of immigration and high fertility rates, and the latter as a consequence of intergenerational socioeconomic mobility.

The women in this book, like others before them, worked hard to obtain the skills provided by higher education, which can lead to success. Each woman defined success in her own words, and the definitions varied. One author (Hochschild, 1995) defines success as the attainment of a high income, a prestigious job, and economic security but adds that material well-being is only one form of accomplishment. Her definition includes measurement as well as content. Success can be absolute, reaching some goal of well-being. Success can be relative, that is, becoming better off than at some comparison point. Success can be competitive, achieving victory over someone else. Millions of immigrants and internal migrants may pursue their American Dream, and they may reasonably anticipate success as a reward for their hard work. Since success indicates virtue, one also becomes virtuous.

In the following stories the relationship between mothers and daughters among women of color reflects the many strands that have emerged from the experience of immigration to the United States.

To study this unique sample of women, I chose a method that included recruitment, selection, and personal interviews using selected relevant questions. A discussion of this method follows.

METHODS OF THE SURVEY

Choosing the Women

Potential participants were proposed by a variety of organizations, agencies, ethnic societies, journalists, academic institutions, organizations, and individuals representing women's groups. Participants' eligibility (ethnic group, maternal status, employment, and designation as being "successful" by referral agency) was confirmed by telephone interviews and a résumé. Selection was made following a second interview to determine level of interest, understanding of the project, and willingness to participate. The final sample included 17 women (the mothers) and 19 of their daughters, representing 13 different ethnic groups living across the country. Table I.1 shows the demographic data.

The Interviews/Data Collection and Analysis

A questionnaire was developed containing ten areas relating to the six basic research questions. These questions, some open-ended, formed the protocol for the interviews, which were audiotaped and transcribed for analysis. Subject areas of the questionnaire included education, family composition, parental attitudes, mother–daughter relationships, ethnic values, child raising, parenting, intergenerational relationships, and other socioethnic influences. Brief socioethnographic profiles were composed of the subjects. All semi-structured interviews took place in participants' homes and places of employment. Participants were allowed to edit the case studies before publication.

Questions of the Survey

1. How do participants perceive the mother–daughter relationship?
2. What achievement norms are expected and acceptable?
3. In what ways does the role of working mother impact upon the daughter?
4. How do daughters perceive themselves as functioning adolescents, adults?
5. How do mothers cope with conflict between ethnic values and perceived goals?
6. What are participants' definitions of "success"?

Results

Mother–Daughter Relationships

The age and level of maturity of daughter had significant impact upon perceptions of the mother–daughter relationship. For example, six daughters below the ninth grade enjoyed shopping, cooking, storytelling, sewing, and having fun with their mothers. At this age level, mothers planned "special" carefree time and activities for mutual enjoyment. As the daughters reached a critical period—adolescence—they began to assert themselves and voice opinions that were frequently critical of, or in opposition to, their mothers' judgment. Mothers and daughters reported fits of temper, anger, and frus-

Table I.1
Demographics—Mothers

No. of Mothers	Ethnicity	Birthplace	Age	Marital Status	No. of Children	Residence
1	African American	U.S.A.	57	Married	3	Glenarden, MD
1	African American	U.S.A.	45	Married	2	Brooklyn, NY
1	Asian Indian	India	43	Married	2	Sparkhill, NY
1	Chinese American	China	54	Married	2	New York, NY
1	Chinese American	U.S.A.	46	Married	2	San Francisco, CA
1	Cuban American	Cuba	45	Married	2	Miami, FL
1	Dominican Rep. American	Dominican Rep.	53	Married	3	Miami, FL
1	Filipina American	Philippines	50	Divorced	2	San Diego, CA
1	Filipina American	Philippines	48	Married	2	Paramus, NJ
1	Haitian American	Haiti	48	Divorced	2	Brooklyn, NY
1	Japanese American	Japan	50	Divorced	1	New York, NY
1	Japanese American	U.S.A.	55	Married	1	San Francisco, CA
1	Korean American	Korea	62	Married	2	San Francisco, CA
1	Mexican American	U.S.A.	40	Married	1	Los Angeles, CA
1	Native American	U.S.A.	42	Single	2	Great Neck, NY
1	Puerto Rican	U.S.A.	36	Married	3	New York, NY
1	Vietnamese American	Vietnam	43	Married	5	Houston, TX

tration displayed by both. As the young woman moved away from her parents' philosophies and values and into her own, conflicts increased distance between them. In the case of the older daughters (11), all reported a hectic adolescence that eased as they grew older and entered college or married. Eight reported satisfying to good and rewarding relationships. Three revealed some continuing differences of opinion with their mothers that they did not see as severe. Omitting the period of adolescence, 95% of all daughters described their mothers as loving, kind, creative, caring, intelligent, loyal, and compassionate and in other laudatory terms.

Achievement Norms Expected and Acceptable

Within all 13 ethnic groups, academic achievement is valued. Beginning at an early age, all mothers were achievers. The vocations of their own parents included five teachers, four administrators, a publisher, two engineers, one police chief, and one contractor. One mother was valedictorian in kindergarten at age 3, and two gave the valedictory address at their high school graduations. All mothers except one continued on to earn higher degrees (see Table I.2). Of the daughters, 16 were outstanding students at the elementary and secondary levels at public, private, parochial, and home schooling. Thirteen were exceptional and made the dean's list and French Honors Club and received several awards. Two were listed in *Who's Who* (a national directory of bright adolescents) and were members of the National Junior Honors Society. Their best subjects were foreign languages, English, mathematics, and sciences (physical and social). Table I.3 shows the achievement and extracurricular activities of the daughters. All daughters were encouraged to excel, as their mothers and grandmothers had before them.

Working Mother/Role Model

Mothers of seven of the sample were employed outside their homes, leaving grandmothers to provide major child care. These mothers grew up very knowledgeable about work schedules, shifts, paydays, flexible supper times, and mothers being out of the home for long periods. As a result, they not only performed household tasks and did baby-sitting and shopping but also became responsible adolescents. The benefits of this early training were influential in raising their own daughters, who developed leadership, problem-solving, and decision-making skills as preadolescents. Raised by a working mother, 80% of the sample mothers were career-minded, goal-oriented, and self-sufficient. All sample mothers perceived their employment as having a positive impact upon their daughters.

As to role models, three sample mothers named their mothers as role models, and six considered their grandmothers as performing that role and having the major influence on their lives. Four others didn't remember having any role model.

Eighty percent of the sample daughters considered their mother as their

Table I.2
A Profile of Achievements of Mothers

Cognitive Ability	The Women's Careers
Above Average Intelligence	Academic Dean
Special Skills/Talents	Consumer Affairs Director
Ability to Focus	County Supervisor
Drive	Criminal Court Judge
	Dir. Health, Welfare & Social

* Academic Achievements of
Mothers (No. of Mothers)

Personality Traits	Programs
Creativity	Hotel/Housekeeping
Enjoys Challenge	Journalist
Flexibility	Medicine
Perseverance	Pianist, Teacher & Director
Motivation	Pharmacist
	Real Estate Broker

Years of School Completed
1 Less than 4 yrs. of HS
1 Community College
1 Two yrs. of College
6 Bachelor's Degree
2 Master's Degree +
1 Doctorate

Positive Self-Image	Registered Nurse
	Registrar's Office Clerk
Achievement Oriented	Senior Program Officer
Effective Problem Solving	Supervisor of Education
Self-Confidence	U.S. Congresswoman
Self-Esteem	Editor/Publisher
Sets Goals	

Graduate of Professional School
1 School of Nursing
1 School of Medicine
1 School of Law
1 Academy of Music
1 School of Pharmacy

Environmental Influences
Changes in Public Image of Women
Economic Need/Market Demands
Feminist Movement
Family Support (Nuclear & Extended)

High Level of Satisfaction
Enjoyed from Community
Contribution

main role model and influence on the daughters' motivation and drive. Twenty percent named a teacher, mentor, and grandmother as being idolized as role models. One daughter perceived her mother's job as being too stressful. Two others admired their mothers but didn't want to be a "copy" of the mothers and, at times, resented some pressure, imagined or real, to become identical. Even when not named as a main role model, mothers received high praise for understanding, patience, and love.

Functional Adolescents, Adults

The rate of independence does not appear to vary between the transition to middle adolescence and the transition to late adolescence. Older adoles-

Table I.3
Academic Achievement and Extracurricular Activities of Daughters

Leadership Role Played	Honors Awards Received	Special Talent	Potential Career Choice	Type of School All Levels
1 Capt. Football Team	1 Gifted Classes	1 Cello	2 Business	9 Public
1 Capt. Basketball	4 Honor Roll	3 Piano	2 Education	5 Parochial
Team	3 Dean's List	2 Violin	2 Law	6 Private
1 Capt. Track Team	1 Award-Art	1 Opera	2 Medicine	1 Home
1 VP Student Act.	1 Award-Poetry	2 Orchestra	1 R.N.	
1 Pres. Sophomore	1 Who's Who	1 Flute		
Class	1 French Club (Hon.)			
	1 Nat. Jr. Hon. Soc.			

Extracurricular Activities	Years of School Completed	Graduates of Professional School	Vocations
Ballet	1 4th Grade	1 School of Law	Investment Banker
Baseball	1 5th Grade	1 Conservatory of Music	Lawyer
Camping/Hiking	1 6th Grade	at San Francisco	Legal Assistant
Cheerleader	3 8th Grade	1 Oberlin (Music Major)	Library Assistant
Dance	1 9th Grade		Mezzo Soprano
Debating	2 10th Grade		Music Teacher, Celloist
Drama	1 12th Grade		
Girl Scouts	1 College Sophomore		
Gymnastics	2 College Junior		
Paintings	1 College Senior		
Pottery			
Sailing			
Swimming			
Track			
Jewelry Making			

cents are given more independence because they have more advanced cognitive skills, greater access to resources outside the home, greater responsibilities and capacity for judgment, and greater contact with institutions outside the family and because of societal age norms that prescribe greater rights inside and outside the home. Early adolescent daughters felt that parental control and supervision were too rigid and limiting. Because of the urban situation, one teenager is escorted on the subway. As girls grow up, they are less likely to be given more freedom. This was true across all racial groups, except African Americans and Hispanics. In late adolescence, girls were allowed to enjoy more social activities outside the home. Asian adolescents do not date as individuals but enjoy group dating. They did not appear to see this as a problem. Non-Asian teenage daughters were permitted to date and hold part-time jobs outside the home.

Ninety-seven percent believed that they had successfully made the transition from late adolescence to adulthood and college. Three percent considered themselves as still growing and searching.

Coping with Ethnic Values and Perceived Goals

Although the role of women has changed, some areas can still cause problems even in these modern times. One is women's desire to seek fulfillment through careers. Even though personal satisfaction is by no means the only reason women seek employment, for an increasing number of women, individual satisfaction is maximized by combining family roles with employment outside the home. This is a combination that has long been viewed as optional for men; it therefore could be argued that the extension to larger numbers of women constitutes a major advance in personal well-being.

The conflict occurring among the sample women is related to the mothers' seeking higher education and employment when apparently her spouse considers his income sufficient to cover family expenses. The mother may agree but is looking ahead to the children's college education, buying a home, planning family vacations, or getting a better position.

The most important strategy they used is a well-planned discussion noting the benefits for all family members. This discussion is "everybody wins," in contrast to a win-or-lose situation. Both parents have to win rather than one winning at the expense of the other. Main methods include active listening, paying close attention, and letting the spouse know that one has heard what the other has said. These discussions are planned to occur when both are relaxed and comfortable. They can extend over several weeks. Both must understand and respect each other's feelings before discussing possible solutions. It is vital that the spouse be able to maintain his position in the family and not lose "face" or self-esteem.

In one case, the church was involved. The wife was elected director of Sunday school. A degree would help her to carry out responsibilities with greater success and would enable her to assist her young children's academic progress. Her husband was respected by the ministry, and his wife's position would add to his status. The spouse became an active partner in additional child care and household tasks as his contribution to the family's well-being.

In another instance, the help of a mother-in-law was sought. Although the older woman held traditional values, she had secretly longed for a career earlier in her life. She became an advocate for the mother. Seeing his mother's interest and support helped the spouse to understand his wife's needs. The grandmother willingly helped with part-time child care services for the family.

Other mothers convinced their spouses through carrying out work, household duties, and college responsibilities at the same time. Seeing success in this multiple role helped to convince the spouse. Some spouses welcomed the additional income, which relieved them of underlying stress. They also learned to respect the wife's efforts and contribution to the family as a whole. A supportive network of kin and friends can contribute to the husband's acceptance of his wife's goal.

Because racism and sexism are so closely intertwined, women of color often go through mental gymnastics that occur on a daily basis of decoding which type of discrimination lies behind which interaction and then deciding whether to respond, how to respond, or being too overwhelmed by strong feelings to respond at all. In an academic or work situation, many women report a syndrome involving switching gears and rotating alliances between various groupings of men and women. This is a survival technique that is quite stressful but necessary. The women literally "fine-tune" and "adapt" themselves in trying to negotiate various work environments. These efforts to decrease the effects of discrimination and conflict, to acclimate in a suitable fashion, and to work more smoothly with others in the workplace are deemed essential as ways to add to overall work effectiveness. Many women of color see these requirements as a way "to keep their jobs" or "not cause waves."

This behavior is not necessarily something one is comfortable doing but is something one automatically finds oneself doing as an option to being confrontational or hostile all of the time. It involves employing various styles, depending on the "norm" of the group, and incorporates a "healthy paranoia" as a survival skill in learning whom to trust, how to read people, and how to cushion disappointments. At one time or another, each mother had to deal with discriminatory remarks or acts. They tempered such instances with a smile or a witty remark or by ignoring the situation.

Coping Strategies Used by Mothers

These strategies were suggested as useful by mothers: (1) be aggressive but appear assertive; (2) be resilient in situations of turmoil; (3) always keep your goal in mind; (4) seek out resources and use them; (5) remain self-confident and optimistic; (6) exercise all options; (7) keep informed and be flexible; (8) use conflict resolution techniques; (9) keep communication lines open; (10) deal with problems and move on; (11) have faith and pray a lot; (12) be patient; and (13) maintain a balance.

Mothers' Definition of "Success"

Each participant was asked to define "success" in light of her personal work experience and private life. Each answered in her own unique way. All reported separating career from personal life in their deliberations. Although 11 out of 17 mothers unequivocally said they were "successful" in their ca-

Table I.4
Mothers' Meaning of Success

Do You Feel Successful?

Answer	PROFESSIONALLY No. of Mothers	PERSONALLY No. of Mothers	HOW MOTHERS DEFINE SUCCESS
Yes	11	11	Influential in Helping Others I Feel Empowered A Satisfaction That Goes beyond Achievement Having a Balance and Enjoying What I Do
Possibly	1	1	Doing What Comes Naturally Qualified in 3 Professions, Involved in Community Volunteering and I Paint
Work in Progress	2	2	A "Qualified" Yes: I Have Some Unfinished Business Work Has Brought Joy and Personal Growth
Could Be Better	2	2	I'm a Successful Survivor I'm at Peace with Myself I'm Happy and I'm Serving People in Need
Just Functioning	1	1	I'm Fulfilled

reers, they found an equal amount of "success" in their private lives. However, when defining "success," their definitions clearly revealed how important feelings, caring, and relationships were to them. For this group, "success" as an individual appeared to be more valued than "success" in a career. Table I.4 displays the variation of definitions.

In some chapters, the Case Studies section is followed by a contributed Personal Reflections section whose writer discusses his/her feelings and experiences with living in a multicultural society.

REFERENCE

Hochschild, J. *Facing Up to the American Dream*. Princeton, NJ: Princeton University Press, 1995.

PART I

BLACK AMERICANS

1

African Americans

The term African American refers to the approximately 35 million Americans of African descent living in the United States in the 1990s. This term was revitalized in the 1980s. During the 1960s, a similar self-description was popular in the black community: Afro-American. While African American is a popular term utilized by many Americans, the term "black" is the most preferred self-description, according to one survey done by a black research think tank (JCPES, 1992).

While both terms are considered interchangeable, it has been pointed out by some observers that "black" is more appropriate, because it reflects the broader African diaspora and longer history than that associated with African Americans. Others have also expressed a preference for "black" because it includes many African descent groups living in the United States that do not use "African American" as a racial or ethnic self-description. One example of such is the case of Haitians, who may identify themselves as black, but not necessarily African American (Cashmore, 1994).

Despite popular conceptions, the first blacks really arrived in the New World as explorers, laborers, and servants, not as slaves. While some historians question whether one of Columbus' sailors was black, there were 30 black sailors with Balboa when he discovered the Pacific Ocean in 1513 (Gonzales, 1990). Six years later when Cortés landed in Mexico, several of his men were blacks (Franklin, 1997). However, the best-known black explorer in the New World was Estevanico, who founded the states of Texas, New Mexico, and Arizona for the Spanish (Gonzales, 1990).

European slave trade was profitable not only in terms of the value of the "black cargo" but also in terms of the exchange and transportation of products. By the 18th century, the English had a very lucrative "triangular trade system." This system allowed them to exchange commodities produced in Britain, such as textiles, guns, and spirits, for slaves captured on the West Coast of Africa. For this purpose they established "trading posts" in Africa, where they exchanged their goods for slaves. Local African chiefs were commissioned to capture members of rival tribes, who were then incarcerated and sold to British slave traders (Gonzales, 1990).

Justification for slavery was based on two points: first, that blacks were a separate species and therefore experienced a totally different genesis; and second, that they were heathens who had to be Christianized (Jordan, 1968). Some have observed that racism, as an ideological position, may have existed prior to the institution of slavery, but the institution of slavery ensured the growth of racism in America. This was essential for the general acceptance of slavery.

In 1780 the new Massachusetts Constitution stated that "all men are born free and equal," which marked the beginning of the end of slavery in that state. New York and New Jersey granted slaves freedom by the end of the century.

The publication of David Walker's *Appeal*, a strong antislavery narrative written by a free black from North Carolina, set the abolitionist movement in action. At the same time, the publication of William Lloyd Garrison's *The Liberator* (1831) focused national attention on the slavery question. However, it took the impact of Nat Turner's rebellion in Southampton County, Virginia, in 1831 to finally bring the nation to the brink of panic. This act of open rebellion struck terror into the hearts of all southerners (Litwack, 1967; Gonzales, 1990). The abolitionists were joined by former slaves who became full-time propagandists, for example, Frederick Douglass, Theodore Wright, William Jones, and Charles Gardner.

Lincoln issued the Emancipation Proclamation, which freed all slaves, on January 1, 1863. For Lincoln, this was just a military strategy, as he wanted to strip the South of "slave power." He was not particularly interested in freeing slaves (Gonzales, 1990). By the end of the war, more than 186,000 blacks had served in the Union army in segregated units led primarily by white officers (Franklin, 1996). This was the second great war in the history of this young nation in which blacks were asked to sacrifice their lives for the preservation of "democracy."

Gradually, in the 1880s the whole grim business came to an end. Almost four and a half centuries since Captain Antony Gonsalves in 1441 snatched his first captives on the shores of Mauritania, the last ship crossed the Atlantic (Davidson, 1971).

Life for blacks during the Great Depression was oppressive. They faced discrimination in labor unions and relief organizations. New Deal programs helped, but not enough to bring the country out of depression. The tragedy of Pearl Harbor (1941) turned the American economy around. During the first year of the war, more than 370,000 blacks joined the armed forces, and at the peak of the war (1941), there were 700,000 blacks in uniform (Franklin, 1996). Over 1 million blacks served their country during World War II (Gonzales, 1990).

In the following decades, school integration caused violence and mob reaction at schools and colleges throughout the South. Central High School, Little Rock, Arkansas, received national attention when the president ordered 1,000 paratroopers and 10,000 National Guardsmen to the campus to ensure entrance by nine black students who were enrolled. At the college level, it was necessary to station 12,000 federal troops on campus to ensure James Meredith's entrance to classes at the University of Mississippi. But Rosa Parks' use of civil disobedience in refusing to give up her bus seat to a white man in Montgomery, Alabama, on December 1, 1955, led to a year's boycott of buses and ended in a Supreme Court ruling that racial segregation on buses was unconstitutional (Gonzales, 1990). The boycott led to the involvement of Reverend Martin Luther King, Jr. (1921–1968), a Baptist minister who led the first successful boycott based on the philosophy of nonviolence, which has six key elements: (1) active resistance to "evil"; (2) attempts to win one's opponent through understanding; (3) directing one's attack against forces of "evil," rather than against people; (4) willingness to accept suffering without retaliation; (5) refusal to hate one's opponent; and (6) the conviction that the universe is on the side of justice (King, 1958).

Dr. King began a series of marches in Birmingham in April 1963. Police chief Eugene "Bull" Connor used dogs and water cannons on the marchers, including women and children, in full view of national media coverage. In May 1963 Medgar Evers was shot and killed outside his home in Jackson, Mississippi.

The killing of Evers was followed by significant tragedies, like the bombing of the 16th Street Baptist Church in Birmingham, in which four young girls were killed in Sunday school. Over the summer of 1963 other senseless violence occurred in retaliation for the civil rights marches. Thirty-four churches and homes were firebombed, and more than 20,000 demonstrators were arrested (Pinkney, 1975). Late in August, Reverend King made his famous "I Have a Dream" speech in Washington, D.C. A few months later, President Kennedy was assassinated, leaving the future of civil rights unclear.

The most radical of the black nationalists, or separatist movements, was the Nation of Islam under the leadership of Malcolm X, known as the Black Muslims. The Black Muslims believed that whites were devils who were created to be the enemy of blacks for 6,000 years, a period that ended in 1914 (Draper, 1970). Their goal was to establish a separate black nation within the United States.

The Vietnam War became the most important issue in the late 1960s and early 1970s. Many who were active in the Civil Rights movement now supported the antiwar movement. This caused the loss of support from white liberals and college students. It was also clear that other social movements, like the women's movement, the ecology movement, and the antinuclear movement, had attracted many potential supporters of the Civil Rights movement (Gonzales, 1990).

Within the black community, the family is one of the strongest and most important traditions. How much of this tradition is based in African customs and how much was developed in the New World are impossible to determine; it is doubtlessly some of both (Franklin, 1997). African American families grew out of African institutions brought to the Americans by enslaved populations over a period of centuries. Over time, the transplanted African families evolved into African American families. Wherever the enslaved Africans settled, they were forced to accommodate and adapt to whatever European law and tradition prevailed. The similarities evident in family life among people of African descent throughout America are a testament to the strength and viability of the extended family, which is one of the most important bases for kinship groupings throughout sub-Saharan Africa (Sudarkasa, 1997).

"The" black family is itself a fiction. Different family forms prevail at different class and income levels throughout our society (Willie, 1970). Andrew Billingsley in his book *Black Families in White America* (1968) provides a detailed description of the structure of black families and notes that there are three major types of family structure in the black community:

1. The nuclear family, husband and wife and their own children, with no other relatives present;
2. The extended family, including other relatives or in-laws who share the same household;
3. The augmented family, including individuals who are not related to the family but who share the same household.

Some of the sharpest differences between the family lives of blacks and those of other races can be found in the living arrangements of young children. The most extreme contrast is found among children living with a mother who has never been married; in 1992, three of every five (59%) of these children had a black mother. In fact, more black children live with a never-married parent than with a divorced or separated parent (31% and 21%, respectively). By comparison, about two-thirds as many children of all races were living with a never-married parent as with a divorced or separated parent (8% versus 13%) (Glick, 1997).

Changes in family income by race during recent years have been profoundly affected by the shift in family types, as well as by a higher proportion of wives in the labor force. Figure 1.1 shows median weekly earnings of full-time wage and salary workers by race and sex in 1995.

Figure 1.1
Median Weekly Earnings of Full-Time Wage and Salary Workers by Race and Sex: 1995

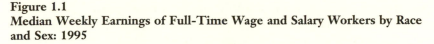

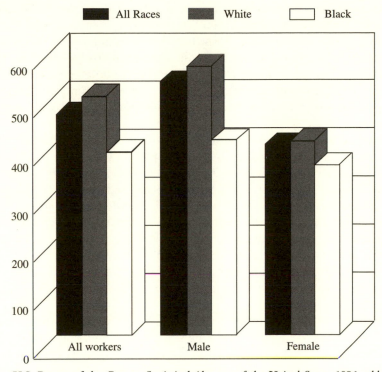

Source: U.S. Bureau of the Census, *Statistical Abstract of the United States 1996*, table 653, p. 426.

America's racial paradox is reflected in the nation's educational system. The gap in school enrollment between African American and white children is rapidly disappearing. Despite much progress in the area of education, many of the nation's public schools remain segregated as predominantly white, black, or Latino schools. Seldom can one find a public school in a major American city where black and white students have opportunities to interact as classmates in the same programs. Continuing disparities in educational experiences of black children and youth are taking place in a national context where the proportion of black children composing the entire public school population is about 16% and increasing rapidly.

In higher education, blacks now attend colleges and universities that were hostile to their presence in earlier periods. The attitude of the northern institutions toward blacks varies from tolerance to active hostility. Calls for multicultural curricula that reflect the growing ethnic diversity of the society, as well as black studies, are resisted by significant sectors of faculty, staff, and leadership of many of the nation's public and private institutions of higher education (Cashmore, 1994). See Figure 1.2.

Poverty of families continues to show significant discrepancies. In 1993, 31% (or 2.5 million) of all black families were poor, compared with 9% (or 5.4 million) of white families. Black families were more than three times more likely to be poor than white families and four times more likely than non-Hispanic white families (8%) in 1993. This ratio is somewhat larger than the 1969 level, when the poverty rate for black families (28%) was three-and-one-half times that for white families (8%). Figure 1.3 shows these differences.

Reviewing the social and economic conditions of black Americans in 1997, many felt that very little had changed in the past 30 years. The poverty rate had not changed, the unemployment and underemployment rates remained, and the income gap was still present. Research (Sudarkasa, 1997) suggests that families focus on the family values and extended family structures of African family life to help them cope with the disturbing circumstances in their lives. The seven values that are proposed are respect, responsibility, restraint, reciprocity, reverence, reason, and reconciliation. Sudarkasa also proposes that professionals working with families look to the inclusive, mutually supportive household and family structures that proved their effectiveness in the past.

In the late 1980s, two major national studies focusing on the status of African Americans were published. One study was commissioned by the National Academy of Science and is entitled *A Common Destiny: Black in America*. This study represents a reexamination of the status of blacks in America, within the framework of the classic study by Gunnar Myrdal, *An American Dilemma* (1944). The second major study was sponsored and conducted by a black research think tank based at the University of Massachusetts, the William Monroe Trotter Institute. The study is *An Assessment of African Americans in the United States* (1989).

While there were important differences in how these two studies approached issues related to black life in the United States, there was at least one important similarity. Both studies concluded that, while blacks have realized important progress in many arenas such as education, politics, military, government, housing, and the economy, many blacks have yet to enjoy social equality with whites. In other words, while there has been some progress and improvement in matters related to race, there still exists an entrenched racial divide and hierarchy in the United States. While some, like Gunnar Myrdal in the 1940s, have referred to this racial paradox as an American "dilemma," others, like Malcolm X and Martin Luther King, Jr., in the 1960s, have described it as "America's hypocrisy."

Figure 1.2
Educational Attainment of Persons 25 Years Old and Over, by Race and Sex: 1980, 1990, and 1994 (in percent)

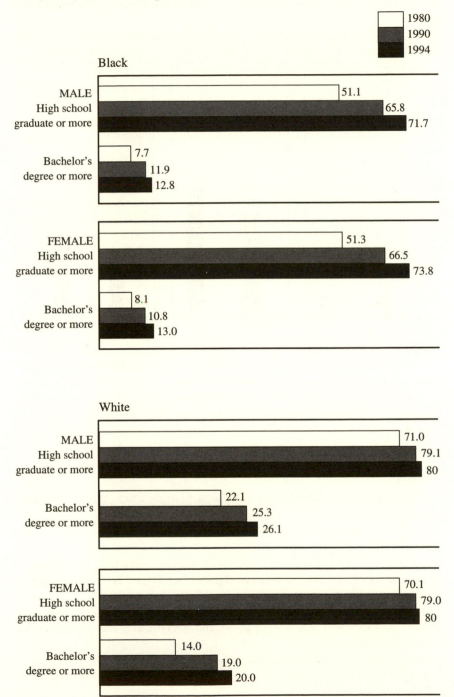

Source: U.S. Department of Commerce, Bureau of the Census, *The Black Population in the United States* (March 1993, 1994).

Figure 1.3
Poverty Rates, by Type of Family and Race of Householder: 1979 and 1993
(in percent)

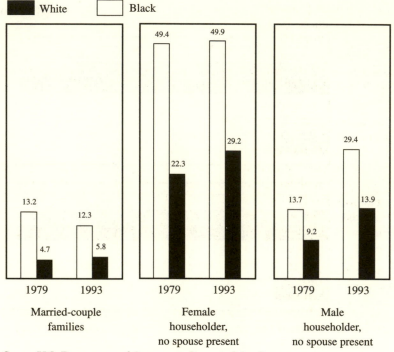

■ White	□ Black	

Source: U.S. Department of Commerce, Bureau of the Census.

CASE STUDIES

Cheryl

A 34-year-old woman, waiting patiently for an uptown express train, is suddenly pushed forward from behind. She screams loudly, purse flying, and her body hits the gleaming steel tracks with a loud thud. The perpetrator is quickly wrestled to the ground by irate bystanders.

Two teenagers, speeding in a stolen van, recklessly mount the sidewalk, crushing a 68-year-old great-grandmother to death. The young men are arrested by police as they attempt to flee the scene.

A 25-year-old waitress is accused of killing her 32-year-old live-in lover. She interrupted a love tryst with her best girlfriend and plunged a 14-inch knife into her boyfriend's back.

A 28-year-old man, known as the East Side Rapist, is arrested by the police. It is alleged that he committed a dozen assaults on women living in the Turtle Bay section of New York City.

These are the kinds of cases on the docket for a cloudy, windy April morning in 1997. The wooden and metal seats of the courtroom are filled with relatives, friends, and lawyers for the defense and the prosecution. The buzz of murmured conversations comes to a sudden stop as the clerk approaches the bench. In a loud, resonant voice ringing with authority, he announces, "All rise! Hear ye! Hear ye! The Criminal Court for the City of New York is now open for the transaction of all such business which may come before it. All those with such business may come forward, draw near and ye shall be heard."

All heads turn to watch the figure in a long, black robe step quickly toward the bench. A concerned-looking face beneath attractively coiled and braided hair reveals how seriously she contemplates the tasks before her. She is the judge—the Honorable Cheryl E. Chambers.

On the bench and in chambers, Cheryl presents an impressive figure. Her voice, low and modulated, is lightly laced with authority. She is not foreboding, but stern. Her mission is clear, and her manner reflects it.

Born in Brooklyn Jewish Hospital, the third of a family of three children, Cheryl has an older brother and sister. She was the baby of the family. Her mother was a schoolteacher, and her father was employed by the New York City Transit Authority. He started as a mechanic and rose through the ranks to an administrative position. Because her siblings were older by five and seven years, Cheryl lacked built-in playmates. She recalls playing alone and being creative with toys. She also spent an inordinate amount of time with her mother and learned the tasks of cooking and housekeeping at an early age. Later the family adopted a young girl, and Cheryl became the little one's primary caretaker.

Cheryl attended Midwood High School in Brooklyn; the school had an outstanding reputation for academic achievement and excellence. Pupils were largely white and Jewish, but African Americans were represented in fairly large numbers. Cheryl attended Midwood during the height of the Civil Rights movement, and the community spirit toward minorities was quite positive, she recalls. Cheryl's school activities included playing the violin with the orchestra and some management tasks for the orchestra. "The conductor was dedicated and committed, so we practiced a great deal." Cheryl also performed school service in assisting teachers and the guidance counselor. Outside school, there were many church activities that she enjoyed.

Cheryl's brother and sister entered the medical field and became doctors. "I really had no particular career objective, although I loved political science, economics, and debating. I liked to talk a lot," she laughs, remembering. Her parents encouraged her to become a doctor, too. Cheryl liked the biological sciences but had stronger interests in the social sciences, politics and government. The legal profession became her choice.

Cheryl sought advice from her mother, peers, and girlfriends, but not always in that order. For a while, Cheryl and her mother went through a period of determined, strong-willed, obstinate behavior. "In fact, she thought I was awful," Cheryl admits. "We still don't see ourselves as equals—not quite. I'm still very positive and determined to follow my own mind." Her family was very religious. Cheryl was brought up in the church. She remembers the choir, Sunday school, and youth programs that took place every Sunday.

The family valued excellence and ambition. "My Mom always told me, 'Whatever it is, do your best.'" Above all else, a positive attitude and a good character, which included loyalty, reliability, and honesty, were characteristics her parents valued.

Cheryl lived a mile from Brooklyn College. "I just had to take the bus. With two other children seeking higher education, the cost was affordable." The period was the 1970s, and Cheryl was desirous of making the world a better place for black people and helping them to become empowered. She was an avid follower of the movement. By the end of her sophomore year, Cheryl knew she would become a lawyer. She enjoyed all of her prerequisites, like political science, government, history, sociology, and economics, and maintained a high B average.

Her first job out of law school was in a bank. "It involved working in a management training program. It was excellent and prepared me for business school," says Cheryl, whose plans included an M.B.A. at that time. She graduated from Boston University's School of Law. Cheryl also earned a master's degree in business from Rutgers Graduate School of Management. Her first legal job was an assignment in the Office of the Deputy Mayor for Criminal Justice. The job offered experience in policy making and planning and in the management side of criminal justice. Cheryl was appreciative of the opportunity but was somewhat insecure. "I didn't feel that I had enough experience to make the kind of decisions that would impact upon the system," she says soberly.

Her parents were overjoyed when Cheryl began to consider marriage. She was in love with a fellow student whom she had dated in college. Her mother was persistent with questions like, "What are you waiting for?" The wedding was spectacular, with bridesmaids, ushers, a ring bearer, flower girls, and a formal reception. The couple honeymooned in the Virgin Islands.

Parenting is a 24-hour job; there are no shortcuts. So Cheryl followed her mother's example. "I had two children close together in age. So I took five years off and devoted myself to their care and training. This prepared them for my return to work." The children were breast-fed, and Cheryl enjoyed the closeness and nurturing. She planned well and made certain that the children had "quiet" and "quality" time. Presently, her two teenagers are given special attention, as they attempt to separate themselves from their parents and develop as individuals. "At times, parents have to provide a little 'slack' and let them experience their own decision making. These years are critical," she says gravely.

Cheryl speaks of the Million Man March in Washington, D.C., as very significant. "Many black men have been the target of racism, bias, indifference, and injustice. I believe it showed many men that they have a responsibility to provide leadership in their communities and support for the wives and children. Our young black people need proper role models, if they are to be successful and contributing members of society." The "fallout" of the march brought positive reactions from men all around the country as they began to identify ways and means of contributing their efforts and skills locally.

Bigotry, especially in the workplace, can be subtle, Cheryl believes. "I once had a supervisor who said, 'How you evaluate a person depends upon how you look at him.' If you don't see his positive aspects, how can you evaluate anyone? Still, most white people, when observing a black person in a position of authority, believe that tokenism or a special program is involved. Many find it difficult to believe that black people have talent and skills," Cheryl says without bitterness and adds, "Or you have to prove that you're capable by some subjective measurement."

For recreation, the family reads or watches television together. The children are learning to play tennis now. When possible, the family takes short trips together to Kiawah Island, South Carolina, a private beach community, and relaxes.

Cheryl's most important value that she tries to instill in her children is a belief in God and a belief in themselves. "I told my son recently about God and his special design and purpose in him, and it should be his goal to discover what it is," she says with emphasis.

Although the dominant culture proclaims that the man is head of the family, the major wage earner, and decision maker, Cheryl doesn't adhere totally to this practice, and decisions are made jointly. Cheryl is married to Seymour W. James, Jr., who is attorney in charge of the Queens Office of the Legal Aid Society Criminal Defense Division. They have three children: Christopher, Cheryl Allison, and Carole. She hopes that she and her husband have been living examples of shared responsibility, role flexibility, sharing, mutual respect, and commitment to each other and their children.

A senior colleague, Edith Miller, retired justice of the Supreme Court Appellate Term, fondly remembers Cheryl as follows.

What I like best about Cheryl Chambers is that she is an integral part of the African-American lifestyle that has insured our survival from the seventeenth century up to the present time. The media focuses on black superstars in sports and entertainment and on dysfunctional individuals overwhelmed by despair seeking solace in drugs, alcohol and gambling. Extremes, however, can never represent any group nor provide an understanding of the group culture. Cheryl Chambers represents the majority of African-Americans, whether they are professional or non-professional, who have learned to triumph over adversity.

In the nine years she worked as an Assistant District Attorney in Kings County, she received several promotions and rose through the ranks to become Chief of the Domestic Violence Bureau. For the first African-American to become a Bureau Chief, it was a personal triumph. However, she was not content merely to be an inspiration to other young lawyers and law students by her accomplishments. In the African-American tradition of "lifting as we climb," she found the time to help others through the New York County Lawyers Association. She organized a course to teach minority law graduates how to successfully prepare for and pass the Bar Examination. She also was a mentor for the Practicing Attorneys for Law Students Program.

When Cheryl Chambers was elected to the New York City Civil Court in November 1994, she became one of the few judges of that court to hold a graduate degree in business. However, because of her outstanding background in criminal law, she was designated to sit in the New York County Criminal Court. Her court proceedings have been featured on local news broadcasts and she has made other television appearances. She has also lectured on law, domestic violence and religion. She enjoys a reputation for being knowledgeable, well prepared, and for giving thoughtful responses to questions.

The Criminal Court in New York County is one of the busiest and most stressful courts in the judicial system. I think that what sustains Judge Chambers is her belief in God and family. Not only is she a member of the Bridge Street AME Church in Brooklyn, she is also an officer of the church.

When I first met Cheryl Chambers, she was at the beginning of her career. At that time, I was the Administrative Judge for the New York City Family Court. When this stunningly beautiful woman walked in to discuss career development, I was very much impressed by her seriousness. This was at a time when women lawyers did not have the cachet they experience today. I knew that she had the ability to succeed, because not only was she knowledgeable about substantive and procedural law, but she realized that to succeed in law, you had to be concerned about continuing education. Cheryl Chambers is at the middle of her judicial career, and I am confident that she will have a long, distinguished career.

Cheryl is a member and former chairman of the Board of Directors of the Metropolitan Black Bar Association. She was a member of the Criminal Court Committee of the Association of the Bar of the City of New York and is now chair of the Program Committee of the Brooklyn Women's Bar Association.

The judge's future hopefully holds an opportunity to teach in a law school. She is particularly dedicated to ethics and the law and the combination of religion and the profession. In order to make it, Cheryl suggests that a person take one day at a time and have a network of friends upon whom one can rely and an intact family if possible, or a dependable substitute.

As to success she says, "If you're really passionate about what you want to do and do it to the best of your ability . . . you're a success."

Cheryl Allison

Cheryl the younger, like her mother, strives for excellence. In the eighth grade, she was enrolled in advanced-level courses in mathematics, science, and English. Cheryl ranked at the top 1% of her class in her private school. There, she was an active leader and member of the National Junior Honor Society for Academic Excellence and of the Debating Team. Now at age 14, Cheryl is a sophomore at Midwood High School—where her mother did so well many years ago. She continues to enjoy music and dance and appeared in several musicals at Midwood. Cheryl plays the flute and is a member of the Black Arts Alliance.

She plans to follow her uncle and aunt into the field of medicine. Mathematics and science are her favorite classes. One summer, Cheryl attended a seminar called "Science Kids" at Downstate Medical College with other potential doctors. The students observed young doctors at work and learned about life in a health field. Cheryl has elected orthopedics as an area of specialty. "Helping people who have been injured or have crippling diseases will be my goal," she states, being aware of the hard work ahead and seeming to be prepared for it. Cheryl is not satisfied with just getting good grades. "I work to improve myself in every area," she says modestly.

Cheryl is friendly and has lots of friends. She would choose friends over money. She enjoys being with an individual, like one of her best girlfriends, or with groups of young people. Cheryl thinks her mother is overprotective. "I don't use the subways or travel alone. My mother drives." When discussing some of the ills of a big city, Cheryl admits that one has to be aware of possible crime or injury. "Maybe she is right," she concedes with a wide grin. At home, she is responsible for cleaning up her room. Cheryl often cooks breakfast. She likes Italian food best. She has no bad habits but used to have a bad temper. Her brother is a best friend and is always available if she needs him.

Cheryl enjoys being with her family, whether at home or on vacation. She thinks that her mother is a good role model for her. "She's hardworking, always makes time for us, and is dedicated. She remembers her own years of growing up and understands us. She can balance a career, husband, and three children quite well." Cheryl has no favorite movie star, singer, or sports figure. She enjoys reading and reads classics and authors like Richard Wright.

Five years from now, Cheryl hopes to be in college, doing well and looking forward to medical school. "And I may have a boyfriend," she adds.

Dorothy

Glenarden, Maryland, could be a bedroom town for those who spend their nine to whatever hours working for the U.S. government in Washington, D.C. Its quiet, tree-lined streets feature attractive, well-kept, moderately priced, single-family homes. One such house, located on a corner, is occupied by Dorothy Graves Kenner and her husband, Oliver. The furnishings, dually designed and created, reflect the skills and love enjoyed by its residents. The setting also is a statement of success after years of sacrifice, saving, and commitment to an achievable goal envisioned by Dorothy many years ago.

Dorothy was born to Connie and Lettie Middleton on June 26, 1940, in Pikesville, North Carolina, a sleepy southern town. Five more children would join the family before Mrs. Middleton's untimely death in 1946. Dorothy was sent to live with her grandmother. She remembers the house as being small but comfortable and in the country. When Dorothy was not attending the rural two- to three-room elementary school, she played under the house with the family dog.

Several years later, Dorothy joined her father and stepmother in Goldsboro, North Carolina, where she attended Dillard High School. As the oldest girl at home, Dorothy missed many school days because she was needed to care for her younger siblings. Despite this, she was an excellent student; she did well in mathematics, typing, and home economics. In the latter course, she made an apron (required also of male students) and cooked spaghetti. Dorothy had a special girlfriend, Bessie Jones, and Dorothy admired her cooking skills in home economics. During the last two years of high school, Dorothy developed a stuttering problem. Although she received no professional help, Dorothy worked hard toward correcting it. She worked even harder when the teachers chose her to be valedictorian. Prayers and belief in God saved the day. Her speech was perfect!

After graduation, Dorothy's stepmother suggested a nursing career. But this did not appeal to the teenager. Dorothy was caught between appeasing her stepmother or leaving home. Afraid to leave home, she opted for the test. On the way to the test, she kept repeating to herself, "I'm going to fail. I'm not going to pass." She thinks that a strong belief in self-determination worked for her, as she failed the test. With no plans for work or education, Dorothy decided to go to Washington, D.C., and join her older sister. A big city would offer more opportunities, she hoped. Instead of employment, she found a potential husband—young, romantic, and charming. Dorothy found Charles to be just what a young woman needed. After a short courtship, they married. Three children in three years brought stress, frustration, and abuse. Unfortunately, Charles turned to alcohol for solace. Unprepared for family, children, and responsibility, they separated. "If we had waited, had counseling, or even openly discussed our problems, the marriage might have worked. We didn't know each other, except physically," Dorothy explains. Her parents and siblings "rallied round" with offers of money, food, and child care. But their love and emotional support were the best gift.

Life as a single mother caused additional problems of child care, employment, and homemaking. Dorothy, ambitious and with a strong sense of responsibility, began work in a local laundry. The work was hot, hard, and repetitious, but it meant food on the table and keeping the family together. "I began on an assembly line as a collar and cuffs starcher." Dorothy grasped the collar and cuffs of the shirt and dipped them into a liquid starch mixture. A quick squeeze, and then the shirt was passed to the next worker. "Within a year, I graduated to sorter." A sorter threw shirts into a lettered bin. "My last job was working on a conveyor belt. As the box of shirts came down the belt, I quickly put on the lid and tied up the box." One night, after the children were in bed, Dorothy contemplated her future. "I didn't want a life in a laundry. I worried about my children's future, their education, their exposure to a nonachieving model." She decided upon a job change.

Through friends, Dorothy learned of job openings at Federal City College, now called the University of the District of Columbia. With confidence, she applied and was accepted. Fortunately, Lois Kahn, the college registrar, believed in helping people help themselves. She encouraged all the staff to upgrade their skills through education. Kahn became Dorothy's mentor by allowing Dorothy to take a course during lunch and finally an evening course. This meant that Dorothy had to make special plans for the children. First, she arranged for a neighbor to "look in on them" in Dorothy's absence. The children were kept in the bedroom, away from the kitchen's hazards and the living room's access to the front door. They were not permitted to allow entrance to the apartment to anyone. Dorothy carefully taught them self-care, simple first aid, emergency techniques and telephone numbers, selected games to play, books to read, puzzles to solve, and simple household chores. Denyce was in charge. At times, Dorothy would rush home from work and spend a couple of hours with her children and then rush back to an evening course.

To increase the family's income, Dorothy took on a second job. She and her sister decided to operate a shopping delivery service. "First, my father sold his station wagon for $200 and sent me the money." Next, they managed an arrangement with a large supermarket. Dorothy would be a "transportation lady." Many shoppers welcomed a chance to have their groceries arrive at their suburban homes without delay. One of the children always accompanied her to help and give driving directions. Dorothy could never remember locations, because she focused on her safe driving skills. The business thrived, often bringing in several hundred dollars a week.

"Single mothers need someone with commonality," Dorothy believes. A friend who is a single parent with several children is of value. Dorothy found one. They would provide sitter services for each other, combine shopping trips, and cook and eat meals together with their combined six children, and the children played safely with playmates known to the mothers. A strong sense of spirituality existed in both families.

Dorothy has been active in church since childhood. She served as Sunday school teacher, sang in the choir, worked as secretary, and participated in fund-raising. "I always felt a need to have God in my life—to guide me—to keep my children going in the right direction," she states. Mentors like Lois Kahn and her stepmother have played major roles in Dorothy's life. Dorothy married Oliver Kenner in 1981. They had a wonderful ceremony, with both of them dressed in white. They made a splendid couple, and their portraits are proudly displayed above the living room fireplace. He is a loving father and grandfather to her children. In 1992 Denyce treated the family to a ten-day tour of Europe. The group included her parents, sister, brother-in-law, aunt, and brother. They had a wonderful trip, and exciting, colorful prints are reminders.

The children have never been in trouble. Dorothy believes it is the result of loving discipline, growing up in a fundamentalist Baptist church, welcoming their friends to her home for pajama parties, trips to the circus, joining in their activities, and having open and honest discussions. "I have always been available to them, even now," she concludes.

"Do you think of yourself as a success?" Dorothy is asked. She thinks for a moment and then replies, "Perhaps. I'm not finished yet. The college is downsizing. I expect to spend about two more years there. Then I would like to start a family business. My husband is a chef, and we're talking about a catering service maybe, or a laundromat. I love being with my family. We get along, and it's fun." With a slow wink and a wide grin, she says, "Come back in five years and ask me the question again."

Denyce

"As far back as I can remember, I always enjoyed singing. There came a point in my life when singing became a joy to feel and to express." The tall, willowy, model-like figure tosses her shoulder-length hair before continuing. Denyce's voice is vibrant with precise enunciation, revealing her years of training. The previous evening, Denyce sang at the White House, where President Clinton entertained the prime minister of Canada, Raymond Chretien. She was still savoring the honor. "As a child, my sister, brother, and I played church rather than doctor and nurse, mother and father, or teacher and pupil. We all sang in the church choir, including my mother."

Denyce sang before she was born, Dorothy laughingly reveals. "I cannot remember a time when she wasn't singing. She's also a trouper. When she had a thyroid problem, which affected her voice, Denyce decided to give up singing and do secretarial work. But word spread about her talent, and the music world was not ready to accept her retirement. The Houston Grand

Opera called repeatedly to ask her to appear in a program designed for young artists. The family and friends begged and coaxed her into accepting. She did well, and the second chance for a career was under way."

Denyce's relationship with her mother has been special. "As the older girl, she acted as substitute mother, handling responsibilities effectively and thoughtfully. I could always depend upon her. She graciously accepted the supervision of her brother and sister and never complained." Dorothy pauses. "One special story comes to mind. As far back as I can remember, she had a flair for fashion. I mean the 'whole nine yards.' Her hair had to be in place. She was always in the mirror combing her hair and tying a colorful scarf around her neck. Her clothes had to look good! When we went shopping, as soon as we entered the store, Denyce would see an expensive item. She never even looked at price tags. If she really wanted the outfit, Denyce would promise me that if I purchased it for her, she would not want anything else for a long time. She was the same way with her hair. I remember that when she became a teenager, she wanted to go to the beauty parlor to get her hair done professionally. One Christmas, I gave her $100. She went to Natural Motions. When she came home, her hair was so beautiful. She was one happy young lady."

Denyce recalls going on her first date. "I was 15 and attended a concert with a son of a family friend. His father accompanied us." Before they left, Mrs. Kenner took Denyce into the bedroom for a quiet chat. She cautioned her daughter about going out on a date without money. "Take this 'mad money,'" her mother said, putting several 50¢ pieces in Denyce's purse, which increased its weight considerably. But Denyce felt grown up—cool, she remembers, showing a happy face.

When describing her mother, a seriousness enters her voice. She says, "My mother has great strength and a sense of family unity. She believes in a greater power, i.e., whatever you believe in can happen. Being able to be free to dream is very important to her." Denyce thinks that her mother is a very kind, generous, talented, and nurturing person. "My ability to understand adversity, my sense of commitment and perseverance were values taught by my mother."

Besides her love of music, Denyce likes to read autobiographies, novels, and inspirational and motivational stories. The credit for help with her success goes to Mrs. Judy Grove-Allen, who guided her career from elementary school through Duke Ellington High School for the Performing Arts in Washington, D.C. "She came into my life as a divine inspiration," Denyce enthuses. As principal of the school, she encouraged Denyce to apply for admission. Not only was Denyce accepted, but private instruction was offered, too. She recalls the visit for her audition. "The environment was so contagious. Everyone worked to capacity. Being a competitive person, I quickly captured the spirit of hard work, intensive study, and practice. This was the norm for the school. Everyone pushed for excellence all the time."

Denyce was startled to see young and older students stretching, vocalizing, limbering up, and practicing on instruments—and this was at lunchtime. She was in awe of such devotion and began to realize what it took to make it. While a student, Denyce attended her first opera performance; it was a dress rehearsal of Beethoven's *Fidelio* at the Kennedy Center. She enjoyed every note of it. Trying to project herself into the future, she wondered if someday she might be on that stage.

When asked about her first solo, Denyce laughed heartily. "It came as a surprise to everyone, especially me." Mrs. Kenner and the children used to practice music at home on Thursday and Saturday evenings in preparation for Sunday services. But this one Sunday, as they stood before the congregation, Mrs. Kenner whispered to Denyce, "I want you to sing the solo today." Denyce was shocked. "Today?" she asked in disbelief. "Today, now!" her mother responded. By now they had the attention of the congregation, and people were calling out, "Sing, sweetheart. Praise the Lord!" There was no place to run or hide. "So I had to go with it," she says. Later, when she thought about it, Denyce was quite pleased with her performance, and so was everyone else.

Denyce has a vivid recollection of a conversation with her mother. "She casually told me that earlier in her life, she had dreamed of becoming an opera singer." Mrs. Kenner spoke without feelings of regret or bitterness, but with feelings of love and happiness. Denyce was amazed to learn of her mother's secret hopes and dreams. They embraced warmly, without words. Denyce believes that children are the first ones to absorb the karma of the parents. Through the entire development process, a child is very close to a parent, giving and receiving love; the parents' hopes and dreams are unconsciously communicated to the child vicariously.

The first time Denyce appeared in an opera happened when she was a student at Oberlin. The college was celebrating its centennial anniversary, and there was high-profile media attention. Denyce created her role, the Queen Mother in Conrad Cummings' *Eros and Psyche*, which added to the significance of her appearance. She remembers that it was a cold, snowy Ohio night, and driving alone to the theater was not pleasurable. Most of the students were busy studying and couldn't attend. But three friends did, and they shared champagne with her after the performance. She drove home alone and got into bed just as the Johnny Carson show was about to be shown. Listlessly turning on the television, Denyce suddenly realized that she had just passed a milestone! She gasped, "Wait a second. I was in my first opera tonight, and here I am watching Johnny Carson . . . just like nothing happened!" She fell back on the pillows, laughing at her ludicrous behavior. But that night made a big impact on her life.

"The greatest honor ever paid to me was given by some prisoners at the Missouri State Prison in St. Louis," she claims. This was a captive audience that didn't choose to listen to some strange woman who was going to sing, of all things, opera. Denyce was advised to just stand in front of them and sing, which increased her nervousness. She prepared herself for groans and boos. "But when I looked at the facial expressions, I envisioned confusion, anger, and hopelessness." Denyce became aware of the distance between their separate worlds. If anything was to be realized, she would have to make the first move. "These are human beings with feelings. I must approach them on a human level," she thought. Denyce slowly began the aria "Habanera" from *Carmen* and consciously walked among them, gently touching a shoulder or patting a back. As she reached out to them with her voice and her body, the room became cathedral-quiet. The men were straining to understand the words and music. They relaxed against the folding chairs. "When I finished, there was hesitant applause, which grew until it filled the room. The men rose as one and came forward to shake my hand and thank me. One said in a husky voice with tremors, 'We won't be getting out, but we wish you all the luck.'" Denyce is quiet for a moment and then says, "This was a highlight of my life and theirs too."

Harassment occurs in the world of opera, just like everywhere else. "People are people, with insecurities, hurt feelings, perversions, and mental illnesses," she says. Denyce believes that some people tend not to trust themselves. They worry about what others might say. For example, she describes an audition before a group. "Afterward, there may be disagreement among them, and they can be swayed from a positive position to a negative one." Denyce prefers auditioning before an individual. Although the final decision depends on the opinions of others, influences beyond one's control do persist, like the desires of wealthy patrons. Denyce feels that each person has a responsibility for art. "I believe that if I get my foot in the door, it's my job to make sure that I stay in the room!" she exclaims with a glint in her eyes. "But the hardest part is getting recognition." She welcomes the change of attitude that is now seen more frequently. To prevent subjectivity, musicians are auditioned behind screens, so the performance is judged purely on merit.

One of the happiest evenings of Denyce's life was her debut at the Metropolitan Opera House in October 1995. Most of her neighbors, family, and friends were aware of her singing opera, but few had ever visited an opera house. On a Saturday evening performance, October 7, 1995, their dreams were realized when Denyce made her debut in Bizet's *Carmen*. They came by automobile, bus, and train, more than 100 of them, to hear the local girl make good. The tumultuous standing ovation she received convinced them that she was an opera star. "I was so proud. Some remembered me as a child, teenager, church soloist, college student, friend, neighbor, and just the 'girl next door.' All those brown faces in the audience were a first for the Metropolitan. Their mere presence made a statement. For me, it was a gift from heaven. They came to see me, Denyce."

Another proud moment in Denyce's life was her appearance at the celebration of what would have been Marian Anderson's 100th birthday at Carnegie Hall in February 1997. A *New York Times* reporter, Allan Kozinn,
wrote, "It must be daunting for a singer to pay tribute to a predecessor whose
style and sound were so distinctive, and there are few stylistic links between
Anderson and the singers who honored her. One exception was Denyce
Graves, a mezzo soprano whose tone has the depth and roundness one associated with Anderson and who offered a gorgeous, passionate account of
Saint-Saens's *Mon coeur s'ouvre à ta voix.*" It was particularly meaningful,
since Denyce was a recipient of the Marian Anderson Award in 1991, which
was presented by Miss Anderson.

Denyce's career profile could be a chapter in "Who's Who in Opera."
Recognized worldwide as an outstandingly talented mezzo-soprano, she has
performed throughout the United States' and Europe's opera houses, including La Scala, Paris, Geneva, and Covent Garden. Her numerous concerts in major cities include appearances with well-known artists like Placido
Domingo, Luciano Pavarotti, and Jose Carreras. She was heard in recitals
at Kennedy Center in Washington, D.C., as well as Musashino Hall in Tokyo. Her recordings include a solo disc of French arias, *Hamlet, Otello, La
Vestale, Rigoletto,* the newly released *Christmas from National Cathedral,* and
a solo disc of spirituals on the PBS label. She has been the recipient of the
Grand Prix du Concours International de Chant de Paris, first prize Eleanor
Steber Music Award, a Jacobson Study Grant, and the Grand Prix Lyrique,
to name a few.

In the fall 1997 opening of the Metropolitan Opera House, Denyce appeared with Placido Domingo in *Carmen,* a revival production. As for her
future, Denyce would like to be in a position where she could have more
artistic control. She explains, "Sometimes you are engaged to sing with
someone unknown to you in a new production, and you're not fully convinced of that person's motivations. You often have to stand behind things
that you really don't believe in. There are certain performers who can help
you . . . inspire you. But there are others who can pull energy away from . . .
harm you. If you're fortunate, you meet someone with whom you can sing
well and are comfortable. It helps both performers and the performance. But
under every circumstance, you remember to be true to yourself, your art."

Denyce would like to see more "brown" faces on the stage and in the
audience. "Children should be exposed to all kinds of music early in life,
particularly that which is beautiful and lasting. I like to see English subtitles,
because it helps people understand the story of opera."

Does her future include children, a family? Her mother smiles and points
to a beautiful wedding picture of an attractive couple—Denyce and David
Perry. "If she ever slows down, I may become a grandmother." Denyce grins
widely and nods in agreement.

Gloria and Shani

"Shani Akilah means marvelous and intelligent in one of the African languages," explains the tall, slim 19-year-old woman who is a freshman at Mercy College in Westchester, New York. Gloria, her mother, a social worker, holds an administrative position in the governor's office. This single, African American mother and her only child have developed a clear, reciprocal relationship. "We talk endlessly about the importance of education, how to have positive relationships with peers, and how racism impacts upon our lives." Because Shani lives in a dormitory, subjects like drinking and driving, acquaintance rape, and drugs are important to discuss. Shani neither drinks nor smokes and chooses friends who don't indulge, either. She knows how to assess a potentially dangerous situation or person. Last year Shani taught sex education to adolescents. The experience reinforced her personal knowledge of AIDS and sexual behavior.

Gloria identifies herself as a responsible role model for her daughter and other young women. "I try very hard to present and expose her to acceptable behavior for a single mother." Gloria is successful in her dual role of a professional and a parent. "Shani always accompanied me to professional meetings where I made presentations in Albany, Washington, D.C., Philadelphia, and other cities. For vacations we travel to California, Myrtle Beach, South Carolina, Canada, and Barbados with friends." Very early in life, Shani learned that education is vital if a minority woman hopes to succeed in a vocation and in life. Gloria is warm and demonstrative, rewarding Shani for excellence in behavior and work. "I may give her a small gift, take her to the opera or a concert, or plan dinner in a special restaurant. I tell her how proud I am of her with lots of kisses and hugs." Gloria's eyes are filled with tears of happiness. Communication flows easily between them regarding choice of boyfriends, dates, employment opportunities, and career choices.

As to Afro-ethnicity, Gloria loves the long, free-flowing, colorful African dress and dons the Gallee, a colorful print cotton head wrap, on special occasions. A memorable learning event was a trip to South Africa several years ago. Three generations (Gloria, her mother, and Shani) experienced a sense of "coming home" in this distant land. "The music and architecture and sculpture were spectacular. Everyone was receptive and so friendly, and it was so comfortable to see so many dark faces," Gloria explains. Within the extended family, many of the old customs of the freed slaves are remembered and honored, like quilting, family reunions, eating soul food, gospel singing, oral history, and family saving clubs. Today, it is not unusual to hear girls' names like Lawanda, Tamekekia, Tashima, Keisha, Takisha, and Jahlhiejah, especially among young African American families, many of whom had ethnic marriage services, that is, with ancient dress and ceremonials.

Women are said to be the "backbone" of the black church. It is common to find mothers and daughters singing in the choir, serving as ushers, and teaching Sunday school and as members of youth groups and other-church related organizations.

Shani believes that Gloria is incredible and takes her role of motherhood very seriously. "She is hardworking and responsible. She shares her knowledge with me, which accounts for my success at school. She's beautiful inside and outside. I hope to be as open-minded and affectionate with my own children. My friends often talk of their parents being cold and selfish; they envy me."

REFERENCES

Billingsley, A. *Black Families in White America*. Indianapolis, IN: Macmillan, 1968.

Cashmore, E. *Dictionary of Race and Ethnic Relations*. New York: Routledge, 1994.

Davidson, B. *Discovering Our African Heritage*. Boston: Ginn, 1971.

Draper, T. *The Rediscovery of Black Nationalists*. New York: Viking Press, 1970.

Franklin, J. H. "African American Families." In *Black Families*, ed. H. P. McAdoo. Thousand Oaks, CA: Sage, 1997.

Franklin, J. H. "A Brief History of the Negro in the United States." In *The American Negro Reference Book*, ed. J. P. Davis. Englewood Cliffs, NJ: Prentice-Hall, 1996.

Glick, P. "Demographic Pictures of African American Families." In *Black Families*, ed. H. P. McAdoo. Thousand Oaks, CA: Sage, 1997.

Gonzales, J., Jr. *Racial and Ethnic Groups in America*. Dubuque, IA: Kendall/Hunt, 1990.

JCPES (Joint Center for Political and Economic Studies). Washington, DC, 1992.

Jordan, M. D. *White over Black: American Attitudes toward the Negro. 1550–1812*. Baltimore: Penguin Books, 1968.

King, M. L., Jr. *Stride toward freedom: The Montgomery Story*. New York: Harper and Brothers, 1958.

Kozinn, A. "Spiritual for a Symbol of Triumph." *New York Times*, March 1, 1997.

Litwack, L. *North of Slavery: The Negro in the Free States. 1790–1865*. Chicago: University of Chicago Press, 1967.

Pinkney, A. *Black Americans*. 2d ed. Englewood Cliffs, NJ: Prentice-Hall, 1975.

Sudarkasa, N. "African American Families and Family Values." In *Black Families*, ed. H. P. McAdoo. Thousand Oaks, CA: Sage, 1997.

Willie, C. W. *The Family Life of Black People*. Columbus, OH: Charles E. Merrill, 1970.

Woodward, C. V. *The Strange Career of Jim Crow*. New York: Oxford University Press, 1966.

U.S. Bureau of the Census. *Poverty Rates by Type of Family and Race of Householder*. 1979 and 1993.

PERSONAL REFLECTIONS
by Regina Jennings

THE ENDURING LEGACY: AFRICAN AMERICAN WOMEN TRANSMITTING VALUES: NEW WAYS TO RESTORE THE FAMILY

Since her transportation from Africa to the Americas, the African woman has had to transmit nontraditional values to her children. I say nontraditional because this woman had to shift African traditions into ways that did not insult a racist and slave-producing society. The overarching structure of society controlled the general habitation and lifestyle of the enslaved woman. The enslaved African woman lacked control over her body, her labor, her offspring, and her husband. How does one continue to function under such conditions that no other group has been forced to endure? One shifts her personal system of values into behaviors that can manipulate a hostile environment. African American women enabled their offspring to survive in America by teaching them to masquerade, assimilate, invert white assumptions, and network within the African community. Such tactics should be considered today as we struggle to direct our youth away from drugs, improper behavior, and disrespect.

When African American mothers taught their children to masquerade, they did so for the sake of longevity. During slavery, children (also adults) were unable to speak the truth to the master class. Therefore, slave children had to be taught the necessity to bind the tongue to, as Harriet Tubman says, see and hear more than they say. They learned to function within an unjust system that described them as inferior. They had to (re)interpret and return the ideology of white America in order to function and to survive with minimal molestation. Thus, black children had to learn to read their environment more deeply than did their white counterparts. They had to mask their own realities and "function" inside a vision or image imposed by enslavers. If the children misstepped the masquerade, they could be sold away, or they could be consistently, physically harmed.

These practices taught black children to immediately learn how society and environment operate. Mothers, knowing the importance of education, when possible encouraged children to read. Even though blacks lacked access to education in many states, they worked through kinship structures to obtain literacy. In *Incidents in the Life of a Slave Girl* (1861), the author and protagonist, Linda Brent, is a case in point. Her parents made sure that she and her siblings learned how to read. The enslaved people knew that being able to read opened new worlds. They could not be tricked as easily, and if they could write, they could make preparations for escape by writing passes.

Education, therefore, was seen as an avenue of assimilation that would help not only the individual black but the group as well. Today, black people and black educators need to work more closely together. My southern colleagues tell me, for example, that when they were students, teachers used their own money to purchase necessary books. They say that their teachers always provided them with extra time and encouragement.

These old, southern teachers definitely understood the necessity to fortify students against American racism and its residue: black inferiority. They knew from history that inverting the reasoning of white America had taught the enslaved people how to critically read their environment in ways unknown by the master class. For this reason and others, blacks developed a kinship interrelationship that extended beyond the immediate family. It extended into the larger black community. A prime example of this kinship relationship is the language of the 1960s. During the 1960s, black people referred to one another as "brother" or "sister" whether or not biologically related. Early in American history, black people developed a collectivity based on racial distinctiveness. Within the closed group they reinforced themselves, particularly their cultural traits. When in the group they sang in that particular black way. They also danced and worshiped in a spiritual manner indicative of black people. It was a form of communication signaling the time for escape, and it was a mode of comfort to sing while one worked. Working within the kinship network, blacks sanctioned their own specific way of being and thereby ensured their longevity.

These efforts are still in effect today, culminating into a reach toward Africa evident in the new black holiday called Kwanza. This holiday, created by Maulana Karenga in 1966, starts after Christmas and lasts seven days. Each day is a reminder and celebration of a universal, African principle. For example, the first day of Kwanza is Umoja, which means unity. To celebrate this Swahili word and concept encourages participants to unite their own community. The purpose is to unify around issues that directly relate to black people. Such unification strengthens the black community, bringing back the importance of kinship. To establish enduring values within the black community, both men and women have to become leaders in initiating the fundamentals. The idea is not unlike the African proverb that "each one teach one."

Being responsible for one another fosters the values that our late 19th- and early 20th-century thinkers adhered to when fighting for the human rights of blacks. Individuals like Carter G. Woodson, who started Black History Week, and Ida B. Wells, who investigated lynchings, were called "race" people. They openly advocated for the betterment of the race. Woodson explained how education should assist intragroup development. Wells' activism included lecturing and writing articles that dispelled myths and stereotypes about black people. Before the postmodern epoch, many black leaders were unapologetic and bold in their responsibility to and for the collective. This sentiment, which peaked during the 1960s, needs to spread once again throughout contemporary America. Men and women have to undertake this challenge. Values that encourage an Afrocentric education, for example, should be instituted in every predominantly black neighborhood. What I mean is this: African-centered thinkers can coordinate community education programs that offer study avenues for neighborhood youth. Any church or mosque can house such programs. These educational and vocational activities will empower our next generation. Additionally, teachers become respected elders as they act as role models, and young black men and women desperately need role models. Gender-specific courses are important, returning young men and women to particular tasks. Because of the power and numbers involved in both the Million Man and the Million Woman marches, sometimes gender isolation is healthy.

People must extend themselves beyond biological kinship. For example, successful parents should reach back and assist struggling parents with young children. All adults can provide children with literature, picture books, African-centered entertainment and learning. Networking within churches or other organizations can locate people ready to help the disadvantaged.

Our youth today need real people to talk to and "be" around. They need more visions than those displayed in the media. To restore values within our community, we have to recognize that we are all the makers and shapers of our future world. To develop the needed link of continuity, severed since enslavement, we have to reach back to move forward.

2

Haitian Americans

Haiti was discovered by Christopher Columbus in 1492, when, in the course of his first voyage in search of a route to Asia, he landed on the northern shore of the island. Columbus named it La Isla Espanola; the island later became known as Hispaniola. The island became the first permanent European colony in the Americas (Santo Domingo). The western part of the colony of Santo Domingo was to become a French colony (Saint Dominique), which in 1804 became the Republic of Haiti, while the eastern part eventually became the Dominican Republic.

Unions of French and blacks in colonial times produced a mulatto element that became an elite class. Throughout the history of the republic, the rivalry of mulattoes and blacks has resulted in struggles for power and prestige involving assassinations, insurrections, and civil wars (Weil et al., 1995).

During the early years of the republic, powerful leaders undertook to direct economic and political life along definite lines, but it soon became obvious that planned social structures would not remain intact. Subsequent developments in the political and economic life of the country were largely unplanned, and in the 20th century, standards of living, compared with those of many other countries, were low.

Turbulence has played a prominent role in the history of Haiti, beginning with the annihilation of the Tainos by the Spaniards and the establishment of the first permanent settlement by the French and English pirates. The slave rebellion that drove out the French at the end of the 18th century, invasion of the Dominican Republic, revolutions supported by mercenary Haitian guerrillas, and rulers who have exercised dictatorial powers ruthlessly—all have contributed to instability and uncertainty in the lives of the people. After the rise to power of Rafael Leonidas Trujillo Molina in 1957, peasants continued to cling to their small plot of land; the mulatto elite maintained its prestigious position; and black leaders remained politically powerful (Nicholls, 1996).

Through Haiti's history, its social system has been marked by a dual heritage—that of the French colonial and that of the African slave. The social and racial configuration was introduced during the colonial period when a small minority of wealthy whites held sway over the lives of their black slaves. A rigid, color-based stratification system evolved that enhanced initial cultural differences. An independence was ushered in, and the white elites were ushered out, giving Haiti the opportunity to develop new values and institutions. The new mulatto elite opted for the social model of their predecessors, however, and kept Roman Catholicism, the French language and culture, and light skin color as criteria of high social position.

The slave masses that fought alongside the mulattoes gained little more than emancipation and subsistence plots after independence. The lifestyles that had evolved during slavery were adapted to their new peasant status with only minimal changes. They maintained their own religion (voodoo) and their own language (Creole) and continued to center their lives on African and slave-based family and market patterns. Little has changed in the peasants' isolated, rural existence since slave days; they remain outside the national economy and political life and are virtually untouched by modern technology or social change.

The 20th century has seen the initial erosion of the traditionally dichotomous society and the emergence of a nebulous middle class. The rise in black consciousness and nationalism has brought an increased awareness of the African heritage by Haitian intellectuals—as witnessed by the liberalizing of official attitudes toward voodoo and sporadic attempts to bring greater prestige to Creoles. Expanding economic opportunities have caused differentiation within social strata, and political awareness has given impetus to the incipient middle sector. Geographic isolation and regionalism are breaking down as rural inhabitants become more mobile and seek opportunities outside their ancestral villages. Although members of the elite retain their exalted position as the last bastion of prestigious French culture, the group has opened its ranks to wealthy, educated nonelites, forming a broader-based upper class (Dorsinville, 1975).

Haitians became one of the newest immigrant groups in the United States during the 1990s. In New York City, they have established themselves in almost every job, career, and profession. They are factory workers, housekeepers, nannies, doctors, college professors, social workers, engineers, schoolteachers, police officers, cab drivers, and entrepreneurs. Many social scientists cite Haitians' use of welfare as being among the lowest (Miller, 1994). Of Haiti's estimated 7 million people, more than one-seventh have emigrated. They have settled in other Caribbean and South American countries, in Canada (primarily in Quebec and Montreal), in France, and in several French-speaking African nations (former colonies of France and Belgium), but mostly in the United States. Although the 1990 census figures report that only 289,521 Haitians live in the United States, in the Haitian community the figure is estimated to be about a million. New York counts about 500,000 Haitians; Florida, 300,000; smaller numbers live in Washington, D.C., Massachusetts, New Jersey, and Illinois.

Haitian immigration to the United States can be divided into four major waves. The first group of Haitians was composed of colonists who were fleeing the Haitian revolution of 1791, free mulattoes, and slaves who had escaped or who came along with their masters. The second major wave of immigration came during and after the U.S. occupation of Haiti between 1915 and 1934. After months of turbulence and instability, the United States invoked the Monroe Doctrine, and U.S. marines occupied Haiti for 19 years. This group (Laguerre, 1984) settled mostly in Harlem and integrated into the mainstream of U.S. society. They were mostly businesspeople, professionals, and politicians. They participated actively in the cultural and political activities of the Harlem Renaissance and the notorious Marcus Garvey's well-known, historical Universal Negro Improvement Association (UNIA) Back to Africa movement. Since they tended to be better educated than the majority of Harlem blacks and were generally more leftist than their American neighbors (Reid, 1939), they were able to obtain white-collar jobs. Immediately after François "Papa Doc" Duvalier's ascendance to power in 1957, a large number of Haitians left for the United States. This third wave initially consisted mostly of the elite or political rivals of Duvalier. Soon after, members of the middle class followed. Their main motive was fear of political reprisals and economic instability.

The fourth and largest wave of Haitians came after the death of "Papa Doc" Duvalier, when his young son, Jean-Claude, was named "president for life." Many of the new arrivals to the United States included working-class Haitians, disgruntled by their economic situation under the new regime (Dreyfuss, 1993). Most were unskilled or had limited skills (Laguerre, 1984) and suffered a kind of double invisibility (Brice-Laporte, 1972). They could not work readily because of their undocumented immigrant status, their lack of English-language proficiency, and their blackness. Many risked their lives on small boats to reach the United States, thus the name "boat people." Others died at sea and never reached shore. The great majority, as many as 35,000, settled in or near Miami (Dewind, 1991). About 10,000 to 15,000 moved to the greater New York area. As the Haitian population increased, there was a tendency toward greater social stratification in New York City and elsewhere. Middle-class Haitians always differentiated themselves from the poorer Haitians, who were the majority (Joseph, 1997).

Sixty-five percent of all Haitian immigrants reside in New York City

(Schiller et al., 1986). New York City is the second largest Haitian Creole-speaking city in the world, after Port-au-Prince, the capital of Haiti. Service providers, including school personnel dealing with the Haitian community in the United States, have now realized that these recent immigrants speak only Haitian Creole, which is a distinct language from Creole. Haitian Creole has finally been recognized for what it is, and not as "Haitian French," as it used to be called. Though this difference has come to light, and despite the fact that Haitian Creole has become an official language in Haiti, Haitian Creole is still seen by many as a lower-status language. Haitian Creole is still predominantly an oral language and is the language of choice in the personal domains of family, friends, intimate relations, and religious observances among a mostly young, first-generation, immigrant community (Joseph, 1992). In the more formal domains of school, work, and neighborhood and with professionals, English is the language most often used.

Although it is believed that the future status of Haitian Creole must derive from developments in Haiti, it is clear that Haitians living in the United States have been instrumental in pushing for change in the role that Haitian Creole plays in society. In the United States, particularly in New York City, Haitian Creole has slowly come to be accepted and used in official domains as the bona fide language of Haitians. A popular Haitian proverb, "deye mon, gen mon"—"beyond mountains, there are mountains"—taps the innermost complexity of being Haitian. There is more to a Haitian than meets the eye (Joseph, 1997).

CASE STUDIES

Carole

It was a noble mission—a college deliberately located in a low-income neighborhood and the first to offer courses in both English and Spanish. The proposed focus was a curriculum especially designed to best serve immigrant students. At Hostos Community College, the answer was to offer many courses, from music to health sciences, in both English and Spanish, while simultaneously teaching English in separate classes. This was in 1970, when the college opened in an abandoned factory in the South Bronx.

In 1997 the almost 78% Spanish-speaking student body is debating the importance of students' proficiency in English as a graduation requirement. Students, faculty, and administration are rethinking the bilingual mission of this college. Some say the environment does not foster bilingualism and does not prepare students for employment or higher education. Others would like special treatment for the adult, poor, working, and family-oriented student population. The college's mission is to provide access to a population that has traditionally been denied access to higher education.

In this often volatile environment Carole Berotte Joseph works as an administrative faculty member—associate dean of academic affairs.

Carole's office is typical of one found in an artificial setting of an old factory building. Painting, shades, lighting, and other amenities have not quite erased the industrial appearance. She sits behind a large desk cluttered with reports, printouts, and correspondence that indicate the interdisciplinary aspect of her responsibilities. "I was born in Port-au-Prince, Haiti, on January 3, 1949, but in 1957 my family immigrated to New York," Carole begins. "It was the time when Duvalier was elected. It was a very frightening time, and I remember standing on the balcony of our home and witnessing several bodies being dragged through the street. The sight of blood, the sound of gunfire, and the tension of curfews stayed with me for a long time." Carole's rapid-fire, whispery voice communicates latent fear. Carole's father was a teacher, but he was also a diplomat who traveled to foreign countries. As a young man, he won scholarships to colleges in West Virginia and Belgium. His area of specialization was agronomy. Her father was also trained in carpentry and cabinetmaking and had his own shop. "All of our furniture was made by him in his shop, where he also taught many apprentices. After a teaching appointment in a technical vocational school, he was awarded a diplomatic post. After becoming a U.S. citizen and continuing his education, he was a junior high school teacher of industrial arts in Brooklyn."

When her family left Haiti, they left everything behind, including clothing. Carole's father had preceded them by several months to look for living quarters. Because he had lived in the United States, he was aware of the difficulties that faced immigrants. "One thing he discovered," Carole says, "was that most people were reluctant to rent to families with several children." He was finally successful in finding an apartment in the Bushwick area of Brooklyn—an almost 100% Italian neighborhood with lots of children. There were four children in her family, but Carole's father told the landlord of only three, in an attempt to minimize the family. To avoid trouble, the children were warned to keep very quiet, walk rather than run down the stairs, and not slam doors. Carole's mother was very anxious to learn English. "She had a bilingual (French/English) dictionary, and we were constantly asking her the meaning of words in order to communicate with our newly-made friends."

There were no English as a second language (ESL) classes in those days. The children knew no English, so all four were placed in a grade below their achievement levels. After six months, Carole's mother enrolled the children in parochial schools. In Haiti only children who can't afford private school attend public school. Carole and her siblings had attended parochial school in Haiti and were excellent students, but making the transition in America was difficult. Carole remembers the confinement of that time. "We would come back home from school, eat dinner, study, and go to bed. We didn't speak English, had no friends in classes, and didn't know the city."

Carole's mother had studied nursing in Haiti. "But when we came to America, she was a homemaker until my youngest sister was in high school. She then returned to her profession," says Carole. Carole attended All Saints

Commercial High in Brooklyn. She did quite well and graduated with a Regents diploma. Carole explains the reason. "When you immigrate and have had some education, and your parents are educated and middle-class, the transition is not that difficult." As one who experienced complete immersion in English, Carole speaks with knowledge.

She remembers being very organized as an adolescent, which helped her in school. Her reports were always turned in promptly, and homework was always up-to-date. At All Saints High School, she also excelled at secretarial work and won several awards in her secretarial courses. All of the children went to parochial high schools, except a younger sister who had musical talent. "My mother wasn't eager to let her attend Music and Arts High School. But all of us convinced my parents that it was the best way for my sister to develop her talent, so my mother finally agreed," Carole notes. In high school Carole was active in volleyball, swimming, crocheting class, and glee club. She had studied piano and violin beginning at the age of 4. Her great-aunt was an accomplished concert pianist in Haiti. But at All Saints, Carole played the bass drum. "I guess I must have joined the band late, because it was the only instrument left," she laughs robustly.

In the old tradition of family members helping each other, Carole's grandmother assisted with the down payment on a private house for the family, on Washington Avenue near the Brooklyn Museum and the Botanical Gardens. "These grounds became our playground. Many happy moments were spent there playing outdoor games. I had become a great ice skater." At home, Carole's father was the main disciplinarian. "But my mother was pretty strict too," Carole recalls. Since she was the oldest, her parents frequently reminded Carole of her responsibility of setting a good example for the younger children. "They always praised me when I accomplished goals or used effective judgment. Their guidance and support were most helpful. My adolescence was pretty smooth," she remembers. "My father always encouraged us to aim for the highest achievement possible. 'Never settle for a lesser goal,' he advised."

Carole was accepted at Queens College but attended York. "I heard that York would have small language classes, as well as teacher education, so I was interested. As a child, I always played school with my dolls or with other children, but I was always the teacher. On rainy days, when outdoor play was impossible, I would line up my playmates on the stairs in a modified classroom setting and act as teacher. I loved it!" Carole is ecstatic in describing it. Several faculty members of York praised Carole for her teaching and her administrative skills.

Carole fell in love with the son of a family friend. They met when the young man attended her high school graduation party. "He was attending college in France. His mother was not prepared for him to get involved with anyone until his graduation," Carole goes on. She was completing her junior year and desperately wanted to get married. Her parents also were against an early marriage. Their dating was very formal, limited, and under supervision. This made the young couple very unhappy and even more eager to marry. Both of their parents finally gave in to the pleas of the young people. He transferred to Baruch and continued his studies in New York, and Carole completed a summer semester of advanced courses. "We were married when I was a senior. Unfortunately, there was some sadness, because my sister-in-law-to-be died a month before the wedding date. The plans had been made for a large, elaborate affair. Because the family was still in mourning, we agreed to have a modest celebration."

Family life has always been vitally important. "There is a closeness between us. Parenting and child care were shared by aunts, grandmothers, cousins, and friends. Since my parents had a house, most holidays, birthdays, and other celebrations were held at our home with my mother organizing the dinner and the entertainment. In the Haitian community, much like African Americans and Hispanic Americans, friends and neighbors take turns caring for each other's children," Carole remembers.

Carole is aware of the practice of voodoo, but the family never followed it or became involved with the religion, although she is aware of many cultural practices that have roots in the voodoo religion. "As children in Haiti, we were Protestants. But when we enrolled in parochial school in Brooklyn, we were baptized into the Catholic faith."

As newlyweds, Carole and her husband planned to postpone a family until they were financially prepared. "We both worked and saved for our first home. I didn't have my first daughter until we were married for three years. With savings, I was able to stay home and bond with her. Later, we shared part-time parenting practices and worked different shifts. I was teaching school days, and my husband worked in banking, evenings. Since my mother lived nearby, she helped out occasionally."

At York, Carole was fortunate to have a professor of Romance languages who encouraged and advised her regarding course possibilities. "She was a wonderful mentor, and we became friends. She even came to my wedding," Carole adds with a smile. Later at City College, a professor of bilingual education took an interest in Carole. He also provided advice and was instrumental in getting teaching positions for Carole.

Carole expresses resentment about her treatment as a young faculty member at City College. "I worked eight hours a day for five days a week. In addition, I was assigned to numerous committees, which were time-consuming and often nonproductive. The senior faculty never helped or advised me about future possibilities or the importance of writing or doing research. I developed and established important programs that I took pride in, but those did not count as much. I found a great lack of leadership in the administration." Carole is not bitter but is disappointed in the quality of mentorship and lack of support rendered. "As a result, I enrolled in a doctoral program in 1977 and didn't finish my dissertation until 1992," Carole explains. "What hurt me most was the insensitivity of senior minority faculty, especially the African Americans. They never reached out to me," she adds sadly. This experience didn't prevent Carole from responding to the needs of both undergraduate and graduate students and younger faculty members; she demonstrated concern, interest, and fellowship to all.

The dissolution of Carole's marriage, she thinks, was a result of youth and lack of experience. "I was right out of high school, he was my first boyfriend, and I was very naive," she recalls. "Because you plan, work, and save doesn't guarantee a long, happy marriage." Now Carole understands how all that energy led to chaos. Her husband not only supported her search for advancement but encouraged her efforts, until they became threatening to his masculinity and esteem. He saw her progress interfering with what he considered her duty as a wife and homemaker. He had a bachelor's degree, and she held a doctorate. Although he had advanced to become vice president of a bank, he saw her gains as too competitive. She was moving ahead too quickly and leaving her husband behind. They became incompatible, and their frustration often ended in anger. Carole suggested professional marriage counseling, but he wasn't interested and didn't really believe in seeking help. Carole gave up some of her professional and community activities to appease him, but that didn't save the marriage. Carole and the girls were helped by counseling during the one-year separation. "We really had many good years together." It was difficult to dissolve a marriage that everyone thought was "made in heaven." But at the end of a year of court appearances, broken promises, and delays in child care payment, Carole sought a divorce.

Unfortunately, the divorce came at a bad time for the adolescent daughters. The oldest, Marjorie, blamed Carole for breaking up the marriage. Since the children didn't witness any major verbal or physical abuse between their parents, they saw no need for the separation. But Carole explained the circumstances thoroughly to them. The youngest daughter felt closer to Carole. "I told them, 'When you are older, you'll understand,' and they did." Carole admits that during this period there were outbursts and tears at times, but when the girls entered college, the mother–daughter relationship became close and happy.

The associate dean's prospects appear bright right now. Although Carole has received offers of positions elsewhere, she is not really looking for a change. "I was recommended for this position by the college's president. I earned a master's degree in curriculum and teaching at Fordham University and a Ph.D. in bilingual education, and I've had many administrative experiences. What I think I need most now is experience in research and writing." Carole stops for a moment and takes a deep breath and at a rapid pace continues. "I aspire to be a dean but now it looks like I may extend my aspirations toward administration. I recently completed an application for a

Kellogg Foundation Fellowship for Leadership in Higher Education, and I've been selected." She laughs at her dilemma. Eventually, Carole would like to teach again. But for now, unfinished business at the college needs her talents. Helping to make changes in Hostos Community College's bilingual education curriculum is one of the challenges that she now faces.

When asked, "What did you learn from your mother and pass on to your daughters?," Carole thinks briefly and says, "Accept responsibility and do the best that you can. Have pride in your work. Complete your tasks today. Don't put things off. Be generous and caring. Organize your thoughts and behavior. Have respect for yourself and others."

This energetic, articulate, and personable young woman is finding happiness in her personal life, too. She has a relationship with an older man who is sympathetic, supportive, and caring.

Carole feels that she is successful. "My personal satisfaction goes beyond professional achievements. I've taken responsibility to speak, offer my services, and be an advocate for my community. They have shown appreciation for my efforts that makes me happy. I am a proud mother of two 'really together' young ladies. Deep down, I'm happy and at peace with myself," Carole concludes.

Carole has received many academic and professional honors, including New York State Association for Bilingual Education (NYSABE) Gladys Correa Award, 1995; Twentieth Century Award for Achievement, 1992; Excellence Award for Leadership; New York City (NYC) Haitian Educator's Association Award; Baruch College's Haitian Cultural Society Award for Community Service, 1987; and the Rockland County Dr. Martin Luther King, Jr., Award for Outstanding Community Service, 1986. She is an honorary member, Golden Key National Honor Society, 1991–present; and member, NYC Chancellor's Advisory Board on Multicultural Education, 1990–present.

She also holds memberships in many professional organizations, has written several articles and chapters, and has served as editor for bilingual Caribbean literary publications.

Carole's latest publication is "Haitian Creoles in New York," a chapter in *The Multilingual Apple*, edited by O. Garcia and J. Fishman. She was recently elected president of Haitian Studies Association, a professional international educational organization that promotes research and encourages discussion and debate on Haiti and Haitian society, in Haiti and in the diaspora, from various perspectives.

Marjorie

Marjorie Anne is the oldest of Carole's daughters. She was born in Queens, New York, on May 2, 1973. Carole remembers Marjorie as a lively youngster who was attracted to everything. Since she was only 20 months older than her sister, Claudine, they shared toys and played together. Their relationship was loving.

Growing up, Marjorie was one of those children who constantly ask, Why? What? Who? Later, she would challenge the answers. In high school, Marjorie's requirements for friendship were loyalty, honesty, creativity, and intelligence. There were quite a few who met those requirements. She met them in activities like Varsity Athletes against Substance Abuse, National Honor Society, Drama Club, French Honor Society, football, basketball, and cheerleading (in which she was co-captain and captain).

Academically, Marjorie claims that she was a great student. "But I don't do well on standardized tests," she admits. Her greatest strengths have always been in English and social studies in high school and in college. Marjorie graduated in 1995 from Pennsylvania State University with a political science major and a double minor in African studies and African American dance. Among Marjorie's personal achievements, she has received the Editor's Choice Award two years consecutively from the Library of Congress for published poems and has made the dean's list.

At one point, Marjorie considered athletic training or physical therapy as career choices. "I loved biology but despised chemistry," she says, so she decided to return to her youthful desires to pursue the profession of law. Marjorie now works as a legal assistant in an entertainment law firm and hopes to enroll in law school in the fall 1998 term. She still asks questions and feels secure in challenging the answers.

One family value she adheres to is strong kinship. "I believe attending gatherings and celebrations with family is vital to maintaining a tightly knit family," Marjorie says. "When I need advice, I usually seek it from my parents or sister and close friends."

The characteristics she admires in Carole include "generosity in helping others in need, fighting for what she believes in, and the ability to make it happen, whatever it may be." Carole is Marjorie's role model. This daughter was very proud when her mother was awarded the Ph.D.

Marjorie doesn't think independence and responsibility can be taught as such but are adopted because of one's natural makeup or characteristics. She explains, "You can have a very 'together' parent with children whose actions are unexplainable. It is my very nature to be independent and responsible. Maybe it's in the genes."

Carole's career influenced Marjorie in several ways. "We were exposed to the many facets of her working life and her interests. She was great in stimulating and cultivating our minds. Consequently, dance and piano lessons were encouraged." Marjorie thinks a few seconds and adds, "Her career life has been positive in that my mother's continuing education and achievements have only served to push me forward in life." Like Carole, Marjorie is a leader who shuns conformity. "I admire my mother's persistence and drive. She never gives up. To see her succeed and be dignified in failure has been great. Negatively, one cannot ever have everything in life, and balance seems to be a never-ending process. At times, I felt like we got the worst of her, while everyone else got the best. This makes sense; when a mother comes home after a hard day's work, she's tired, frustrated, running late, and her day is not over, with cooking and housework facing her," Marjorie says philosophically. "But my Mom almost always prepared meals in advance and made sure that we were properly cared for."

Marjorie describes her family as close-knit, in which the women have always been strong and successful in whatever they do. "Although my grand-mother was not career-oriented, she successfully raised five children—one of the best careers available," she says. "Independence has always been en-couraged. However, if your personality or nature was not to be independent, love was unconditional. When one is ready to fly, he or she will fly!," says Marjorie brightly.

Claudine

Claudine Marie is the younger daughter of Carole. She was born Novem-ber 16, 1974, in Queens, New York. She agrees that her relationship with sister, Marjorie, has always been warm and loving. "She's available for a chat always. It could be a real problem or a simple situation." Claudine's favorite toy as a child was a pencil, because she was always sketching or doodling. She enjoys volleyball and loves animals, especially dogs.

This young woman differentiates between friends and associates. "I am very particular in choosing friends. You can always find associates, but friends are hard to come by." Claudine likes people who are outgoing, fun, energetic, and, of course, talkative. She is also a leader.

In high school, Claudine demonstrated her physical prowess by gaining positions of captain of the varsity volleyball team and captain of the track team. She was honored with a golden pin presented by the city for her academic achievements. Claudine's name appeared in *Who's Who* of high school collegiate students. The African American Club, Culture Club, and AP (Advanced Placement) Art Club listed her as an active member. She made the honor roll in almost all of her high school years, although she does not claim to be a high-achieving student. "I always did my homework but had to study quite a lot to get good grades. My best subjects were advanced economics and history, but I really enjoyed my advanced art class, from which I won numerous awards," Claudine says, smiling broadly.

Claudine cannot rate any of her teachers. She feels that they were all qualified and prepared. "I love to be challenged. I am competitive and hard-working. I think that my teachers recognized that and looked forward to teaching me." At the University of Maryland Eastern Shore, Claudine was president of Student Activities, vice president of the Student Government

Association, and president of the sophomore class. She is proud of these prestigious positions. "It means that not only was I popular, but thought to be capable," she cites with candor.

Currently, Claudine attends the Fashion Institute of Technology in New York City, where she previously earned an associate degree in fashion buying and merchandising. She now is working toward a bachelor of science degree in marketing and international trade. Claudine hopes to work in corporate America in a fashion-related company or corporation that will lead to increased knowledge of worldwide operations.

Claudine says that her mother is strong and determined and an inspirational person who has taught her to be responsible and independent. "I share everything that goes on in my life with her, from boyfriend problems to stress and special advice needed in college," the young woman reveals. She believes that Carole instilled in her all the values needed to go forward in her life and career. "She is my best friend and role model. I think I'm very much like my Mom and will probably imitate everything she has taught me." Because Carole is an educator, both daughters are grateful for their mother's support in the choice of colleges and careers. "She's given me the motivation that I need to finish college." Claudine nods, reinforcing her words.

Mother and daughter are quite close. "I missed her terribly when I went away to college. I'm closer to my mother than I am to my father. Marjorie is just the reverse. She's closer to our father. But Mom loves us equally." When her parents divorced, Claudine was sad, confused, and angry. The loss brought her closer to Carole. "She's my guardian angel and is with me in spirit all the time." Claudine likes to buy special things for herself, like special treats to enjoy, "but they could not replace my Mom."

On Mother's Day, the daughters planned a special day for Carole, but due to a chronic back problem, Carole was forced to remain at home. The next day, everything went off as scheduled—flowers, gifts, and dinner at a fancy restaurant.

Carole has inspired her daughter to make a difference in the world. Claudine wishes everyone could be like her mother, because it would be a different world. This youthful, cheerful, and energetic young woman obviously adores her Mom. "She is the ultimate best chocolate chip cookie. That's my favorite. My Mom's my ideal, and she means the world to me." Claudine beams.

Carole, Marjorie, and Claudine

Among Haitian Americans, it is not unusual to discover very close intergenerational mother–daughter relationships. Carole's mother has influenced the lives of her daughters as well as her granddaughters, Marjorie and Claudine. When the family migrated to the United States, Carole's mother postponed employment in order to ensure a sound educational start for her girls.

As a professional nurse, there were employment opportunities available, but she chose to be a homemaker and supervise the children's homework, library assignments, and a strict schedule of study and recreation. Being bilingual, the mother eased the transition for the non-English-speaking girls. They did well, and Carole received a Regents diploma upon her high school graduation. After a family conference, Music and Art High School was chosen for another daughter with musical talent.

Following family tradition, Carole's grandmother helped the family with a down payment for a private house. Haitian kin always assist family members in need.

During Carole's junior year at York College, she met and fell in love with the son of a family known to her parents. Both sets of parents wanted the young couple to delay marriage until graduation. But love prevailed, and they were able to convince their parents to agree to an early marriage. Family life is prized by Haitians. "I will always remember holidays, birthdays and weddings as being joyous occasions celebrated by groups of relatives at our house where my mother organized dinner and entertainment," Carole recalls.

Carole thinks several things caused the dissolution of her marriage. "I had no experience. He was my first boyfriend. My advanced degree threatened his bachelor degree status. I was moving ahead too rapidly and leaving him behind," she explains. He refused professional counseling, but she and the girls received help for one year. Despite a thorough explanation of the facts, the daughters suffered emotionally for quite a while. The professional support was supplemented by counseling and understanding from Carole's mother and other female kin.

When both girls enrolled in college, things changed. They were older, were having relationships with young men, and were emotionally mature. Mother–daughter relationships again became close, realistic, loving, and happy. One important piece of evidence is the fact that both girls have accepted Carole's "boyfriend" and encourage the relationship.

REFERENCES

Brice-Laporte, R., Jr. "Black Immigrants: The Experience of Invisibility and Inequality." *Journal of Black Studies* 3 (1): 29–56, September 1972.

Dewind, J. "Haitian Boat People in the United States: Background for Social Service Providers." In *Social Work Practice with Refugees*, ed. D. Drachman. Washington, DC: Institute of Mental Health, 1991.

Dorsinville, M. "Haiti and Its Institutions: From Colonial Times to 1957." In *The Haitian Potential: Research and Resources of Haiti*, ed. V. Rubin and R. Schaedel. New York: Teachers College Press, 1975.

Dreyfuss, N. "The Invisible Immigrants." *The New York Times Magazine*, May 23, 1993.

Garcia, O., and Fishman, J., eds. *The Multilingual Apple*. Berlin, NY: Mouton de Gruyter, 1997.

Joseph, C. "A Survey of Self-Reports of Language Use; in Self-Reports in English, Haitian and French Language Proficiencies, and Self-Reports of Language Attitudes among Haitians in New York." Ph.D. dissertation, New York University, 1992.

Joseph, C. "Haitian Creole in New York." In *The Multilingual Apple: Language in New York City*, ed. O. Garcia, and J. A. Fishman. Berlin, NY: Mouton de Gruyter, 1997.

Laguerre, M. *American Odyssey: Haitians in New York City*. New York: Cornell University Press, 1984.

Laguerre, M. "The Haitian Niche in New York City." *Migration Today*, September 1984.

Miller, J. "One Answer to Haitians' Crisis: Let Them In." *Wall Street Journal*, August 3, 1994.

Nicholls, D. *From Dessalines to Duvalier: Race, Color and National Independence in Haiti*. New Brunswick, NJ: Rutgers University Press, 1996.

Reid, I. *The Negro Immigrant: His Background, Characteristics and Social Adjustment, 1899–1937*. New York: Columbia University Press, 1939.

Schiller, N. G., et al. "Home Ties: The Relationship of Caribbean Migrants in New York City to Their Countries of Origin." New York: Columbia University Center for Social Sciences, 1986.

Weil, T., Black, J., Blutstein, H., Johnston, K. McMorris, D., and Munson, F. *The Dominican Republic: A Country Study*. Washington, DC: U.S. Government Printing Office, 1995.

PERSONAL REFLECTIONS
by Carolle Charles

HAITIAN ETHNICITY

What do Haitian women do to help maintain Haitian culture within the many Haitian communities within the United States?

There is no unique recipe, as there is no single answer to that question. What exists, however, is what I would describe as the multiple facets of Haitian motherhood. This mothering is a form of loving, nurturing, and parenting that encompasses emotional, social, cultural, political, and economic relations. It is a form of mothering that is illustrated in a story published in the *New York Times* on January 13, 1998. This was a story about the ordeal of a Haitian woman, MFB, and in particular about her achievements. As the article recounts, MFB had been mentally sick for more than a decade. In 1983, after giving birth to her third child and unable to stay focused because of her internal demons, MFB decided to kill herself and her children. She started a fire in her apartment, but as the flames erupted, she became conscious of the atrocity of her action and called for help. For the next seven years, MFB spent days and months in mental hospitals. Her children were sent to foster care and her husband asked for a separation. Yet, during that ordeal, what MFB never missed were the scheduled visits with her children. She did more than visit. She sometimes brought gifts to the foster parents because, as she stated, "I knew they were helping me because I could not take care of my children." In 1990, with the help of an agency, MFB began to receive day counseling and medication outside a mental institution. She was able to secure a new apartment and a part-time job. Last July 1997, 14 years later, MFB was reunited with her children. She has worked hard to regain their trust. Today, as the article reports, when night falls, instead of struggling to quiet her demons, MFB listens to Zelda, her now 14-year-old daughter, who wants to become a singer and who practices in the house singing in the shower. As the article revealed, this is a story about a special kind of bonding. It is a story about how Haitian women conceive of motherhood as a form of devotion to their children so that they can become successful citizens. For most Haitians, a mother's dedication to her family, particularly to her children, represents something fundamentally Haitian. Moreover, the Haitian mother plays the central role as the gatekeeper and the promoter of these cultural values.

Awareness of being Haitian begins in the family, with the appreciation of ethnic food, language, music, and values. Within the family one may objectively differentiate one's experience from another's, and one can assess the limits, strengths, and weaknesses of one's cultural traditions. Although these experiences vary greatly with class background, as well as length of time living in the United States, Haitian women are the most important agencies in transmitting these values. In most Haitian households, the encounter with Haitian culture begins with the lullaby. Every Haitian child has been exposed to the soft and charming lyrics of "Haiti Cheri" or "Ti Zwezo," two of the most popular songs of the musical repertory. Through the cooking by Haitian mothers and Haitian sisters one comes to appreciate the richness of Haitian culinary arts. In the kitchen of Haitian mothers, aunts, and women friends the cooking lessons of how to make "di ri ak djon-djon" (rice and Haitian black mushrooms), "griot" (fried pork), "marinades" (codfish fritters or dumplings), "soup joumou" or "poisson gwo sel" (salt fish), "blanc manje" or "pain patate" (sweet potato bread). In the warm confines of the kitchen every Saturday night while listening to a Haitian radio show, mothers begin to prepare the Sunday early dinner. Around the kitchen table every Sunday morning, right before going to the Catholic mass, Haitian mothers serve strong demitasse of dark coffee, hot cocoa, milk, and "pate chaud" (meat pattie) while listening intensely to the latest news about Haiti from a radio station at Columbia University.

Being Haitian is more than keeping Haitian culture. It is also being very political. From the first phases of the Haitian immigration experiences in the United States, Haitian women as mothers, daughters, sisters, aunts, and "comrades" have been very forceful and visible in denouncing the Duvalier regime, a dictatorship that lasted 30 years, from 1957 until 1986. Haitian women, through their political work, raised consciousness and maintained hope for the coming of democracy in Haiti. Haitian women created many feminist organizations, among others, the Union des Femmes Patriotiques (Union of Women Patriots), Neges Vanyan (Strong, Vibrant Women), Ralliement des Infirmieres (Group of Women Nurses), Ad Hoc Committee for the Decade, and Point de Ralliement (Rallying Point). These organizations struggled for the betterment of, and respect for, Haitian women, for social and political changes in Haiti, and for the maintenance of Haitian culture in North America.

The Haitian woman's role has been crucial in keeping and using the extended family structure by creating transnational household networks. Examples abound of mothers sending their children to maternal grandparents in Haiti or to sisters and aunts in Montreal in order for them to receive a "better" education. This, in fact, really means the possibility of learning French and Creole. Haitian women are also the most important cultural agents as healers, as community and spiritual leaders. In particular, as *mambo*, or priestess, of the voodoo religion, they reproduce the culture, acting as confessor, doctor, magician, confidante, and adviser to the members of their temple and/or group. Because the office of *mambo* is usually hereditary, it gives to the *mambo* a lot of authority.

Finally, Haitian women are the creators of Haitian transnational networks. Haitian women constitute about 55% of the migration flows. In many Haitian households that arrived before 1980, the process began with the departure of a mother or sister or aunt. Haitian women are also more open to new Haitian friends and neighbors who may become part of the extended networks, sharing reciprocal services in baby-sitting, borrowing money, and organizing trips to Catholic places of worship or special events. Interestingly, one of the important Haitian cultural artifacts is the "Fetes des Meres," a famous Mother's Day celebration that is celebrated simultaneously in Haiti.

Thus, through Haitian women, in particular through their roles in the family, the household, and the community, Haitians begin to objectively differentiate their experiences from those of "others" and can also assess the limits, strengths, and weaknesses of their cultural traditions.

PART II

ASIAN AMERICANS

Asia, with more than 3 billion people from many different cultures and countries, is home to nearly two-thirds of the world's population. The United States has drawn from these countries and cultures its Asian Americans, some with recent attachments to the continent and some with very distant connections. In the world of social science and educational research, Asian Americans are frequently represented as one group and summarized in one number, like an arithmetical average. Yet Asian Americans think of themselves as (and are) quite different from one another.

Over the past two decades, Asian Americans have been the nation's fastest growing minority group. Like African Americans and Latinos, their potential for growth during the next decade is enormous, given that Asian Americans currently represent 38% of all immigrants to the United States. Accordingly, it is important to learn more about the commonalities and differences among Asian Americans.

Chilton Williamson, writing in *The Immigration Mystique*, claims that the history of immigration to the colonies of North America and later to the United States may conveniently be divided into eight periods. The first begins with the settlement of the North American colonies by the English, the Spanish, the French, and other Europeans and extends to 1783, by which time Professor R. Mayo Smith (professor of political economy and social science at Columbia University), writing some generations ago, says, "the state was established, and further additions to the population had little influence in changing its form or the language and customs of the people" (Williamson, 1996: 23). The second period, from 1783 to 1820, was one of slight immigration, when an average of 10,000 people arrived annually in the United States. The third, 1820 to 1860, was an era of heavy immigration, mostly Catholics from Ireland and Germany. In the late 1820s, the federal government began to compile statistics relating to immigration, and by the 1850s nativism had become a powerful political movement.

The sectional crisis culminating in the Civil War brought immigration to a temporary halt, but between 1865 and World War I vast numbers of immigrants arrived from Central, Eastern, and Southern Europe, among them many Jews and still more Catholics; on the West Coast, the appearance of the Chinese, the Japanese, and other Orientals provoked the exclusionary movement. The period after World War I commenced with the powerful restrictionist impulse that produced the national origins system as incorporated in the Quota Acts, which were fortified by the Great Depression and helped to keep immigration to the United States nearly nonexistent until shortly before the outbreak of war on the Continent, when a substantial number of refugees from the Third Reich were admitted.

But in the two decades between the end of World War II and 1965, American immigration policy was subjected to drastic and finally revolutionary change, beginning with the Act of 1965, which replaced the national origins system with a nondiscriminatory one that emphasized family reunification. The period from 1965 to 1990 witnessed the unforeseen consequences of the 1965 Act, as tens of millions of Third World immigrants, Congress, and the executive branch attempted to grapple with the crisis in a politically acceptable way. Thus, in the eighth immigration era, the United States struggles to solve problems and difficulties and reconcile concerns that were familiar to our forefathers for more than a century and a half before the American Revolution (Williamson, 1996).

President John F. Kennedy's study *A Nation of Immigrants* was the basis for the proposed immigration reforms that he sent to Congress on July 23, 1963. The chief executive described three criteria for admission: skills, family reunification, and priority of application.

He asked for no significant increase in the numbers of immigrants admitted, merely a modest increase from the present level of 156,700 per annum. When President Kennedy sent his historic message to Congress in 1963, calling for a complete revision of the immigration law, he decided it was time to revise the book for use as a weapon of enlightenment in the coming legislative battle. The phrase "weapon of enlightenment" was especially well chosen. The Immigration and Nationality Act of 1965 is unquestionably John F. Kennedy's direct legacy, passed as a tribute to his memory.

During the last two decades, the number of Asians and Pacific Islanders in the United States doubled from 1.5 million in 1970, to 3.7 million in 1980, to 7.3 million in 1990. The percentages of Asians and Pacific Islanders in the total population also nearly doubled during the 1980s from 1.5% to

2.9%. The dramatic increases are the result of increased immigration from China, India, Korea, the Philippines, and other Asian Pacific Island areas following the adoption of the Immigration Act of 1965 (Min, 1995).

Fifty-four percent of the Asian population lived in the West in 1990, compared with 21% of the total population. Approximately 66% of Asians lived in just three states—California, New York, and Hawaii—but the concentration varied by Asian group.

In 1990, 78% of all Asians 25 years old and over were at least high school graduates; the national rate was 75%. Education is highly valued in Asian communities, but the educational attainment of different groups varies widely. The proportion completing high school or higher was 88% for Japanese, compared with 31% for Hmong. In general, Asian men had higher rates of high school graduation than Asian women: 82% versus 74% in 1990. Japanese women had a high school or higher completion rate of 86% compared with 19% for Hmong women. At the college level, 38% of Asians had graduated with a bachelor's degree or higher by 1990, compared with 20% of the total population. Asian Indians had the highest attainment rates, and Cambodians, Laotians, and Hmong had the lowest.

SOCIOECONOMIC STATUS

Although economic motives are the determining factor for the most recent Asian immigrants, structural factors—political, military, economic, and cultural connections between the United States and various Asian countries—also influence Asians' propensity to immigrate to the United States, explaining why some countries send more immigrants than others. Among Asian countries, the Philippines has annually sent the largest number of immigrants over the last two decades.

The large number of interracial marriages, providing the basis for subsequent kin-centered immigration, continues to affect immigration statistics. South Korea was the second largest source country of U.S. immigrants from Asia during recent years. Similar structural linkages between the United States and South Korea have contributed to that exodus. It is also important to note that the normalization of relations between the United States and China in 1979 opened the door to immigration for people of China.

With the high unemployment rate in the United States because of the economic recession in the mid-1970s, the federal government severely restricted the admission of occupational immigrants—those primarily seeking employment. The government discouraged alien professionals from immigrating by passing the Eli-Berg Act and the Health Professionals Educational Assistance Act in 1976 (Agarwal, 1988). The former required alien professionals to have job offers from U.S. employers before they could gain admission as legal immigrants. The latter, in effect, removed physicians and surgeons from eligible categories of labor certification. Since the late 1970s, the U.S. Department of Labor has discouraged other types of occupations by not issuing labor permits to many qualified prospective immigrants.

As a result, the proportion of occupational immigrants, including professionals, has decreased since the late 1970s. During the last ten years, most Asian immigrants (more than 85%) have been granted permanent status based on family reunification. This change in Asian immigration patterns has led to a change in the immigrants' socioeconomic background. More recent Asian immigrants are more diverse in their socioeconomic status than the Asian immigrants admitted in the 1970s (Park et al., 1990).

THE GHETTO—AN ETHNIC ENCLAVE

The minority community as we know it today had its origins in the ghettos of the first generation of ethnic enclaves established to meet the needs of their alien residents. Their way of life was adapted to their shared experiences in a new world. Indeed, their alien status became the basis of integration for their community, since traditional values eventually lost their meaning in a secular society (Kramer, 1970). Nevertheless, these values were significant in the emergence of the ghetto. The existence of the ghetto tempered the transition from one culture to another, buffering strangeness with communal familiarity. Uprootedness was the characteristic quality of the immigrants' community, no longer situated in its accustomed land; the changed life transformed its institutions over time, but the initial intent of the first generation was to keep intact those institutions it could, thereby sustaining its cultural identity.

The ghetto community of the first generation continued to embody the traditional values of its country of origin, even though some institutional reorganization was required to do so. The principle of closure in the ghetto operated to protect its cultural insulation and social isolation. Avoidance of all but the most impersonal economic contact with the dominant group (and even that was not always necessary) minimized the potential for cultural conflict and thus helped to preserve the distinctive values of the ethnic group.

Chinatown has long been one of the most exclusive ethnic communities in American society, a tight-knit, ingrown ghetto that is only now beginning to lose members of the younger generation in greater numbers. The Chinese population has tended to concentrate in segregated areas in large cities such as New York, Los Angeles, and, most particularly, San Francisco. Although a smaller proportion now lives in Chinatown than formerly, its social structure has remained largely the same, with only some modifications in institutional functions. Until recently, the Chinese have been highly insulated, maintaining their own distinctive organizations, which, among other things, mediated indirectly the instrumental relationships with the dominant community that were unavoidable (Marden and Meyer, 1962). There were relatively few Chinese, and they were determined to preserve the way of life and the language of their ancient culture. Although much like the Jews in this respect, their reasons were different; they did not conceive of themselves as permanently exiled: they still hoped to return to their homeland.

SECOND-GENERATION ASIANS

Mobility paved the way of the second generation into the middle class, all the more quickly for those groups whose values supported mobility. Indeed, the stronger these values, the greater the seed for their disintegration by the very success they made possible. Out of this mobility, however, emerges the prototypical minority community in which ethnicity begins to lose its traditional meaning (Kramer, 1970). Most recent Asian immigrants, unlike those who came earlier, are not trapped in ethnic ghettos and can afford to reside in suburban areas by virtue of their high socioeconomic background.

Several critical issues regarding integration of Asians have been addressed (Furuto, Muras, and Ross-Sheriff, 1992). One is public confusion about, and resistance to, Asians and other people of color. There is concern about whether these people will be able to integrate into American society the way Europeans have or whether they will polarize neighborhoods linguistically and culturally. These fears result in anti-Asian sentiments and sometimes violence, making it difficult to develop harmonious relationships between Asians and other Americans. However, the prevailing view is that the new Asian immigrants and refugees, like their conationals who have resided in the United States for several generations, will succeed economically, socially, and politically at the expense of established communities (Schwartz, 1985).

Contrary to economic analysis (Borjas, 1989), many Americans still believe that Asian refugees and immigrants are taking away their businesses and jobs. Those Asian immigrants and refugees who work at low wages in the service industry are accused of depressing wage rates and utilizing social welfare and income-maintenance services that are much needed for nonimmigrant, low-income Americans (Borjas, 1989). Through their hard work, long hours, cultural practices, and family ties, Asians are acquiring businesses and accumulating wealth at a faster pace than their indigenous counterparts. This creates fear and also resentment in local residents of inner-city neighborhoods. Many believe that the Asians are exploiting the poor without making a contribution. Lately there appears some indication of understanding on both sides. Employment of residents and contributions to community projects have led to respect in both camps.

Prejudice against Asians is also based on resentment of the academic and economic success of the group. Rather than admiring or emulating the characteristics of hard work, self-discipline, family cohesiveness, achievement orientation, and respect for education associated with Asians, some Americans convince themselves that Asians must somehow be dishonest and need to be punished. Such convictions perpetuate the hostility and acts of racism that have been directed toward the group historically and that continue to affect the adaptation patterns of Asians in the United States.

Some studies (Furuto, Muras, and Ross-Sheriff 1992) suggest that more knowledge, awareness, and understanding of diverse Asian groups are required for both Asians and other Americans to facilitate Asian integration into American society and to dispel myths related to Asians. Research knowledge should guide policy and human relations. Social work services and programs, whether for the newly arrived young families or for established elderly Asian groups, should be guided by an understanding of cultural practices and traditions of diverse Asian groups. Like all other groups, Asians experience the stress of life. Service delivery models based on an understanding of cultural background, history, and specific life experiences are more likely to meet the needs of new immigrants as well as established Asians.

REFERENCES

Agarwal, Bina, ed. *The Structures of Patriarchy: The State, the Community and the Household*. London: Zed Books, 1988.

Borjas, G. *Friends or Strangers: The Impact of Immigrants on the U.S. Economy*. New York: Basic Books, 1989.

ETS (Educational Testing Service). *Policy Information Report*. Princeton, NJ: ETS, 1997.

Furuto, S. M., Muras, K., and Ross-Sheriff, F., eds. *Social Work Practice with Asian Americans*. Newbury Park, CA: Sage, 1992.

Kramer, J. *The American Minority Community*. New York: Thomas Y. Crowell, 1970.

Marden, C., and Meyer, G. *Minorities in American Society*. 2d ed. New York: American Book, 1962.

Min, P. G., ed. *Asian Americans*. Thousand Oaks, CA: Sage, 1995.

Park, I. H., Fawcett, J. T., Arnold, F., and Garden, R., eds. *Korean Immigrants and U.S. Immigration Policy: A Predeparture Perspective*. Honolulu: East-West Center, 1990.

Schwartz, D. F. "Immigration and Refugees: Issues, Politics and Democratic Pluralism." Paper presented at the National Immigration, Citizenship Forum, Washington, DC, 1985.

Williamson, C., Jr. *The Immigration Mystique—America's False Conscience*. New York: Basic Books, 1996.

3

Asian Indian Americans

While Asian Indians have had a history of migration since the time of Christ (Kondapi, 1951), their modern period of emigration from India is marked by the introduction of the "indentured labor" system by the British. The British introduced this system as a substitute for slavery, which they abolished in 1834. Therefore, indentured labor was similar to slavery, with the exception that after working out their contract, the laborers were simply "released" or reemployed under a new contract (Gangulee, 1947). The result was an Asian diaspora that supplied the necessary labor for the extraction of raw materials that were essential to the maintenance of the British empire (Gonzales, 1990).

The first Asian Indians to arrive in North America were Sikhs, who settled in Canada in 1904. Between 1905 and 1907, some 5,134 Asian Indians arrived in Canada (Chadney, 1984). They were attracted by the employment and economic opportunities available in British Columbia. Unfortunately, their welcome was very short-lived, as the Canadian government prohibited their immigration in 1908, which met with strong resistance and political action from Asian Indians in British Columbia (Buchignani and Indra, 1985).

Although Indians did not emigrate to the United States in large numbers until 1904, they arrived in North America as early as 1750. A man from Madras may have been the first Indian to travel to the United States. A group of approximately 200 Parsi (Zoroastrian faith) merchants designed a plan to emigrate from Bombay, perhaps inspired by the earlier emigration of Gujaratis to other British colonies. Also, isolated individuals such as sailors were brought to the United States as indentured servants by captains of merchant marine ships in New England; some of them were sold into slavery and moved to Salem, Massachusetts, as well as to other parts of the Atlantic seaboard and the South (Jensen, 1988).

During the period between 1820 and 1870, 196 Indians, mainly from the state of Punjab, came to this country. Indian merchants were reported in Philadelphia in 1889 (Jensen, 1988). The number of Indians in the United States reached 5,000 by 1910, and a total of 8,000 more Indians had arrived by 1924. However, due to the enforcement of the Asiatic exclusion provision of the national origins quota system, only a little more than 100 Indians came to the United States during the 1930s. More than three-quarters of the East Indians in the United States in the early 20th century came from Punjab; others came from Gujarat, Oudh, and Bengal (Banenjes, 1969). Most Indian immigrants came directly from India to the Pacific Coast, and others came through East Asia (Sheth, 1995).

The early Indian immigrants can be divided into two groups: (1) farmers and laborers and (2) middle-class students, elites, and political refugees. The middle-aged farmers and laborers from Punjab were mainly attracted to Canada. They were rejected from entering Canada and formally barred in 1908. From 1908 to 1920, a total of 5,391 Indians were admitted to the United States, although more than 3,000 were prohibited from entering, and nearly 1,700 went back to India (Das, 1923). However, it is reported that some 3,000 Asian Indians entered this country illegally, mostly via Mexico between 1920 and 1930 (Jacoby, 1956).

Partly in response to the role that the Indian government played in assisting the United States in the defeat of Japan during World War II and the indefatigable lobbying efforts of prominent Asian Indians, the federal government did make some major changes in the immigration laws. With the passage of the Luce-Cellar Bill in July 1946, Asian Indians were freed from the barred-zone immigration restrictions and were given an annual quota of 100 per year. Of equal importance, this bill finally granted Asian Indians naturalization rights. In retrospect, the immigration ban of the Pacific Barred Zone had been in effect for 25 years and almost succeeded in bringing about the demise of the Asian Indian community in America.

The real victory for Asian Indians was the ability, after 30 years, to send for their wives and children. This meant that, for the first time, they could establish families and bring the second generation of Asian Indian Americans into being. In contrast to this second wave of immigrants, the third-wave Asian Indians were young, well educated, and heavily concentrated in the professions. They were also more likely to arrive as family units, to have an urban background, and to be fluent in English.

A study conducted by the Immigration and Naturalization Service found that of those Asian Indians who had become naturalized citizens in 1981, half (49.3%) held professional or technical positions (*INS Yearbook*, 1981). Another study found that since 1965, India was America's major source of scientists and engineers. In 1965 only 84 scientists or engineers arrived as immigrants from India, but by 1970 there were 2,900 (Pernia, 1976). This high concentration in the professions reflects the high proportion of well-educated and highly skilled immigrants among the third-wave population. But this also conforms to the typical "brain drain" phenomenon found among the new Asian immigrants.

In real numbers, this means that approximately half to two-thirds of Asian Indian immigrants who settled in America over the past two decades were professionals. For example, between 1977 and 1981, a total of 98,748 Asian Indians arrived, for an annual average of almost 20,000 per year. This means that approximately 10,000 to 15,000 professionals arrived from India each year (Gonzales, 1990).

India has been one of the major source countries of foreign students in the United States during recent years. Of the more than 400,000 foreign students who entered the United States during 1990–1991, about 7% were from India (Dodge, 1991), making India fourth among the 67 countries that sent students to the United States during that period. Because of the professional prestige of science-related occupations and their practical applications for India, engineering was the most popular field of study among Indian students until the 1970s. However, recently, the fields of business and information science have replaced engineering. Unlike the patriotic motive for the freedom and economic development of their home country, post-1965 students have as their primary goal enhancing their own professional careers (Sheth, 1995).

Post-1965 Indian immigrants have generally come from large cities in all parts of India. They represent several religious and linguistic groups, although the main language is Hindi. The major religions of Indian immigrants include Hinduism, Islam, Sikhism, Christianity, and Jainism. Another important characteristic of post-1965 Indian immigrants is that most of them are fluent in English. As a result of the British colonization, English is still spoken as one of the official languages of India.

By virtue of their high educational level, Indian Americans generally hold good jobs and earn a high income. Based on the results of regression analysis (Barrenger and Kassebaum, 1989), Asian Indians were paid well but less than their education and occupational concentration would produce if they were not a minority in the United States. Moreover, although Asian Indians are concentrated in professional occupations, 7% of Asian Indian Americans were living at the poverty level in 1990, which was as high as for white families. This indicates that even an affluent immigrant community can have many poverty-stricken families.

Indian and other East Asian immigrants continue to suffer from personal prejudice as well as institutional discrimination, even when they are highly educated and qualified. Denial of admission to medical school by select universities partly due to racial bias is well known, as well as discrimination against Asian Indians at work and in the community and personal mockery (e.g., "dot bustering" or ridiculing Indian women for the beauty mark on their forehead).

The sources of Indian ethnicity are Indian religions, languages, families, and specific Indian values, such as nonviolence. Asians express pride in their history, civilization, and values, as well as their scientific, educational, and professional achievements.

In the early 20th century, the major political issue was U.S. citizenship; in the 1990s, it is dual or multinational citizenship. This contrast may indicate the expertise of the new Indians in making international demands and their need to maintain Indian citizenship and identity. Indian expatriates, called nonresident Indians (NRI), have raised the issue of dual citizenship in India and the United States in an increasingly global economy.

Since ancient times, traditional customs relating to marriage and the family have been the foundation of Indian social life. In Indian history, marriage was both monogamous and polygamous. The structure of the Indian family was joint (extended), patriarchal, patrilineal, and patrilocal. Jati endogamy and village exogamy were the rules. Selection of a mate was with parents' supervision only. Presently, this ideal is only partly realized. Industrialization and urbanization in India have changed the family structure and functions and the gender divisions of labor and authority structure in the home, favoring more egalitarian relations between husband and wife (Sheth, 1995). A sizable number of Indian immigrants seek mates through advertisements, either in Indian newspapers during a short visit home or in Indian ethnic newspapers in the United States; they also use referrals from friends and relatives and marriage brokers to find mates.

The second-generation Indian Americans of both genders born or raised in the United States are in schools and universities or just beginning professional careers and marrying Indians or Euro-Americans with similar qualifications. Although most of them are successful, many of them also suffer from pressures to succeed and other social problems. They have quickly realized some contradictions with their parents, as well as with American society (Agarwal, 1991). In spite of generational and cultural conflicts, they have somewhat compromised with both. Several youths have decided to work with politicians and run for political office as a means of increasing the clout and equality of the Indian community within American society. Second-generation females have closed the gender gap almost completely in education and occupations, in contrast to the immigration generation. Young women experience the double standard in mating and marriage with the young Indian males and in freedom from their parents. Yet, second-generation Indian Americans have more freedom in choice of education, occupation, and marriage than the immigrant generation (Sheth, 1995).

CASE STUDIES

Lincy

The trip from the suburbs had been uneventful, especially for a Monday morning. Lincy parked her 1995 Honda Accord LX in the parking lot next to the hospital. It was exactly 7:40 AM when she arrived at the Pharmacy Department in the basement of the large metropolitan medical center. Several staff members were already busy with the day's work. Except for the sound of a ringing telephone, the whole extensive department was silent. Lincy removed her jacket and donned a freshly-ironed white lab coat. She glanced at the work sheet. Before the unit became too busy and noisy, Lincy would prepare IV (intravenous) chemotherapy drugs for several patients being treated by the Oncology Program.

The large, 800-bed hospital in several buildings depends on the Pharmacy Department for all medications ordered by the medical staff. The pharmacy is open 24 hours a day. Later in the day, there may be visits to patient care areas to review drug orders, do inspections and solve problems, monitor drugs used in the hospital, monitor drug and food interactions, inspect patients' medications, distribute narcotics, and check doctors' orders for patients' drugs. These are some of the tasks of a pharmacist in a large hospital. There are 35 male and female pharmacists in the department besides Lincy. She has enjoyed and applied her professional skills at this hospital for about ten years. Her supervisors describe Lincy as an efficient, reliable professional who has a pleasant disposition and is a well-liked colleague.

Lincy was born in 1954 in Kerala, a southern state in India, to Varghese and Elizabeth Mammen. Lincy was the younger of two girls born to the couple. One thing still prominent in Lincy's memory is the mile-long walk to her all-girls elementary school. The teachers were strict. The students wore uniforms. Science was Lincy's favorite subject. No single teacher affected her, but she enjoyed interaction between teachers and students. Elementary school included grades one to five; then girls began high school from grades five to ten. Subjects included languages like English, Malayalam, and Hindi, as well as biology and history. In high school, students were scheduled for an outdoor program in physical education in which they performed exercises; on Fridays there were singing, elocution, and Girl Guides, which are equivalent to Girl Scouts in America. "We made knots, which is universal," Lincy laughs, "just like in the States."

Young people did not date. "You get married instead," Lincy says with a giggle. The tradition is for both sets of parents to meet and discuss social background, finances, education of the young couple, and health. "The parents make the choice. The couple meet for the first time after these discussions. It can be rather awkward trying to start a conversation, especially when both sets of parents are present. But it is the tradition," Lincy explains. "Your elders are wiser than you and have the experience of making choices and decisions. It is expected, and no one complains." The practice continues in some parts of India today.

Lincy, however, completed work for her B.S. degree at Trivandrum Medical College in Trivandrum, Kerala, India, and then came to the United States to seek employment and additional education and training. She obtained her license and was employed at King's Harbor Care Center in the Bronx for three years. Lincy met Samuel, her husband-to-be, in the United States and returned home to India for the wedding. Although she was 25 and Samuel was 27, traditional practices were followed. "My father gave several thousand rupees as a dowry and presents to Samuel. At the wedding, I wore a white sari, and the groom wore a Western suit. I also wore lots of gold jewelry, rings, necklace, and bracelets, which were gifts from my father," Lincy recalls. There were 700 people celebrating the ceremony. There was a great feast, but there was no drinking or dancing. Since Lincy was the first girl to marry, her folks went to great lengths to make the occasion memorable. After a few days, the couple returned to New York City and their new home.

When Lincy became pregnant, tradition called for more gold jewelry to be presented to Samuel by Lincy's father. Gold jewelry was again given to Samuel by her father when the child was born. Her son was born in 1982 by cesarean delivery, followed by an infection that prevented Lincy from breast-feeding. Lincy's mother came to New York to help out and provide child care. Lincy's son was the first male in the family, and grandmother was delighted to care for a male child, since her own children had been females.

Sherin was born in 1984. Lincy and Samuel were able to work split shifts to provide child care for the baby and her brother, a toddler. Samuel, a teacher of special education, cared for them evenings while Lincy worked at the hospital. "It was difficult, but we managed," Lincy says.

Lincy finds it particularly difficult to raise a girl in the United States. "Growing up, my life was restricted to home and school, but I must allow my children more freedom than I had. The restrictions used in India cannot be applied here." With working parents, it takes careful handling to let children enjoy some of the pleasures their playmates enjoy and still follow traditions. Fortunately, Samuel lived in America before their marriage, so he is aware of the needs of adolescents. "We talk about our hopes and plans and make joint decisions. We belong to the Church of God, an apostolic faith, which is very traditional. We keep the lines of communication open between the children and parents."

Family unity is very important to Lincy and Samuel. Most of the time away from work is spent together. She considers him the head of the family and respects his opinions. For example, Samuel would not approve of Lincy's spending evenings "with the girls" or joining social clubs or any activity that takes her away from her family—her main obligation. "I would not go against his will, because that is the way I was raised. Samuel is quite liberal in some ways, but again he is the head of our family. I am happy with this arrangement," Lincy states firmly. There are no special ethnic holidays to celebrate, but American holidays like Thanksgiving and Christmas are enjoyed by the family. However, Lincy does prepare Indian food as well as American food, which everyone likes.

Lincy's children accompany their parents to church services and many other church-related activities. The children have chosen friends from the congregation whose parents are known to Lincy and Samuel. Lincy makes a point of inviting the children's friends to her home for family entertainment.

Lincy's relationship with her daughter is fairly open. "She hasn't talked to me about sex yet. But I had prepared myself even earlier. I will give her the opportunity and let her know that I'm there for discussion." Lincy did not have personal marital education before marriage. "We just learned as we went along. Things turned out happily for us." Lincy laughs at her embarrassment.

Her future may include a master's degree. But that will wait until the children are older. "I'm satisfied with my life and think I've been successful in what I do. Perhaps I could do more. The future will tell. My husband is supportive in whatever I want to do, and that's important to me." She ends with a happy, wide smile.

Sherin

Sherin, Lincy's daughter, has features similar to her mother's—wide smile, soft dark eyes, long black hair, and a shy, genteel overall appearance. She was born June 25, 1984, in the Bronx, New York. Eugene, who is two years older, shared computer games with his sister. But he spent most of his time enjoying sports. At times, Sherin played outdoors with him when she was a preteenager. Sherin also played Monopoly and Scrabble. Her pet stuffed bear was an unnamed favorite. Most of her friends lived in the neighborhood or attended her school.

Sherin is in the eighth grade at Tappan Zee School, where she excels in mathematics. It is her favorite subject. Her worst subject is art. "I'm all thumbs with no imagination," she admits. Sherin is an avid reader and enjoys biographies, adventure stories, and historical novels. Agatha Christie mysteries and Shakespeare are prominent among her favorites. She and her friends enjoy popular music, like rhythm and blues and rap. "Blue is my favorite color," she confides. When not in school, Sherin can be found wearing blue jeans and a T-shirt. Best-liked television shows include *Fresh Prince* and *Spin City*.

Her extracurricular activities include the Community Service Club, National Junior Honor Society, Chorus, and Mathematics Club. Parents and children spend time together at concerts, picnics, and visiting with other families. Sherin insists that her friends have a sense of humor and enjoy activities similar to hers.

As for ethnic traditions and values, Sherin is convinced that she will never wear a sari when she becomes an adult. It is almost certain that her own marriage will be a consensual one, since she isn't influenced by tradition very much.

When faced with a problem, Sherin usually thinks things through and comes up with a proper solution. There are times, however, when she consults the wisdom of her mother, whom she admires very much. "She is loving, but strict. She also has determination, works hard, and cares for people. I would like to be like her when I grow up," says Sherin in a voice that is soft and serious.

This young woman hopes for a career in law. When asked about American values and culture, she replied, "I like the freedom and equality in the United States very much."

REFERENCES

Agarwal, P. *Passage from India: Post-1965 Indian Immigrants and Their Children: Conflicts, Concerns and Solutions*. Palos Verdes, CA: Yuvati, 1991.

Banenjes, K. K. *Indian Freedom Movement in America*. Calcutta: Jignasa, 1969.

Barrenger, H., and Kassebaum, G. "Asian Indians as a Minority in the United States: The Effect of Education, Occupations, and Gender on Income." *Sociological Perspectives* 32 (50): 1–52, 1989.

Buchignani, N., and Indra, D. M. *Continuous Journey: A Social History of South Asians in Canada*. Toronto: McClelland and Stewart, 1985.

Chadney, J. G. *The Sikhs of Vancouver*. New York: AMS Press, 1984.

Chandrasekhar, S., ed. "Some Statistics on Asian Indian Immigration to the United States of America." In *From India to America: A Brief History of Immigration, Problems of Discrimination, Admission and Assimilation*. La Jolla, CA: Populations, 1982, 11–25.

Das, R. K. *Hindustani Workers on the Pacific Coast*. Berlin: De Gruyter, 1923.

Dodge, S. "Foreign Students in the United States." *Chronicle of Higher Education*, 1–33, 1991.

Gangulee, N. *Indians in the Empire Overseas*. Bombay: New India Publishing House, 1947.

Gonzales, J., Jr. *Racial and Ethnic Groups in America*. Dubuque, IA: Kendall/Hunt, 1990.

INS Yearbook. Washington, DC: Immigration and Naturalization Service, 1981.

Jacoby, H. "A Half Century of Appraisal of East Indians in the United States." Sixth Annual College of the Pacific Faculty Research Lecture, University of the Pacific Immigration & Naturalization Service (1979–1992). *Statistical Yearbook*. Washington, DC: U.S. Government Printing Office, 1956.

Jensen, J. M. *Passage from India: Asian Indian Immigrants in North America*. New Haven, CT: Yale University Press, 1988.

Kondapi, C. *Indians Overseas*. New Delhi: Indian Council of World Affairs, 1951.

Pernia, E. N. "The Question of the Brain Drain from the Philippines." *International Migration Review* 10: 63–72, 1976.

Sheth, M. "Asian Americans." In *Asian Americans*, ed. P. G. Min. Thousand Oaks, CA: Sage 1995.

4

Chinese Americans

The first Asian group to immigrate to the United States consisted of the Chinese. A small number, 43, lived in this country before 1850. With the discovery of gold in California in 1848, the numbers migrating to the United States increased significantly. In the following three decades, more than 225,000 Chinese immigrated to this country; most were single men from the provinces of southeast China—Kwangtung and Fukien—which had for centuries sent laborers overseas to other places such as Southeast Asia (Chen, 1980). Many were married and left wives and families behind in China. The poor economic and social conditions in China—drought, overcrowding, rebellion, incursions by foreign troops, and natural disasters—encouraged many men to come to try their luck. They were not truly immigrants who came to remain in the United States. These men came to make enough money to return to China, buy land or a business, and live a prosperous life. That is why when they set sail for the "Mountain of Gold," as the men called it, they left their families behind (Sung, 1977; Dinnerstein and Reimers, 1998).

Occasionally, the men made trips back to China. By necessity, these were few and far between, as the distance was long, and the trip was costly. But the greatest deterrents were the harassment of the Chinese at the ports, when they tried to reenter the country, and the fears that they could not come back (Sung, 1972).

During the next decade, 1850–1860, Chinese immigration increased dramatically. Building upon an initial 43 before 1850, 41,397 Chinese immigrated to the United States in the 1850s, and another 64,301 arrived in the 1860s (Gonzalez, 1990).

The Chinese who arrived during the 19th century were predominantly illiterate peasants who established a community of men, without wives or families. This shortage of women presented a very serious problem for the cohesiveness and stability of their community.

The Chinese Exclusion Act of 1882 was passed by Congress after much pressure by groups and individuals. It was the first and only immigration act to specifically designate an ethnic, racial, or nationality group from exclusion. The act prohibited all Chinese laborers, whether skilled or unskilled, from entering the United States for ten years. All other Chinese entering the country had to have identification certificates issued by the Chinese government.

Besides mining and farming, the Chinese worked in other occupations. For example, in 1870 Chinese were heavily concentrated in the cigar-manufacturing industry, representing 91% of all cigar makers in San Francisco (Coolidge, 1969). Chinese were strongly represented in the woolen and boot industries, where they constituted two-thirds of all employees in the former and 19% in the latter. During the same period, it is reported that there were 1,200 Chinese storekeepers and 1,500 factory and mill hands in San Francisco (Cather, 1932). Because the Chinese workers were more efficient, worked faster, and worked longer hours than their competitors, they were successful.

Surprisingly, domestic service provided the greatest source of employment, primarily because of the scarcity of women. Prior to the arrival of the Chinese, it was the custom of socialites in San Francisco to send their laundry to Hawaii to be washed by Polynesian women. The first Chinese laundry was established at the corner of Dupont and Washington Streets in the spring of 1851 by an immigrant called Wah Lee.

Chinese restaurants were popular, since they offered a very good meal at a modest price. Most of the vegetables, greens, and fruits came from small farms cultivated by the Chinese, and there was a variety of fresh fish caught by Chinese fishermen in San Francisco Bay (McLeod, 1947).

The Chinese were involved in many occupations that were critical to the economic development of San Francisco. Gonzalez relates one important contribution to this development of the West in his *Racial and Ethnic Groups in America*. The decision to hire Chinese laborers on the Sierra Nevada section of the transcontinental railroad was made early in 1865 by Charles Crocker, following a number of engineer problems, labor difficulties, and management problems that had put Central Pacific behind schedule. When construction was completed in May 1869, more than 14,000 Chinese had been on the payroll (Saxton, 1971). "Crocker pets," as they were called, were paid $428.00 a month, with Sundays off, and they had to supply their own food and tents (Chen, 1980).

Many were attracted to the burgeoning agricultural industry of California, where they were first to clear the land, dig the canals and reservoirs, plant the orchards, and harvest the crops. After all, the completion of the transcontinental railroad made it possible for California farmers to sell produce in the East. As a result of their labor, the annual fruit production in California increased from 1.8 to 12 million pounds between 1871 and 1884 (Chen, 1980).

Passage of the War Brides Act in 1945 allowed approximately 6,000 Chinese women to enter the United States as brides of men in the U.S. armed forces. In 1946 an amendment to this act put Chinese wives and children of U.S. citizens on a nonquota basis. As a consequence, almost 10,000 Chinese females migrated to the United States in the next eight years. This influx had a tremendous impact on the demographic structure of the Chinese American community (Wong, 1995).

By abolishing the national origins system, the Immigration Act of 1965 was probably the first immigration policy that practiced the principle of racial equality and the first real immigration reform in over a century. The most significant consequence of this act for Chinese was the dramatic increase in the number of Chinese immigrants to the United States (Wong and Hirschman, 1983).

Another consequence of the act was its influence on the changing nature of family life for Chinese in the United States. With its emphasis on family reunification, this act granted each country a quota of 20,000 immigrants per year. Since 1968, when the law went into full effect, approximately 22,000 Chinese have immigrated to the United States each year. Unlike the pre-1965 immigrants, who came over as individuals, most of the new Chinese immigrants have come as family groups—typically, husband, wife, and unmarried children (Glenn, 1983; Sung, 1977; Wong and Hirschman, 1983).

The Chinese American family can best be viewed as a product of the complex interaction between structural factors (i.e., restrictive immigration policies and racism) and cultural factors (i.e., Confucian ethics). Because these factors are constantly changing, the Chinese American family is not a static entity but one that is also undergoing constant permutations and adaptations to a changing society (Wong, 1995).

The traditional Chinese family exhibited a patrilocal residential pattern. Grandparents, unmarried children, and their married sons together with their wives and children all lived in one household. The more generations living under the same roof, the more prestigious the family; married daughters lived in the household of their husband's parents, and this extended family provided additional laborers needed in an agriculturally based economy and provided the members with some degree of economic security (Wolf, 1968).

The Chinese system of descent was matrilineal, with the household property and land divided equally among the sons. In exchange, however, the sons were to reciprocate by sharing equally in the responsibility for the care and support of their parents in their old age (Nee and Wong, 1985).

The Confucian practice of ancestor worship was observed in a traditional Chinese family. It was believed that a Chinese male could achieve some sense of immortality only if his family line was continued (i.e., if he bore sons). In fact, it was believed that one of the greatest tragedies that a man could suffer was to die without having any sons to carry on the family name and perform the ancestor worship ritual of burning incense over his grave (Wong, 1995).

The modern Chinese American family can be classified into two major types. The first type, referred to as the "ghetto" or "downtown" family (by Glenn, 1983, and Kwong, 1989, respectively), consists of the new immigrant Chinese family living in or near Chinatown in the major metropolitan areas of this country. Both husband and wife are employed in the secondary labor market or enclave economy, in the labor-intensive, low capital service, and small manufacturing sectors, such as the tourist shops, restaurants, and garment sweatshops (Wong, 1983). Husbands and wives are equal breadwinners in the family. Unlike the small-producer family, however, there tends to be a complete segregation of work and family life. Moreover, it is not uncommon for parents to spend very little time with each other or their children because of different jobs and schedules (Wong, 1988).

The second type of Chinese family is the "uptown," middle-class, white-collar, or professional Chinese American family that has moved away from Chinatown to the surrounding urban areas and suburbs (Kuo, 1970; Kwong, 1987; Yuan, 1966). These Chinese families are modern and cosmopolitan in orientation and view themselves as more American than Chinese (Huang, 1981). However, there is a tendency for these Chinese to be "semiextended" or to reestablish a Chinese community in the suburbs (Huang, 1981).

Educational Testing Service (ETS) produced a study in 1989 with language minority students—Hispanic Americans. Now they have completed a similar one of Asian American high school students' educational characteristics. Heather Kim (1997) examined differences among six major ethnic groups of Asian American high school seniors in their socioeconomic characteristics, parent expectations and involvement, educational values, school behaviors, academic performance, and educational expectations. These differences are examined according to ethnic group and by whether students were foreign- or native-born. While most Americans know that an average is simply a convenient statistical representation, it tends to convey an image, particularly when it is pointed out, over and over again, that the average achievement of one group is higher than that of another. A large proportion of Americans know that Asian Americans, on average, score higher on a wide range of educational assessments than any other ethnic group. This tends to promote a stereotype of Asian Americans. Some, in fact, have referred to Asian Americans as a "model minority."

The model minority stereotype emphasizes Asian Americans who are college graduates and/or have high-status occupations and high incomes. But the stereotype often does not consider the substantial number of uneducated, illiterate Asians and those who have low-paying jobs.

When we compare the education levels between the sexes, it is clear that there are as many female college graduates (49.7%) as male college graduates (50.3%). This compares to 21.3% of the males and 13.3% of the females in the general population. But a far greater number of Chinese males (65%) obtain graduate degrees, as opposed to females (35%). This, in part, reflects their traditional family orientation and the general feeling that men should obtain as high a level of education as possible (Gonzalez, 1990). Because of their upward mobility and achievements, the future of the Chinese American population in American society appears bright.

CASE STUDIES

Spring

The fall of 1965 was eventful for Spring, because she left Taiwan for the United States. She had been an excellent student and was awarded a scholarship to the University of Wisconsin. She looked forward to her life in the United States. Spring enjoyed exciting and new experiences and expected more of the same.

At an early age, Spring demonstrated her independence. She was named Josephine. But after reading *Little Women*, Spring decided that her name was too somber and didn't fit her exuberant nature. "I changed it to Spring, because I was born on the first day of spring when plants shoot through the earth and birds take flight." Her laughter is robust. Born in Chungking, China, and raised in Taiwan, Spring was the middle child in a family of five children. She was never placid or compliant like her siblings. "I was the dark horse," she explains with a giggle. Spring's father was a reporter for a newspaper and gradually advanced to the position of editor, editor in chief, and publisher. Her mother was an administrative assistant in a business office, but due to poor health she worked infrequently. The family lived in a large compound, with many other families providing lots of playmates. Spring remembers the families enjoying Chinese New Year and Full Moon Festival. There was a day in June when everyone celebrated by eating a special kind of rice, too. Spring's childhood included church activities, choral groups, "Girl Scout"-type clubs, and summer camp. All were fun and enjoyable.

Her problems began in an all-girl high school that required uniforms and strict adherence to a code of behavior. Spring found school too traditional and boring. She didn't join any social groups but enjoyed sports and Reserve Officers' Training Corps (ROTC), which appealed to her energetic temperament. She was inattentive in class and did not receive high grades. Her father was proud of her athletic skills, which earned awards, but he couldn't understand her disorderly behavior. Spring's mother frequently took gifts to the teachers. "I'm sure she was trying to pacify them and compensate them for enduring all of my bad behavior," she says and grins. She recalls family relationships as happy and satisfying. Until her two younger sisters' births, she was pampered as an only child. But adolescence was quite trying for her. "I was very critical, independent-minded—a real troublemaker," Spring recalls. To her parents' consternation, she "chased" boys aggressively—demonstrating seemingly un-ladylike behavior.

However, she matured somewhat at National Taiwan University, where her major was sociology. Her achievements won her a scholarship to the University of Wisconsin. After graduation from Taiwan University, like most new graduates, Spring searched for employment. However, the country was poor and undeveloped. Most of her classmates managed to go to the United States to continue their studies. So, Spring decided to take advantage of the honor she had received at National Taiwan University and leave for Wisconsin.

When the plane landed in San Francisco, Spring really had no urgent plans. The next four days were spent riding across the countryside on a Greyhound bus to Wisconsin. At the university, Spring continued the study of her favorite subjects—political science, economics, and sociology. No instructor gave her either academic encouragement or moral support. Spring feels that her critical mind, questioning, and argumentative discussions often earned her a B instead of an A. But she holds no hard feelings. "Probably a difference in culture, concept, and beliefs," she concludes. Her inquisitiveness led to doctoral studies, but she never completed the program. Instead, she accepted a teaching position in New York City, actually an assistant professorship at City College of New York. Spring spent two years there teaching political science and sociology. Meanwhile, Spring renewed and strengthened family ties and relationships during a return trip to China.

Spring met her husband-to-be in the early 1970s. Both were activists in the fight to improve the lives of citizens and others in the Chinatown community. It was a love match celebrated in a simple, quiet ceremony. Two children, a girl, Lee, and a boy, Jimmy, were born within three years. Spring continued her community work day and night. Her commitment grew, and she found it necessary to take the young children with her to meetings. "During this period, the mid-70s, everyone was socially active in the Civil Rights and antiwar movement, so I wasn't unusual," Spring explains. "Being Asian, an independent thinker, and female was not uncommon," she adds with pride in her lusty voice. She also notes that a lot of changes have taken place in China. Women there are now more educated than men, are expected to work and study more, and working women are considered the norm.

Spring worked before and after marriage and after the birth of her children. "The children became part of the movement, because we took them everywhere." While the adults were having their meetings, the children were supervised and cared for by responsible child care workers in the same building. The children and the home were always Spring's responsibility, even when she worked. Her husband, a traditional Chinese man, did not get involved with children and household tasks.

Traditional values and cultural activities are still practiced by the older generation. For example, Spring's mother-in-law is traditional and not equipped to cope in today's world. Although Spring's husband practically grew up in the United States, when it comes to male–female relationships, his perception is purely traditional. An Asian man might have difficulty in building a loving relationship with a woman because of his conception of family. A family mainly consists of responsibility toward one's parents and one's children. This very feudal definition has much strength in that it binds the family together; nevertheless, it often prevents a meaningful relationship from being developed between man and woman. "In his whole concept of family relationships, his mother comes first, then the children; the wife is last. My son will probably be different, because of the influence of television, his peers, and movies," she reasons. "You want to marry your own people, but most take them as you find them. I made my choice. My husband was raised in the traditional manner where the male child is very important, the decision-maker, the head of the family." Despite the lack of intimacy, Spring believes her marriage is strong, secure, and viable.

The family usually goes out as a unit to dinner or movies. At home, English is spoken mainly, but Spring grew up with Mandarin. She enjoys jazz, Channel 13, PBS, and reading mysteries.

Her relationship with Lee has reached a pleasant plateau after years of frequent highs and lows of adolescence. "We are beginning to see each other as women and are able to accept or reject what we like or dislike in each other," Spring says in a matter-of-fact tone.

At times, Spring has encountered bias. Usually, it was in the classroom because of different values and strong viewpoints. Although she did well in courses like political science, the instructor awarded her a B. Discrimination was felt on a more personal level. "When I picked up my children at play school, staff thought I was the baby-sitter or maid. Snobby Park Avenue doormen always gave me a quizzical look as they hesitantly opened the door. And once an employer asked, 'Could you find a good Chinese maid for me?'" It's annoying, but Spring has learned to live with insensitive people.

Spring is still active in community affairs and works as a realtor. She takes her role of leadership very seriously. "Sometimes you feel that you're out there all by yourself. You're carrying the burden, and it's too much. But it passes."

Is she satisfied with her life? Spring feels luck has been with her. The family is healthy, and the children have had no serious problems. Her husband, a social activist, realized that he must change with the economy and is trying to earn money to support his family. However, he wants to get rich quickly. "You have to adjust to societal change, but you can't lose your own bearing—otherwise, you throw the baby out with the bathwater. You must put family, career, and your own desires in perspective," she warns.

Does she feel successful? Spring has managed career and motherhood, but she hesitates to answer. "You must ask yourself from time to time—Have I done all that I wanted to do? What have I missed? What could I have done differently? Then you can answer realistically," she sums up.

The concept of the traditional role of wife and mother is changing in the United States and China. Mothers want their children to be well rounded, well balanced. Spring advises her children to be bold, to scale the heights and find the proper balance. "I'm a better mother because I have had so many other interests that affect my decision making. It's manageable—you just have to search for it. Being a role model is a grave responsibility. The children gained, too. We used to drop them off at the 'Y' after school. My son read every book in the library. Children need to grow up in a diverse environment. It broadens their development and circle of friends and gives them the opportunity to develop leadership and independence."

What does Spring see in her future? She would like to have more time for workshops for mothers focusing on child care and to continue her social activism. "I would like to establish a foundation that would facilitate programs or institutionalize ideas one always dreamed possible."

Lee

"My name is Lee, and I'm 18 years old. I'm completing my freshman year at Yale University." Her rapid, breathless speech is pitched whisper-low in contrast to her athletic appearance. Lee is two years older than her brother, Jimmy. Since they spent much of their growing up together, they are very close. "My mother was always very busy with several agendas operating at the same time. She's strong, has great endurance, and works a lot. But she can be bullheaded. She's a pragmatist, and I admire that. She's very busy and gets a lot done. My mother needs to be efficient. As a daughter, I felt neglected at times. I wonder about pragmatism being an overwhelming value," she finishes, with a deep sigh.

What is their relationship like? "Well, I'm not pragmatic like my mother. She's a strong personality. I don't feel that I have to be a strong personality in order to live with her. My Mom is also a strong organizer with a long history of fighting 'causes.' She's effective! At times, I'm a little turned off by her organizing." Lee pauses as if thinking what she should say next. Without waiting for the next question, she continues. Lee explains that her mother approaches any discussion or problem they have with a suggestion that they make a list of the three most important things. "I think that's a little grotesque—sometimes," Lee says with a hint of irritation in her voice. Her quick grin reveals that her irritation is not deep-seated. She offers another example. "After I come home from a long trip, she'll ask me to name the three most exciting moments of my trip. This makes me quickly review the whole trip in my mind, before I can answer. Of course, some of her organizing rubbed off on me. As a matter of fact, I'm good at assessment and note-taking, so I guess it isn't so bad," she says, laughing at her own conflicting statements.

Lee remembers being left alone frequently by her parents, who were committed to social action groups that helped Chinese on the Lower East Side of Manhattan prepare for citizenship, register to vote, unionize, and find housing. There was no money for baby-sitters, so sometimes the youngsters accompanied their parents. Being exposed to their parents' activities had a positive effect on both children. As they grew older, both saw these activities as sincere and worthwhile. Both children developed a social responsibility for others as a result. Also, Lee has become involved with school and her own life for the past two years and has proved to be capable. Her Mom is employed but continues with her community work. "I learned to function independently very easily and quickly—all because of my parents' lifestyles," Lee maintains.

As the older child, Lee has always assumed responsibility for her brother, Jimmy, almost 17 years old. He's a junior at Dalton, a private high school in Manhattan. "He needs my mother and, at times, feels neglected." Since both children enjoy each other's company, Lee and Jimmy get along well. "I'm sort of a role model for him in a way. A couple of years ago, he went through a period in which he considered himself a 'black nationalist.' He became an expert on Malcolm X. He's still committed but now uses his energies in a more relevant way," Lee says in a voice and smile laced with caring.

For a long time, Lee and her Mom had a very close relationship; she used to tell her mother everything that happened in school, out of school, and with girlfriends. But when Lee reached midteens, things changed. "My Mom regarded me as a prude and very conservative. This surprised me, since she had been a rebellious teenager, a tomboy, going out with boys who rode motorcycles, etc., all unheard of and unacceptable in those days." Lee thinks that her mother didn't understand Lee's need not to be so "outgoing." Also, Lee was a maturing adolescent in a period when the values and rules of peers become more important than those of parents.

Lee considers herself politically liberal-minded but somewhat traditional. She thinks that the biggest concern of teenagers today is the tremendous amount of pressure to work hard, excel, and succeed. Problems evolve around a shrinking economy and the diminishing opportunities that accompany it. She thinks of herself as being more "blessed" with many opportunities than some adolescents growing up in a more disadvantaged environment. "There is a general problem of how to fit your talent into a land of great opportunity. For my generation, there are few role models around. We know this, and it leaves a tremendous vacuum in our lives. Then with world confusion, young people don't have much faith in their elders or leaders. This leads to activism. There are a significant number of young people who are socially oriented, want a better life for all people. Their efforts are often dehumanized, ridiculed, and ignored." Lee's sincerity and concern appear obvious and are well expressed.

In her personal life, Lee enjoys most types of music, particularly classical music like Bach. At Yale, many students waltz beautifully to tuneful, quiet music. "I buy well-made, finely-tailored clothing—mostly classical and expensive—a taste that I inherited from my mother." Lee never wears jewelry. But she does like to eat. Her choice is not gourmet restaurants. Her choice is fresh, simply prepared foods. "We grew up enjoying a variety of food mostly, since my Mom worked and didn't have time for cooking. We rarely have Chinese food, but my Mom stir-fries fresh vegetables and cooks rice. Robert loves to cook and shows some skills in that direction." She feels that a movie date is a waste of time—a most asocial occasion. "You don't get to know someone by going to a movie with him," she says, frowning at the idea. "My favorite date is a long, relaxed dinner of simple food, cooked well, and plenty of stimulating conversation."

This young woman is not focusing on a career yet. Her interest is not in business or any office job. Since her parents have been activists and idealists, they want their children to have some real skills, solid jobs with a future. Lee plans on a broad major like history or English. "I don't want to get caught up worrying about graduate school and the future." She believes advocacy structures one's entire life. "My parents taught us values of social consciousness, an awareness of justice, and the needs of human beings. Although I may appear to be critical of my Mom, I know that if I could be even half as good a mother as she, I would be truly fortunate."

Talking with Lee several months later, we learned that Lee completed her freshman year at Yale very successfully, with good grades and some new friends. She joined the Asian American Students Association, worked as a reporter for the *Yale Daily News*, and became involved with photography. She left New York in June for China, where she will spend two months studying at the Beijing Foreign Language Institute, where she will take Chinese and other courses and will live with relatives.

Adrienne

In San Francisco, television weatherpersons expire of boredom, as the report is usually the same. "Coastal fog morning, clearing by noon; temperatures in the low 60's—warmer inland." The coldest months are June, July, and August, when the Central Valley heats up and pulls in the cool, gray ocean fog. The warmest months are September and October. Unique to San Francisco is the Bay to Breakers Run, held in May. The participants run dressed as Dolly Parton, as cocktail weenies, as the Golden Gate Bridge, as Venetian blinds, and as blind Venetians. They even run wearing nothing at all. It's Bay to Breakers, San Francisco's answer to the world's great foot-races, the country's largest participatory sporting event. Bay to Breakers attracts some 70,000 serious runners and weekend warriors each year. It begins at the docks on the Bay at 8:00 AM and winds 7.5 miles through the city to the edge of the Pacific Ocean. This year's race was May 18, 1997, and I enjoyed a visit with the Ponses after the race.

"I was born in San Francisco, California. I am a middle child with two brothers—one older and one younger. My father was a Chinese immigrant but never spoke Chinese at home. He was very Westernized and unconventional. My mother, on the other hand, was born in the United States, a second-generation citizen, but used old Chinese maxims all the time. We had a kind of mixed upbringing," Adrienne says. "I remember when I was 3 years old, my mother came home from the hospital with a new baby boy. He looked like a long, thin doll dressed in clothes that were two sizes larger than him. The baby had a necklace of tiny blue beads on his wrist that spelled out his name. My parents began to remove the bracelet, and my Mom kept warning, 'Don't cut him. Be careful.' Today my brother tells the story as if he remembered it." Adrienne's laugh is humorous.

Adrienne attended a high school that was college preparatory and traditional. Although her teachers were excellent, she can't identify one that impressed her. But she enjoyed class discussions in subjects like civics, world history, and world literature, which allowed students to get different perspectives of people and events.

During her junior and senior years in high school, Adrienne served as a mentor or junior guidance counselor for a nonprofit community agency. She escorted youngsters to activities, games, and concerts and, in the summer, worked in the day camp. There she met her future husband. Adrienne had many friends but never became attached to any one clique. "I moved in and out of various groups, enjoying them all."

Adrienne earned her master's degree in public affairs while working a full-time job and raising a family. For her undergraduate education, she chose San Francisco State University, where she majored in community health education. "I wanted to work in and for the local community in a hands-on occupation. Although I wasn't particularly interested in health, my future husband was, so we had something in common." Adrienne continued her relationship with the same young man she had dated in high school. After high school graduation, the couple decided to marry. They had a small family wedding at a Presbyterian church. There was no honeymoon.

Adrienne comes from a family with a long history of working with nonprofit volunteer groups in the Asian Pacific American community. Her father was prominent in the local Toastmaster's Club. At that time, very few people of color were involved. Her mother was president of the Parent-Teacher Association (PTA) even after her children graduated from public school. Since her early teen years, Adrienne has been involved with all kinds of nonprofit community agencies.

Adrienne's parents can be considered her role models. Both have encouraged and supported her interests and concerns. In addition, her husband maintains a longtime friendship with one of his high school teachers, who taught Mandarin. When Adrienne entered college, this particular teacher "adopted" them and became their counselor. "We call her our third mother, and I believe she has influenced me as well," Adrienne says softly. This relationship afforded a different approach to dealing and coping with situations. "Unlike my own mother, who was diplomatic, genteel, and polite but oblique, this friend is a no-nonsense person, a 'Put it on the table,' 'Say what you mean,' and 'Mean what you say' individual. She provided a balance for me," Adrienne maintains.

Before entering college, Adrienne gave birth to a daughter, Tiffanie. It was a very happy event, and Adrienne and her husband became involved in parenting at the beginning. "We prepared well. My husband and I shifted our work schedules so that one of us was always at home." Adrienne gives credit to her mother, who taught her children three basic concepts: treat people with kindness, don't be snotty, and serve others. Her mother also encouraged the children to solve their own problems by thinking of alternatives and planning effectively. "My mother was nontraditional," Adrienne adds.

The family has two chow dogs and a cat. She notes, "The children are responsible for their care, since they wanted them." The family attends and enjoys community events. Since Adrienne's job includes working with community groups, she involves the whole family, including her 25-year-old son, in clothing drives, concerts, festivals, "walkathons," and fund-raisers. At home, they work on upkeep projects. All the Ponses join in the painting, designing, and refurbishing.

Adrienne and Tiffanie have a closer relationship than Adrienne had with her mother. Adrienne describes Tiffanie as very artistic and creative with the temperament that usually accompanies an artistic person. "She's determined about her roles and involved in what she shares with others. She wants to be one of the crowd, whereas her brother enjoys being his unique and inimitable person. Although we brought them up to be individualistic, Tiffanie prefers to identify with others." Adrienne feels that Tiffanie has not explored her artistic talents fully. "She's a whiz at mechanical things. At the age of 2, she could easily open a childproof cap on the aspirin bottle," recalls Adrienne.

When a preteenager, Tiffanie used to follow her mother around the house, even into the bathroom, discussing the events of her day. She would occasionally seek advice or an opinion from Adrienne. At about 15, Tiffanie suddenly didn't appreciate advice or feel the need for it. She told her mother, "Just listen; don't tell me what to do!" Adrienne understood that their relationship was changing to a more mature one.

About 15 years ago, Adrienne and her husband immersed their children in ethnic studies to expand the children's knowledge of Chinese and other cultures. "We began with Chinese art and history and then proceeded to Japanese and other cultures. At home, we follow some Chinese traditions but add a modern touch. I will eat Chinese food only prepared at home. Restaurant food has a lot of additives, salt, and sauces. My mother-in-law is quite a good cook. I enjoy her meals. On the other hand, my husband eats anything and everything—even a dish we call 'soul food'; it's equivalent to the chitterlings southerners enjoy," Adrienne relates with refreshing laughter.

Adrienne's children, as fourth-generation Chinese Americans, have very positive and warm intergenerational relationships with grandparents and their late great-grandparents, which reinforce a sense of ethnic identity and culture. "Our own friends are of Chinese, Japanese, Filipino, and African American heritage. We have no problems of relating to each other," states Adrienne.

Adrienne recalls an early incident of bigotry that saddened her. She was about 8 years old. Her neighborhood was fairly well integrated with the Caucasian majority. Borden's Milk Company was giving away samples of a new product. All the children lined up to accept a gift. Adrienne joined the line. When she reached the sales representative, the woman looked at her quizzically and asked in an irritated voice, "Didn't I just give you one?" Adrienne explained that she and her mother had just arrived before she joined the line. The woman thrust the ice cream bar toward Adrienne and said in a frustrated voice, "Oh well, all of you Oriental children look alike to me!" Adrienne remembers feeling sad and uneasy. "I didn't like the feeling, but I didn't know how to answer her." Although her parents never discussed racism, Adrienne sensed this as her first racist experience. She believes that racism is "alive and well" in San Francisco; it is subtle—but just as strong as in the South. Even today, it exists in the workplace. Adrienne reveals incidents where the opinions or ideas expressed by people of color are not given credence.

The future holds promise for Adrienne to be involved in leadership training for girls and young women. "Most young people today do not give enough recognition to the work of their elders that gave them so much freedom and civil rights. They must fight for legislation to ensure the gains that have been made." She is emphatic.

Adrienne is external affairs director for Pacific Telesis Group. As the corporation's liaison to statewide and national senior, health, and Asian Pacific American organizations, she is responsible for analyzing public policy issues, developing corporate strategies, and working with community leaders and advocates for the economically at risk. She also develops models for new trials and innovative projects, such as Voicemail for the Homeless.

Prior to the assignment, Adrienne was personnel manager and education relations director for Pacific Bell's Management Recruitment Department. She has also served as the company's statewide local government manager for California cities and counties.

Adrienne is a longtime community supporter and a believer in building networks between the corporate and nonprofit sectors. She is active in several organizations, including being president of the San Francisco Civil Service Commission; chairperson for the National Asian Pacific American Women's Leadership Institute; board director and past chair of Asian Americans/Pacific Islanders in Philanthropy; board director and former officer for Leadership California; member of the Corporate Task for Kimochi, Inc., a senior service organization; and advisory member to the National Asian Pacific American Legal Consortium. This is just a sample of her commitment to women, community, and leadership.

"I feel that success is using all your influence in helping others. In that sense, I feel very powerful," Adrienne says proudly.

Adrienne remembers a quote from one of Malcolm X's speeches: "Sitting at the table doesn't make you a diner unless you eat some of what's on that plate. Being born in America doesn't make you an American." What she is referring to is that for people of color, it seems it doesn't matter if people have been here for hundreds of years or a few generations; they still have a long way to go to be regarded as full and equal participants in the democratic process. Moreover, Asian Pacific Americans are still considered "other" or "foreign," and this is what many leaders are working to change.

Tiffanie

Born in San Francisco on January 15, 1970, Tiffanie is the older of Adrienne's two children. "My earliest memory is the wonderful Sunday mornings when my brother and I would wake up very early and run to our parents' bedroom. We would shake them not too gently to wake them up and then jump into the bed. Once they were awake, there would be hugs and kisses. Then we would all be talking at once about how to spend the day. Those close and happy moments will stay in my memory forever." Tiffanie's remembrance leaves her face glowing with pleasure.

Tiffanie's relationship with her brother is not as close as she would like it to be. "We are similar in lots of ways. Yet we are different in others. It is this difference that keeps us from being close. There is, however, a great deal of respect and admiration for each other," Tiffanie explains.

"As a child, my favorite toy was any type of puzzle. But when Rubik's Cube came out, it became my favorite—after microscopes." Tiffanie didn't have a favorite doll, since she rarely played with dolls. Today if she were a child, she would probably choose a stuffed animal. But she does have one old doll—a Raggedy Ann. "It was given to me by my mother when I was a baby. It is a keepsake." Tiffanie also had a pet goldfish, which was won at a local fair. Her favorite television show was *Quincy*. She loved it and was upset when she missed the show. "My folks thought I was a little strange," she says. Tiffanie's favorite classes in junior high were science, metal shop, wood shop, home economics, art, and mathematics. "We were always doing something, and it was fun," she remembers.

Tiffanie's favorite course in high school was chemistry, but her highest grades were in psychology. Family life was another favorite. Her favorite teacher taught the psychology course. "He was a teacher who identified with his students and was also a good mentor," she recalls. Tiffanie has not given much thought to role models. "When I think of role models, I picture someone on a pedestal. The closest person whom I would put on a pedestal would be my Mom. She's done more than I could ever do." Tiffanie was an excellent student and participated in the Gifted and Talented Education Program (GATE) from elementary through high school. She speaks a limited amount of Cantonese and Japanese as second languages.

In high school and college, Tiffanie's average was 3.0, or B. She also made the honor roll in high school. She is not definite about a future career but is thinking about one that will allow her to build something, tangible or not, to help better someone's life. Perhaps it may be education or teaching. During her entire college career, she worked at a nearby Safeway store as an assistant manager, while carrying maximum credits. Tiffanie's volunteer work included being camp counselor, peer counselor, and aide on a pediatric surgery ward.

Although she's highly social, Tiffanie doesn't date very often. "But when I do, I look for someone whose appearance is presentable and is honest and charming," she says, grinning shyly. The best date for her, Tiffanie believes, is somebody who likes to have fun and doesn't expect much more from her except good company. "I like him to be motivated and somewhat attractive. I also have a weakness for mixed races. I don't know why. But more important is his ability to converse. I don't like one-way conversations. I enjoy talking with someone and not to someone!" Tiffanie is explicit.

About values, Tiffanie isn't too sure about "Chinese" values, except those that relate to family. "Family comes first, serve everybody else first, and work hard. My family always comes first. They are my support. I try to make sure others are taken care of before me. When others are happy, it makes me feel good. I always work hard—an example set by my parents. I like to be efficient and work hard. This way no one can say I didn't complete my job. I know that I did, and that pleases me," Tiffanie says.

This young woman has many friends who represent different ethnic groups. Approximately 50 percent are third- and fourth-generation Chinese American. Another group is Latino, and another group is Caucasian. A smaller group is of mixed heritage. "I get along well with each group. But if they were all in one room together, they probably wouldn't get along with each other." Yet Tiffanie enjoys her multiethnic friends and wouldn't want to change anything. "They are part of the reason I love life," Tiffanie proclaims seriously.

Her plans for the future include travel and graduate school. She would like to enjoy life before settling down to marriage and family but would love to continue learning forever.

When an adult single woman still lives at home, there is bound to be some friction. Tiffanie believes conflict arises because Adrienne treats her like a child, although she brought her up to be independent and strong. "The flip side of that is I think she would like me to act like an adult, but doesn't give me the freedom to be one. I love my Mom and admire her for wanting all that she wants for me," she admits. It's this confusion of roles that both are working to untangle.

Adrienne taught her children to be strong and believe in themselves. "How I choose to deal with daily activities and conflict depends upon the paths and direction my life takes. We are responsible for our mistakes and our achievement. I am open to learning new things, ideas, and skills because of my mother's example and guidance." Tiffanie tells of earlier times while dressing for work and school. "This was our 'quality' time. We talked about almost everything. Since our schedules are different now, we don't get together very often." Tiffanie admires her Mom's strength and business proficiency. "Nobody can fool her. I like that," the daughter emphasizes.

Like her mother, Tiffanie plans to be a working mom with a career, but one that will allow her to spend a great deal of time with her children. She is adamant about this condition.

Tiffanie thinks that the most meaningful part of their mother–daughter relationship is their likeness. "I believe that as I get older I become more like my mother, both physically and in personality traits. Perhaps someday I can have half the strength she has." While growing up, what Tiffanie loved most was her mother's interest in stimulating her children's interests. Tiffanie remembers singing, drawing, and playing games, along with other activities. This is one practice she will utilize when she becomes a mom. Tiffanie promises to be gentle, kind, and compassionate, as were her parents.

Tiffanie has mixed feelings about Chinese culture. Although she learns about this culture from second- and third-generation Chinese American friends, she feels far removed from Chinese American cultural practices. She is fourth generation, and this may be the reason. Unfortunately, some first-generation Chinese Americans who are traditional look down on ABC (American-born Chinese). They laugh and tease her because of her unfamiliarity with Chinese customs, food, or language. As a result, Tiffanie is more comfortable with people of mixed races, like Japanese Americans, African Americans, and Latinos, than she is with Chinese people. She admits that this is a problem. "I am constantly looking for a place to belong—a box to check that doesn't say 'Chinese'—a connection or an identity. I feel very much American but am confronted daily with an identity crisis." Her analogy for this is the Orthodox Christian versus the "Christmas-Easter" Christian. "I am the 'holiday' Chinese versus the Orthodox Chinese. For now, though, I am content being an ethnic Chinese, fully practicing American." Tiffanie seems relieved after airing some thoughts about her confusion. She relaxes against the cushions of the overstuffed armchair.

When asked about success, Tiffanie pauses, and a serious look appears on her face. "My definition of success is to be happily surrounded by friends and family and to live with little money. Money and material things are nice but do not offer me anything but a false sense of success—something I can show to others. All I want and all I need to feel successful are my friends and family and the ability to do something for somebody," she sums up.

Penny and Lisa

Lin and Fu (1990), in a comparison of child-raising attitudes, found that Chinese Americans were more controlling, more achievement-oriented, and more encouraging of independence than were Caucasian parents. But what style of parenting do you follow when you are Caucasian, and your daughter is from mainland China? This is the situation of Penny and Lisa. Brooks (1991) reports that parents develop their own parenting theory based on their cultural and reference group socialization, in addition to individual and family experience and personality, style, and characteristics of their children.

Beautiful, 6½-year-old Lisa smiles and greets the visitor with one of her magic tricks. Lisa is a casualty of China's one-child policy, still strictly enforced in China's largest cities and an ancient tradition that favors boys. Penny's strong desire to experience motherhood resulted in her joining several thousand U.S. Caucasian women who traveled to distant China for adoptable baby girls.

Lisa proudly hands Penny, a single mother, a bright pink balloon that she inflated to full size. Lisa's shining dark eyes twinkle out of a heart-shaped face with deep-set dimples. Her black, Dutch-cut hair tosses freely as she leaps to bounce the balloon off the ceiling. "She's a happy and delightful child," Penny says in a voice filled with pride. Penny would like Lisa to be both bilingual and bicultural. "The earlier a child learns a foreign language, the more fluent he or she is. Children who learn a foreign language later, at 10 or 11, may have accents," she advises. "Most Chinese American children are not fluent in their parents' mother language, and there are so many dialects. . . . Mandarin, Cantonese, and etc. I would like for her to learn

Mandarin, and she was tutored for a while, but Cantonese is more popular in New York. Right now exposing her to Chinese culture and tradition is more important. We'll worry about the language later," Penny concludes.

Penny and Lisa visit Chinatown and shop there. They celebrate Chinese New Year and other events. Lisa knows some Chinese history and uses chopsticks to eat Chinese food. Lisa has made many friends among other adoptees. "There is a young girl Lisa's age who lives in Massachusetts. Both girls were born on the same day at the same hospital and ended up at the same adoption agency. They call each other sisters. We visit her and her parents often," Penny reveals. There is frequent eye contact between Penny and Lisa signaling messages of love.

So far, there has been no racial or ethnic question asked. Lisa is comfortable with children in her multicultural class at school. During her first two years of life, Lisa had a Chinese nanny, whom she adored. She is accustomed to Penny's work schedule, because she had excellent caretaking from her nanny in preschool and in kindergarten. Lisa adjusts well to any changing or new situation.

Penny considers herself fortunate. "When they brought Lisa to meet her new mother, everyone was amazed. She was standing unsupported in the palms of the nurse's hand. Only six months old, the act was considered spectacular." Penny laughs heartily. Lisa continues to be spectacular in sports, arts, and ballet. The summer of 1999, she attends an all-day summer school, while Penny works for a foster-child agency.

The hours after 6:00 PM are special for mother and daughter, who discuss the events of the day, new friends, and new activities. Lisa and her large, nondescript cat nestle with Penny in a large, overstuffed chair. They may watch a television show or listen to Penny read a story. Weekends are spent visiting with friends, walking, enjoying picnics or movies together.

"She's a lovable, creative, easygoing kid. Our dreams include college graduation, a profession, and family." When adopting, there is always a chance of the unknown surfacing and causing troubles. But Families with Children from China, a group founded in 1993 by a few families and now with 89 chapters in North America and Europe, is supportive. The group sponsors panel discussions, publishes a newsletter, and provides advice. Thus far, everything has been smooth sailing for this mother and daughter, and they hope to build upon their foundations.

REFERENCES

Brooks, J. B. *The Process of Parenting*. Toronto: Mayfield, 1991.
Cather, H. "The History of San Francisco's Chinatown." M.A. thesis, University of California, Berkeley, 1932.
Chen, J. *The Chinese of America*. San Francisco: Harper and Row, 1980.
Coolidge, M. R. *Chinese Immigrants*. New York: Holt, 1969.

Dinnerstein, L., and Reimers, D. *Ethnic America: A History of Immigration.* New York: Harper and Row, 1988.

Glenn, E. N. "Split Household, Small Producer and Dual Wage Earner: An Analysis of Chinese American Family Strategies." *Journal of Marriage and the Family* 54, 1983.

Gonzalez, J., Jr. *Racial and Ethnic Groups in America.* Dubuque, IA: Kendall/Hunt, 1990.

Huang, L. J. "The Chinese American Family." In *Ethnic Families in America*, ed. C. Nendel and R. Habenstein, 2d ed. New York: Elsevier, 1981.

Kim, H. "Diversity among Asian American High School Students." Princeton, NJ: ETS Policy Information Report, 1997.

Kung, S. W. *Chinese American Life: Some Aspects of Their History, Status and Contribution.* Seattle: University of Washington Press, 1962.

Kuo, C. "The Chinese on Long Island." *Phylon* 31, 1970.

Kwong, P. "The New Chinatown." *Newsday*, March 10, 1989.

Lin, C. C., and Fu, V. R. "A Comparison of Child Rearing Practices among Chinese, Immigrant Chinese and Caucasian American Parents." *Child Development* 61: 429–433, 1990.

McLeod, A. *Pig Tails and Gold Dust.* Caldwell, ID: Caxton Printers, 1947.

Nee, V., and Wong, H. Y. "Asian American Socioeconomic Achievement: The Strength of the Family Bond." *Sociological Perspectives* 28, 1985.

Saxton, A. The Indispensable Enemy: Labor and the Anti-Chinese Movement in California. Berkeley, CA: University of California Press, 1971.

Sung, B. L. "Changing Chinese." *Society* 14(6), 1977.

Sung, B. L. *The Chinese in America.* New York: Macmillan, 1972.

Wolf, M. *The House of Lin.* New York: Appleton-Century-Croft, 1968.

Wong, M. G. "Chinese America in Pyong Gap Min." In *Asian America: Contemporary Trends and Issues.* Thousand Oaks, CA: Sage, 1995.

Wong, M. G. "The Chinese American Family." In *Ethnic Families in America: Patterns and Variations.* 3d ed. Ed. C. H. Mindel, Jr., R. W. Habenstein, and R. Wright. New York: Elsevier, 1988.

Wong, M. G. "Chinese Sweatshops in the U.S.: A Look at the Garment Industry." In *Research in the Sociology of Work*, ed. R. L. Simpson, Vol. 2. Greenwich, CT: JAI, 1983.

Wong, M. G., and Hirschman, C. "The New Asian Immigrant." In *Culture, Ethnicity and Identity: Current Issues in Research*, ed. W. S. McCready. New York: Academic Press, 1983.

Yuan, D. "Chinatown and Beyond: The Chinese Population to Metropolitan New York." *Phylon* 2(4): 1966, 321–323.

5

Vietnamese Americans

Unlike the Chinese and Japanese, the Vietnamese do not share a history of several generations in America marked by incidents of discriminatory treatment and exclusion. Also, unlike other immigrants, such as the Filipinos, they are not veterans of years of direct U.S. colonization. Unlike other Asians, too, most Vietnamese came to the United States as political refugees, not immigrants. They entered the United States outside regular immigration channels as part of the largest refugee resettlement program in U.S. history (Rumbaut, 1990).

The Vietnamese people trace their origins back to a mythological time when a fairy princess or angel married a dragon. From this union, the fairy laid 100 eggs, which bore 50 sons and 50 daughters. The mother took the 50 daughters and went to the mountains and established a matriarchy. The father took his 50 sons to the coastal area and established a patriarchy. The Vietnamese claim to be descendants of the sons of the dragon, a belief widely held today and transmitted through oral history.

The first Vietnamese dynasty, or the Hong Bang Dynasty, is believed to have had its origins in this mythological time. Although these early accounts of the origins of Vietnamese culture are significant in the history of the nation, the actual historical documentation of Vietnam begins in 221 B.C. during wars of conquest by the Chinese.

Following the common practice of the Chinese, subjugated populations were encouraged to adopt elements of Chinese culture. Consequently, the Chinese introduced agriculture and made various cultural contributions. These included the areas of governing practices, education systems, writing, literature, religious practices, and art. During the initial contact period and the subsequent 1,000 years of Chinese domination, the Vietnamese were greatly influenced by the Chinese. However, the Vietnamese managed to maintain their own national identity and eventually drove out the Chinese in A.D. 938 (Hickey, 1964).

The maintenance of a distinct Vietnamese identity has been attributed to their adoption of Chinese administration methods with the utilization of Vietnamese administrators. Adoption of the Chinese system called for the establishment of a civil service of bureaucrats and administrators recruited through literary examinations as in China (Huynh, 1979).

As many as a few thousand students were given the examinations at one time, and testing periods would last several days. Those who succeeded in passing the exams would go on to the next level for more testing. Ultimately, a great number of students would be reduced to only the best. Licenses or degrees were awarded, and candidates were able to secure a position in the national administration.

In traditional Vietnamese culture, teachers and scholars occupied the highest position on the social hierarchy, and teachers were more revered than one's parents. This long tradition of high regard for education and respect for teachers still persists in Vietnamese culture. Vietnamese encourage their children to study and excel in their education. This culture places a high value upon education, rather than upon material accumulation. Social status has been dependent on education and academic performance and reflects the continued importance of the Confucian system.

Confucian teachings have become an integral part of Vietnamese character and family observances. The importance of history and remembering ancestors was a major concern for Confucius. This influence is still seen in Vietnamese culture.

In order to achieve human perfection, one must follow the established codes of behavior of Confucianism, which include reverence for ancestors and respect for elders. Acceptable behaviors emphasize the ideal of a virtuous person who acts politely and moderately in all instances. Important are not the individual's accomplishments but one's duty to family and society. Paramount in this tradition are the son's obedience to his parents and a daughter's obedience to her parents until she marries. Following the marriage, she must obey her husband. After his death, she continues obedience to her eldest son. In this system, a code of appropriate behaviors regulates the relationships between "king and subject, parent and child, and husband and wife" (Tran, 1982).

The influence of Taoism has also found expression in Vietnamese culture. The acceptance of one's fate as unavoidable and the importance of maintaining harmony with nature and between people are understood as elements of this tradition.

The Vietnamese household traditionally follows the extended multigenerational pattern. The parents, their sons, their sons' wives and children, and any unmarried siblings usually constitute a Vietnamese household. One is expected to make personal sacrifices for the benefit of the family. Permission must be received from the family for what Americans would consider individual expenditures or decisions. The family determines what members buy, whether one works or continues one's education, and whom one will marry. The family institution is indispensable in the maintenance of Vietnamese culture.

The highest status in the Vietnamese family is given to the father. The husband traditionally provides the main source of income. His position and authority as provider are unchallenged. Although he secures financial support for the family, the husband gives his complete income to his wife, who budgets it for the household. When he needs money for small expenditures or spending money, he takes what money his wife gives him. The Vietnamese wife keeps all the money for the family; the husband is not expected to do household chores, cook, and so on. All this is taken care of by his wife and daughters. Vietnamese women have traditionally been subordinate to the men of the family. According to the Confucian code, a woman must first obey her father and then obey her husband after marriage. When her spouse dies, the surviving widow must be obedient to her eldest son, who assumes the role of the family head. Women are expected to excel in housekeeping, cooking, and raising children.

Women do not traditionally work outside the home. Some may enter business for support after the spouse's death. Others teach elementary school or care for children in schools. Children respect their parents, elders, and teachers and have a high regard for education. The continuation of these traditions and values is linked with the survival of Vietnamese culture in the United States (Muzny, 1989).

In 1979 Charles C. Muzny became an instructor in the Vietnamese American Association. He was training coordinator for Indochinese counselors. As a visiting teacher with access to the homes of the Vietnamese population, his interest and interviews became a study, *The Vietnamese in Oklahoma City* (1989). Muzny collected data over a five-year period. The first portion utilized life histories, surveys, observations, and informal interviews and general background information. Later data collected focused on public and private sector behavior and value changes among Vietnamese.

The objectives of the study were to identify the initial changes that first-generation Vietnamese individuals have experienced and to investigate the development of group organizations among Vietnamese following their arrival in Oklahoma City.

All participants were from various sections of the city and represented a cross-section of the current Vietnamese population in the city. The subjects were first-generation Vietnamese who were born in Vietnam and arrived in the United States between 1975 and 1983. The informants were extensively interviewed to retrieve preimmigration experiences and to clearly document types of habit and value changes that had occurred in the public and private sectors since their arrival.

Muzny reports his findings and conclusions in two parts: public sector and private sector changes. Associations with American groups and organizations were limited and confined to the areas of work and church attendance. The Vietnamese were not significantly involved with larger American groups. Participation in the public sector and contacts with other Americans appear to be primarily limited to the workplace. The family, its activities, and success are the main concern for most Vietnamese in Oklahoma City.

In the private sector, the family system in Vietnam was an intricately organized institution in which each member knew his or her position and duty. The linkage of the individual households into one network enabled the family to function as one entity. The Vietnamese family has been described as a "mini-commune; a maternity center; a funeral home; a religious place; an adoption agency; a court room; a welfare center; a hospital; a nursing home; an educational institution; and a bank" (Vuong, 1976). These many functions were carried out through the cooperation of the many members. Mutual assistance and linkage with other component households were necessary for the continuation of this family system.

In Oklahoma City Vietnamese women began to work, and children went to American schools. The traditional family roles and behaviors had begun to change. Children learned English and became familiar with American attitudes and behaviors. The presence of young children was identified as a significant influence in effecting change within the family. When children are small, usually Vietnamese is spoken only at home. After the children begin school, more English is gradually spoken in the home. Many Vietnamese children have lived in the United States for the majority of their lives. It is common for children under age 13 to speak Vietnamese but not read or write this language.

In addition to changes in roles and language usage for family members, traditional family ceremonies were observed to differ. The factors of expense, distance from family members, and conflicting work schedules were indicated to contribute to these changes. Engagement procedures, marriage ceremonies, and observances for the dead have been modified, abbreviated, or even eliminated in Oklahoma City.

The least area of change was in the ideas and values of parents, who prefer to keep a Vietnamese lifestyle within the home. The important issue for Vietnamese is not the continuation of the complex, extended family system but the maintenance of individual households and their Vietnamese home life.

The researcher adds that some Vietnamese informants characterized their existence in America as a dual experience and identified with the public and private distinction in their daily lives.

After arrival, individuals commonly studied English, improved employment, learned to drive a car, and made accomplishments in the economic area of the host society. These public sector changes were cumulative in effect and were perceived to be the beginnings of continued changes. This study has identified some changes experienced by Vietnamese during their first years of life in America.

CASE STUDIES

Vu Thanh Thuy

Imagine fleeing war-torn Saigon.

Imagine being terrorized by rape-seeking Thai fishermen, turned pirates.

Imagine being jailed by the communists.

Imagine drifting on rough seas with 77 refugees for ten days in a small boat.

Imagine all of this happening to a petite young Vietnamese journalist, wife, and mother who was able to survive these and more horrors and escape to the United States to freedom. Her name is Vu Thanh Thuy, and this is her story.

Born in 1950, one of five children, Thuy grew up in a city where war was a normal condition. Her father was a teacher, and her mother was a school administrator. Being part of the middle class, Thuy's early life in Hanoi was quite routine. In 1954 she followed her family to Saigon when the country was divided into North and South Vietnam. She attended local elementary and high schools. Her parents believed that all children should be educated, so their oldest child, although a girl, went to college. Thuy was prepared to follow the same path. But at the end of her senior year of high school, Thuy happened to walk past a newspaper company and see a "part-time help wanted" advertisement. Thuy applied and was accepted. At the time, she was just interested in learning about newspapers. Thuy didn't tell her parents, because they wanted her to go to college. Fortunately, her parents were out of town, and she was living with her grandmother in Saigon. Thuy saw no reason to worry them with her decision. Traditionally, girls who do not go to college were supposed to marry and raise families. Once a girl married, she usually did not work outside the home.

Thuy was fascinated with the environment and the excitement of the news agency and quickly went from a part-time to a full-time position. She worked as a news translator, translating French wire news into Vietnamese. During her third week on the job, there was an urgent need to send a reporter to an important military operation meeting in Cambodia. Despite her inexperience, Thuy was selected. "Just listen and write down what you hear," was her instruction. At the meeting, she followed this advice but soon became involved and began to ask questions. At the close of the meeting, Thuy was approached by a three-star general who was chief of command. He was impressed by her interest and desire to learn more, so the general invited Thuy to join journalists at the front line. Thuy was flattered, but she noticed male staff members laughing in the background. "It was only much later that I learned that the general was a 'womanizer,' " she says, laughing at her naïveté.

Thuy believes her youth, energy, and enthusiasm made her fearless. She was chosen to accompany the chief of staff in his helicopter to the front line. Thuy observed many casualties and learned about actual combat conditions. One woman, an Italian journalist, Orianna Fallaci, was greatly respected for her courage, intelligence, and ability. She was the only one privileged to interview high-level communists. Thuy recalls riding with her to the front line in a tank. "The tank was fired upon and, in an instant, Fallaci was gone. I was devastated. But I called out to her, and she answered." Fallaci was unhurt and was found huddled under the shell of the tank. The journalist said to Thuy, "You will understand when you get older." Thuy realizes now how her teenage sense of immortality and autonomy protected her from reactions to reality. Some time later, the helicopter in which Thuy usually rode with the chief of staff was fired upon, and all those in it were killed. "It was the one time that I didn't make the trip with him," Thuy recalls remembering their loss.

Although Thuy attended college, she never graduated, because she continued working as a journalist. She met Phuc, her husband-to-be and also a journalist, on the front line. They became acquainted while dressed in camouflage fatigues and crammed into a bulletproof truck reserved for the press. Phuc and Thuy were married by a priest in a small chapel in 1974. The couple had planned an intimate affair, but since both came from large families, the wedding was traditional, with all the trimmings, for example, bridesmaids, big reception, and music. The groom's family paid for everything, the bridal gown, wedding rings, and even the honeymoon. In addition, the groom's family brought very expensive gifts in traditional Vietnamese manner. "It rained the entire two weeks of our honeymoon." Thuy laughs lustily. "Thuan An was the result," she continues, laughing. Their daughter was born two weeks before the fall of Saigon. Thuy's sisters left the city a week before the disaster.

Thuy was hospitalized for the birth, but the government staff abandoned the hospital and the patients in fear of being captured. Thuy and her infant joined Phuc's relatives for safety. Thuy's parents also helped and wanted the young family to leave Saigon with them. Traditionally, a new mother spends one month in a hospital with complete care. Phuc wanted to stay because, as a journalist, he felt a responsibility to document the conditions of the war and its impact upon people. Unfortunately, his patriotism resulted in incarceration in a "reeducation" camp for the next two years.

Meanwhile, Thuy was left to care for her child alone. "I was very scared.

Many young mothers turned their children over to grandparents. It is common for grandparents to raise and care for grandchildren if parents cannot manage. When the child is six years old, he or she is returned to the parents." Thuy was desperate and lonely—often to the point of considering suicide. She bought books on child care and faithfully read every page. In the end, she joined a group of young mothers whose husbands were also imprisoned, and together they learned about, and shared, child care.

Every day, Phuc was sent to the forest to chop down trees, which supplied lumber for the prison camp. Every day, Thuy scouted the area and tried to pass a note to Phuc. For the next two years, dodging the authorities, Thuy planned and plotted Phuc's escape. She tried smuggling all details about an escape plan to him, but the notes were found. Eventually, she was seized and imprisoned. Phuc was confined to a four-by-six-foot cage, from which he managed to escape after enduring much torture. Their captors believed that the couple were working for the U.S. Central Intelligence Agency (CIA). When Thuy was finally released, the couple found each other and went into hiding. "I had to leave my home because the police were following me all of the time," Thuy remembers with a grimace.

For the next two years, the family was intact but on the run. Living under less than safe, sanitary, or comfortable circumstances, they had a second child, Chun-Giao. An old friend of Thuy, a physician, helped her to deliver the baby in the hospital under a false name. The close-knit family was exhilarated but frightened. They used all of their energy in trying to find passage out of the country. After more than 22 attempts to flee, Thuy and her family, along with 77 other refugees, crowded into a small fishing vessel and set out for Thailand. The year was 1979, and the price was ten gold pieces, about $5,000 in U.S. money. Within one week, the engine failed at sea, leaving them without power in a boat hardly seaworthy. During those horrible days, Thuy witnessed and suffered pain, fear, and abuse. "There was no privacy; all were exposed to the indignity of relieving themselves over the side of the boat before an audience. Food and water were scarce and rationed. The hot, blistering, sunny days were infrequently relieved by brief, torrential rain. And there was always the black, eerie darkness of night. One learned to sleep standing up or leaning in a 24-inch space. Children cried from hunger, thirst, and lack of comfort." They drifted for ten days and nights.

On the 11th day, they sighted a fishing boat. Everyone cried with happiness and screamed for help. Unknowingly, they were about to become victims of the infamous fishermen pirates who scouted the seas looking for victims to rob and rape. The pirates towed them to the deserted isle of Ko Kra off the coast of Thailand. For more than three weeks of hell, the pirates tortured the men and raped the women. The fishermen fished by day, but at night they came back to the island to have a good time. The women had to hide or be raped. "I was so cold because I had only one shirt. It was November. We had to help each other, so I shared my shirt." Thuy shudders as she vividly recalls her experience. "I huddled in the crannies of sheer cliffs, determined to jump to my death in the sea rather than be brutalized by the drunken pirates." Thuy thinks her religious background and faith in God helped her maintain her sanity. She prayed constantly for the sight of a ship that would rescue them.

Their plight came to an end when a U.S. vessel sailed into view and rescued them. All were taken to the Songkhia refugee camp. Thuy weighed only 75 pounds. Life in the camp was "heaven" after their ordeal. Once settled, Thuy served as a medical interpreter and radio broadcaster. Thuy and Phuc composed the "Open Letter," a statement describing the plight of the boat people that was eventually read in a United Nations press conference in Thailand in December 1980; for the first time, the victims themselves alerted the world to these horrors. Thuy and her family arrived in the United States in 1980 and settled in Rancho Penasquitos, San Diego.

Their small, one-story house on a quiet, suburban street is "child-friendly," with skates, balls, and bicycles crowding the flower-strewn front yard. Bright red bougainvillea flourish on both sides of the doorway trellis. In bright, hand-printed letters, a banner is strung across the arched entrance. It reads, "Home Is Where You Hang Your Heart." The living room is neatly furnished with childproof sofa and chairs. Religious statues are prominently displayed on the mantel over the fireplace. But what is most notable is a large banner hung above the door that reads "Happy Anniversary." Thuy and Phuc celebrated their 23d wedding anniversary in 1997 with a trip to Las Vegas.

The house is alive with beautiful girls with sparkling dark eyes and long, thick, and shiny black hair. They are happy, laughing children. One is Mai-Kim, who is playing *"Für Elise"* at the small, upright piano. When she haltingly finishes, everyone applauds, and Phuc serves coffee to the adults.

"Family is the most sacred value of Vietnamese. It's top priority. The individual is secondary," Thuy says, looking around at all the happy faces. Although Phuc tends to be traditional, he is mellowing. Thuy says, "He may make the major decisions, but I make the day-to-day ones. He shares parenting, too, and is becoming more flexible." Phuc smilingly agrees. "I've gone against so many traditions—like naming my children. It's supposed to be bad luck to name someone after a dead person. But I did." The children:

Thuan-An	born 4/15/75	"named after a central beach where we first met."
Chun-Giao	born 6/26/79	"named after the two cities where we both were imprisoned and escaped."
Binh-Minh	born 8/27/85	"named after our best friend who perished at sea."

| Trang-Thu | born 8/7/87 | "named after my two sisters who are deceased." |
| Mai-Kim | born 10/28/90 | "named after my two grandmothers' maiden names." |

Thuy is called "the Dragon Princess," jokingly, by some friends, because she has five girls.

The family enjoys outings and trips with the children, school and church activities, weddings, and parties with friends. "We are blessed," Thuy says in a quiet voice. "My faith in God sustained me. My strength and resourcefulness come from him."

Thuy's future includes advances in her career at the San Diego Union, perhaps a book, and continued work as a volunteer with Boat People SOS Committee. She is modest about the many honors and awards bestowed upon her: the Roger E. Joseph Prize, the Woman of the 21st Century, Freedom Foundation at Valley Forge, the Silver Star for Valor, an honorary doctorate from Marist College in New York, and coauthorship of a book, *Pirates in the Gulf of Siam.*

"I would call myself a successful survivor," Thuy murmurs humbly. "My hardships made me more loving and gave me a greater appreciation for life," she adds.

Chun-Giao

Chun-Giao, or Sue, as she is more frequently called, was born while her parents were in hiding after their release from captivity. She has no distinct memories of her early years, but occasionally there are flashbacks of crowds, loud noises, and flight.

Sue attends a parochial school and has fond memories of one of the nuns, not only a great teacher but a kind, friendly person. She had lots of patience and tried to help everyone. Sue enjoys school, especially poetry and music. "I choose people for friends who have the same interests as mine. This way we can get along together," Sue states rather positively. This rather quiet, soft-spoken, low-key young woman has no real favorite idol but likes popular writers including Stephen King.

She enjoys coed activities like sports and birthday parties but has no special boyfriend. Because her parents work and attend many meetings, Sue does a lot of child caring. She isn't too happy about this because at times it means forgoing some activities with friends. "But I try to work it out. We can't afford baby-sitters, so that's my contribution to the family," she explains. Sue also does household chores, because of her working parents.

At times, her relationship with her Mom is "testy," as it is for most adolescents. "For a long time, we didn't get along. She gave too many orders.

Although I admire her, I'm not like her and don't want to be her 'shadow,' "
she proclaims with emphasis, "but lately, we have been getting along. I just
want to be me, myself, not a carbon copy of her. She understands now and
has not pressured me so much." Sue appears embarrassed about her honesty
and turns aside for a moment. In fact, Sue was commended for an essay she
wrote called, "The Person I Admire Most—My Mom" for an English class.
Thuy was flattered and gave Sue a big hug. New Year's Eve is one celebration Sue enjoys, as well as doing things with her family, like shopping and
taking trips.

She admires her Mom for being conscientious, industrious, people-loving,
ambitious, and caring. Sue thinks her Mom is the disciplinarian in the family.
This young lady has no firm plans for the future. "I don't worry about it.
I'm going to get two years of college before I decide what to be. About my
Mom being a Dragon Princess, she's not a dragon, but she is a princess,"
she states with a half grin.

REFERENCES

Hickey, G. *Village in Vietnam*. New Haven, CT: Yale University Press, 1964.
Huynh, S. "Literature and the Vietnamese People." In *An Introduction to Indochinese
    History, Culture, Language, and Life*, ed. J. Whitmore. Ann Arbor: University
    of Michigan Press, 1979.
Muzny, C. *The Vietnamese in Oklahoma City*. New York: AMS Press, 1989.
Rumbaut, R. "Vietnamese, Laotians and Cambodian Americans." In *Asian Americans*,
    ed. P. G. Min. Thousand Oaks, CA: Sage, 1995.
Tran, V. T. *Vietnam and Its Culture*. Hayward, California, Office of Refugee Reset-
    tlement, Region VII, Alameda County Schools, Instructional Support Ser-
    vices, 1982.
Vuong, G. *Getting to Know the Vietnamese*. New York: Frederick Unger, 1976.

PERSONAL REFLECTIONS
by Thanh-Thuy Nguyen

THE WAVES THAT CARRY ME

It is my right to be uncommon—if I can.
I seek opportunity—not security.

My past is an ocean of memories wrought by the circumstances of war.
Its waves carry me up and down in its rhythms, but always moving forward
in time. I came to the United States at the age of 8 in December 1981. I,
black, cropped hair, brown eyes, round face, and big cheeks. With me are
my two brothers, ages 4 and 6, and my father. From the airplane window,

I saw white snow! Oh, joy!, I thought. Once we arrived, a group of international refugee service workers greeted us and provided warm coats to battle the winter in the United States. I felt very alone without my mom, very tired from the 24-hour trip. My eyes were puffy from crying on the plane. My dad had left me sitting with two white strangers while he sat with my brothers.

My father worked as an airplane technician for Vietnam Airlines during the war and was sent to reeducation camp after the war. We lived in Vietnam for another six years before we became "boat people" fleeing on fishermen's small boats that could barely handle the waters of the rivers but somehow traveled through the blue ocean waves of the South China Sea for a week.

We arrived in the land of opportunity, but I did not fully understand the voyage, or why we had taken such a dangerous trip. My father has often tried to explain: "If you stay here, the tyrants will kill you. If you try to leave here, the might of the blue sea will kill you." During the many nights and days at sea, we learned of human insecurity, selfishness, and frailty, the weakness and powerlessness of human beings against nature's blow, how terror and fright can move the smallest creatures to doing the greatest evil.

> I want to take the calculated risk,
> to dream and to build, to fail and to succeed.
> I refuse to barter incentive for a dole.
> I prefer the challenges of life to the guaranteed existence,
> the thrill of fulfillment to the stale calm of utopia.

We arrived in Philadelphia, the "city of brotherly love," where I learned, explored, and proclaimed myself to be a Vietnamese American. Elementary school was a hard time in my life. I felt very awkward in my clothes, my shoes, and my life. Without my mom, I usually did not wear the right-size shoes; I was always scrunching my toes away in shoes that were too small. My clothes were hand-me-downs from local charities that were ill-fitting and were rather boyish. My brothers and I were left alone most of the time because my dad was busy working two jobs to take care of us. I was left to take on the role of the mother in the family—cooking, cleaning, taking care of my brothers, and assisting my dad in his daily activities as a translator. At that time, I didn't think I was being cheated out of a normal childhood. I was my own self doing the best that I could for my family, knowing that the tradition of being a Vietnamese meant sacrificing and suffering in order to survive as in our history and great literary tales. But the residues of those events left emotional scars of abandonment and worthlessness in my later days. I saw myself as an outsider in America knowing that I didn't speak the language or know the environment and that I acted differently, took on roles different from other students, and had a different skin color from the "native" students.

The Vietnamese community of Philadelphia was growing and burgeoning fast when we arrived. It had a Vietnamese church community that provided cultural activities and educational classes for the young so that we wouldn't lose sight of the virtue of our ethnic heritage. We had Vietnamese Franciscan brothers from the area Catholic high school who put together summer and after-school programs to tutor us and sponsored sports tournaments for youths to participate in. During this part of my life, I was still closed off to the outside community.

Blacks and whites were considered "other" people, and I learned to be afraid of black people in elementary school. I was teased and taunted in elementary school by a black girl who also called me "chink." It was hurtful because I didn't do anything specific to provoke such treatment. She just wanted to play with my hair, and when I said "No," she got aggressive. Moreover, I saw that white kids had it fairly well; I remember seeing them succeed in school and considered them to be a more "noble" race. I felt the inequality and injustice among races; I saw myself as a focus of racial prejudice.

During high school, I was able to come out of my shell a little more and mix with different people. Nonetheless, the human connection between me and blacks and whites was still not smooth—very clumsy and ungraceful. It was almost a task to talk to someone of another ethnic group. I did not consider myself an American.

When I finally entered college, I started to think more critically and examined who I was because of my interactions with others. They reminded me constantly that I was an outsider through their looks and their apparent discomfort in dealing with me. The feelings of alienation were very strong. I felt closed off from the city's diversity, surrounded by rock fences and manicured lawns, a "safe" environment, and a sea of white faces. Students with their blank stares were hesitant to acknowledge me or talk to me. Those with some courage brushed by quickly and ran off to their more familiar territories. Very few students were of my color or interests. My thoughts about being an American were pushed aside because I still considered America to be the land of the whites. I didn't feel any inclusion or being a member of the American fabric. When I walked down the street, I was considered a foreigner. When I went to classes, I was characterized as an Asian first. When I met people, they greeted me with the old stereotypes of a submissive Asian female without voice or opinion. Even today, many of those behaviors still occur to me.

I didn't feel connected with most of the people around me—I felt a sense of being stewed in a pot of soup where I was supposed to blend in with the "white" broth, but instead I kept my flavor and identity as a Vietnamese.

By my senior year in college, I saw two parallel lines running through my life steadfastly and never faltering behind one another. Yet, many times the two lines crashed into one another or ran side by side. I saw my values, my ways, my beliefs, my lifestyle, my principles, and my mind going in two distinct ways in everything I did—one was Vietnamese, and one was American. For example, in Vietnamese culture, one does not talk about one's accomplishments or discuss one's successes, but when it came time to apply to college, and one had to give and show these examples, I had a terrible time deciding what I should say or whether I should include an award or a scholarship I had or the achievements that I had made, coming from an immigrant family. I had to put aside the lessons of humbleness and do what it took to get into college. I learned to decipher more and more which was the right road for me. I learned to accept who I am and which roads deterred me from growth and which brought success. I learned to take from both cultures and at times to stretch a few lines to see where it would take me. The self-realization of being Vietnamese American gave me comfort to understand who I am, my ways, and people's perceptions of me. With this knowledge, I was moved to take on leadership roles on campus to heighten awareness of Asian cultures. I helped sponsor multicultural events and charitable events. But the most exciting part was working on a proposal with the dean to have courses in Asian history. I was elated when a course on the history of Vietnam and the war was offered and courses on Asian art became available during my senior year. I overcame my fear of blacks because black students and other minority students groups supported my activities tremendously; and we were in cooperation with each other. I finished my college journey with the completion of my senior thesis on the Vietnam War. In addition, I was naturalized as an American citizen. I was conscious of that decision, really analyzing my values and growth in America, and saw myself as a participant and an actor in this giant play of American history.

> I will not trade freedom for beneficence
> nor my dignity for a handout.
> I will never cower before any master
> nor bend to any threat.

My appreciation for being a Vietnamese American only heightens through my growth. I enjoy the beauty in the elegant flows of an *ao'dai*, Vietnamese paintings of the sinewy back of a Vietnamese woman and her long, flowing, black hair, the sensuality in the poems by Ho Xuan Huong, the mouthwatering *canh chua* and *ca'kho to^*, and the painful yet powerful history of the Vietnamese people. My Vietnamese heritage has been fundamental to my development.

I have also come to appreciate my parents' sacrifice, my father's dedication and devotion to my brothers and me through the struggles to make ends meet. The risk that he took in bringing us here and raising us moves my soul to remember always his love. He strived through the hard times with the physical challenges of a new environment, language, culture, and the psychological challenges of war stress, assimilation, and prejudice. My mother, who sacrificed almost ten years of her life being alone without her children or her husband in Vietnam, risked her life by traveling through the beaches of Vietnam and the jungles of Cambodia to find a way to America and endured the loss of seeing her children grow and provided me some healing with her here by my side.

The war and the waves of the South China Sea with its torrents and turbulence taught me a lesson of resilience and strength. The ashes of the Vietnam War have resulted in a tumultuous life for me, being a woman, a refugee, an immigrant, a Vietnamese, and an American. It has made me strong, capable of withstanding the bludgeoning of circumstances, and still finding happiness through the tears. Thus,

> it is my heritage to stand erect, proud and unafraid,
> to think and act for myself, enjoy the benefit of my creations
> and to face the world boldly
> saying, this I have done.
> All this is what it means to be an American.
>
> Dean Alfange, "My Creed"

6

Filipina Americans

The Philippines consists of a cluster of 7,000 tropical islands located in the South China Sea. However, 11 islands contain 95% of the landmass. The Philippines was a Spanish colony for more than three centuries following Ferdinand Magellan's landing on the island in 1521, when he claimed the territory for Spain. The islands were named for Prince Phillip, who encouraged Spanish exploration and settlement. One lasting effect of almost 400 years of Spanish domination was the conversion of Filipinos to Catholicism. The church owned vast tracts of land and controlled the educational system. Today, 83% of Filipinos are of the Catholic faith. Manila became an important port for the Spanish galleon trade between Asia and the New World. Under Spanish rule, the majority of native people were reduced to landless, peasant sharecroppers (Karnow, 1989). Several cultural influences come from Spain and can be found in Filipino food, songs, and dances (Agbayani-Siewert and Revilla, 1995).

The majority of the Filipino population are basically of Malay stock with intermingling of Chinese, Spanish, Indian, and American. There are eight major ethnolinguistic groups, consisting of some 200 dialects; Filipino, the native language based mostly on the Tagalog dialect, is the most politically prominent. Language and the region of origin are two main differentiations among Filipinos in the Philippines and abroad (Alcantra, 1975).

The victory of the American navy over the Spanish in the Battle of Manila Bay brought the Spanish-American War to an end in 1898. The Treaty of Paris (1899) formally ended the war and transferred control of the Philippines to the United States in exchange for $25 million. President McKinley announced that the islands would be an American protectorate until the Filipinos could establish a stable constitutional government. In September 1900, the president appointed William Howard Taft as the first provisional governor of the Philippines (Melendy, 1977).

However, possession of the islands by the United States was resisted by Filipinos, so it took four years of savage, guerrilla-type war before the entire country was relatively peaceful. This situation added to centuries of Spanish colonial rule followed by years of war for independence; change from family-sized farms and slave labor plantations to large-scale agricultural, horticultural "factories," or agribusiness; and finally, the acquisition of the Philippines by the United States.

This made the islands a ward of the United States and provided the political, economic, and social linkages that allowed the "internal" and "voluntary" migration of Filipino labor to the U.S. territories and mainland without the domestic and diplomatic difficulties associated with the immigration of other alien workers, such as the Chinese, Mexicans, and Japanese.

FOUR PERIODS OF IMMIGRATION

Historically, the *pensionados* (students) were the first group of Filipino immigrants. They constituted the first wave in a four-stage immigration process. The *pensionado* stage lasted from 1903 to 1924. The second wave consisted of farmworkers who arrived in Hawaii and California between 1906 and 1934. The third wave was composed of Filipino war veterans who arrived between 1946 and 1964. The fourth wave consisted of the "brain" immigrants who arrived after the immigration reforms of 1965 (Gonzalez, 1990).

Regarding the first wave, in August 1903 the Pensionado Act passed by Congress provided support for selected young Filipino students to pursue college education in the United States. The *pensionados* were enrolled at elite institutions like Harvard, Cornell, Stanford, and the University of California at Berkeley. The goal was that they would absorb the principles of democracy and return to their homeland as representatives of the American way. These students were actively involved in student activities at their campuses. Initially, the Pensionado Act allowed 100 Filipino students to attend colleges and live with American families. In addition, some 14,000 "self-supporting students" entered the United States between 1910 and 1930. But only 10% of these actually enrolled in colleges (Catapusan, 1941). After completion of their studies, they returned home to be social, political, and economic leaders. However, their pioneering efforts were continued as thousands of young Filipinos, inspired by the success stories of the *pensionados*, came to the United States in search of education (Agbayani-Siewert and Revilla, 1995).

The second wave consisted of farmworkers and included many potential students who couldn't afford the cost of education and other young men seeking employment. Because of the protectorate status of the islands, Filipinos were made "nationals," which meant that they could travel freely and without immigration restrictions to any state or territory of the United States. This was good news to the growers in Hawaii, who would gain access to an unlimited supply of low-cost labor without the complication of immigration restrictions (Gonzalez, 1990).

The first recruitment of Filipino laborers by agents of the Hawaii Sugar Planters Association occurred in the spring of 1906. Only a few hundred Filipinos arrived in Hawaii between 1907 and 1909; the serious flow began in 1910, when 3,000 arrived. Between 1909 and 1920, a total of 33,273 arrived, for an average of 2,800 a year. Between 1921 and 1932, a total of 15,163 arrived, for an average of 7,100. During this period (1909–1932) a grand total of 118,430 Filipino laborers arrived (Sharma, 1984). By 1935 approximately 58,000 returned home, and another 18,500 migrated to the mainland (Sharma, 1980).

The laborers traveled from season to season, from one farming community to another, following crops. Stereotyped as good for "stoop labor," Filipinos harvested crops like asparagus, grapes, lettuce, carrots, and beets. The farmers were believed to have the ability to withstand the peat dust and became invaluable to asparagus growers. Since they were smaller than white laborers, the growers also were convinced that the Filipinos could stoop more easily. Their backbreaking work schedule was ten hours a day for 26 days a month, with an occasional Sunday or holiday off (Agbayani-Siewert and Revilla, 1995).

Third-wave immigrants (1946–1964) were primarily Filipino war veterans who were granted citizenship and allowed to bring their families to America. Up to this time, Filipinos were considered "nationals" and were eligible for citizenship. However, a law passed in 1925 allowed them to become citizens only after serving three years in the U.S. military.

Earlier, thousands of Filipinos from California and Hawaii joined the specialized Filipino units to fight the guerrilla war in the Philippines. At the end of the hostilities, these units were among the most decorated. In recognition of their services, they were granted citizenship and allowed to settle their families in the United States. In addition, on July 2, 1946, two days before the granting of independence to the Philippines, Congress approved legislation that made all resident Filipinos eligible for citizenship. For the first time, Filipinos were allowed to apply for American citizenship, either as veterans or as legal resident aliens (Vallangca, 1987).

Between 1946 and 1965, 35,700 Filipinos were admitted to the United States. These third-wave immigrants were different from the farmworkers, as they were veterans and could take advantage of veterans benefits. They had learned to read, write, and speak English and had learned a good deal about the American way. They secured employment at military installations and in the industrial sector. By 1950, 60% in California were urban, which increased to 80% in 1960. They also abandoned farmwork and moved into industrial jobs; 62% were farmworkers in 1940, but this dropped to 11% by 1960 (Smith, 1976).

Strong family units and blue-collar jobs meant that second-generation, American-born children could take full advantage of the educational opportunities available after the war. Veterans could use their veterans benefits to secure technical training or a college education.

The fourth-wave immigrants may be called the "brain drain" generation, as they arrived after the immigration reforms of 1965, which gave preferential treatment under the family reunification policy to those with professional and technical skills (Pido, 1980).

The reform acts set a quota of 20,000 immigrants per year for all countries and a total of 170,000 per year from Asia. The impact was threefold: (1) it resulted in a very significant increase of Filipino immigrants; (2) it attracted highly skilled technicians; and (3) it allowed legal resident aliens or naturalized citizens to sponsor their relatives for immigration (Portes, 1976). In the 1980s more than 100,000 Filipinos applied for tourist visas each year in Manila, and between 40,000 and 50,000 applied for immigration on the basis of family ties in the United States (Mangiafico, 1988).

One of the interesting characteristics of the fourth wave is that more females have immigrated than males. For example, in 1965 two-thirds of all Filipinos admitted were females. In 1980 the sex ratio among foreign-born Filipinos was 86.4 males for every 100 females, compared with 95.4% in the U.S. population. But this imbalance is offset by the large number of Filipino women who marry American men, both in the Philippines and in the United States. For this and other reasons, the Filipino "mail-order bride system" has become the focus of considerable criticism in recent years.

Perhaps the most distinguishing characteristic of fourth-wave immigrants is their level of educational achievement. Of all Filipinos over the age of 25 (in 1980), 87% were high school graduates, and 47% had four or more years of college. This compares with 66.5% and 16.2%, respectively, for the general U.S. population. It is also interesting to note that more Filipina women graduate from college (43%) than men (34%). It is also important to note that most Filipino immigrants arrive with college degrees (58% in 1980), as opposed to obtaining their education in the United States (Gonzalez, 1990).

All indicators reveal that Filipinos in the United States have very stable families. The rate of marriage among Filipinos is higher than that of the general population (68% compared to 58%), and their divorce rate is half of the national average. They are also less likely to be separated. This high level of family stability can be attributed to their religious beliefs (Catholicism), to the fact that divorce is not legally possible in the Philippines, and to strong family bonds that work against the possibility of divorce. However, divorce rates are higher among those who marry exogamously and tends to increase with length of residence in America (Posadas, 1981).

The need for political power and a sense of discrimination may be the key factors that foster unity and cooperation among Filipino Americans. Within the last decade, Filipino Americans in major Filipino centers like Hawaii, Los Angeles, San Francisco, and Seattle have successfully united to elect Filipino Americans to political offices. Organizations based on professional ties have been formed to lobby for less restrictive legislation aimed at immigrants who practice medicine and law. In addition to possible changes within the Filipino population, more attention from business, government, and academic researchers will influence the ways that Filipinos cooperate with one another to protect common interests. As their numbers grow, and common issues emerge, the sense of Filipino community will most likely increase (Agbayani-Siewert and Revilla, 1990).

CASE STUDIES

Maria

Sometimes called the "Jewel of San Diego," La Jolla offers beautiful beaches and many cultural sights and sounds in fine arts, antiques, museums, wildlife, sea life, and music. Its playhouse is 3,000 miles away from the bright lights of Broadway, but this widely praised regional theater has become the West Coast's own "Broadway by the Beach."

Dr. Maria Mason, a pathologist, leads an active professional and volunteer life in this attractive artistic section of San Diego. She was born in Manila, the Philippines, June 11, 1951, to Ernesto and Generosa Reyes, who were chief of police and Spanish teacher, respectively. Maria was the fourth of ten children. Her academic life began early, when, at the age of 3, she entered kindergarten and was graduated with a medal after giving the valedictorian speech! Maria also marched to a different drummer, making up her own rules as she progressed. She recalls trying to enroll in the Girl Scouts at the age of 8, although she knew the rules required a girl to be 10 years old. Maria played with paper dolls but would have preferred a doctor's kit. Her pre–high school activities included sewing, needlepoint, acting in plays, dancing, and helping hearing-impaired children, while serious studying earned her honors.

From age 11 to 14, Maria attended a private Dominican university. She was one to two years younger than her classmates but was competitive and won honors in geometry. She participated in acting and dancing and won oratorical contests in three languages—Tagalog, Spanish, and English.

Her role model was a Spanish teacher. "She was gentle, kind, beautiful, and patient," Maria recalls. "She became my best friend." Maria had two other close friends, the valedictorian and the president of the student body. "We vowed to become physicians and planned to get together at some future date. I chose them for friends because they were intelligent and sweet; we spent a lot of time together." In high school, Maria was interested in poetry and often, as a volunteer, taught catechism to young children. Although she was too young to date, she was very pretty and feminine, and Maria remembers boys trying to get her attention. The valedictorian sent her love letters, and other boys often slipped chocolate bars into her notebooks. "My mother was very strict," Maria says. "Only once did she allow me to go on a picnic with a boy, and boys have to make formal visits to our home—with chaperones, of course."

Maria always wanted to become a physician and was ready to go directly into a premed program. But her mother and aunt advised that she major in medical technology to assure employment possibilities in case Maria changed her mind about medicine. In college she was a brilliant student but had difficulties adjusting socially because of her young age. "I began college at age 14 and graduated at 18, magna cum laude," she explains. "I concentrated on my studies and was the number one student in the entire college for three years." Maria was class president and represented the college in oratorical contests in three languages and won them all. In a citywide oratorical competition, she represented the college and won second place.

Studious Maria was a member of several clubs, a news reporter, religion editor of the newspaper, and a member of the debating club and Pax Romana, a religious group of student leaders. Although her parents didn't allow dating, Maria had a lunch date when she was 16 years old. On her birthday, her friend joined her for lunch. The young man was not liked by her parents, because he was poor, not handsome, and dark-skinned. She recalls an important incident. "My sister informed my parents, who sent my three older brothers to the college to bring me home. They came right into the classroom, and the teacher excused me. I thought that an emergency had happened at home. When we reached our home, my mother slapped me, pulled my hair, and called me horrible names. I was hysterical. She had never hit me before. All I could do was cry and scream. No one said why I was being punished. My father finally stepped in and sent me to my room. Later he consoled me and asked that I break off the relationship with the young man. I pretended to follow his request but instead continued to see my boyfriend." Maria stopped this revelation and took a deep breath before continuing. "I never forgave my mother until just before she died. I also vowed that I would never hit my children, and I didn't. I kept that promise." Maria appears thoughtful for a moment.

After graduation, Maria wanted to enter medical school. She won a partial scholarship, but her parents thought that 19 years was too young for such a big step. They suggested a trip to the United States in the interim.

Maria came to San Jose to attend an aunt's wedding in 1970. She liked California and took the examination for a license in medical technology, which would enable her to work. Maria found employment, but soon the immigration authorities alerted her to the need for technologists in Fresno, California, and ordered her to go there. Despite a petition from her employer, who cited her trilingual ability and superior skills, Maria was forced to accept a position in Fresno. "This was my first discriminatory experience," she remembers.

At first the hospital staff thought Maria was a family member of one of the administrators, because she looked like a young teenager. Within a few weeks, Maria demonstrated knowledge and skills at such high levels that the staff welcomed and respected her. Guy Wesley Mason was an intern in the hospital's Medical Laboratory Department program. He was seven years older than Maria, but they fell in love. Guy was completing his degree after a hiatus with the air force. Maria's parents were against their marriage, but Maria was determined; so the ceremony took place on June 10, 1972.

The wedding, in a Catholic church, was formal. Maria's mother attended, but her father was prohibited from leaving the Philippines, which was under martial law. The entire small town participated by providing a community hall and a lavish reception. The couple left for San Diego immediately after the ceremony. Both were, fortunately, scheduled to begin work that week.

In 1974 Maria had a son. Two years later, a daughter was born. Maria breast-fed both children—her son for five to six months and daughter Lisa for three months. Maria didn't work for six months after her son's birth and stayed home for three months after Lisa's birth. "It was hectic. Most of the time I worked at two jobs. I would pick up Pap smears from the clinic and read them at home while my son slept. With Lisa, I worked the graveyard shift, so I could be with her during the day. In addition, I completed all the household chores and made the children's clothing," Maria says with nostalgia creeping into her soft voice.

When the children were young, Maria provided most of the child care and nurturing. Guy was helpful in many ways. "We used to read to our children. We began when they were infants, and it became a nightly ritual. We enjoyed picnics and vacations visiting his parents."

When Lisa was 2 years old, Maria decided to enter medical school. She and Guy had separated. Despite Maria's excellent college record, she was not accepted by a medical school in the United States. She believes that because she was older and a mother, admissions officers didn't see her as a viable prospective candidate. Women who were mothers and older were not seen as positive candidates in those years. Maria returned to Manila, retrieved her scholarship, and entered the University of Santo Tomas in Manila. She completed three and a half years there and one-half year in a rotating internship in San Diego. Upon graduation in 1983, Maria received honors of Benemeritus (the equivalent of summa cum laude).

All during her medical education, Maria had problems with child care and an ill mother. After the first six months, the children went back to the United States and were cared for by their father. Maria's mother was diagnosed with an eye melanoma and was dying. As the oldest girl, Maria was designated to escort her mother back and forth to Los Angeles for scheduled chemotherapy treatments. Maria was determined to complete medical school, despite the circumstances. "I missed my children, who were in the United States. I missed so much of their growing up," she says with sadness in her voice and in her facial expression. Maria was able, however, to spend four months in the United States with the children each year. "Not only was I lonely for the children, but while in the Philippines I began to feel out of place in the Filipino community, too," she adds.

After a year, Maria was accepted at St. Louis University Hospital in Missouri for a four-year residency training, which she completed in 1988. The family relocated to St. Louis. "Although Guy and I were separated, we decided to make our children's lives our first priority and work together raising them. We lived in the same house but were separated as far as marital relations were concerned. Guy lived in a basement apartment," Maria says wryly. Since both parents were concerned about their children's upbringing, they presented a uniform approach with lots of love and family activity. Several years later, they divorced.

Unfortunately, during Maria's residency, the chief was neither friendly nor even cordial. Maria thought his opinion of foreigners was quite low. It equaled his feelings about women. "I worked twice as hard as my Caucasian colleagues," she says. When Maria requested a fellowship, a committee interviewed her, and her request was approved despite the resident representative voting against her. Maria became politically active and represented the hospital at the Resident Physicians Section of the American Society of Clinical Pathologists and eventually served as its chairperson. "But I always had to 'prove' myself before being nominated for office, it seemed," she recalls.

Maria wants her children to follow Philippine customs and traditions of the extended family. She realizes that this comes as a hardship for them, since they live in an American environment. "But our ethnic practices have maintained family bonds," Maria believes. "It is also important that children show a deep respect for their elders," she adds.

As to the mother–daughter relationship, Maria and Lisa talk openly about everything. They confide in each other and share happy and sad experiences with laughter and with tears. Maria's attitude is nonjudgmental. "At times, I feel that I have overburdened her young mind with my own problems. I hope this has allowed her to experience and learn from them. Lisa asks my opinion on many facets of her life. I try to share my thoughts with the premise that Lisa will be the one making the decision."

Maria thinks Lisa's temperament is similar to hers. "Lisa has a zest for life; she's vibrant and alive. She loves to dance and talk!" Maria glows, and her dark eyes light up as she describes her daughter. Lisa shares interests with her father; she enjoys camping and nature. She is competent and reliable and completes her tasks at home and at school. "I think she is somewhat of a feminist. She believes in equal rights and equal treatment," opines Maria.

Their relationship has not changed over the years. Maria admits that she has had to make adjustments as Lisa matures into a young adult. "It's hard to let go. I perform rituals like moving her things out of her old room." Maria would like Lisa to have a stable life. Presently, she vacillates about possible career choices. Maria hopes Lisa will be able to find her way soon. "I can only be here to support her decisions," Maria says softly.

What does success mean to Maria? "When I feel pleasure after an accomplishment," she offers. "I am successful in many ways. I'm a qualified pathologist and a teacher. I'm a leader in the Philippine community and hold many positions, and I volunteer with the American Cancer Society. I am an active participant in several committees of the San Diego County Medical Society and the Philippine Medical Association and am on the Board of Directors of PUSO Philippines (a Filipino nonprofit organization), and I am president of the American Cancer Society, San Diego Unit."

"As a mother, I think my children are humble, good-natured, kind, and intellectual. I struggle as a woman, because I am assertive, and in my culture, this is unacceptable. I have had some success as owner of a laboratory business. I struggle as an artist, because I don't have time for my poetry or writing. There are times when I feel that a simple life would be a blessing. But yet—would I be happy?" Maria answers the rhetorical question with a shrug of her shoulders and a quizzical smile.

Lisa

Lisa's memory of her early years is rather distant and vague. "I was born in San Diego, California, in 1977. When I was very young, my mother entered medical school. My brother and I were cared for by my father." Lisa attended a private elementary school, where she made friends and enjoyed all subjects. She learned to play piano at the age of 6. Lisa's middle years were spent at public schools, where she was an honor student and won several science fair and mathematics contests. In addition, she excelled in oratory. Lisa graduated from Bishop's High, a private school in La Jolla, where she was inducted into the Cum Laude Society. As a teenager, she enjoyed outdoor activities like kayaking, camping, and hiking, as well as music, including the piano.

What characteristics does Lisa look for in prospective friends? "I look for friends who are active in their daily lives, who enjoy thinking about, and discussing, a variety of subjects, who are confident, and who are caring and loving," Lisa says cynically and questions, "Wouldn't it be great if all of my friends were like that? But neither any of my current friends nor I fit this description 24 hours a day. We are forever learning, growing, and changing," Lisa says gravely.

As a teenager, Lisa could have been a "social butterfly," but for parental restrictions. She had lots of boyfriends, but a chaperone had to be present when boys visited her at home. Lisa's first date was at age 13. Maria told

Lisa about her own experiences as a teenager, whose three older brothers acted as constant escorts. "Consider yourself lucky," Maria told her daughter.

Lisa talks about ethnicity and friendship. "Until college, I had only one close friend who was Filipino. It was during the 8th grade, and I have pleasant memories of our boy-crazy conversations and dancing together in a Philippine dance troupe." In college two of her closest friends are Filipinos (one is "half"); both were born and raised in the United States. They met as freshmen but became friends only through membership in the college Philippine Association. "Both live near Philadelphia and have welcomed me to their homes and families—a home and family away from home," she marvels.

Lisa found her relationship with Maria, overall, stimulating, challenging, and positive, although passionate at times. While Lisa was in high school, Maria and Lisa lived alone. Maria worked long hours, leaving Lisa responsible for her own meals, classes, and free time. "This freedom and trust that my Mom gave me definitely contributed to my growth. However, what affected me more was the time that we did spend together. We always met for coffee once or twice a week. We would chatter away about our experiences, our problems, and our plans. I felt that I was having 'adult conversations' with my Mom while my friends were still hiding secrets about drinking, drugs, or whatever from theirs. My mother trusted me as an adult and sought my opinions. Concerning my questions and problems, she simultaneously voiced her opinions and trusted in my ultimate decisions."

However, the closeness of their relationship also created conflict. Back then, Lisa considered her Mom an equal and would, at times, challenge her authority with her voice and actions. "She would say that I did not respect her, followed by 'I would have been slapped by now if I'd said that to my mother,' to which I would reply that she did not raise me the same way her mother had raised her. I felt that my Mom was raising me to be independent and yet wanted the same respect and authority of the parent–child relationship she grew up with. What she did not understand was that I always loved and respected her strongly, but, at the same time, felt capable of questioning her and asserting myself because of our closeness—a closeness that she did not have with her mother. The closeness allowed me to see her as 'my mother,' 'a friend,' and 'another human being' with weaknesses who makes mistakes just like me."

Lisa speaks of the changes in their relationship now that she is an adult. "I am in college, and my mother is active in several organizations outside her work. We are both busier than ever, but thanks to technology, we keep in touch through e-mail and an occasional telephone call. The conversations usually focus on a problem or concern in one of our lives. We still use each other as outlets and look to each other for advice, but the daily details of life are missing in these conversations. I no longer know everything that's going on with her laboratory, or how she's doing with her significant other. I am still getting used to this.

When I am home for a visit, I become like a child, cooing for attention and affection, letting my Mom take care of me once again. This surprised me at first, and I tried to ignore it, but now I enjoy it without questioning it."

Lisa thinks that the most important gift parents can give to their children is unconditional love. She admits that this is something that she doesn't fully understand and, at times, has criticized. However, Lisa believes that it is what has helped her trust in herself, push ahead through difficult times, and begin to truly love others.

Lisa has had few problems adjusting to a different culture or lifestyle. She grew up in several different states and spent time studying and living abroad. The only problem she has is in Philadelphia, where she attends college. It's the "city attitude" she encounters daily in her interactions with people. Often, people are distant, rude, and not helpful, especially during 9–5 working hours. To cope with this, she tries to be patient and friendly, but sometimes she slips into her own "distant" mode as a way of ending the interaction as quickly as possible.

Lisa has no role model, so to speak, "other than my constantly changing vision of 'the ideal.' " However, the more complete truth is that that vision is a composite of aspects of several people: "my mother's dedication to helping other people, my brother's intelligence, my friend's generosity, my own honesty."

At 20, Lisa appears quite mature about some things. But a career choice is not one. She ponders about possibilities these days quite often. "I imagine that five years from now, I will be working in public health in a Spanish-speaking country, involved with the growing acceptance of 'alternative medicine' in the United States, or entering medical school. My interest in a health-related career has definitely been shaped by observing my mother's practice and admiring her service for her community. However, through my studies in college and my recent experiences studying abroad in Mexico, I have realized that there are a variety of ways to get involved with health and that right now I am not capable of choosing which way to pursue. My Mom likes to tell me, 'Oh, just get your M.D. now and decide later if you'll use it or not.' I laugh. It is a ridiculous suggestion, because I would probably fail out of medical school for lack of attendance. They would find me volunteering in a variety of health centers because I am itching for more clinical experience."

In addition to being impressed with her mother's outstanding achievements in medicine, Lisa finds other sterling qualities. "My mother is amazing! She is a leader in the community and in her profession. She is an orator, a singer, a journalist, and a poet. She is incredibly busy, and frequently stressed, and yet she makes time and does thoughtful things for everyone around her, loved ones, friends, acquaintances, and strangers. This thoughtfulness is what I hope to develop." Lisa pauses. She is impressed and wonders if she has forgotten anything.

Lisa believes she's still growing positively and negatively. "I hope that I never stop," she says. She thinks that self-discovery and self-challenge are two of the most wonderful things that she experiences in her life.

Some years ahead, Lisa hopes to become a parent. Will her mother's parenting influence her? She responds, "My mother likes to remind me in a 'you'd better thank me' voice, that she raised me very differently, that is to say, much more liberally, than the way other Filipinos living in the United States raise their children. I thank my mother for her choice, and I imagine that I will follow her style of parenting while adding one modification [rigid structure], which deals with education." Lisa's face reflects concern.

Lisa has lived in many different cities and countries. She has experienced life as the child of a working mother and a single mother. But the most influential experience she's had occurred early in life. "It was in my junior year chemistry class in high school. The teacher made us think about those chemical reactions. He challenged us to answer questions and solve problems in class in a 'do it or sit down and be quiet' situation. It made me curious, and it made me want to think for the first time. It was an awakening, which has spread beyond classroom walls into all aspects of my life."

Lisa admits that she doesn't know Philippine values and practices, except in a superficial way. She believes this is the result of the circumstances of her childhood—living with a Filipino mother and an American father, far from other relatives, in predominantly "white" neighborhoods. "I never perceived clashes between my parents about values. They both value love and support within the immediate and extended family, and so do I. They both value education and working hard, and so do I. However, there are two values that I associate with my mother and Philippine values that I do not appreciate—special respect for elders and strong religious faith. I have 'made mano' (raised his hand to my forehead) to my Abolito [own God] because that is the custom and because it makes me and my fair skin and brown hair feel more accepted in a room full of morenos [Filipinos]—but the truth is that I do not feel greater respect for my elders in general than I do for other human beings, despite the years and wisdom that my elders may have. Likewise, I respect my mother's Catholic faith, but right now it is not something I accept in my own life. Initially, this hurt her and she would not discuss it with me. Now she is more open and welcomes many forms of spirituality."

Lisa says this interview brought her subconscious realizations to the surface. It has made her think and clarify some of her true feelings.

If asked to say "thank you" to Maria, what would Lisa say? "I would say thank you for being yourself, for showing me all the greatness that one human being can accomplish and do for others and for herself. Thank you for loving me always." Lisa's voice is whispery soft and gentle.

Lisa's definition for success—"To succeed in life is to be happy once in a while—the kind of happy where you feel alive all over your body and you say, 'This is right.' It is not something to be constantly felt, for no personal or social progress would be made. But it is something that anyone can achieve if they have dreams, work hard for them, take time for reflection, and laugh at themselves along the way."

Cynthia

When two people work closely in a collaborative effort, at times almost thinking the same thoughts, sharing the same interests and the same goals, they need a creative, inspiring environment, one that is pleasing to the eye, soothing to the spirit, and stimulating to the mind. Such a place is the De Leon Music Studio, located in suburban New Jersey. Large, airy, and decorated in soft earth tones, sea and sand colors splashed with pink and blue pastels, the studio features a baby grand piano and other musical instruments. Shelves of sheet music, tapes, and cassettes hug the beige walls, beneath several colorful, framed pieces of artwork mostly made by the De Leon family members themselves. In this beautiful setting, Cynthia and Sarighani De Leon teach and play beautiful music. For this mother and daughter, music-making has enhanced their loving relationship.

Cynthia was born in the Philippines, the eldest of four siblings—two girls and two boys. Her father, Gaudencio, was an engineer and worked with the U.S. Air Force and the airline industry. Her mother, Nieves, was an English teacher. Migration to the United States in the 1970s was, to her parents, a golden opportunity for education and personal growth.

As children, the siblings got along quite well with each other. "I was 11 years old when my sister was born, and there was a difference of seven years between her and the third child, my brother. Although there was no one in my family actually involved in playing a musical instrument, my father listened to classical music all of the time." Since Cynthia was the only daughter for a long time, her parents gave her a lot of attention. She spent most of her out-of-school time with them.

Cynthia really became interested in music at the age of 8, when her friend was taking piano lessons that interfered with their playtime. "I watched her, and it seemed rather easy. So I asked my mother if I could take lessons, too," Cynthia says with quiet laughter. Her mother was hesitant, because the family didn't have a piano at that time, and she feared that Cynthia's interest would be short-lived. But after a year of lessons, Cynthia demonstrated skills that convinced her parents to buy her a piano the next year. Cynthia's first teacher gave private lessons as a community service, but her second teacher, Marina Diokno, really was responsible for developing Cynthia's skills as a pianist. "She taught at my school and made sure I got sponsors for my numerous recitals. I would say she really built the foundation for my career. I began my first lesson with her when I was 9 and had my first recital when I was 11 years old. For my graduation recital, my husband, Bayani Mendoza de Leon, conducted the orchestra. He was from a musical family. His father, Felipe Padilla de Leon, is a composer and National Artist of the Philippines. His mother, Iluminada, is a pianist."

One person who impacted upon Cynthia's life was Philippine president Cory Aquino. "I feel that she's a role model because before she became president, she was a devoted mother and wife. She supported her husband's political endeavors. I can relate to that. For a while, I, too, put my career aside and devoted myself to my husband's career and my children. Only when the children were advanced in school did I return to my music and accept opportunities to perform."

Bayani was Cynthia's first boyfriend. Although she was quite young, her parents approved of the marriage. It is no longer a custom for parents to choose their daughter's husband. Young people choose their mates because they love each other. The only misgiving her parents expressed, like most parents, was a fear for their financial security because "he was an artist, a composer-writer." Cynthia's laughter is charming. The young couple would have preferred a quiet family wedding, but the De Leons opted for a large, traditional affair. Because of the many musicians in the family's circle, it was almost like a showcase for musical talent. Cynthia describes one tradition. "Everyone is in a circle. The bridal party goes around the circle, and every woman who wants to dance with the groom and every man who wants to dance with the bride pins money on the bride's gown or the groom's suit." The food was Philippine, but things like cutting the cake reflect more of the Western influence. Cynthia and Bayani had a short honeymoon in a mountain resort. They settled in San Diego, where there is a sizable population of Filipinos. "My husband studied composition at the University of California in San Diego and had musical interests there. He established several Ethno Music Ensembles there and has continued his association with the groups."

The first child, a honeymoon baby, was born in 1970. "We named him Lakasnubay, coined from Filipino words meaning 'the guiding force.' Three years later, our next child was Sarighani, also coined from Filipino words meaning 'fresh charm.' She was a placenta previa delivery and quite difficult. I wasn't able to breast-feed my children, but I made up for this by extra bonding practices," she reveals.

Regarding Philippine values, Cynthia thinks respect for the family and respect for the elders are very sacred. Being proud of one's Philippine heritage is also important. "You may live in America and adopt some American customs, but you remain Filipino. Just look in the mirror and you cannot deny your roots." Cynthia appears serious and concerned. "We made sure that our children spoke the Filipino language, because I think language is the main connection."

Because Cynthia and her daughter spend so much time together with their shared interest in music, their relationship appears to become closer as they grow older. "She has become my best friend. At times, Sarighani would seek advice from her close friends, because she believed people in her own age group had more relevant experience, and she felt more comfortable with them." Yet, Cynthia recognizes that there are certain subjects about which a mother is the most logical one to supply information. "I respect her for that," she says. Cynthia believes that it is important that Sarighani respect what her parents can give her that would bring meaning to her life. Then she can pursue those concepts for herself.

As to bias or discrimination, Cynthia has never allowed herself to consider any expression or behavior of this type to be criticism of her personally. She has such a deep sense of personal worth that she allows her talent and skills to speak for themselves. "I always wanted people to accept me and what I did on merit. If they didn't, it was their problem, not mine," she concludes with a bright smile.

Cynthia considers herself very successful and lucky. "Success creates a record, and my record speaks for itself. As a musician, I feel honored to be associated with various groups that recognize talent, ambition, and hard work. Many opportunities come my way as a result." Travel is no longer the hardship it was when the children were younger, and music performances were scheduled around the children's needs. With both parents actively involved and engaged in music, it was normal to encourage Lakasnubay in that direction. "When Lakasnubay was younger, he used to ask, 'Why do I have to take piano and violin lessons?' Now he sees the value of that musical exposure and how it has helped him to succeed as an entrepreneurial recording engineer and computer graphics designer."

Cynthia enjoys reading psychology, esoteric philosophy, educational books, and an occasional best-seller, but when the De Leons gather, it is a music-centered affair. Even the near and distant kin participate. They are a clannish group, a close-knit family. Cynthia's parents visit the United States every two years, and she has a brother who lives in Vancouver and a sister in New Jersey. Many of Cynthia's friends are musicians, too.

Cynthia's dream is to have her own music school and really get involved with teaching children. She graduated summa cum laude from Centro Escolar University with a double major in mathematics and piano. She also enjoys the mathematics side of her career as director of finance and personnel affairs for a New York–based executive recruitment firm specializing in the quantitative sciences.

Cynthia has gained special recognition as a fine, sensitive collaborative pianist, performing in recitals with numerous artists, including sopranos Evelyn Mandac and Lani Misenas, violinist Yeou-Cheng Ma, flutist Laurel Mauer, clarinetist Bonnie Sholl, and pianist Karen Beluso, to name a few. Cynthia is currently the director of the Children's Orchestra Society of New York Chamber Ensemble Program, which she helped to establish in 1989, and was on the piano staff of the Mannes College of Music Preparatory Division for several years. She has also collaborated with her cellist daughter,

Sarighani, in a cassette and compact disc recording of *Heartstrings: Philippine Airs for Cello and Piano*. The mother–daughter team, together with soprano Lani Misenas, performed for former Philippine president Cory Aquino during her New York state visit. Cynthia is pianist for the Ma-De Leon Piano Trio (with Yeou-Cheng Ma and Sarighani), which appeared in concert at Queens Theater in the Park and the Gillary Music Gallery on Long Island. She is also pianist for the Mendele Trio (with violinist nephew Asa Mendoza and Sarighani). In addition, Cynthia teaches piano lessons privately and presents her students annually in recitals in Bergen County, New Jersey. She is also treasurer of the Professional Music Teachers Guild of New Jersey.

Cynthia concludes, "As a family, we have always made an effort to maximize whatever gifts and talents we have and share them."

Sarighani

Sarighani's pretty oval face is framed by thick, long, dark brown hair. She smiles easily and frequently. Her fine voice is still girlish. "My name means 'fresh charm,' and I was born April 12, 1973. I started playing piano at the age of 4. In San Diego, I began to learn to play the cello. I really didn't get serious about cello playing until my family moved to Paramus, New Jersey, a few years later." Sarighani completed public school and graduated from Paramus High School. "We lived in a predominantly Italian and Jewish neighborhood. There were very few Asian families, so most of my friends were Caucasians." Mathematics was Sarighani's favorite subject, for which she always received A grades. From age 11 to 14, she was an avid competitor in gymnastics and won recognition in several local events. "But when I began to spend four hours a day in the gym, working out and practicing, my parents decided that I would have to choose between gymnastics and cello. They helped me choose what would have better, possibly lifelong employment opportunities," Sarighani says, laughing girlishly, remembering.

Sarighani graduated from San Francisco Conservatory of Music, where she majored in cello performance, after earning a precollege certificate from Mannes College of Music in New York. After graduation from college, she joined the New World Symphony in Miami Beach, Florida, as cellist. She is considering plans for a master's degree, perhaps in the future, but at present, she is teaching cello with the Children's Orchestra of New York and the Mannes College of Music. Sarighani was a member of the Children's Orchestra herself for many years, through her high school years.

This young cellist has had many accomplishments, beginning in 1990, when she won first prize at the Mannes Concerto Competition and the 1993 Kohl Mansion Competition, and was a finalist in the 1992 Grace Vamos Competition and state finalist in the 1994 American String Teachers Association Competition. Sarighani was featured soloist of the Children's Orchestra of New York and the 92d Street "Y" Symphonic Ensemble, under

Yaacov Bergman. She has attended and performed at the Round Top Music Festival in Texas, the Sarasota Music Festival in Florida, the Aspen Music Festival in Colorado, the New York String Seminar at Carnegie Hall, and the Music Academy of the West in California. Although she performs a lot in recitals and chamber/orchestra concerts, her most significant contribution to Philippine music is the recording of *Heartstrings: Philippine Airs for Cello and Piano*, which received wide circulation in the United States, Canada, and the Philippines. "I feel that my biggest and most significant concerts were in December 1996 and May 1997, when I performed in Carnegie Weill Recital Hall in New York City. I sometimes get nervous before a concert," she admits with a giggle, "but once I start, I feel as one with the music, and the anxiety disappears." Sarighani prefers classical music, especially Brahms. "I also like opera but need to know more about it," she adds. When not practicing, she reads a lot, cooks, and dabbles in interior designing.

Respect for, and honoring, the family are two Philippine values Sarighani admires. "In Filipino families, good friends are like relatives, even though not biological kin. They are extended family." She thinks that her relationship with her parents is "satisfactory and rewarding." Sarighani explains, "In a traditional Filipino family, parents are formal and don't encourage children's opinions. But my parents are open, and we discuss feelings and behavior all the time." Because of heavy schedules of teaching and out-of-town concert engagements, the family has limited time to share each other's activities outside of music. But they manage an occasional movie and dinner in a fine restaurant.

Sarighani has lots of friends and enjoys dining and dancing and attending concerts. Although her mother is available for consultation, Sarighani feels competent in making decisions and choices that are effective and satisfying.

"I would love to play chamber music all of my life," she says emphatically and then adds, "Of course I hope to get married and have a family, too, some day." Sarighani describes her mother as compassionate and giving. "She's devoted to the family but should now give more time for herself, since we're all grown up. Her judgment, flexibility, practicality, sense of giving, and her big heart are characteristics that I would love to have." Sarighani gives her mother a loving smile.

REFERENCES

Agbayani-Siewert, P., and Revilla, L. "Filipino Americans." In *Asian Americans*, ed. P. G. Min. Thousand Oaks, CA: Sage, 1995.

Alcantra, R. R. *A Guided Study Course—American Subcultures: Filipino Americans*. Honolulu: University of Hawaii Press, 1975.

Catapusan, B. T. "Problems of Filipino Students in America." *Sociology and Social Research* 28: 146–153, 1941.

Gonzalez, J., Jr. *Racial and Ethnic Groups in America*. Dubuque, IA: Kendall/Hunt, 1990.

Karnow, S. *In Our Image: America's Empire in the Philippines.* New York: Random House, 1989.

Mangiafico, L. *Contemporary American Immigrants: Patterns of Philippine, Korean and Chinese Settlement in the United States.* New York: Praeger, 1988.

Melendy, H. B. *Asians in America: Filipino, Korean and East Indian.* Boston: Twayne, 1977.

Pido, A. J. L. "New Structures, New Immigrants: The Case of the Filipinos." In *Sourcebook on the New Immigration*, ed., R. S. Bryce-Laporte. New Brunswick, NJ: Transaction Books, 1980.

Portes, A. "Determinants of the Brain Drain." *International Migration Review* 10: 489–568, 1976.

Posadas, B. M. "Crossed Boundaries in Interracial Chicago: Filipino American Families since 1925." *Amerasia* 8: 31–52, 1981.

Sharma, M. "Pinoy in Paradise: Environment and Adaptation of Filipinos in Hawaii, 1906–1946." *Amerasia* 7: 91–117, 1984.

Smith, P. C. "The Social Demography of Filipino Migration Abroad." *International Migration Review* 10: 307–353, 1976.

Vallangca, C. C. *The Second Wave: Pinoy and Pinoy (1945–1960).* San Francisco: Strawberry Hill Press, 1987.

PERSONAL REFLECTIONS
by Rev. Thelma B. Burgonio-Watson

A CHILD OF THE COSMOS: ONE AMONG MANY

As an immigrant in the United States, I struggle to claim and maintain my identity as a Filipina, which in these days for me means to identify with the oppression of women in my homeland by economic poverty, the exploitation of Filipina women workers abroad, the commercial and sexual exploitation of Filipino children, the sexual exploitation of Filipina women by tourism, militarism, and the mail-order bride industry, and the racial and sexual violence experienced by Filipina immigrants in this country. In other words, my identity as a Filipina immigrant is linked with the current struggles of my sisters and their children, whether they are here or there in the homeland or elsewhere abroad working as domestic workers for the world and working for freedom from their oppression and mine. My identity is bound up in the suffering of my sisters. I am not free until we are all free.

This is part of the heritage and the identity that my daughter can claim, young as she is, turning 11 in May 1998. To be a Filipina of mixed heritage in this country is to identify with the oppression of one's foremothers and to see to it that the oppression ends. On the other hand, she can claim equally with pride that she was born in this country with mixed ethnic origins and is empowered to be who she is with the diverse gifts from her mixed cultural heritage. She can be who she can claim herself to be. No one else can tell her who she is. She knows that she can choose who she wants to be. We, as her parents, have instilled in her the sense that she can have control over who she is. As an heir to mixed ethnic origins, she has a deep awareness that she is who she is with her solidarity with the struggles of her mother's sisters in the struggle for freedom from violence and oppression. And yes, she is more than that.

I am more concerned at this point that she know who she is rather than with the question of integration. If she knows who she is, I am not too worried whether she is able to integrate or not. At worst, I am pessimistic that whoever ends up to be the dominant group in this country will allow the rest to integrate. Besides, I am not a proponent of the "melting pot" concept. I prefer the concept of the "tossed salad," where each one is able to maintain one's own identity in the mixing bowl.

It is a gift that I am called professionally to work to end violence against women and children and all those vulnerable in society. I work from an interreligious, educational, feminist, and international setting. This work has brought me into closer contact with the local Filipino community and, together with Asian Pacific Islander colleagues in the field, we are strengthened to address the issues of violence against women in our communities. Our awareness that violence against women is a common thread that binds women's lives together has made our local group only more determined in our community efforts, not only to identify with the victims of violence but to help prevent and end this problem, even as we draw from the life-giving resources of our cultural heritage.

Participating with the local Filipino immigrant community in addressing a problem that affects all communities has brought to the fore those enduring values I have learned from my parents, my elders, the church, and the *barrio* community that nurtured me while I was growing up.

These are the same values that I am imparting to my daughter to ground her to that part of her heritage from me as her mother. Growing up in a *barrio*, I learned to value community. This community may mean extended family. For me, community means sharing and pooling resources; supporting and nurturing relationships; and advocating and working for the good of the collective. In the busyness of daily survival in this day and age in this country, it is not easy to find time for "community." However, for some of us immigrants and communities of people of color, the search for community is a matter of survival. To be able to claim that one is part of an ethnic community is to have a sense of identity and belonging. That is why I need to be in those community gatherings once in a while, and that is why I expose my daughter to these gatherings, that she, too, may literally claim her sense of identity and belonging. These community gatherings can serve as places and events where she can see the diversity of her own people, especially for one like her who is of mixed ethnic origins.

Another value from my culture that I am attempting to instill in her is hospitality. Hospitality is the gift of generosity. It is the ability to be present to the "other." It is meeting the other person's needs. I tell my daughter that we are "gift-givers." We have received love, so we give love. My home, my Christian church, my *barrio*, my extended family nurtured me with this value. It is a value we are modeling for my daughter in our family. This has sustained me in my struggles as an immigrant. This has helped me keep my identity. I know it will sustain my daughter in the face of racism and injustice.

The gift of hospitality extends beyond material gift-giving. However, if it is a bowl of rice that the other person needs, and you meet that need, that is hospitality. But more and more, this value is overlooked, for almost everyone is sufficient unto himself or herself here in America. One may no longer need the hospitality of the other, except for those who are down and out.

However, hospitality encompasses sharing what gives access of life for the other. It is about working for justice for all those who have precious little of it, like poor women and children and people of color in this country. This kind of hospitality is a value that grounds my daughter in her mother's heritage from her own people who fought valiantly to protest the colonization of her native land. So I tell my daughter of a strong woman in her native past so she can also claim this as part of her heritage. I tell her about Gabriela Silang from my hometown, a woman who led a revolt against the Spanish domination in my region.

I tell her of her mother's cultural heritage, that although her native land was invaded by colonizers, the people resisted this domination. Even so, the struggle for women and people of color in this country goes on; she has a heritage of courage and strength to resist oppression and injustice. The struggle for poor women of color may be tripled, but, like her foremothers, she, too, can stand up against injustice. I tell her it is her calling to pass these values to the future generation, to help them keep their identity and their mothers' identity and therefore their heritage. In this way, her mother's strength and courage and her own as well will always be remembered in the future generation.

She is nurtured with a belief system that our family adheres to: "You shall not wrong or oppress a resident alien, for you were aliens in the land of Egypt. You shall not abuse any widow or orphan. If you do abuse them, when they cry out to me, I will surely heed their cry" (Exodus 22: 21–23).

What is helping my daughter maintain a strong identity with her mother's origin are her visits to the homeland and meeting her extended family, her community. She claims the homeland as her own and wants to go regularly. She loves all that she has experienced—the literature, the music, the cuisine, the traditions, the rituals, and, most of all, her own people, her roots.

I nurture her with the stories and legends I have heard from my parents. One among many legends stands out for her, the origin of the first Filipino woman and man, a creation story. The legend tells about a bird that was flying between the heavens and the sea and got tired and rested on floating bamboo. The bird pecked into the bamboo, and when it split, a man and woman emerged. The man bowed to the woman. She recognized him, and then they walked away holding hands.

She is growing up with a clear and profound spirit within her that girls and boys are created equal. She believes no less. She also believes that, being Filipino Scottish, she is one among many kinds of people and as beautiful as any in the cosmos. She is raised with values and new traditions that we as a family are creating for ourselves. We draw upon the mixed cultural heritage that is available to our family. In this sense, she is her own person. She is a person of the cosmos. She is integrated. She is raised with values that cut across all lines, the values of a loving and inclusive, caring community, hospitality, equality, and resistance to oppression. I hope that these values will help her resist the "racial colonizing" of her identity.

7

Korean Americans

Although Korea was historically surrounded by more powerful neighbors like China, Japan, and Russia, it managed to maintain a distinct national identity and culture. Toward the end of the 19th century, China, Japan, and the United States became interested in the natural wealth of Korea and its strategic location in the modern world of global politics (Hurh and Kim, 1984; Gonzalez, 1990).

Like other people of Asian nations, the Koreans were mostly a society of peasants and farmers who were oppressed by a small number of social elites, where the hierarchy was headed by the royal family, or *yanghan*, and accounted for 3% of the population. The largest group was the *sangmin* class, who were 75%–80% of the population. These were farmers, fishermen, merchants, and laborers. The social castes at the lowest level were the slaves, entertainers, monks, and butchers (Chang, 1974).

The Koreans were plagued with inflation and high taxes. "Tax farming" allowed noblemen and others to collect taxes from private land and agricultural holdings. Constant taxes, increasing labor demands, inability of farmers to pay, and political corruption left the country open to foreign exploitation (Kim and Kim, 1967).

Although China was a powerful neighbor, Koreans feared the Japanese more. When the Meiji Dynasty came to power in 1868, the Japanese began to search the Far East for new sources of raw materials. During the next few years, Japanese purchased rice directly from Korean farmers at inflated prices. By the 1880s Korean farmers and the nation's economy were dependent on Japanese rice merchants for survival. These sales often resulted in mass starvation in the Korean countryside (Kim and Kim, 1967).

Korean immigration to America can be classified into three major periods: (1) the period of old immigration; (2) the intermediate period; and (3) the period of new immigration. The old immigration period covers about 50 years between 1903 and 1949. The intermediate period focuses on the 15 years of Korean immigration following the Korean War in 1950. The last immigration period involves a new wave of Korean immigrants, following the enforcement of the 1965 Immigration Act (Min, 1995).

The period of the New Wave of Korean immigration was initiated by the Immigration Act of 1965, which brought about significant increases in numbers of immigrants. They were primarily urban and educated, many with professional or technical backgrounds—all the skills needed by American employers. The Immigration Act allowed family reunification, meaning that immediate relatives of permanent legal aliens and naturalized citizens were granted preferences for admission to America. The effect of this provision is reflected when one compares immigration statistics between 1950 and 1987. For example, between 1950 and 1964, a total of 15,049 Koreans arrived. But between 1970 and 1979, a total of 240,398 arrived. This accounts for almost half (45.5%) of all Koreans admitted between 1965 and 1987 (Gonzalez, 1990).

By 1990 there were approximately 789,849 Koreans living in the United States. Their higher concentration is in California, with Los Angeles having the largest population of Koreans (over 100,000) outside Korea. Their high concentration means that they can promote a healthy cultural support system. Korean shops—bakeries, grocery, liquor, book, and appliance stores, beauty shops, and restaurants—are in abundance along main streets. The 1990 U.S. Census shows New York had 95,648 Koreans; Illinois 47,500; New Jersey 38,540; California 250,951; Washington 29,697; and Hawaii 24,450. The heavy concentration in metropolitan areas is a reflection of their educational achievement, their occupational distribution, and their entrepreneurial ambition (Light, 1988; Schifrin, 1988).

A high majority of post-1965 Korean immigrants held professional and technical jobs in Korea. Most were unable to find similar employment here because of language difficulties and unacceptable certification earned in Korea. Many accepted lower-paying jobs as aides, assistants, and unskilled laborers. Many worked in small, Korean-owned businesses; others became self-employed. As a result of language barriers and discrimination, it was not unusual to find well-educated Koreans working at jobs far below their skills. The extent of incongruous job placement among Koreans was discovered by one study in Los Angeles that found that half of Korean immigrants who were doctors, pharmacists, nurses, laboratory technologists, and medical assistants were working as operators, craftsmen, or salespersons (Kim and Wong, 1977). The end result is frustration, humiliation, underemployment, and poverty, regardless of the fact that both husband and wife work outside the home (Yu, Phillips, and Yang, 1982).

Ethnic identity refers to the reality and the process through which people identify themselves and are identified by others as members of a specific ethnic group (Levinson, 1994). Korean immigrants to the United States maintain a high level of ethnic attachment, higher than that of any Asian ethnic group. Ethnic solidarity refers to the sense and degree of cohesion felt by members of an ethnic group. Most Korean immigrants speak the Korean language, eat mainly Korean food, and practice Korean customs most of the time. Most are affiliated with at least one ethnic organization and are involved in active, informed ethnic networks. For example, Hurh and Kim (1984) report that 90% of Korean immigrants in Chicago speak mainly the Korean language at home and that 82% are affiliated with one or more ethnic organizations.

There are three major reasons Korean immigrants maintain a high level of ethnic attachment (Min, 1995). First, South Korea is a small and culturally homogeneous country, with only one racial group speaking one language. Second, Korean immigrants maintain strong ethnic identity partly because most of them are affiliated with Korean ethnic churches. Some 55% adult immigrants attended Christian churches before emigrating. Third, Korean immigrants' concentration in small businesses also strengthens Korean ethnicity.

The immigration of Koreans to the United States has led to many changes in the traditional Korean family system, but the most significant is the radical increase in Korean women's participation rate in the labor force. Since many women work in family businesses, they do not report their work to the census taker. Min's 1995 survey appears to be more accurate. He found that 79% of Korean married women in New York City were employed, which compared to 57% for U.S. married women in general in 1988 (U.S. Bureau of the Census, 1989, p. 385). Korean women worked an average of 51 hours a week, with 80% working full-time (Min, 1992).

Despite full-time jobs, Korean immigrant women assume responsibilities for housekeeping tasks. Min's New York City survey indicated that Korean immigrant working wives spend 75.5 hours weekly between their job and their housework—12 hours more than their husbands do (Min, 1992).

The lives of battered Korean women in the United States are an extension of thousands of years of subjugation, with the additional conflicts resulting from adjustment to a new culture. The battering of women has been justified by the conventions of Korean culture, which is deeply rooted in the philosophy of male domination. A wife speaks of her husband as *uri chip ju* (the master of the house). She also may refer to him as the *pa kaat yang-ban* (outside gentleman). In sharp contrast, the wife is the husband's *chip saram* (houseperson) or his *an saram* (inside person) (Crane, 1967).

Research reported by Young I. Song Kim (1992) involved a sample of 150

Korean women age 18 years and older who had resided in Chicago for not more than ten years. Three factors appeared to contribute to battering: sex-role past performance and traditional attitudes; cultural factors; and stress-evoking factors.

Korean traditionalism is strongly linked to battered women. Women who adhere to rigid sex roles experience more violence than women who are in households in which tasks traditionally carried out by females are shared with their male partners. Researchers suggest that battered women remain in a violent relationship because of many social and economic obstacles (MacLeod, 1980; Strube and Barbour, 1983), including fear of increased violence, lack of support and resources, and fear of loneliness. The evidence points out that social isolation of battered women constitutes part of both the cause and the consequence (Walker, 1980). The traditional Korean views the wife as causing the abuse. Abuse is seen as a reaction to an unhappy home life. The assumption is that if a man is unhappy enough to hit his wife, she deserves it. Hence, blame and shame are yet other impediments to articulating the problem (Young, 1992).

Young suggests that social workers focus on the strengths of battered women when intervening. Social workers are encouraged to help these Korean women see that the incredible strength they have shown in enduring their problems may be constructively rechanneled to improve the quality of their lives.

Cultural homogeneity and economic segregation help Korean immigrants maintain strong ethnic attachment but hinder their assimilation into American society. Because Korean immigrants were not exposed to significant subcultural differences in their home country, most of them have a low level of tolerance for the cultural differences found in the United States; they are unwilling to learn English and American customs.

CASE STUDIES

Chung Soon

The instructions were clear: "Leave the freeway at Exit 16, turn left for two blocks, then right for four blocks and then left again to Hollister Avenue. Go straight down. It's a dead-end street." The street was almost devoid of traffic. Moderately priced, single-family homes, shaded by large, leafy trees, were observed on both sides of the street. Near the end of the street, the silence was broken by a cacophony of shrill, screeching, joyous laughter and noisy play of happy children. The cab stopped at Bret Harte Children's Center, San Francisco. The youngsters were riding seesaws, climbing jungle gyms, building sand castles, swinging on swings, and playing tag. Their faces, a rainbow of ice cream flavors from pale vanilla, to creamy cafe au lait, to caramel tan, to dark brown mousse, to inky fudge-chocolate, were a delight to behold. Chung S. Cho, smiling broadly, slowly made her way through the group, gently touching and patting heads, arms, or legs in her path. "How do you like my garden of beautiful flowers?" Mrs. Cho is supervisor-teacher at several Children's Centers under the San Francisco Unified School District.

"Chung Soon means 'righteous' and 'obedient,' " she begins. "I was born in South Korea in a city called Samchunpo on September 14, 1935. There were six children in the family, but my oldest brother died of chicken pox during a severe epidemic that killed lots of children." Chung's face reflects sadness as she remembers. The children had a great relationship playing together. The family considered education one of the most valuable tools a child could have. "My grandfather was a scholar, and I remember him surrounded by books. This tradition was passed on to my father, who managed the family farm." English was taught in junior high, and most people had a working knowledge of the language. Chung enjoyed all of her subjects, especially mathematics and history. "It's hard to identify any one teacher as special. I liked all of them. Teachers were considered part of your family. They were strict, demanding, and professional. They loved children." Chung believes her interest and desire to teach came from her family rather than teachers. Her uncles and aunts worked on the farm to provide money for educating the younger siblings. Three uncles graduated from college and became teachers. Teachers were admired and valued. But Chung was not quite ready to pursue teaching as a career. She wasn't mature or informed enough to make a career choice.

Chung's first boyfriend was her husband. "In that era, young people did not date. I went to an all-girl high school in another city and lived in a dormitory. If a student, boy or girl, was discovered dating, expulsion from school followed. But most young people managed to avoid getting caught." Chung was one of them.

Chung's choice of a career was determined by the state of war. Korea was taken over by the communists, and many families lost all of their kin. Chung's family was not spared. "My father had to help everyone escape, including nieces and nephews. He also had seven brothers and sisters who helped in the rice fields." Money was not available, but Chung won a scholarship at her high school. Her family decided to send her to Pusan Teachers College, which was out of the war zone. She graduated in 1958 with a degree in home economics education. Chung really wanted to study law and become a judge. "At that time, a female judge was unheard of. But my family urged me to be practical, for the moment." She remembers her father suggesting that she get her education and then a job so that she could send one of her younger brothers to law school. "This idea was following a family tradition—the older children helping the younger ones to get a higher education degree."

After graduation, Chung taught home economics in a high school in Samchunpo, Korea. From there, she taught at another high school for another two-year period. Her husband-to-be graduated from Seoul National University in Korea in 1960 and then came to the United States and received a master's degree and a Ph.D. at the Maxwell School of Syracuse University. The young couple decided to marry in 1960. Both families were known to each other, so everyone was happy. Since Chung had joined the Catholic Church while in school, a large Catholic wedding in a cathedral was planned with all the trimmings—music, reception, and a three-day trip to Pusan. Chung had envisioned coming to the United States to continue her education, but she became pregnant and remained in Korea to give birth to Miyan. Chung's husband's first job was teaching at the University of Las Vegas. Chung and Miyan joined him. Chung's husband holds liberal points of view in philosophy, theology, and ethics. "The Korean way to confront a problem is to first identify it. The solution depends upon the circumstances and what's involved. One solution may be more effective than another at that time," Chung explains.

In the area of parenting and child care, Chung compares former practices to today's economy. "Women and mothers used to be the main child-care persons but after the war, circumstances and political conditions like depleted economy and shrinking job markets made women seek employment. They had to work to meet family needs. In America and Korea, women's roles changed." Chung breast-fed Miyan for two to three years, partly because of the shortage of fresh milk. Since milk is in abundance in the United States, and solid foods are encouraged early, Chung followed the American practice when she migrated to this country with Miyan, who was 4 years old. Chung had to provide the major amount of child care, because her husband was completing two degrees in four years. He also worked summers to supplement his scholarships. Chung's son was born in the United States in 1966. "I put him in nursery school and joined my husband at the University of Nevada, where he was a professor. Within three years, he joined the faculty of the University of Ohio in Akron. Both children were raised there," Chung explains.

Chung's son is a graduate of Princeton and Cornell Medical School. "He completed his residency at the University of California at San Diego. He holds an M.D. and a Ph.D." His mother's face lights up with pride. He is 30 years old and was married in September 1997. Both are working in University of California, San Diego, General Hospital. "We have met her family, and they are fine people. Unfortunately, both of our children did not attend schools where there was a large population of Koreans. Both young people have medical and professional education in their backgrounds. We do believe they will be happy," Chung says. "Our daughter also married a Caucasian. She's happy and has two beautiful children. Our children are proud to be Korean and honor and cherish their heritage, which they share with their children and mates," she concludes.

The family is the most sacred social value of any Korean. Even when both parents work, family values are carried out, particularly by the mother. "My children observed the manner in which we respected them and Korean principles of hard work, responsibility, and sharing. These became part of their personalities." When her children were young, the family celebrated New Year's Day in a modified, traditional way. In those days, the goal of an immigrant was to become "Americanized" as fully as possible. They came here to live and didn't want to be foreign. For a while, celebrations became fewer and modest. But now in the United States and Korea, many are returning to celebrating in the traditional way. Chung recalls San Francisco in 1989, when the Chos arrived. "We came from Ohio and found life so different there. We built a Korean church, a Korean restaurant, and a Korean grocery store. And we spoke Korean. We were too successful. Now I'm trying to get Koreans in San Francisco integrated into the community at large. They don't speak English, don't vote, and can't read English newspapers. They're so isolated! Children must be immunized, fed properly, and educated. They have to be brought into the mainstream. We have a mission!," Chung says passionately.

Chung believes that some Koreans fear change. The women work outside the home but are also the main child caretakers and homemakers. Change will occur with the next generation of Korean Americans, who will be better educated and assimilated into American culture. "As a teacher, I feel much depends upon our teachers, who must be dedicated to the task. A good teacher must be flexible, committed, willing to work hard, work with all kinds of people, and love the job."

Racism has crossed Chung's path occasionally. She recalls one incident with sadness. "In Akron, Ohio, a student said that her mother would not allow her to continue in my class because I was Korean. The student was tearful, since she liked the course and did well. Several teachers wanted to know if I was Catholic or Chinese. I didn't feel too bad, because I was the only Asian in the school. I feel that if people can't see me as I am, they will just have to work harder." Chung laughs sarcastically.

"I don't know if I'm successful. Inside I feel peace. I go to bed each night feeling comfortable with myself. I thank God for giving me certain qualities like the ability to get along with people, the fortitude to face challenges, the desire to learn, to face and deal with change." After 37 years, Chung is retiring and will accompany her husband to Korea, where he will accept a professorship at one of the universities for two years. Chung will not be idle. Her colleagues feel that this talented and beloved teacher will keep busy making effective changes in the Korean educational system, too.

Miyan

Miyan, Chung's oldest child, was born in Korea in 1961. She came to the United States as a toddler with her mother and was raised in Las Vegas and Akron, Ohio. Miyan remembers being happy and active as a child enjoying the outdoors. Later she rode her bicycle and learned how to skate. As a preteen, Miyan took lessons in ballet and played the piano. She also had a cat; she doesn't remember his name, but she loved him. Miyan did well in school and made many friends. She remembers her best friend, Carole Knobe, who moved away when Miyan was 10 years old.

In high school, Miyan excelled in most subjects, especially in honors classes in English, mathematics, and science. Her role model was her piano teacher, who is now a professor and concert pianist. Miyan had no real career choice, but she began a career in banking by accident. Miyan recently received a promotion at a new financial investment firm as a banking investor. She enjoys her new position.

As a teenager and young adult, her relationship with her mother was quite often stormy. Communication was very difficult with her mother. "My family raised me to be a strong and independent woman, but they wanted me to be a traditional Korean daughter at the same time, which was very difficult, if not impossible," Miyan says. She did not date as a high school student. Her parents didn't approve of young people dating, but occasionally, Miyan was allowed to date in groups of mainly American friends.

Her marriage to William Fellerhoff was very formal and traditional—Western-style, with gown, reception, and music, all carried out beautifully. She met William through business contacts. Miyan believes that, in some ways, their roles are traditional. "I want to do everything," she says. Miyan doesn't envision values being ethnically oriented because there are as many Asians with similar values as Westerners. "The features I respect are honesty, integrity, commitment to family and marriage, respect for one's spouse, family, and children."

Many of her characteristics were inherited from Chung, her mother, Miyan thinks. "I am obsessive-compulsive. I need to be in control of every situation. I am really neat/clean. I am compassionate and caring of others. I want to do everything for my family. I want to take care of my husband and family. In some ways, I practice parenting like most women, but not entirely. I breast-fed both children for two to three months."

Mother–child relationships were weakened by Miyan's fear of telling her parents that she wanted to marry a Caucasian. She wanted to respect their desire that she marry a Korean. "I felt guilty of disappointing them. As a wife and mother, I tried to do too much as I followed my mother's example. I felt failure, because it was impossible. When I decided to do what was best for me and my family, the stress and tension grew less." Miyan was able to express her feelings, and her parents accepted her decisions. Miyan learned that as an adult, she didn't need parental approval—she was an adult! She now seeks advice from her husband, parents, and friends, depending on the situation. Miyan manages as a working mother with live-in help. Miyan says, "My adult relationship with both parents is very close now." In and out of business, there are always some undertones of racial or gender bias. "But I cannot dwell on them. The best approach is to perform at the best of your ability."

For her two daughters, Miyan hopes that they are strong and confident. "I hope they really like themselves." The Fellerhoffs are content with two daughters and do not plan any biological additions to the family but will consider adoption. Although Miyan feels a certain degree of success, she thinks there is still much more to accomplish.

Miseon Chang (the Korean Oprah)

(To get another view of Korean American contemporary life, I visited with M. Chang, a radio personality. She can be called "in transition"—still very obviously a Korean, yet acting very American, too.)

M. Chang, a radio journalist of WZRC-Radio Korea New York, in a soothing voice, cheerfully says, "Ahnyung Haseyo Yo Song Salon Chang Miseon Im Ni Da," roughly translated as, "Greetings, this is the Miseon Chang Show." She is chief production director, a job that requires her to oversee 20 reporters and disc jockeys.

In a low-pitched voice laced with confidence, M. Chang begins her daily program of news, discussion, music, and advice, which is conducted only in Korean. Her show helps Korean immigrants bridge cultural and social gaps. It has become a morning staple of the city's many Korean-owned nail salons, coffee shops, and grocery stores within the last six years. With more than 350,000 Koreans within the reach of the station, which can be heard as far as Philadelphia, the show's popularity has made her a Korean Oprah Winfrey. She left Korea for the United States after 14 years of hosting a variety show. Miseon's nontraditional, outspoken style clashed with the authoritarian government of Chun Doo Hwan, who was given a death sentence for his oppression of the student movement and recently granted amnesty.

By American standards, the advice M. Chang gives her listeners seems like common sense, but to the working-class and elderly women who make up most of the audience, it is almost revolutionary. "But," says M. Chang, "the aim of the show is to help Korean women break away from their traditional roles and become independent and for the men to support their effort."

M. Chang talks about the prominent role males play in Korean culture. "The man is everything! He is the one that gets the education, if parents must make a choice between daughters and sons." Her voice rises shrilly. "Things are changing now in Korea, and women are seeking nontraditional careers. They are becoming educated! Would you believe that men are seeking wives who are educated and who work? It is revolutionary!," she exclaims with a jovial laugh. Not so many years ago, people spoke of the "broken egg" when they referred to a working wife and mother who destroyed her family and gave up her traditional role by working. But now there is equal opportunity, and many women work within and without families. They feel independent and empowered with their own money.

However, tradition dies slowly. "Most women are expected to continue raising children, cooking meals, and doing other household chores," M. Chang says with sadness in her alto voice. "She even turns over her earnings to her husband, in some cases," she adds.

In 1984 M. Chang arrived in the United States and found a job working in a Korean radio station in Philadelphia. "I knew very little about the United States except its size, movies, and television. I believed everyone was rich; there were the million-dollar lottery and Wonder Woman." She lived in a racially mixed neighborhood where many black people lived, too. Her only contact with this racial group in the past had been the U.S. troops stationed in Korea, where many were said to be almost illiterate trouble-makers and potential rapists, according to the media. "I was too frightened to leave my apartment. But I soon learned that I was misinformed. I had an old Chevrolet, which often gave me trouble. When I had a flat tire, a black man fixed the tire and refused to take any money. White and Asian men ignored my plight. Black women helped me shop, befriended me, and most of all, they were intelligent, well spoken, and neighborly. I couldn't believe that I had misjudged a whole group of people unknowingly." She is apologetic in tone. To amend this situation, M. Chang called City Hall and set up a series of discussions on the air by noted black educators and historians, who spoke and informed Koreans of black history and culture. M. Chang is proud of her opportunity to "mend fences."

Regarding prejudice and bias in this country, M. Chang feels most people are so involved with their own affairs and conditions that they really don't have time for, or interest in, other people. "They say, 'How are you?' without even waiting for an answer. It's artificial and superficial—just a saying," she feels. Once M. Chang invited a black businessman to join her at dinner. When they arrived at the restaurant, they were told that reservations were required, even though the room was half empty, and people walking in from the street were seated. She was terribly embarrassed. The next week, she invited a Caucasian friend to the same restaurant. Even though she wanted to make a reservation, the friend insisted that it was not necessary. When they arrived there, the friend led the way, and they were seated promptly. M. Chang has learned that "people are people," some accepting and some not. "This is America," she sums up smiling. She has endured further insults. "When I go to a department store or a boutique, the salesperson will look me over. I may not be dressed up or wearing makeup. She will ask with a smile, 'Are you Japanese?' I'll say proudly, 'No, I'm not.' The smile fades, but she waits on me."

In this country, among Asians, Japanese rank first, Chinese second, and Koreans third. "Of course, this reflects the economy, technology, and Wall Street," M. Chang states understandingly. Her parents live in California, and a sister lives in Washington, D.C. "I like America's freedom, but I also like the Korean ways," M. Chang explains. "The Korean man may make the money, but it is the wife who decides how it is spent." There are complaints from Korean women living in the United States, and M. Chang hears them. In this country, husband and wife work together in a grocery store, market, and so on. They are together almost 24 hours a day. They even go to church together on Sunday. The wife needs "her space," time alone.

There is a lot of networking between New York, Chicago, and Los Angeles, where Korean volunteers help their "sisters" find careers, invest, learn parenting and American culture. This country offers so many options, different lifestyles. There are many things about America that she likes. "In Korea, when relatives, parents die, they are buried a great distance away from the family, and graves are visited only on special occasions. In this country, people tend to want the cemetery quite near, so that they can visit the grave quite frequently. It is better this way," M. Chang believes. Her other gripe is the amount of freedom young children have. "Children call 911 if their parents correct them with physical punishment. Families should discuss discipline within the family and not consult authorities."

In 1989 M. Chang married Dr. Ryang Suh, a Korean-born psychiatrist with two children. Although M. Chang has an hour-long trip from Westchester and is normally in the office at 7 AM, she says she gets up at the crack of dawn to make her husband, Kim Bap, rice balls for lunch. She is conservative, and so is her husband. The children are away at college. M. Chang describes herself as a "bad cook." "On the show, I teach parents how to make American dishes, because the children are tired of rice and Kimchi and want to be part of the mainstream society. This helps them to have a good relationship with their children."

Her suggestion to young Korean women in the United States is to " 'Go for it,' whether it's a career in medicine, science, or teaching. Despite everything, someday you'll be someone's mother and then you can follow your heart or the Korean male-oriented tradition," M. Chang advises.

REFERENCES

Chang, D. "A Study of Korean Cultural Minority: The Paechong." In *Traditional Korea: Theory and Practices*, ed. A. C. Nahm. Kalamazoo, MI: Center for Korean Studies, Western Michigan University, 55–56, 1974.

Crane, P. *Korean Patterns*. Seoul: Hollym, 1967.

Gonzalez, J., Jr. *Racial and Ethnic Groups in America*. Dubuque, IA: Kendall/Hunt, 1990.

Hurh, W. M., and Kim, K. C. *Korean Immigrants in America: A Structural Analysis of Ethnic Confinement and Adhesive Adaptation*. Rutherford, NJ: Fairleigh Dickinson University Press, 1984.

Kim, C., and Kim, H. *Korea and the Politics of Imperialism, 1876–1910*. Berkeley: University of California Press, 1967.

Kim, D. S., and Wong, C. "Business Development in Koreatown, Los Angeles." In *The Korean Diaspora*, ed. Hyung-Chan Kim. Santa Barbara, CA: Clio Press, 1977.

Levinson, D. *Ethnic Relations: A Cross-Cultural Encyclopedia*. Santa Barbara, CA: Clio Press, 1994.

Light, I. "Immigrant Entrepreneur. Koreans in Los Angeles." In *Clamor at the Gates*, ed. N. Glazer. Berkeley: University of California, 1988.

MacLeod, L. *Wife Battering in Canada: The Vicious Circle*. Ottawa: Canadian Advisory Council on the Status of Women, 1980.

Min, P. G. "Korean Immigrant Wives Overwork."*Korea Journal of Population and Development* 21: 23–26, 1992.

Min, P. G. "Korean Americans." *In Asian Americans Contemporary Trends and Issues*. Thousand Oaks, CA: Sage, 1995.

Schifrin, M. "Horatio Alger Kim." *Forbes* 142 (8): 92–94, October 17, 1988.

Strube, M. J., and Barbour, L. S. "The Decision to Leave an Abusive Relationship: An Economic Dependence and Psychological Commitment." *Journal of Marriage and Family* 45: 785–793, 1983.

Walker L. E. *The Battered Women*. New York: HarperCollins, 1980.

Young I. Song Kim. "Battered Korean Women in Urban United States." In *Social Work Practice with Asian Americans*, ed. M. Furuto. Thousand Oaks, CA: Sage, 1992.

Yu, Eu-Y, Phillips, E., and Yang, E. *Koreans in Los Angeles: Prospects and Promises*. Los Angeles: Center for Korean American and Korean Studies, California State University, 1982.

PERSONAL REFLECTIONS
by Pyong Gap Min

HOW TO HELP KOREAN CHILDREN MAINTAIN KOREAN IDENTITY AND YET INTEGRATE INTO THE MAINSTREAM SOCIETY

Many people choose to immigrate to the United States to give their children a better opportunity, although they expect to face many adjustment difficulties. Thus, immigrant parents put a great emphasis on their children's education and social mobility. Yet they also want to transmit their cultural traditions—language, customs, and values—to their children. Most contemporary immigrants have come from Asian and Latin American countries whose cultures differ significantly from American culture with an emphasis on individualism. This suggests that contemporary immigrant parents' efforts to teach their children ethnic traditions are often incompatible with their children's success in school and social mobility.

This is particularly true of Korean immigrant parents and their children. Under the impact of the Confucian cultural tradition, Korean immigrants, along with Chinese immigrants, put a great stress on their children's educational success and social mobility through education, probably more than other immigrant groups. As a result, Korean immigrants are generally successful in their children's college education. For example, according to the 1990 census, the Korean group occupies the second place in young people's (ages 18–24) college enrollment rate, with 67%. next to the Chinese, among all racial and ethnic groups classified in the census.

Coming from a culturally homogeneous society characterized by a single language and lack of subgroup or regional differences and economically segregated from the larger society (concentrated in small businesses), Korean immigrants want to stick to their own cultural traditions and maintain social interactions mainly with other Koreans. This suggests that Korean immigrant parents try to transmit their cultural traditions to their children to a greater extent than do other immigrant groups.

Korean immigrant parents' one-sided emphasis on Korean customs and values in their children's socialization leads to conflicts with their children at home. Several studies have shown that Korean immigrant families suffer from generational conflicts due to the language barrier and cultural differences between parents and children and parents' high expectations of their children to perform well in school. Moreover, Korean parents' "too Korean" child socialization practices can also hamper their children's educational success and social mobility, which most consider the main goal of their children's socialization.

Here I can provide many examples of how Korean immigrant parents' teaching their children Korean customs and values or "too Korean" child socialization practices are detrimental to their children's education and social mobility in American society. First of all, Korean parents' overemphasis on their children's academic success itself and blind worship of Ivy League schools have negative effects, not only on their children's psychological well-being but also on their long-term educational achievements and social mobility. Academically successful children are well rewarded in the family, but students who perform below average or even just at average levels are not rewarded and sometimes neglected by their parents. This benign neglect can stifle their academic interest. Many Korean children who have aptitudes in baseball, football, or other sports are forced by their parents to stop participating in athletic activities to concentrate on preparing for college admission. Most of these students are not academically oriented and lose interest in continuing their studies, while they are forced to stop athletic activities. As a result, Korean parents' academically oriented child socialization practices make their children waste their nonacademic talents.

Most Korean immigrant parents send their children to extracurricular study programs after school to prepare for admission to prestigious schools. As a result of these extracurricular study programs, many Korean students get admitted to colleges and universities whose academic levels are higher than their intellectual levels can match. However, this has more negative effects on the students than positive effects. Some of these students, unable to survive in the schools, give up their college education in the middle. Others who can survive attend college under a great deal of pressure with no extracurricular activities. In an extreme case, a few Korean college students, unable to overcome the pressure to perform successfully in competitive schools, have committed suicide.

I can understand why people in South Korea try to do everything possible to send their children to first-class universities, because graduates from Seoul National University and a few other first-class universities have huge advantages in initial employment and ensuing occupational mobility there. However, Korean immigrant parents should realize that colleges' prestige levels are so diverse in this country that individual talents and achievements outweigh the name of the school in employment and occupational mobility. They should help their children choose schools that match their intellectual levels and interest. Korean students with an average intellectual level can choose moderate levels of colleges initially, and some of them can advance to prestigious graduate schools when they gain confidence in their academic performance. While the name of an undergraduate college has determining effects on one's professional career in South Korea, the prestige of the final graduate school influences one's occupational trajectories most significantly in the United States.

Korean immigrant parents push their children not only to attend prestigious universities but also to choose the fields that lead to high-status, high-paying professional occupations. Medicine and law are the two most desirable major areas, followed by engineering and business. Some Korean children decide to major in a premed or prelaw subject in order to follow their parents' advice and wishes. Others are forced by their parents to it, although they are interested in other subjects. Korean parents usually discourage their children from majoring in arts, literature, social work, and education.

These pressures from parents to choose selected fields of study also have detrimental effects on their children's education and career mobility. Many Korean students lose interest in studying major subjects that have been selected for them against their will or without their personal commitment. Even if Korean students successfully complete graduate school in medicine or law, they cannot enjoy their careers if they are chosen against their interest. Many Korean students change their majors, giving up the career choices expected by their parents. Some of these students have ended up in bad relations with their parents for many years, struggling with a sense of guilt. Korean parents are entirely responsible for this situation. American society provides first- and second-generation Koreans with a wide range of career avenues—journalism, politics, acting, social work, and college teaching—that are typically off-limits to their parents because of their language and cultural barriers. Korean parents should encourage their children to pursue the major fields and careers that best match their intellectual level, aptitude, and interest. When second-generation Koreans enjoy their chosen fields of subjects and careers, they will work hard to achieve.

Following the Confucian norm of children's obedience to parents, Korean immigrant parents do not allow their children to talk back and discourage them from challenging their own arguments. Because of these authoritarian child socialization practices at home, even native-born Korean children who speak English fluently have disadvantages in classroom discussions, compared to white American children. This is one reason Korean Americans, along with other Asian Americans, are underrepresented in social sciences. Korean Americans' weakness in communication and leadership skills can be a greater hindrance to their occupational mobility than to their school performance because these interpersonal skills are often the main criteria for promotion in jobs. Korean Americans' underrepresentation in managerial and high-ranking leadership positions compared to their high educational level is due to their weakness in communication and leadership skills, as well as to American society's stereotypical views of Korean and other Asian Americans as inefficient in communication and leadership. As long as Korean immigrant parents want their children to succeed in American schools and American society, they should help their children to develop communication and leadership skills by encouraging them to talk and challenge their arguments freely at home.

In the Confucian patriarchal tradition, people in South Korea prefer boys over girls and treat boys more favorably. Korean immigrants have changed some of the more traditional gender socialization practices brought from Korea but retained others. Few Korean immigrants seem to prefer boys over girls, as evidenced by many Korean immigrants with two daughters alone. But many Korean immigrants, fathers in particular, put priority on their sons' education. They make their school-attending daughters spend more time helping with housework than sons and spend more money for their sons' extracurricular study programs. In some cases, Korean immigrant parents discourage their academically oriented daughters from going to a graduate school and push their less talented sons to graduate education.

Korean immigrants' unequal treatment of their daughters in education is due to conflicts between their home country and the United States in women's occupational opportunities. Both traditional gender-role orientations and gender discrimination in the workplace discourage women from participating in the labor market in South Korea. Gender discrimination in employment and promotion is severe, particularly in high-level professional occupations, which partly contributes to great gender differentials in a college education. However, women have far more opportunities for professional careers in the United States. In terms of gender-role orientations, a married woman assuming the economic role is almost a norm in contemporary America. Moreover, many professional and managerial jobs are available for women in the United States. In fact, a higher proportion of female workers than male workers holds professional occupations in this country. In addition, minority women, as double minority members, get preferential treatment in employment, although they may encounter barriers in promotion after reaching certain levels. I have seen many second-generation Korean and other Asian American women benefit from affirmative action programs in government, college, and other professional jobs. Korean immigrant parents should give the best education possible to their daughters as well as to their sons, so that their daughters can take advantage of occupational opportunities open in a new society.

Coming from a monorail, homogeneous society, Korean immigrants hold very negative views of intermarriages, probably more negative views than other immigrant groups in the United States. Although only a small minority of Korean immigrants are ready to accept their children's intermarriages, second-generation Koreans have a high intermarriage rate—over 30%, according to one study. Like other Asian groups, Korean women have a higher intermarriage rate than men. Many Korean parents do not accept their children's choice of non-Korean partners, causing serious conflicts with their children. They reject their children's intermarriage, particularly when Latino or African American partners are involved. I know of a second-generation Korean woman who told her father about her marriage to a black man after living with him for seven years.

It is quite natural that Korean immigrants want their children to marry Koreans. However, they should realize that whom their children marry in this country is out of their control. While in South Korea a marriage is viewed mainly as a union between two families, here in the United States it is considered a union between two partners. What is most important for successful marital relations are similarities in personality, the worldview, interests, hobbies, and so forth between the two partners. When a Korean American shares many other similarities with her non-Korean partner, the marriage can be successful. Some Korean immigrants do not accept their children's intermarriages because they believe an intermarriage has a greater chance for ending with divorce than an inmarriage. However, they should keep in mind that intermarriages are, on average, more unstable than inmarriages, partly because of lack of support by parents of both partners. Korean immigrants can make efforts to help their children to find Korean partners. But once their children make a decision to marry a non-Korean partner after a long period of dating and careful consideration, they should give full support. Whether it is an inmarriage or an intermarriage, parents' strong support will contribute to successful marital relations.

8

Japanese Americans

The history of Japanese emigration to America is a relatively short one—little more than 100 years. For over two centuries, no Japanese were allowed to leave Japan by decree of the ruling military government. In 1854 Commodore Perry petitioned the government to reopen the country, and Japanese could emigrate to other countries. Initially, only the upper classes and students were permitted abroad. In 1884 the laboring classes, who formed the bulk of the settlers in America, were allowed to emigrate and came as contract laborers for Hawaiian sugar plantations. Eventually, other Japanese of the laboring class (mostly farmers) reached the mainland United States, either directly from Japan or via Hawaii once their contracts were completed (Kendis, 1889).

The issei were the first Japanese to arrive, and about 200,000 emigrated to the United States between 1890 and 1940. During that period, the total immigration was 25 million. The Japanese were a physically visible population often in a region with a history of anti-Chinese sentiment. They tended to concentrate in a relatively few geographic areas and in a narrow range of occupations. By 1940, 75% of the mainland Japanese had settled in California. More than half were in six counties, where they tended to cluster in enclaves, in both urban and rural areas. Initially, most worked as season laborers in railroading, logging and lumbering, fishing, and farming. In later years, many turned to farming, first as migrant laborers, then as sharecroppers and tenant farmers.

The early immigrants were overwhelmingly single males. Many were second and third sons, ineligible by primogeniture to inherit any of their family's holdings. Like so many immigrants before them, they had come intending to make their fortunes and return to Japan as rich men. Few came with the intention of permanently settling here. However, as the years passed, the immigrants gained some measure of economic stability but, except for a very few, no great fortune. In the early 1900s, realizing their stay would be longer than expected, they sent back to Japan for picture brides.

The Japanese found ways to legally circumvent many of the laws, despite the growing restrictions. Rather than displacing previously established farmers, the issei farmers often opened new farmland, such as the Imperial Valley in California. They were very successful with their labor-intensive, high-yield style of agriculture, as opposed to the resource-intensive methods of American farming.

In the urban sector, the Japanese flourished in some businesses—especially in the wholesale and retail sale of agriculture products. By 1939 there were 149 Japanese-operated wholesale establishments listed in Los Angeles. In 1941 they were estimated to have handled more than 60% of the total amount of business, grossing an estimated $26,500,000.

The nisei were the offspring of these immigrants and were American citizens by right of birth. They were far more educated than their parents. Many had a college education. Although the nisei did well economically, most found it difficult to break out of the ethnic community for better opportunities. There were continuing anti-Japanese discrimination from the outside and pressure for ethnic solidarity from the inside.

Of the nisei who went on to graduate school, only 48% were able to enter the professional ranks immediately. Since it was extremely difficult to succeed outside the ethnic community, many nisei had to remain with the community and under the authority of their parents. It was quite common for young men with a college degree to take jobs as salesmen, fruit stand attendants, and vegetable washers (Kendis, 1989).

The attack on Pearl Harbor by Japan, December 7, 1941, brought new antagonism against the Japanese. On January 29, 1942, all enemy aliens (meaning all Japanese immigrants) were required by the U.S. government to leave the Pacific Coast. Few, however, were able to relocate due to the hostility they encountered when they attempted to enter other states. In March 1942, all persons of Japanese ancestry, foreign-born and American citizens alike, were ordered to concentration camps under the aegis of the War Relocation Authority. In most cases, the evicted people had only one week's notice of their removal. Some had as little as 48 hours in which to sell, rent, loan, store, or give away property and possessions. Administrative defects and the circumstances of the Japanese American population made losses inevitable for even the most sophisticated businessmen. The majority of the population was not equipped to deal with the situation; many were economically destroyed.

The camps did not begin to close until January 1945, when the West

Coast Mass Exclusion Order was rescinded. It was an uncertain period for most Japanese Americans. Many were afraid to return to their former homes on the Pacific Coast. As the years passed, many more continued to return until once again the highest concentration of Japanese Americans outside Hawaii was on the West Coast. As before the war, they tended to cluster in particular counties and cities.

The issei returned from the camps to find their businesses gone. Many were able to reestablish themselves, but others were too old or too discouraged to begin the struggle again. The Japanese business communities never regained their prewar levels of activity.

The nisei, the second generation, however, found new opportunities open to them that by their education they were prepared to take. Rather than filling the gaps left in the ethnic community by the first generation, many preferred to leave and seek professional work in salaried and wage positions in the employ of others. Of college graduates who entered the job markets in the postwar period from 1946 to 1952, 55% obtained high-status jobs, 48% being in the professional ranks versus 10% in the prewar period. Of another 10% who did graduate work, 70% became professionals (1946–1954). In California, nearly one-half of the Japanese American population had been involved in farming. In 1960 less than one-third were still involved, whereas more than 38% were in professional, technical, and white-collar fields (Nishi, 1995).

The years following the war were generally good ones economically for the nisei and their offspring. Many had made it into middle-class security and were seen by the outside society as a "model minority" who succeeded in American society. A study by Schmid and Noble, based on the 1960 census, showed that the Japanese population in America had a greater percentage of college graduates than whites in the white-collar occupations (56.0% Japanese vs. 42.1% white).

Social scientists find that lately the sansei generation have become increasingly indifferent to the traditional ways in the issei sense. They have entered the social and economic networks of the larger society and have moved away from older-style Japanese American identities. In this respect, they follow the fates of so many noncolored ethnic groups; they are in a world that is no longer foreign or hostile to them. The younger ones, especially, think of themselves as Americans, and they are considered such by their friends, neighbors, and associates, particularly in California (Levine and Rhodes, 1981).

Besides, there is the problem of the consequence of sansei outmarriage. The offspring of exogamous unions may have little reason to retain any Japanese American history or identity (and that may depend partly upon appearances). Levine and Rhodes (1981) explored with about 100 children of interracial unions the problems of identity formation and the direction of subcultural commitment that they faced.

Federal legislation of 1965 made emigration more possible for Japanese, resulting in a flow of about 4,000 Japanese immigrants to the United States per year. These immigrants can be added to the many students who come here from Japan, many of whom gain employment and stay. The interchange between Japan, mainland United States, and Hawaii continues. Sansei are bound to be curious and perhaps troubled. Have they been deprived of something valuable that might be regained? In any case, they soon find out; for example, a Japanese contemporary has far different values and style of life distinct from that of the issei grandparents. The latter left Japan decades ago when Japan was still a rural and feudal nation. Today, the young sansei meet sophisticated Japanese youth who share many of the interests in music, the arts, sports—and yet, they are indefinably different. Language, too, is a barrier.

Levine and Rhodes suggest that the very presence of Japanese immigrants and students in the United States can serve to compel even the most assimilated sansei to question their own values, their own identity. Trips to Japan, which sansei (not unlike other Americans) are eager to make, no doubt have the same results.

These researchers noted that Japanese Americans have adapted to America not only better than other nonwhites but also better than many European groups. Social scientists have also observed that there are many areas of value congruence between the white, Anglo-Saxon, Protestant civilization and Japan that have made successful adaptation possible.

The first generation, issei, were preoccupied with economic survival and the question of how best to adapt to America. The second generation, nisei, moved toward this goal. The younger Japanese Americans had three choices. First, they could continue to emulate the dominant white, middle-class culture, while largely discarding their Japanese roots. A second goal, an extension of the first, was amalgamation, whereby a fusion between races and cultures occurs. Absolute entry into white society would be the ultimate result. A third choice could be to move toward a pluralistic position in which components of Japanese culture would continue to influence the formation of self-identity (Nishi, 1995).

Dr. Setsuko Matsunaga Nishi sums up the mixed feelings of the Japanese Americans in the United States in the chapter "Japanese Americans" in *Asian Americans* (1995):

In the last decade of the 20th century, the first generation immigrants are nearly gone. With little replenishment through immigration from modern Japan, two-thirds of Japanese Americans are native born. The unusually age-concentrated second generation are in their old age, while the third generation are approaching their prime years. In their educational, occupational, and residential characteristics, they apparently have attained structural assimilation. Their outmarriage rate is 50%. Particularly their continuing heavy concentration in the Pacific states has enabled a strong presence in Congress and in state and local affairs. The United States has apologized for their wartime incarceration.

Still Japanese-Americans, along with other Asian-Americans, continue to be the butt of the fallout from Japan bashing and antiforeignism. The model minority stereotype is a pervasive source of hostile, resentful attitudes, and obscures attention to their needs as a racial minority in the United States, objects of direct, blatant hate as well as the subtle, sophisticated forms of modern racism—institutional discrimination. The extent of constitutional precedents of the Japanese-American wartime cases symbolizes the fragility of constitutional safeguards of citizen rights in times of crisis. The residue of Japanese-American stigmatization in wartime banishment has yet to be investigated systematically, although anecdotal accounts of the damage abounds. Of greater concern to Japanese-Americans is that most Americans have little knowledge that their incarceration took place on a racial/ethnic basis, with no charge or trial. (129)

Even more burdensome is that because most Americans do not understand the circumstances that led to the gross violation of their constitutionally protected rights, it could conceivably occur again—perhaps to victimize some other group identified by descent and race as an "enemy."

Thus, both as a collective identity seared by wartime events and reinforced in the residues of stigma as well as by a network of communication and social organizations attending to family-learned obligations to each other, Japanese American ethnicity retains a remarkable vitality—despite high structural assimilation and acculturation in American society (Levine and Rhodes, 1981).

Writing some 50 years after the 1943 incarceration, Dr. Harry H. L. Kitano is much more tolerant and optimistic about the past and the future. He writes:

I have arrived at a number of identities. I am a member of the *nisei* generation, a Japanese-American, a former resident of Topaz, and a professor at UCLA [University of California, Los Angeles]. Perhaps my search for identity has been resolved. So, as we near the end of the twentieth century, and look back at the past, it appears that the Japanese-American has done rather well. The interaction with the dominant culture, never very smooth, has had more of a positive nature. The term "Japs" is no longer bandied around as a common epithet, and overt racist remarks against Japanese-Americans are sources of censure. Perhaps the total racial climate has changed, although there are also constant reminders that racism remains an unresolved American dilemma. But would Japanese-Americans trade where they are now with where they were five decades ago? (207)

CASE STUDIES

Cheryl

Some people dream of winning a million dollar lottery, some long for a hole-in-one, others yearn to buy a second home, but Cheryl prays to gain a higher level of spirituality.

After extensive and intensive study with a Zen Buddhist priest, Soko Morinaga, Cheryl has decided to modify her aspirations and fulfill her spiritual needs in a more realistic manner. "With a child and a career, I must arrange my priorities into a practical system," Cheryl says with a half smile.

Cheryl's parents, nisei (second-generation) Japanese, were newly wed when they were assigned to an internment camp in the early-1940s during World War II. Although people suffered horrible indignities, these were hardly mentioned among family members. Confiscation of property, bank accounts, automobiles, and family businesses was experienced by Japanese Americans. They were given little notice, and few were prepared for the move. Within the camp, Cheryl's mother remembers, the lack of privacy was a major inconvenience and humiliation. Cheryl's youngest sister and brother were born under crowded, uncomfortable, debasing circumstances. Shanty-type rooms were divided by thin partitions and open at the top. "My mother spoke of being embarrassed by hearing arguments, personal discussions, and crying day and night. Bathing and toilet facilities were in the open. Sons and brothers were recruited into the military and returned to visit their families behind barbed wire fences. Japanese people tend to be stoic and not complain," Cheryl explains.

When Cheryl's extended family were released, they settled in Chicago. A large number of Japanese Americans chose Chicago rather than return to the West Coast with its haunting memories. Cheryl, sansei Japanese, was born in 1947. Her father was a contractor and a carpenter. He also assisted in the operation of the family-owned apartment houses, vegetable farm, and grocery store. As is typical of Japanese family structure, each male family member made a contribution to the management of the family business. Japanese males are supportive of each other, too. Cheryl's mother was a working mom who began her career when Cheryl was 9 years old, first as a beautician in a Japanese firm and later in the field of social services. Since both of Cheryl's parents came from large families, child care was never a problem. "There were plenty of uncles and aunts available, and one set of grandparents lived next door. We were not latchkey children. Having working parents didn't affect us three children at all," says Cheryl.

Cheryl attended a public elementary school and was later enrolled in a coed private, progressive high school. Both schools offered excellent academic programs and a diverse population permitting interaction with children of several racial groups. Her teachers in high school were extraordinary. "They worked hard with every pupil. They made learning exciting for all of us," Cheryl says, beaming. Because Cheryl's parents were practicing Methodists and advocates of a strong spiritual life, the three children spent a significant amount of time in church accompanied by their parents. Cheryl enjoyed all school activities and made many friends, with some of whom she still maintains contact. She and her friends went out on "group dates," for example, school trips, outings, picnics, and school functions. "Japanese

American teenagers did not date much. I don't recall dating one-on-one until I went to college," she says.

When Cheryl graduated at 17, she entered Oberlin College in Ohio. Her junior year abroad was planned for Waseda University in Tokyo, a large, private, and (at that time) predominantly male university. She enrolled in a special course programmed in the International Division for American students. Most of the courses in Japanese history and culture were taught in English, excluding the Japanese language. The student movement, or *gakusei undo*, was operating in Tokyo as it was in the United States. "All of the students were on strike! So our entire year abroad was spent on campus with Americans speaking mostly English." Cheryl laughs robustly, remembering the ludicrous circumstances. "But, we were able to make some friends with the Japanese students attending club activities on campus." Although Cheryl made many new friends during the year, coming home, she encountered a challenging situation. She had to design her own course of study to coordinate her Japanese experience with the curriculum at Oberlin. "To me the year abroad added substantial growth and knowledge of Japanese life. Being brought up in the United States, I was able to distinguish between the two cultures and lifestyles. I was able to really communicate with my grandparents in the Japanese language, which made us all happy."

Another bonus was Cheryl's insight into differences between Japanese American men and Japanese males born and raised in Japan. "For Japanese American men who experienced internment, this affected their self-esteem. Internment diminished their spirits. In Japan, I observed family structure that had not been interrupted by captivity, despite defeat in the war. Japanese men were proud, with a strongly developed sense of self. Their role as men and family leaders had not been subjugated, or if it had been, the country as a whole shared the same experience," she recalls in a voice tinged with sadness.

After graduation from Oberlin, Cheryl returned to Tokyo. She spent a term at Tsuda Women's College studying English as a second language and over one year teaching at a commercial high school in Osaka. She also taught at two colleges, Heian Junior College in Kyoto, Japan, and another college in Nagoya. When she returned to America, Cheryl entered the University of Hawaii and earned a master's degree in Asian art history in 1972.

Cheryl met Masanobu, her future husband, while both were studying at Oberlin College. He was majoring in music at the Oberlin Conservatory of Music. After graduation, he earned a master's degree at Indiana University. They were married in 1972. Since both sets of parents were Christians, the wedding took place at a Christian church, but the minister permitted the couple to write their own vows, which embraced the spirit of Buddhism.

While Cheryl was teaching in Japan, she began studying Buddhism with Soko Morinaga, a Rinzai Zen Buddhist priest who became very important in her life. Soko was a living example of what it means to be a Buddha. She says, "The concept is that everyone has the Buddha inside, and one has to work hard in order to realize that."

Cheryl continued an intensive study that lasted more than ten years. She and her husband went to live in a communelike community in Maine, where Cheryl taught in their elementary school and worked on the farm and did other community chores, too. Her husband, Masanobu, founded and directed a music festival in the small town, which was home to many artists and musicians. After ten years of complete immersion in the monastic-type life, Cheryl and Masanobu left the commune. "I was finally convinced that I needed more in my life. I wanted a child and could not attend to the needs of a child if I was involved in a program that called for rituals day and night." She left and came back to what she considered the real world of satisfying work.

Miwa, Cheryl's daughter, was born in Japan in 1984 and has dual citizenship. In Japan there is the Family Registry, where babies are registered at birth in their father's hometown, an old practice followed by everyone. Since Miwa's father is a Japanese national, she had to be registered. One could be born in Japan and not be a citizen, but being registered automatically confers citizenship—giving Miwa dual citizenship. In Japanese hospitals, a new mother is hospitalized for a minimum of one week after giving birth. Since Cheryl had a cesarean section, she spent nine days in the hospital. She recalls the understanding of, and caring for, her needs shown by the devoted staff. "I was taught breast-feeding, bathing, positioning, etc. every day. I felt very comfortable handling my baby." Traditionally, upon discharge a new mother goes to her own mother's house, where the instruction continues. This releases and relieves the husband of caring and worrying, so he can apply all of his energies to his work. Cheryl was grateful for all of the support. "In my case, my own mother came from Chicago to help me for several weeks. In the United States, I would not have been so privileged to have such care. After waiting 12 years to start a family, I needed it," Cheryl explains.

The marriage lasted just over 20 years. Cheryl believes her husband's devotion and commitment to his music were partly responsible. "He had to travel frequently, and this wasn't conducive to a strong family life," she says flatly. "We have different personalities, too," Cheryl adds. However, the parents have managed to have an understanding and a relationship in which they share their daughter's life and interests. Miwa is studying violin and viola, which she and her father enjoy playing together, and he often accompanies her when she practices. Miwa understands and accepts these circumstances and makes no excessive demands. "Probably better than I did," Cheryl says rather grimly. Miwa is rather mature for an adolescent, and her mother is amazed that her child is so flexible and can adjust to change so easily.

The only overt incidence of bias happened to Cheryl in, of all places, Japan. "I may have had earlier incidents when I was young, but I don't remember any. However, when I went back to live in Japan for a time, people would say to me in a demeaning way, 'You're not Japanese; you're American,' meaning that I didn't understand what it means to be Japanese." But Cheryl ignored their insensitivity.

Cheryl believes that there is no typical Japanese American. "After World War II, some Japanese left the West Coast. There are major centers of concentration across the country: Hawaii, Los Angeles and other regions of California and the Northwest, Chicago, and New York City. In New York City, the population is considered small. Philosophical differences occur among those born and raised in a non-Japanese community." Cheryl pauses momentarily and then continues, "When I lived in Hawaii, I observed Japanese Americans like those in Japan. They had important roles in high places. The overall picture of Japanese Americans, whether they are male or female, involves the question of an identity, especially when mixed with racial, cultural, and ethnic features. Some remain within the ethnic community, while others may live totally away from other Japanese. Most take a middle position, but all are aware of their relationship to Japan and the United States, share common bonds, and know that a changing society influences their sense of identity," Cheryl sums up.

Cheryl believes that the ten years of studying Buddhism made her life different. Living a monastic-like life had its limitations, but she continues with meditation and tries to eliminate distraction. "Every day is a challenge. I live every day with realistic and obtainable goals. I'm seeking enlightenment and a deeper level of understanding," Cheryl explains.

She recognizes Japanese American values as those that focus on (1) a strong family relationship; (2) a sense of interdependence—helping each other; and (3) obligation to help others—modified community service.

Cheryl thinks that she could be more successful. "I have to balance the family, the spiritual, and the community in my life. I have other priorities. I'm not obsessed with my career. I'd like to spend more time with my spiritual development. I'm a single mom who has a unique set of requirements. I believe that I'm fairly balanced emotionally. Buddhism teaches one to start from inside; if that becomes strong, then all else will follow." As for Miwa, Cheryl thinks she has the inner strength to do whatever she chooses and do it well.

Miwa

Miwa came from the kitchen dressed in her favorite outfit—T-shirt and jeans. She was munching a dry English muffin—her breakfast. The slim, attractive teenager with thick, black, shoulder-length hair, dark eyes, and a mouthful of metal braces is rather shy and genteel.

Miwa is 13 years old and is an eighth grader at the Dalton School, a private institution in New York City. When asked about the new school year, she replies, "The fall started out with classes that seemed very difficult, harder than the seventh grade, but things are falling into place now." Her voice is soft and friendly. "I'm taking mathematics, English literature, French, social studies, science, art, and physical education." Class size is about 15 students, permitting lots of interaction with other students and the teacher. Miwa will advance to high school in the same building with her classmates. "It's comfortable knowing most of the students and being able to stay together as we advance," Miwa adds.

As usual, Miwa spent most of the summer months visiting with her grand-parents and other relatives in Japan. "It's a long 15 hours by airplane, with one stop in California. My mom and I read, slept, played games, and listened to music. We ate some food, but like most airplane food, it was not exciting," she ends with a little laughter. "My grandparents met us at the airport, and we went to their house." Miwa describes her first day. "After breakfast, I tried to converse with my grandparents in Japanese. I'm not too good, but I think they understood what I was trying to tell them. Then we went to Kyoto to visit my aunt and uncle. My cousin, who is a young man of 21 years, is studying music at Rice University in Houston. We enjoyed sushi that afternoon with them."

The next day, Miwa went to visit another aunt in Shizuoka, with whom she stayed for several weeks. "I went to school every day from 9 to 5 for a month. I took classes in Japanese language, English as a second language, and mathematics." Most of the students asked Miwa for help in learning English. She was pleased to act as a tutor. "Helping them and talking with my relatives, who can speak fluent English, helped me learn the Japanese language." She made some friends with whom she will correspond during the coming year. "I already had a telephone call from one of them; I was very surprised and happy she called." Miwa smiles broadly.

An only child can be lonely at times. Miwa thinks that she is bored more than lonely. "There is no one my age to talk with. But it's good in one way. I would not be able to attend private school if I had brothers and sisters. My parents wouldn't be able to afford the tuition for so many children." There are teenage girls living in her housing complex, and sometimes Miwa visits them. She goes with classmates to movies, but that happens infrequently.

After school, Miwa works with clay making pottery, practices soccer, and plays the violin and viola. On Saturdays, she plays in an orchestra at Mannes School of Music and in a string quartet directed by her violin teacher. The young people visit the elderly at nursing homes and entertain the senior citizens. "They enjoy our visits and the music, and we like being with them, too," Miwa reports. The orchestra may give a recital next winter for the public, and Miwa will play the viola.

When Miwa is alone, painting is one hobby she enjoys. Miwa loves to read novels, too. She is responsible for taking care of her clothes and washes them, sorts them, and puts her things away. Miwa also cleans her room and does the dishes and can cook some simple dishes. Since her mother works, she is expected to help out with household chores and shopping. Miwa changes to a blouse and skirt to go out to a Japanese restaurant, where she orders soup, sushi, red bean rice cakes, and tea.

Since biology is a favorite science, Miwa says she may consider medicine as a career choice after graduation from college. "My uncle in Japan is a doctor and lives in a home above his own clinic. We talk about the profession a lot." Miwa likes to paint and was formerly a student at the Art Students League in New York City. Her portfolio contains sketches and watercolors and some still lifes. "At that time, I was considering being an artist," she says. Miwa likes swimming but claims that she's not that great at it. She swims in the Japanese school's pool, a public pool, and in the ocean when she visits Japan in the summer.

There are lots of Asians at Dalton, but not many Japanese students. Miwa is friendly with most of the students. They go out as a class to museums and on field trips. She has a few Japanese girlfriends who do not attend her school. Miwa enjoys pop music and, like most teenagers, dances whatever is "in"; right now, it is line dancing. Her father, a pianist and music director, performs both classical music and ragtime, which Miwa likes also.

Miwa and her mother get along well most of the time. "Sometimes I get angry, but we talk it out and come to a compromise. She's patient and cool. If I have a problem, I feel comfortable talking about it with her. I know that she loves me very much. I'm the only child, and she tends to be over-protective; she still thinks of me as her 'baby,' but I'm growing up and am no longer her 'little girl.' She'll have to accept that."

Miwa attends the New York Buddhist Church every week with her Mom. She finds the services interesting. The one problem in Miwa's life is the limited time she spends with her father. "He travels a lot and is very busy," she complains. She thinks perhaps telling him that she would like to see him more often might help; also planning frequent short visits may be possible, like a breakfast or luncheon date.

"My grandmother in Japan is a retired English teacher, but she would like very much for me to speak Japanese more fluently. She's not like most grand-mothers. She's fun to be with and jokes a lot."

Miwa wears a gold necklace with an opened heart where her name and birth date are engraved in the center. She received it when she was born. What does "Miwa" mean? "Beautiful harmony," she says in her girlish voice. How appropriate.

Janice

Arthur Herbert Gold, author, called San Francisco America's last great metropolitan village. While San Francisco beatnik and Age of Aquarius hippies have died, the bohemian tradition has spread and thrived, giving color, energy, vitality—an ageless youthfulness—to new neighborhoods. Ao Mo, like Soho in New York, is a hip, lively enclave of artists: lofts, trendy restaurants, and cutting-edge clubs, with an avant-garde, multicultural flavor embracing the city's diversity.

"It [San Francisco] is a place that grew up overnight in the din and scramble and mercurial heat of the Gold Rush, only to turn around a century later and launch the decade of Free Love," said Bonnie Wach ("Where San Francisco," May 1997). Its neighborhoods make the city a delightful enigma. Union Square is an example. Located in the center of downtown, between Geary, Powell, Post, and Stockton Streets, the square is at the heart of the city's luxury shopping and hotel district. Union Square is named for the pro-union rallies held there during the Civil War; in the center is the granite Dewey Memorial, capped by the bronze face of Victory, which commemorates Admiral Dewey's triumph over Spain's navy in 1898. One can observe reminders of the past in former hotels that were once "first-class," with faded painted signs on the brick walls announcing "steam heat," "toilets in rooms," and "elegantly furnished at $70.00 a month." They share the streets with massage parlors, rundown bars, Philippine coffee houses, Korean groceries, Chinese take-out restaurants, social clubs, and upscale chain hotels. The area is at the edge of the Tenderloin, San Francisco's meanest neighborhood, a realm of moldering tenements and flea-ridden flophouses, of crack dens and shooting galleries and porn palaces. This is where Glide Memorial United Methodist Church feeds, comforts, and counsels hundreds of thousands of homeless, nameless, gay, straight, prostitute, and multiethnic poor. The church offers 39 programs, including rehabilitation for substance abusers, outreach, workshops for batterers and batterees, anger management classes for ghetto youth, and job skills and computer training for the unemployed and underemployed. The Meals Program feeds 3,500 needy people daily, three times a day, 365 days a year. The church is, according to Reverend Cecil Williams, its pastor, an extended family, where no prodigal is rejected, no dogma is enforced, but certain commandments (beyond the traditional ten) apply.

Everyone in the "Glide family" is expected to be responsible for his or her actions. Everyone is encouraged to volunteer for the church's good works, and most of Glide's 8,200 members do so. Everyone is invited to bare his or her psychic wounds to the congregation and seek healing of them—as Reverend Williams' wife, Janice Mirikitani, did a few years ago, when she stepped to the pulpit and came out as an incest victim. Everyone is expected to reach out across the chasms of color, class, and gender.

In 1982 Janice became president of the Glide Foundation as well as executive director of its programs. She can be found in the pea soup–colored church or church office almost every day at almost any hour. Janice develops the programs from her vision of a multicultural, multiracial, and multiservice institute in San Francisco that promotes gender and cultural sensitivity and empowerment. The walls of Janice's office are covered with press releases, media announcements, photographs of well-known artists and political figures, and reports of church events and functions, as well as numerous accounts of her prolific talents as a poet, artist, choreographer, and writer.

It is 6:30 PM, but Janice is as bright and energetic as if the hour was forenoon. The appearance of this striking, petite woman with a below-the-shoulder mass of black, wavy hair is unexpected. She begins in a modulated voice that is crisp but soft. "I was born in Stockton, California, in 1942. My family and I were sent to the Rohwer Internment Camp in Arkansas shortly thereafter, where we spent the next three and a half years. My parents' marriage was traditional and prearranged, but not a happy one. They were divorced as soon as we left the camp. Like many other Japanese Americans after the war, we settled in Chicago." Janice attended kindergarten while her mother worked. Life was hard for the single mother, but she met Hank, whom she loved very much, and a happy marriage ensued. Hank was born in America but raised in Japan, so his concept of life was rather traditional. After a while, the family moved to a small town outside San Francisco where Janice's maternal grandparents had a chicken farm and where they sold eggs for a living. She remembers the whole family living in a chicken house without plumbing or refrigeration, while the family built a large house.

"It was a hard life, and we were very poor. My brother was born when I was 8 years old, which meant additional work for my mother, who provided most of the child care in the Japanese tradition." Despite the circumstances, Janice's mother stressed hard work and education as a means of improving one's life. "I also worked very hard, was a good student, and graduated at the top of my high school class," says Janice. "I was always an A student." She earned a scholarship as a result. "That was not unusual for Japanese American students. They work for success and want to overcome insecurity through achievements—and break the stigma of being poor," she rationalizes. Her family believed that it was very important to be educated, which would eliminate the stereotype of being seen as unworthy.

Janice attended UCLA and graduated cum laude and then went to Berkeley to earn her secondary teaching credentials in 1963. Afterward, Janice taught high school for a year. "I became disillusioned with the limitations and restricted curriculum imposed on teachers. This was the era of Vietnam, civil rights, and the assassination of President Kennedy. A whole lot was happening. I felt discontented and wanted to go back to college and earn a degree, then teach college-level classes. At that level, I thought things would be more liberated." At college she learned about a part-time job at Glide, which was ideal for a student. Janice pauses in reflection, and her brow wrinkles in a frown. "I was undergoing therapy. My self-esteem was shattered, and I had an addiction problem. The pastor and I became good friends; in fact, he was the best friend that I ever had. Reverend Williams was married at the time. This was 33 years ago. He was surprised that I didn't know his reputation or his name. So he ignored me for a couple of days. Then our friendship developed and grew." Rev. Williams performed the ceremony at Janice's wedding to her first husband. She began work at Glide as a transcriber of tapes of victims of police brutality. "My first job was working with gay youths who were runaways and often addicts and prostitutes," she recalls.

She remembers her relationship with her mother as being rather hostile. "I was angry with her, because I felt she didn't provide protection but rejection when I was sexually abused. Later I realized that she had been abused as a child and had never dealt with, or resolved, her problems. She was in denial," Janice recalls with a hint of sympathy and forgiveness in her voice. Because of her low self-esteem, Janice thinks that she overcompensated. "The sexual abuse that I was experiencing led me to believe that I was acceptable only sexually and physically." She sighs and relaxes a bit. "My mother was physically exquisitely beautiful, and her behavior reinforced an image of women's character that I found unacceptable. She was passive, accepting."

"I believe positive values of a woman were represented by my grandmother, who said to me, 'You are truly beautiful and worthy.' But the words didn't solve my problem, although they brought me comfort." Janice understands now that it was difficult for her mother to be a caretaker when she had so much "personal baggage." Out of this situation came role reversal. Janice spent most of her teenage and young adult years protecting her mother, maintaining the status quo. Part of the solution to her dilemma came from creative writing. "I was extremely shy, introverted. My writing permitted self-expression and a venue for catharsis. It saved my life!" Janice exults. "Through the writing, I was actually sharing who I was, and that's how I survived."

Janice was estranged from her biological father because his second wife did not desire a relationship with her. "He became ill and was hospitalized. I visited him just before he died, but we didn't have time to 'mend fences.' He asked for me and died during my visit. I believe he wanted to see me, and that eases my pain." Her grandmother was the pillar of strength for the whole family. She was the source of inspiration and unconditional love. She wanted to build a happy, loving family. "I believe that it is a memory of that love that helped me embrace the idea of forgiveness. But it has been very difficult. And my search for God has not been easy. As a child, I was very devout and believed that God really loved me. But when my prayers weren't answered, I felt God rejected me. After coming to Glide, it was the community who helped me with my spirituality. The people in recovery who were telling the truth about their pain inspired me," Janice says with a broad smile.

Janice's marriage ended after four years and the birth of a daughter. "That was very rough. I looked upon it as another failure. My daughter is Caucasian and Japanese and very proud of her Japanese heritage as well as her German,

Dutch, and Irish heritages. She is a very strong person, a determined personality."

In regard to Japanese culture and values, Janice appears to have followed her own mind and heart. She has had two marriages, both to non-Japanese men; she not only was a victim of sexual abuse, but she publicized it; she received therapy, dealt with the need to recover from chemical and emotional addictions, and has embraced spirituality. But Janice is quite comfortable with her choices. "Neither the Williamses nor my family members approved or applauded our marriage several years ago any more or less than the community at large accepts intermarriage. But we didn't expect acceptance. Just doing our jobs at Glide is difficult and a struggle, but it is what we want to do," says Janice in a voice full of joy. "Just to witness changes in people's attitude and behavior is so rewarding. We deal with people who have reached bottom or are at the edge of it. We give them hope. We help give them back their lives."

Glide is the dream of a 10-year-old Cecil Williams, recovering from a breakdown. The illness left him with excessive energy and finely tuned emotional antennae; it also took away his fear of death. In 1960 he restored a tumbledown church in Kansas City and filled it with an integrated congregation of 800. In 1966 Methodist authorities tapped him to recover the fortune of another moribund church. Glide's membership consisted of about 40 middle-class whites. On his third Sunday, Rev. Williams tore off his robe and announced, "We're gonna make these walls come down!" The congregation walked out because it didn't like his style. They were replaced by street people, prostitutes, then by San Francisco's hippies. Glide offered jazz services and hosted psychedelic happenings. Expanded social services, celebrity visitors, and involvement in the crack epidemic made Glide a major player on the local political scene. According to a 1997 *Life* magazine article (vol. 20, no. 4) written by Kenneth Mills and entitled "A Church for the Twenty-First Century," the defining moment of Rev. Williams' early years at Glide came in 1967, when he took down the sanctuary cross. The cross symbolized death, the pastor said, and Glide championed life. "You are responsible for your life and the world. You are the cross!" he preached.

Janice considers her grandmother her major role model. Others are close professional friends and her husband. "I gained strength, tolerance, and spirituality from all of them." Although her daughter, Tianne, was raised by a single mother, working and often troubled, she and Janice have a very positive relationship. Janice explains, "Early on, she showed independence and self-determination and the ability to make effective decisions. I tried to protect and guide her, probably attempting to give her what I missed as a child. It was when I approached her as an adult and recognized her maturity that our relationship grew rich and meaningful. She knows all about my past. She understands." Janice's voice is light and gentle.

Janice's 18-hour-a-day schedule at Glide permits little time for family activities. "But we're into physical fitness and have a treadmill. We work out together, and I try to run 25 miles a week. Late at night, I write poetry. I cook Japanese food, which we all enjoy—it keeps the heritage alive," she says jokingly. "Tianne is my best friend, and we're happy. She is my confidante."

Janice has administrative, fiscal, and supervisory responsibilities for the 39 programs. She hopes that increased fund-raising and donations will permit Glide to employ personnel to assume some of these responsibilities. The goal for Glide is to create and develop self-responsibility and direction within their clients. "For myself, I would love to publish another book, a novel this time."

Janice has published three novels: *Awake in the River* (1978); *Shedding Silence* (1987); and, most recently, *We, the Dangerous* (1995). She has also edited several landmark anthologies, including *Time to Greez: Incantations from the Third World*, poetry and prose by major writers of color; *Third World Women: Ayumi-Four Generations of Japanese in America; Making Waves*, an Asian women's anthology; and a collaborative project, an anthology of work by survivors of incest and abuse, entitled *Watch Out, We're Talking*. She has been published in numerous anthologies, textbooks, journals, and magazines in the United States and in Japan. She is also a noted dancer and choreographer.

Does she consider herself successful? "A work in progress" is what Janice calls herself. "Sometimes you have to climb a mountain to get to another place. Right now, I feel that I'm at the steepest grade of the mountain." This extraordinary, sensitive, and intelligent woman has successfully climbed many mountains, and her future holds many more potential conquests. She is truly "a work in progress."

Tianne

"I would have loved to have had brothers and sisters, especially when I was younger," Tianne begins. She was born 29 years ago in San Francisco. She appears much younger, with long tawny hair and fair skin. As she was growing up, Tianne remembers Glide Memorial Church as a special place. "I had many friends and knew everyone there. I was quite comfortable in that environment."

High school for Tianne was four years of scheduled classes and homework. She made no special friends, nor can she remember any particular teacher. Education was stressed by her parents and maternal grandmother. "I found school routine. It was not difficult to graduate. The work was not that challenging." Tianne laughs, remembering the monotony. "I guess because I always worked after school, I didn't have the time to get involved with any school activities." Tianne now attends San Francisco State College but still works part-time. "I've worked all my life, it seems. But I'm a senior and almost finished," she says with a deep sigh.

Most of her employment has not been career-oriented but work to cover college and living expenses. Jobs held include McDonald's boutique sales, and car washing. Her major is industrial management and occupational psychology. Tianne is people-oriented, and if she goes to graduate school, her goal would be helping people choose careers that fulfill their lives. When she has time, Tianne reads novels of every kind.

At the moment, Tianne shares an apartment with several girls. "It's fun, and we get along well." Tianne dates but with no one steadily. "I want to get my life focused and organized and also complete my education before I consider marriage."

While she was a teenager, Tianne was somewhat rebellious. "I used to cut classes once in a while and had difficulty communicating with my mother. But that's over now. We get along just fine now," says Tianne, her face brightened by a wide smile. "I quit smoking," she adds. "When I moved out, real changes occurred. I had to assume responsibility, and I proved to myself and my mother that I was capable."

Tianne admires her mother's strength and creativity. She writes poetry and nonfiction, which people admire. "My mother is multitalented. I don't think I could be like her, but that's OK." Tianne loves San Francisco but would love to try living elsewhere, although she doesn't have any city or state in mind. "Moving away would be another step in maturity," she concludes.

"I would not bring up my children the way that I was raised. First, I would want to have at least three children; in that way, they would have someone else in their lives and not have to depend upon friends but have a real family. My mother had many hardships that affected her as a woman and a mother. She was a great mother. She protected me. I knew that I was loved. But I would not want the struggles she had to overcome. Perhaps I would not have the strength," Tianne says wistfully.

About Japanese culture and traditions, Tianne thinks most fourth-generation Japanese don't feel traditional as such, especially those who are not adults. "When I was young, my Mom made me rice cakes, terriyaki chicken, sushi, soups, and other Japanese food I enjoyed." Regarding her own appearance, "My father is Caucasian, and my hair is light brown, because the beautician 'highlights' it. My mother's life and environment are filled with many ethnic groups and many cultural practices." She would love to learn Japanese. Tianne's grandparents told her about her Pennsylvania Dutch father. Tianne feels fortunate that she has so many different ethnic groups in her background. "That's a lot of people who love you," Tianne says with a smile. Tianne admires her mother's intelligence, academic achievements, conscientiousness, practicality, and passion about what she does. "Five years from now, I would like to be focused with a positive direction in my life. This will make me successful."

REFERENCES

Kendis, K. P. *A Matter of Comfort: Ethnic Maintenance and Ethnic Style among Third Generation Japanese Americans.* New York: AMS Press, 1989.
Kitano, H. H. L. *Generation and Identity: The Japanese American.* Needham Heights, MA: Ginn Press, 1993.
Levine, G. S., and Rhodes, C. *The Japanese American Community: A Three Generation Study.* Westport, CT: Praeger, 1981.
Nishi, S. M. "Japanese Americans." In *Asian Americans: Contemporary Trends,* P. G. Min, ed. Thousand Oaks, CA: Sage, 1995.

PERSONAL REFLECTIONS
by Hiroshi Fukurai

IDENTITY, CULTURAL ADAPTATION, AND ACCOMMODATION OF A JAPANESE FAMILY LIVING IN THE UNITED STATES

When our first son was born five years ago, we felt a great concern about how he could retain a Japanese identity and still integrate within the main culture in the United States. Since then, we have added two daughters to our family. It has been a constant struggle, thinking and wondering whether we have made the right decision to maintain cultural ways and beliefs intact, inculcating them in our children.

We have had to make a number of critical decisions about child raising and specific ways that our family should be designed to feel secure in America. From the first time we discussed child raising, we decided to make our home much like the way we knew it when we grew up in Japan. We felt that any type of unnatural pretension or artificial home atmosphere would affect our children negatively. We also decided to make our home a sanctuary, away from the strains of racism and socioeconomic inequality that permeate U.S. society. And the motto of our revered home was simple: be comfortable and act naturally.

Translating the motto into our daily activities meant that we decided to communicate in the Japanese language, eat Japanese food, watch Japanese television programs, and maintain the Japanese way of life that we understand and are confident in providing to our children. We also thought that it was important to make clear personal and social distinctions between what we do at home (*honne*) and how we live outside home (*tatemae*). Luckily, access to Japanese ways of life is not difficult to come by in California.

Japanese towns are nearby, and ethnic foods are easily accessible. Even television programs from Japan are accessible for almost 24 hours a day, thanks to satellite relays and today's ever-advancing technological innovations in telecommunications (Pollack, 1995).

Another important decision involved our efforts to give our children constant exposure to the Japanese language, people, culture, and tradition. After our son was born, I asked my father to spend at least three months a year with our children in the United States. We also invite my wife's parents to Santa Cruz annually to spend a month with our children. My father-in-law, who suffered a stroke eight years ago, visits us in a wheelchair and enjoys his stay because of the greater accessibility to various public and private facilities. In Japan the physically handicapped are still considered outcasts, and, while great strides have been made in recent years to make public facilities accessible to physically handicapped individuals, the United States offers them greater opportunities and accessibility to both private and public facilities. With both of our parents coming to the United States regularly, they make strong cultural connections with our children, giving them constant exposure to the Japanese language and a Japanese way of life.

We also tried to take advantage of maximizing cultural exchange with Japanese visitors through my university. Since there is always a small group of Japanese visiting scholars and their families in the area, we routinely arrange parties, dinners, and picnics with them. Almost all of them bring small children with them, increasing the opportunity to interact and play with our children. Another benefit of interacting with Japanese visiting scholars and their families is that they often come back to Santa Cruz after their initial appointment is completed. I often end up making necessary accommodation arrangements for them. And every spring, we have a reunion with former visiting scholars and their children in Santa Cruz.

We have also decided to spend a couple of months in Japan every summer. While international travel remains expensive, we find the traveling and staying in Japan very rewarding to our children because the trip gives them an important opportunity to interact with different Japanese adults and children, making them aware that there are a large number of "real" Japanese-speaking people out there who, besides us, the parents, communicate in the Japanese language. Fortunately, our cousins also have children who are at the same age as ours, giving them the opportunity to play, talk, and interact.

In Santa Cruz, we also decided to teach some conversational Japanese to preschool children and teachers because my son is one of a few students, if not the only one, able to speak and understand the Japanese language in class. The preschool is run by the university and often enrolls children of non-English speaking parents. Given the preschool's multicultural environment, many teachers appear to be very sensitive to cultural differences and language difficulties faced by the children.

Several times in the past, we have been invited to teach children and teachers Japanese children's songs and conversational Japanese. When we take our son to preschool every morning, for example, we say, *"Ohayo-gozaimasu"* ("good morning") and give Japanese greetings to children and teachers, and they often respond to us in Japanese as well. All children and teachers sing a Japanese song several times a week. We were also asked to teach them traditional paper arts called origami. Our involvement in pre-school and the teachers' willingness to accept Japanese culture have helped create the preschool's multicultural environment, so that our son feels less isolated culturally and linguistically (Smith, 1995).

At home, we have made efforts to celebrate many Japanese festivities and conduct cultural rituals. In appreciating a festive occasion for Japanese girls, for instance, my wife's parents helped celebrate Girls Day (a Japanese national holiday celebrated with special dolls that remain in the family for years) on March 3 by sending us the decorative dolls, called *Ohinasama*. On May 5 we also celebrate Boys Day by making large carp flags (three-dimensional flags containing the emblem of a fish, the symbol of strength and endurance) to pray for our son's health and life's success. As well, we have built a small shrine at home where my wife and I make a daily offering of a fresh glass of water and a small rice dish to the spirit of our ancestors to pray for the good health of our family and loved ones. Our children also participate in this brief morning ceremony by clapping their hands and meditating for a brief moment, a practice of belief that is part of the spiritual ritual in Japanese custom and tradition.

Because small children's stories and Japanese songs are an important part of raising children at home, we also brought with us from Japan both books and audiocassettes of most major Japanese small children's stories and songs. We play them almost daily and read the stories before they take a daily nap or go to bed in the evening. We also frequently play Japanese small children's songs and traditional music. Not only do our children enjoy listening to traditional Japanese songs and small children's stories, but we the parents also enjoy them. We feel that it is important to let our children know that we as parents also enjoy the traditional songs and stories. After all, living the motto, we must feel comfortable and be natural at home.

All these measures to make sure that our children have constant exposure to Japanese culture and a Japanese way of life come directly from my own personal experience in the United States as a foreign student and then a professional scholar. I was fortunate enough to have the opportunity to meet a large variety of people from different parts of the United States, as well as the world, carefully observe their experiences and methods of coping, and examine their strategies in dealing with differences between their own cultures and those of the United States. I have also experienced racism, and such experiences have made me aware of my ignorance of racism at home and the effect it has had on Japan's racial minorities and their children. While I considered myself a member of Japan's racial majority, I found myself and my family as members of a racial minority in the United States, and such an identity shift and racial awareness made me more sensitive toward racial and gender inequality and how these influence children and affect family and the social environment where children are brought up.

In order to understand my approaches, cultural adaptation, and efforts to create Japanese-conscious domestic and social environments for our children, it is important to disclose something about my personal background.

I was born as a son of a working-class family in 1954 in Sendai, a city of a half million population, located approximately 200 miles north of Tokyo. After completing a study in metallurgical engineering, I came to the United States in 1976 and completed a doctoral degree in sociology at the University of California, Riverside, in 1985. I first taught at Texas A&M University for two years, then moved to Santa Cruz, California. My decision to return to California was prompted by my desire to be close to Japanese communities, cultures, and a way of life where I could easily meet and share ideas with people of Japanese backgrounds. The fact that I was still single and in search of a lifelong partner also played an important part in my decision to return to California.

During 1990 and 1992 I returned to Japan and served as a senior policy adviser at a Japanese branch campus of Texas A&M University. Texas A&M University, one of three government-sponsored, American universities that launched their first international campuses in Japan, opened its branch campus in 1990 in Koriyama, a town of 320,000 population. Koriyama is located near Sendai, where my parents were still living, and the geographical proximity to Sendai was another important factor for taking the advisory position at the branch campus.

While taking a leave of absence from my university and working as an adviser in Koriyama, I met and married a then 32-year-old former television reporter in 1992. The encounter was set up according to a Japanese traditional, arranged way, called *omiai* in Japanese, in which a go-between makes a reservation at a respectable restaurant for a couple to meet and talk. We then fell in love and married five months later. The following year, our son was born, followed by two daughters.

Once in the United States, our decision and plan to act naturally and comfortably at home and maintain the Japanese way of life were also closely related to my wife's limited language skills and her lack of international experiences. As a college graduate, despite having taken English courses since junior high school for a total of ten years, she could barely engage in English conversation. The greater part of her failure to communicate in English stems from the Japanese educational system's emphasis on learning the grammatical structure of the English language, rather than on teaching students to express their ideas and thoughts through conversation and communication. Given her very limited language skills, I felt that it was imperative to create and maintain a family environment where she feels safe and comfortable so that, despite living in a foreign land, she does not feel pressured to act pretentiously at home or in social settings.

The fact that she had never lived outside Japan played an important part in creating the Japanese-specific cultural environment at home for our children. Her limited international experience also forced both of us to make certain personal sacrifices and collective decisions. When she was seven months pregnant, for instance, we both decided and agreed that she should return to Japan to have our first baby. She had been taking private English conversation courses in Japan and attended adult school in the United States. However, her language skills were still quite limited. So, when we discovered that she was pregnant, she became concerned about her limited language ability and felt that she might not be able to communicate effectively with hospital personnel when going through the last, critical moments of childbirth. The practice of a Japanese woman to return to her hometown is neither new nor an anomaly but is still considered a traditional part of Japanese culture in which daughters often return to their parents to have babies. My younger sister, for example, returned to Sendai and had her first two sons there. For her third baby, she decided not to return, only because our mother passed away the previous year, and my sister did not feel comfortable in the absence of our mother.

My wife's limited language skills ultimately led to different approaches to cultural adaptation, leading to my increased involvement with the daily activities of my wife and our children. Ever since the beginning of our marriage, for example, I always had to accompany her and our children practically everywhere, due to her and my children's lack of language skills. Such daily activities included shopping, doctor's visits, preschool, and counseling. While my wife's language began to improve significantly, going places together still remains the routine and integral part of our daily activities. It is still my responsibility, for instance, to take our children to see doctors. I go with my wife and children on most shopping expeditions. For academic conventions or conference presentations, the entire family travels with me. Even for a routine physical checkup for my wife, I go along and take our three children with us. All doctors and nurses at the clinic know every member of our family and play with our children in a waiting room or in the doctor's office.

So my place is different from that of most Japanese men. The gendered role of Japanese male is that of "sarari-man," devoting his life to work and spending almost no time with his family. Well, the changing environment and planned strategy to adapt in a new environment with my Japanese wife and children have led to my greater involvement in family affairs and daily activities, contrary to the stereotypic image of a work-crazed Japanese husband (Krooth and Fukurai, 1990).

While I feel that I succeeded in creating a much kinder and friendlier family atmosphere and culturally robust domestic and social environment, there are always some areas that I may have overlooked. For instance, the most difficult part of carefully thought-out strategies to make a homey and soul-resting environment for my wife and our children comes from my dealing with people who do not share the Japanese language or culture. With respect to preschool teachers and children, we have made a conscious effort through our greater involvement at preschool to make sure that our son does not feel physically and intellectually isolated from other children. However, with respect to my colleagues and students, most of whom do not share the Japanese language or culture, I often find myself communicating with them in English in the presence of our children. I always wonder how our children view my interaction with people in English and their assessment of my dealings with English-speaking strangers. They may see me with a double personality—one at home speaking Japanese and the other, outside home, speaking a foreign language.

My decision to communicate in the Japanese language at home and speak English only when children ask English-related questions comes from my assumption that children will eventually acquire English-language skills at school (Wright and Taylor, 1995). For example, I often overhear my son communicating with his sister in English, though she has yet to attend preschool. The English language, I assume, can be acquired through my children's continued process of socialization at school and interaction with their friends.

My decision to speak Japanese at home is also based on the suggestions given by a large number of Japanese American friends who indicated that their parents pushed them to learn the Japanese language and a Japanese way of life when they were young. However, their frustration in dealing with two separate languages and cultures forced most of them to reject and abandon the cultural learning experience. The irony is that when they grew older, they felt remorseful and even angry because their parents failed to push them hard enough to keep up with the Japanese language and culture.

Another major concern or fear that I have is that because of my children's demarcated lifestyles between home and outside, they may end up developing no true identity (Hobsbawm, 1996). Development of no ethnic or strong racial identity is a true worry for us as parents. We call it *nenashigusa*, the duckweed of the grass without its roots. No matter how much we try to impose on them a Japanese way of life at home or create a domestic and social environment promoting the understanding of Japanese culture and language, there is a certain limit to what we can do as parents. Though racial identity is an integral part of American life, they may fail to develop a strong sense of social or racialized identity, perceiving themselves as neither Japanese nor American. Once they grow up, they may feel alienated and even become angry that we as parents failed to make them feel either Japanese enough or American enough.

The only hope that my wife and I have is that when they grow up, they read these words and try to understand the struggles that we their parents had to go through to create the "right" and "comfortable" environment for them and their future.

REFERENCES

Hobsbawn, E. "Language, Culture, and National Identity." *Social Research* 63:1065–1080, 1996.

Krooth, R., and Fukurai, H. *"Common Destiny: Japan and the United States in the Global Age.* Jefferson, NC: McFarland, 1990.

Pollack, A. "Time-Warner in Venture for Cable TV in Japan." *New York Times*, January 10, 1995, C2, D2.

Smith, S. M. "Cross-Cultural Issues and Racism in a Multi-Cultural Society." In *The Emotional Needs of Young Children and Their Families: Using Psychoanalytic Ideas in the Community*, ed. J. Trowell and M. Bower. London: Routledge, 1995, 237–246.

Wright, S. C., and Taylor, D. M. "Identity and the Language in the Classroom: Investigating the Impact of Heritage versus Second Language Instruction in Personal and Collective Self-Esteem." *Journal of Educational Psychology* 87: 241–252, 1995.

PART III

LATINO AMERICANS

Unlike Chinese or Japanese, the Latino population is composed of a diverse collection of national origins fragmented by class and generation (Bean and Tienda, 1987). The category "Latino" does not really exist apart from the classification created by federal statisticians to provide data on people of Mexican, Cuban, Puerto Rican, Dominican, Colombian, Salvadoran, and other extractions. Although "Hispanics" in theory includes all those who can trace their origins to an area originally colonized by Spain, in practice, this definition delineates few common traits and embraces tremendous national diversity.

With heterogeneity in national origins comes great variation in the timing of each group's arrival in the United States.

- Cubans arrived largely between 1960 and 1990.

- Mexicans have been migrating continuously since around 1890.

- Southwestern Hispanics were forcibly annexed to the United States in 1848.

- Dominicans, Salvadorans, and Guatemalans have just begun migrating to the United States within the past two decades.

The differences between the countries appear to be more important than the commonalities, even when within single countries. Five differences, according to most scholars, are:

1. obvious differences in geography, language, race, ethnicity, and culture
2. there are degrees of industrialization and wealth among nations, including amounts of natural resources capable of generating full-scale industrialization
3. Latin American nations differ in their actual forms of government, whether dictatorial or democratic
4. although nationalism is usually known as a commonality, the difference is in their approaches or selection of national "enemies"
5. there are major differences in political tradition and values even within regions (Cockcroft, 1989)

In the last third of the 20th century, three highly publicized elements of Latin American politics emerged. First, there were violence and state terrorism of strong right-wing governments or armed violence of their guerrilla opponents. Second, there were the human rights and peace movements leading to a Nobel laureate for Latin Americans—Costa Rica's president Arias' 1997 Nobel Peace Prize. Third, there were the "theology of liberation" and its curious alliance with the new Marxism. However, the reform efforts of the theology, which overlapped with the Civil Rights movement, achieved the most success in actually reaching large numbers of people.

One important commonality in Latin American history is the reliance on one or two dominant export commodities, for example, oil, coffee, and minerals. Another is stepped-up militarism in countries with decades of stable civilian rule, for example, Mexico and Panama.

Through recent decades, several commissions (the Rockefeller Report, the Linowitz and Kissinger Commissions) have called for reforms with U.S. aid in Latin America. None were acceptable by Latin American countries.

In order to concretize what a future U.S.–Latin American relationship might look like, advocates of change cite a number of realities and possibilities. An official alliance between more forward-looking U.S. policymakers with Latin America's younger technocratic elites and entrepreneurs, leaders of the widespread popular mobilizations, and representatives of the new ideological amalgams of the theology of liberation, Marxism, and nationalism, would give the United States a new and favorable image. In turn, by breaking the old, bankrupt alliance with outmoded elites, terrorists, "national security states," aging gangster-style labor leaders, and corrupt bureaucrats, costly military adventures could be avoided, and long-run peace and stability could be achieved (Cockcroft, 1989).

REFERENCES

Bean, F., and Tienda, M. *The Hispanic Population of the United States*. New York: Russell Sage, 1987.
Cockcroft, J. D. *Neighbors in Turmoil in Latin America*. New York: Harper and Row, 1989.

9

Cuban Americans

Cubans who immigrated to the United States during the late 1950s and early 1960s were predominantly professionals and entrepreneurs who fled Cuba when Castro came to power. Their background, coupled with their being granted refugee status and subsequently resettlement assistance by the U.S. government, has meant that Cubans have done relatively well economically. As their migration occurred during an earlier period, Cuban immigrants are not as young as other Latinos. This predominantly urban population settled primarily in Florida. In the early 1980s, another influx of Cubans entered the United States. Commonly referred to as "Marielitos" because they left from the Cuban port of Mariel, this group has not fared as well economically because they were of lower socioeconomic status than the previous Cuban immigrants and also did not receive such extensive resettlement assistance (Portes and Bach, 1985). During a five-month period (May to September 1980), 125,000 refugees arrived. While most Marielitos were similar in some ways to other Cuban exiles, some were detained in government camps, as they were suspected of being convicts or mental patients. Most were men (85%), most were single (65.5%), most were blue-collar workers (86.2%), many were black (40%, compared to 4% of U.S. Cubans), and a small percent (16%) came from Castro's prisons (Bach et al., 1981). Of these, only 4% were "hard-core" criminals (Boswell, 1985).

Historically, Cubans have had a natural attraction to south Florida, as some 40,000 lived in Miami prior to the revolution. Many of the pioneer refugees settled in Miami, considering their stay temporary, as they were waiting only for the "inevitable" overthrow of Castro's regime (Azieri, 1981).

Furthermore, the dynamic density and cultural supports available in Miami naturally attracted other Cuban refugees.

Most refugees were attracted to south Florida by the availability of government assistance programs. As early as 1959, President Eisenhower allocated $1 million for refugee assistance, while the Kennedy administration provided millions more for education, job training, welfare benefits, and housing programs (Pedraza-Bailey, 1985). Today it is estimated that 70% of all Cubans live in the Miami area. Another reason for their concentration in Miami is the absence of a language barrier and the general availability of jobs. "Little Havana" is an area where Cubans can live and work in a totally Spanish-speaking environment (Fradd, 1983). Furthermore, it is customary for Cuban businessmen to hire their compatriots, as the refugees give them their loyalty, and the Cuban entrepreneurs guarantee them jobs. Unfortunately, these ethnic loyalties sometimes result in wage and labor abuses (Wilson and Portes, 1980).

When compared to other Hispanics, the Cuban American population must be considered the most economically advanced. Part of the reason for their success is the selective nature of their immigration, the advantages received from government assistance programs, and their strong economic base in Miami. Among Hispanics, Cubans had the highest average family income, $27,294 in 1987 (compared to $30,853 in the United States). But this level of income is achieved only by combining individual family members' incomes (Perez, 1986). But this still leaves an income gap of $3,559 when compared to all Americans. The higher economic standing of Cuban Americans can be attributed to their higher positions in the labor force, the higher percentage of women who are employed full-time (47.1% compared to 40.1% U.S. women), and a greater number of workers per family (18.6% had three or more workers per family compared to 12.5% U.S. women) (Perez, 1986).

The healthy representation of Cubans in white-collar positions is, in part, attributable to their educational achievement. Among Hispanics, Cubans have achieved the highest level of education. Part of the reason for their success is the higher social status of the pioneer refugees who encouraged their children to pursue higher education. They also valued the opportunity to attend a public institution of higher education. Consequently, they were highly motivated in their pursuit of a higher education (Portes et al., 1982).

As is generally true among Hispanics, Cubans place great importance on family relationships. In the Cuban enclave today, the family plays a particularly important role as a result of the refugee experience. Over the years, Cubans have worked assiduously at "family reunification" (Richmond, 1980).

Professor Mercedes Sandoval, anthropologist at the Inter-American Center of Miami Dade Community College, wrote about Cuban cultural contributions to south Florida. "The impact that Cubans have had in South

Florida is observable in all areas of life and is manifested in all aspects of culture including economy, politics, education, religion, entertainment, sports, the arts and the media." The most obvious contribution by Cubans has been in the economic section, largely as owners of large businesses and firms. Cuban Americans have been involved in the development of banking, insurance, and real estate firms.

The presence of Cubans changed the electoral statistics of Dade County from a solid bastion of the Democratic Party to only a slight majority in 1998.

In the area of religion, Cubans' presence has changed the religious picture of south Florida, since the majority of them are either nominally or practicing Catholics. The huge influx of thousands of Haitians and Nicaraguans has added to the increase of Catholics in the area, too.

New generations of Cuban American writers spread their wings, a literary tradition nourished by authors in south Florida, who write in a bilingual mode, and a bicultural context is emerging. Their work is enriching the literary world of this area with wide perceptions of a transcontinental worldview, soul, and flavor (Bertot, 1990).

In the sports arena, Cubans are noted for their skill in baseball. José Conseca has left his mark as the first player to have batted 40 home runs and stolen over 40 bases during the same season.

Bilingualism is at the root of the change that transformed Greater Miami from a resort and retirement area to a cosmopolitan region catering to the needs for goods and services of large segments of the population of the Americas. Public schools and the media have stressed teaching a second language and/or maintaining the mother language.

Cuban culture has been quite eclectic, the product of the syncretion of different cultural traditions (Sandoval, 1985). "Some basic values such as the strong family orientation, personalism, a joyful view of life, where human and active socializing play an important role, serve as sensor or watchdogs allowing or inhibiting the entry or exclusion of new cultural elements which were not congruent with these values," says Professor Sandoval.

CASE STUDIES

Ileana

Although it is early April, sharp winds blow across the Potomac River, leaving dancing whitecaps in their wake. Bright sunlight offers little respite. Blossoming cherry trees bend against sudden gusts showering pink petals into the air. Men and women step rapidly, leaning forward to push against the Arctic-like blasts. Clutching bulging briefcases and dark attaché cases, they race up the steps of the Rayburn Building. These constituents—farmers, health care providers, educators, firefighters, and law enforcement agents—have come from near and far to present their concerns to members of Congress. Ileana Ros-Lehtinen is one of them.

Oversized flags of the United States and the state of Florida hang at the sides of the ornate oak doors to the congresswoman's offices. With a bright, welcoming smile, a receptionist escorts visitors into a large, sunny room. Almost immediately, one learns that the congresswoman is very family-oriented. Beautiful, colored pictures of her family, including her husband, two daughters, and parents, are everywhere, leaving little space for official photographs, citations, and plaques. The pictures reveal happy moments at home, entertaining, enjoying recreation, and relaxing on their boat. Ileana Ros-Lehtinen's firm handshake is a surprise. She is petite, attractive, and energetic.

"I was born in Cuba on July 15, 1952. My parents were Enrique and Amanda Ros. My parents own a courier business. I have one brother, whose name is Henry. My parents, brother, and I all came over from Cuba by plane. The family planned to stay in the United States for a few days." But days turned into weeks, and weeks turned into months, and months turned into years, and years turned into decades, and they are still here. "It was a time of chaos. Castro had taken over the government and was confiscating everything—homes, businesses, banks, and property. There would be no more elections, and life would be unbearable." Ileana pauses a moment. "We still have a part of our Pan Am return flight ticket. It's framed and hangs in my office."

"In terms of my elementary education, I attended Southside Public Elementary School and started to learn English at the age of 7, once I arrived in the United States. I had some problems adjusting to life in America, because there were a new language, a new culture, and new children at school. I received a lot of help at school from teachers and from my classmates. I was very shy when I was in school, so I spent a lot of my out-of-school time reading, which I think was indispensable in sparking my interest in education in English." Ileana takes a deep breath and continues, "My high school years were not especially eventful, in terms of sports, clubs, or major social events. My best subject was English. I enjoyed reading, and to this day, I still read my favorite author, Walt Whitman, diligently. I also liked romance, action, and drama movies."

During her college years, Ileana's main subject was English, a subject in which she majored and received her B.A. degree. Her parents were key in influencing her career choice, especially her father, who, being a teacher, registered accountant, and college graduate himself, instilled in her the need to receive higher education in order to get ahead. Later, Ileana earned a master's degree in education at the same local state university.

Before becoming an elected official, Ileana was a teacher for many years in private and public schools. At one point, she had her own school, Eastern

Academy, in Hialeah, Florida, which is part of Dade County. It was a small facility specializing in bilingual education.

Ileana had to put her doctoral studies on hold. "I haven't taken a course in a while, because Claude Pepper died, and I decided to run for the vacancy." She hopes to continue working on her doctorate in educational supervision as soon as possible.

In Florida, Congresswoman Ros-Lehtinen began her political career by being elected to the Florida House of Representatives in 1982, becoming the first Hispanic woman elected to Florida's state legislature. She had been a strong lobbyist for educational changes and decided that perhaps she would be more effective if she became a part of the system. She served until 1986, when she became a state senator. As a state legislator, she supported legislation to promote drug-free workplaces and a tuition assistance program for Florida college students. She served as state senator until 1989, when she was elected to the House of Representatives to fill the vacancy caused by the death of Claude Pepper.

Congresswoman Ros-Lehtinen serves on the International Relations and Government Reform and Oversight Committees. Her seat on the International Relations Committee is of particular importance to her Cuban American constituency. In her second term, she played a key role in the discussion of the Cuban Democracy Act, which became part of the 1993 defense authorization that prohibits subsidiaries of U.S. corporations from trading with Cuba. There has been some discussion about relaxing some of these regulations. In this Congress, she became the first Hispanic woman to chair a subcommittee (Africa) and was designated vice chair of the Western Hemisphere Subcommittee. Her assignments have provided the opportunity for Ileana to fight for the causes in which she believes—like freedom, democracy, and human rights.

Her district includes Little Havana, South Miami Beach, Coral Gables, Coconut Grove, Key Biscayne, and suburban Miami, Florida. She works hard for her constituents and has been unopposed in the last two elections. "I'm a very homegrown legislator. I am in Miami more than I am in Washington. I never forget my roots. I've never left home," she says loud and clearly. Ileana represents Florida's 18th district, where, according to the 1990 census, 67% of the population is Hispanic. In Congress, she has continued her support of legislation dealing with education.

For women to succeed in politics, they must be prepared to undertake an arduous task. "First there are fund-raising and getting the people to support candidates. Most people think that the male candidate will win. But changes are happening. The public is beginning to be supportive of women and thinks that women candidates are to win rather than lose. Women are getting more support today. I've been in politics about 14 years, and I see the changes. Women are being taken seriously as more women run and are successful."

Ileana is very happy in her present position. This position is manageable, and it's what she likes to do. With a husband and two daughters, Amanda and Patricia, it would be difficult for her to balance family life and political life in other positions. "This is what I want to do and would like to stay for a few more years and keep working toward that freedom."

The congresswoman is fortunate enough to have parents who live near her home in Florida. The semiretired couple are devoted to their grand-daughters; they provide continuous and excellent child care in Ileana's absence. The children have their own rooms and playroom in their grand-parents' home. "I'm not a typical working mom who has to constantly worry about what's happening to her children. My family support makes everything possible. I couldn't manage without them."

In the Spanish community, men are beginning to accept women's work-ing. The economic factors have caused many women to seek employment as a necessity, and the men are beginning to accept the idea that some women enjoy and want to work as well. "It is becoming more positively acceptable for Spanish women to work and run for elective office," Ileana explains.

The Lehtinens purchased a sailboat for Christmas, and the family enjoys sailing now. The girls are learning to sail, too. Besides attending an occa-sional movie, the family stays home and reads together. They find pleasure in this joint activity, Ileana says. "I have to be away so much that when Congress is not in session, I want to spend time with my family at home and not get on another airplane to go somewhere."

Ileana was unable to breast-feed her children because they were born after she became a state representative, and with her commitments it would have been impossible. They were both bottle-fed.

Although Ileana has lived in the United States for many years, she feels very much a part of the Spanish culture, and so do her children. Both chil-dren speak Spanish fluently and are proud of their Cuban American back-ground. "Traditionally," Ileana explains, "the woman is the focal point of the family, so it's difficult to balance home and job responsibilities when you have children. Fortunately, I have an understanding husband. We met in the state legislature when he was in politics, so he is aware of the demands and is supportive. I feel that his support is the key to my success. He supports all three of my roles—wife, mother, and politician."

In Congress, there are few women, and their male counterparts are still not aware of women's capabilities. They are not used to having women around. The women have a challenge ahead to enlighten their male col-leagues. Sometimes, Ileana is approached as if she were someone's aide. When women become more vocal and involved, the men will eventually give them the respect they deserve.

Her children see her as a mom and also as a working mother. Ileana spells this out. "I'm a Girl Scout troop leader and meet with the Scouts twice a month. In fact, I was the leader of my younger daughter's troop, and this year I'm the leader of the older daughter's troop." Since birth, the children have been exposed to the media, camerapersons, television crews, and reporters at Mom's interviews and committee meetings; they know that all of this is part of Mom's life.

Ileana hopes that the girls think of her as a role model, not because she's a congresswoman but because she loves them and does the best she can do for them.

The congresswoman speaks of her work as very rewarding. Having a balance and enjoying what you are doing are the crux. Reducing the level of stress in one's life and family gives one a sense of satisfaction. Having a feeling that what you do matters is important to others as well as to yourself. Therefore, the Welfare Bill is of great concern to her. She voted against it, because she believes it hurts a lot of her poor constituents and legal residents who would lose their benefits. "I always tell my female colleagues that we need to look at advances for minority women especially and women outside of the United States as well. I was happy about our First Lady's recent trip to Africa and her emphasis on helping women. I think it's important to help women all over the world," she pauses to add. "People, especially women, need to know more about women in politics. Opportunities for participation are growing daily."

For her children, Ileana would like them to do whatever is comfortable with their lifestyles. "Getting a good education is important. One wants to be a teacher. The other leans toward becoming a congresswoman. Both indicate my impact upon them. These are their choices for the moment. But whatever they choose to do is all right with me," Ileana says happily.

Amanda and Patricia

Although Ileana's daughters are less than two years apart, their likes and dislikes sharply contrast. Amanda, age 11, is in the sixth grade; she really enjoys Girl Scouts, could live in blue jeans, and is comfortable in T-shirts and sneakers. Amanda also favors the color blue.

Patricia, or Patty as she is called, is in the fourth grade, prefers skirts and very pretty, feminine dresses, and has a penchant for the color purple. Even in food preferences, they differ. Both will order grilled cheese sandwiches, but Patty really goes all out for hamburgers. Her interest is playing baseball or soccer.

In out-of-school activities, both girls like ballet and have appeared in several recitals. They enjoyed reading *Hundred Penny Box* and the *Boxcar Children* series.

In terms of personality, some people think Patty is more like her mother— affable, loquacious, and amiable. Amanda, on the other hand, is more like her father, Dexter—reticent, contemplative, and reflective.

While the girls differ from each other in their tastes, interests, and personalities, they do agree on one vital thing. "We are each other's best friend, because we spend so much time together and are able to share so much as a result of our closeness in age," the girls say.

What they like best about their mom are her energy, spirit, and desire to participate in any event or project that either daughter is involved in. The girls note, for example, how their mom always takes them shopping or to the movies, reads with them, and even takes them to congressional events. Although Ileana is away quite often, she is always available to help them by phone, even when in Washington. "It's easy to talk with her and get her help in solving problems," the girls say.

What they hate most about Mom's being a congresswoman are her regular and sometimes long absences. However, they do feel that her time spent in Washington is made up by the fact that when she is home, she always makes time to spend with them and join in their activities. They feel, in some ways, that they are luckier than their classmates who, while having parents around all the time, have parents who are not involved like their mom.

Both girls agree that the most important value that they have learned from their parents, grandparents, stepbrother, and stepsister is that family is the key to everything.

REFERENCES

Azieri, M. "The Politics of Exiles: Trends and Dynamics of Political Change Among Cuban Americans." *Cuban Studies* 11: 55–73, 1985.

Bach, R. L., Bach, J., and Triplett, T. "The Flotilla 'Entrants': Latest and Most Controversial." *Cuban Studies* 11: 29–48, 1981.

Bertot, L. *Images of Cuban Literature*. Paper presented at the Distinguished Visiting Professors Series sponsored by Miami Dade Community College, Miami, 1990.

Boswell, T. D. "The Cuban American." in *Ethnicity in Contemporary America: A Geographical Appraisal*, ed. J. O. McKee. Dubuque, IA: Kendall/Hunt, 1985.

Fradd, S. "Cubans to Cuban Americans: Assimilation in the United States." *Migration Today* 11: 34–42, 1983.

Pedraza-Bailey, S. *Political and Economic Migrants in America: Cuban and Mexican*. Austin: University of Texas Press, 1985.

Perez, L. "Immigrant Economic Adjustment and Family Organization: The Cuban Success Story Reexamined." *International Migration Review* 20: 4–20, 1986.

Portes, A., and Bach, R. *Latin Journey*. Berkeley: University of California at Berkeley, 1985.

Portes, A., Clark, J. and Lopez, M. "Six Years Later, The Process of Incorporation of Cuban Exiles in the United States, 1973–1979." *Cuban Studies* 11: 1–20, 1982.

Richmond, M. L. *Immigrant Adaptation and Family Structure Among Cubans in Miami, Florida*. New York: Arno Press, 1980.

Sandoval, M. C. *Mariel and Cuban National Identity*. Miami, Florida: Editorial SIGI, 1985.

Wilson, K. L., and Portes, A. "Immigrant Cubans in Miami." *American Journal of Sociology* 86: 295–319, 1980.

10

Dominican Republic Americans

Most historians believe that Christopher Columbus discovered this island about the same time that he discovered Haiti, which occupies the same territory. The Dominican Republic is a Hispanic country forming a part of Latin America, despite its location in the Caribbean. It is, in fact, the modern version of Spain's first colony in the New World; its culture represents more than a 500-year continuum since the conquest in 1492. At the same time, the Dominican Republic is an African American country. Due to the early demise of the large Native American (Taino) population by disease and warfare, as early as 1502 African slaves were imported into the island as a labor force, largely for cultivation of sugarcane. Africans were later taken to other areas of the Caribbean, likewise for sugarcane cultivation. So, despite the European colonial rule and official language, African heritage is the cultural common denominator that unites the Caribbean as a culture area. In the Dominican Republic, African culture merged with Spanish culture to form the rich hybrid illustrated by the oral musical traditions of today.

The island of Hispaniola was a single colony, Santo Domingo, for over 200 years. But after Spain discovered greater riches in Mexico and Peru, Santo Domingo was left as a backwater. This neglect allowed France to get a foothold on the island. In 1697 Spain ceded to France the western third of Hispaniola, called St. Domingue (the French translation of "Santo Domingo"). Unlike Spain, France developed St. Domingue as the jewel in its crown. Development at that time was based on tropical agriculture using an African slave labor force. So, tens of thousands of Africans of various ethnic origins were brought in from West and Central Africa. In this way, the racial and ethnic composition of St. Domingue and the population density itself grew to be very different from those of Santo Domingo, which remained sparsely populated and quite European, racially and culturally. This marked racial and cultural difference between the two countries has remained despite certain influences that have remained in the country and that are represented in aspects of contemporary festivals.

The African slaves of St. Domingue liberated themselves from the French yoke in 1804, forming the second free republic in the Americas (the first being the United States) and adopting for their country the Taino Native American name of Haiti, meaning "mountainous land." Dominican independence from Spain in 1865 likewise led to the renaming of Santo Domingo as Dominican Republic.

Since then, the population growth in Haiti has exhausted the natural resources and caused a state of chronic poverty to develop. (The Dominican Republic is following the same course but lies behind Haiti because of its initially low population density.)

By 1996, Moss and other researchers at the Taub Urban Research Center say, foreign-born persons headed 35% of black households, 47% of Hispanic households, and 27% of white households. Together, immigrants and their children make up 56% of the city's population, the researchers found, and more than 46% of the city's school-age children live in households headed by an immigrant.

The study's findings showed that the dynamics at work in New York City are changing. "The traditional black-white racial image of cities doesn't work for New York anymore," says Mitchell L. Moss, director of Taub Urban Research Center (Halbfinger, 1997:4). "Ethnicity is much more important. And the political leadership has yet to understand the magnitude of the change and to incorporate these groups into the political system." For example, no Asian Americans have been elected to political office in New York City.

Demographers say it can take as much as a generation or two for the political system to catch up to population trends, since new immigrants must first wait to be naturalized and then are slow to register and to vote in politically effective numbers. Despite two decades of heavy immigration from the Dominican Republic, for example, only two Dominicans have been elected in New York.

That lag can clearly be seen in Manhattan, where 30% of residents now are Hispanic, up from 25.5% in 1990, and 18% are black. Despite the large numbers of Hispanic residents of the borough, blacks retain a large share of political power through their traditional power base, Harlem.

A new study says New York City has failed its Dominican immigrants, allowing nearly half to live in poverty, while many others struggle for a shrinking number of blue-collar jobs. "Unless the situation improves, we are going to have a very ugly picture in the future," says Ramona Hernandez, a City College sociologist who coauthored the study (Hernandez and Rivera-Batiz, 1997:61). The report calls for a major investment in education, including adult literacy and bilingual education programs to address the ills afflicting the city's fastest growing ethnic group.

Hernandez and Francisco Rivera-Batiz also called for improved job training, business incentives, and relief for overcrowded public schools, where a disproportionate number of children are Dominicans. New York is home to some 495,000 Dominicans, the second largest Hispanic group in the city after Puerto Ricans. Per capita household income among Dominicans between 1990 and 1996 plummeted more than 22% to $6,094, compared with a 4.6% increase in income for non-Hispanic whites, the report said. Just over 45% live below the federal poverty guidelines. Dominicans also have the highest unemployment rate—19%—among major racial and ethnic groups.

Recently, scholarly developments and data on the unique health and human services needs of Latino families and children provide a relevant base from which to shape appropriate, effective, and responsive services for Latinos (Furino, 1992; Furino and Munoz, 1991). In effect, what is abundantly clear is that health promotion involves improving the standard of living and is the most important area of public health policy in this decade. Terris (1990:43) succinctly states the core of the solution:

The concept of health promotion refers to the development of healthful living standards. These have a profound effect on positive health, which is not only a subjective state of well-being (including such elements as vitality, freedom from excess fatigue, and freedom from environmental discomforts such as excessive heat, cold, smog and noise), but also has a functional component, namely the ability of an individual to participate effectively in society; at work; at home; and in the community.

Improvements in the standard of living are crucial to Latino families and children, but equally important is access to primary and preventive services. All current data on use of public health and social service programs show that Latino families and children are not receiving needed services due to lack of awareness of services, lack of understanding or eligibility, and sociocultural and language barriers that impede access.

In addition, immigration status and the effects of differential eligibility within a single family are economically and psychologically damaging to Latinos. Immigration status is an obstacle to health care access and clearly an obstacle to maximizing contributions to society. For example, differential definitions of "resident" for purposes of eligibility for county-funded services lead to inequitable access to health and family support resources (Zambana, Dorrington, and Bautista, 1995).

CASE STUDIES

Nury's

Nury's is 52 years old. She divorced her husband after 25 years of marriage and now lives in Miami with her youngest daughter. Although Nury's works in the Housekeeping Department of the Marriott Hotel, she plans daily "quality time" for her 2-year-old granddaughter. Nury's continues a warm relationship with family and friends in New York City, where she lived for more than two decades. Her "good deeds" are not forgotten by that community. Whenever she feels lonely, Nury's retrieves her karma—the little bottle of Caribbean Sea and the package of sand from the beaches of the Dominican Republic. With closed eyes and holding her karma, Nury's retreats into her own world of love and family.

"I was born on August 16, 1944, in the Dominican Republic. My mother was Angélica Ramona Martinez, and my father's name was Gabino Nuñez Martinez. He was a well-known politician and radio personality in the valley town of Moca. My mother died during childbirth at the age of 25, giving birth to my younger sister, leaving me an orphan, since my father had abandoned her. I was 3 years old. After my mother's death, my father remarried, and my life became a series of challenges because of the many incidents of child neglect that I encountered." Nury's' story begins slowly. She was raised mostly by a grandmother who died about three years ago at the age of 107. Her grandmother and great-aunt worked as domestics. They were dark-skinned and identified with black Dominican Republicans who were descendants of a settlement of runaway slaves. This great-aunt lived to be 112 years old. "Because my skin was dark, my immediate family rejected me and my sister, even though she is light-skinned. For a time, we were hidden from the public eye in the cellar of a coffee plantation. But my grandmother rescued us and took us to my grandaunt, who raised us both." The memory causes Nury's to frown.

In high school, Nury's fell in love with a handsome young man. "At the time, I wanted to be a dancer," she says with a smile. "But a dancer was not an acceptable occupation for a young lady. So at the age of 17, I married." Nury's had a diary that she carried everywhere and in which she wrote down experiences and thoughts for the next generation. Her life was plagued with miscarriages. "My first pregnancy ended in a miscarriage, Angélica became my second, followed by another miscarriage, then a son and another daughter." Nury's husband was an economics and computer science teacher at a technical school in the Dominican Republic. Later on, he worked for IBM as a computer technician in the late 1960s. "During an islandwide economic slump, my husband lost his job because of the recession." To provide a family income, Nury's demonstrated her latent skills of entrepreneurship by baking cakes for daily use and special occasions, making and selling meat pies, creating flower arrangements, teaching neighborhood adolescents how to cook, and selling cosmetics. The family house was large and set back from a front lawn. Nury's grew coffee plants to remind her of her childhood and planted a garden of pretty, colorful flowers to provide inspiration and beauty in her life.

Nury's was an independent spirit and wanted independence and self-reliance for herself and her children. To accomplish this, she went to live in Puerto Rico with a friend who helped her find employment as a domestic. During her absence of more than a year, she wrote weekly to Angélica, reminding her of her responsibility as the oldest to keep the family unit together.

After 18 months, Nury's and her husband came to the United States to seek a better life for themselves and their children. They lived in Washington Heights in upper Manhattan. They shared an apartment with a cousin and found employment in a factory for Nury's.

Although Nury's had dreamed of living in New York City, she was unprepared for what she would encounter. "I couldn't sleep day or night. The piercing, shrill sirens from police cars, ambulances, and fire trucks were heard so frequently that I thought they were scheduled. Also, the noises coming from the apartment—loud music, arguments, babies crying, and kids playing in the street—continued round-the-clock," Nury's reports and then adds, "Two unpleasant things I'll always remember—my first ride on the subway and the feel of wet snowflakes brushing my cheeks." Nury's had some pleasant moments, too. "Hearing our music and eating our food and talking our language helped to ease the homesickness. I missed my children so much."

Angélica kept her mother informed of events back home via her own journal. She took pictures of the family and of a mango tree Nury's had planted years earlier. The tree was bearing fruit for the first time. Valentine's Day is also known as Friendship Day in the Dominican community. Angélica baked a large, heart-shaped cake and decorated it. She took pictures of it and sent them to Nury's with love.

Despite long hours in the factory, Nury's began work with local youth in after-school programs of remediation and recreation through the church. Nury's joined the International Ladies' Garment Workers' Union (ILGWU) and worked 20 years until an economic slump hit the manufacturing sector in the 1990s. Nury's' involvement in the community grew to include counseling of battered women, a relief society, a food pantry, and extensive church activities. Nury's' husband opened a superette with a deli in the Bronx. The area was considered risky, with a high crime rate; her husband was shot four times during his five years of operation, but he survived.

Meanwhile, Nury's continued to keep her journal, noting her and her children's experiences. She created what she called a "Life Line" on a piece of cloth that can be attached to any wall, featuring the children's pictures and birth dates and their accomplishments and family involvements, emerging from a picture of Nury's. This timetable of events kept all in touch with her. This chart symbolized their presence, even in their absence.

Because of her youngest daughter's almost tragic, premature birth, Nury's felt a closeness to this child. She was the first child to join her parents in New York City. Angélica and her brother followed shortly afterward. Before they arrived, the children's father returned from the Dominican Republic and met them at the airport.

Nury's' relationship with Angélica was very close. She supported Angélica in every way possible. Often Angélica's boldness in speech got her in trouble. Nury's would counsel Angélica and encourage her to be honest and outspoken. She felt Angélica had a mission to demonstrate leadership to her own people and family. Nury's continues to support Angélica's endeavors.

Nury's left New York City in 1995. She has continued her work with youth, the homeless, and immigrants like herself in Miami. In June 1997 Nury's completed her requirements for citizenship in the country that had brought her so much success. Nury's believes that Angélica was chosen by God to be the one who will help open doors for the family and other Dominicans by her activities. "Angélica will lead the way," she says in a voice filled with pride.

Angélica

"My family will never forget my birth or birthday," she begins. "I was born January 7, 1964, in the Dominican Republic, the day following 'Three Kings Day,' a big holiday for us. Because my mother had suffered miscarriages earlier, it was decided that this delivery would take place in a clinic. Labor pains decided to begin a month later. I was born with a particularly funny-shaped head—like a cone. It was said that a large amount of blood was concentrated in the front, which gave my head that conical appearance. All during my early years, children called me 'Pujita,' meaning cone head." Later, Nury's gave a more acceptable explanation. "It indicates that you will be smart, because it's on the best part of your body. My relatives called me a 'Black Angel,' a gift from God to the family celebrating Epiphany. My skin was darker than most of the members of my family, like my maternal grandmother."

Angélica began school at the age of 4. She learned to read and write as a preschooler. Her mother was her teacher. She attended parochial schools through elementary and her first year of high school in the Dominican Republic.

Angélica speaks lovingly about her mother. "She is sweet, caring, and beautiful. My mother never abused me physically or verbally. She always called me 'Viva,' meaning 'alive.' She encouraged me in every way. At the age of 7, I used to be interested in a talk show that was political. Neighbors thought I was too young for such exposure. But my mom encouraged me to be aware of civic and political issues. 'Never clip her wings,' she used to say when people criticized my interests. She's a free spirit and outspoken, but very sentimental. My mom often took me to political rallies. I never played with dolls like other young girls." Nury's stressed such values as family being the most important. Children's needs and stability came first, before individual needs. Sacrifice your life for your children was another value she supported. Individuality was important. Strive to excel. She veered away from tradition in some ways. One was that women should follow in the footsteps or shadow of their husband. She preached that women should be strong and have independent thoughts. Angélica and her mother did many things together. She says, "At 9, I learned how to make meat patties and bake cakes. Other girls would come to our house, and my mother would also teach them." She remembers when her mother went to Puerto Rico. A friendly nun became Angélica's surrogate mother. "I missed my mom very much. But as the eldest, my responsibility was to keep the family intact."

Angélica attended school in the morning from 9 to 12 and in the afternoon from 2 to 5 and then came home to care for the needs of her elderly great-grandmother and great-aunt. The young girl did some of the cooking and housecleaning before doing her homework. At 11, she was the head of a family of two young children and elderly relatives. On Parents Night, her great-grandmother and great-aunt would visit the school and talk with Angélica's teachers. "I was so proud of their support and interest," she beams. In the Dominican Republic, Valentine's Day or Friendship Day is celebrated. Angélica baked a cake and took a picture to send to her mother when her parents were in Puerto Rico and New York. "I took pictures of everyone and everything, even a mango tree that my mom had planted years earlier. When the tree bore its first fruit, I sent the picture to her." Although her mother telephoned every two weeks, at times it was too painful for her daughter to speak with her. She became too emotional just hearing her mom's voice.

Preadolescence was trying for Angélica in several ways. She had her first menstrual period at the early age of 8. At 11 years of age, she was surrogate mother to a younger sister and brother and was supervising a household of children and elderly adults. She recalls having menstrual cramps and her great-grandmother's preparing tea to ease the pains and insisting that Angélica rest for several hours. "They felt that I needed to be strong for the life that was before me—the one who would lead the family out of darkness into light." Angélica's speech is almost rapid-fire with her desire to ventilate her feelings. "When a girl menstruates, she is considered a woman, even when she is very young. When people called me a little girl, I would respond, 'Don't call me a girl. I am a woman.' I was very proud of the role assigned to me by my family." Meanwhile, Angélica's father sent money to pay for her lessons in English and writing. Angélica worked with a tutor and learned rapidly. She also received the best elementary education at home.

Another symbolic incident remains in her memory. "When we were very young, my mother used to take us to the beach. We loved to play in the sand and the sea. After my parents left to live in Puerto Rico, an aunt took us to the beach. I located the very spot my mother visited with us. In my childish mind, I tried to capture the sun and sand. I filled a small bottle with ocean water and an envelope with sand bathed by the bright sun. This and my mom's favorite candy were my gifts for her." Angélica recalls the 3½-hour plane ride to New York from the Dominican Republic as being endless. "When the taxi finally reached the apartment house, I ran up the five flights. I was breathless. My mom was still beautiful, and we hugged each other and cried with happiness."

Angélica was 13 years old when she arrived in New York City to become a "Dominican York," as Dominican Republicans are called in New York. She registered for classes at George Washington High School. At 13, she was already "socialized" and had overcome many challenges. "I discovered that some Dominican values were not for me. My mother always preached self-reliance, independence, and self-fulfillment. She encouraged me to be opinionated, but intelligently so. Be a leader and not a follower of a man." "Live your life to the fullest," Nury's had advised her.

The teenager was academically advanced when she arrived at the high school in New York and was eligible for the 11th grade. She was an avid reader and always spent at least two hours reading after school every day. At the Bachillerato (high school in the Dominican Republic), Angélica had been a teacher's aide, helping the nuns even after school. She enjoyed learning. Her mother became active in the PTA. Early on, when Angélica was 7 years old, she announced that she would be a "woman lawyer" and someday be president of the Dominican Republic. The adults warned her that women could never have such an important job. But her mother supported her by replying, "Perhaps when you grow up, impossible things will be possible."

Her first week at George Washington High School was traumatic. A chemistry teacher gave a pretest on the first day. Angélica scored 98—the highest mark in the class. A male student sitting next to her wanted to copy her paper. She refused. The young man scored 19. After class, he followed her to the subway and threatened to beat her up. A woman passing by rescued the frightened, crying Angélica and notified the police, who escorted her back to the school. Her father wanted to place her in a private school, but he couldn't afford to. The school arranged for a security guard to escort her home after school for the next two weeks. For one used to an all-girls parochial school, where girls are taught manners and values, George Washington presented quite a change. "Would you believe that this boy became my good friend and now holds a Ph.D.?" she ends, laughing.

Angélica was an honor student because of her achievement, cooperation with teachers, her doing extra assignments, and her eagerness to learn. "There were ten of us, recent immigrants. We stood out because we were concerned, capable and respected our teachers. Of course, we were called 'teachers' pets.' " Her father was a gypsy cab driver at the time and would drive around, circling the block each morning before dropping her off at the school. "For every grade above 90, my mom always gave me a small present, which was a medal. And she would bake a cake." Angélica's parents were very proud of her school achievement and gave a small party for her upon graduation. There were meat patties, soda, and, of course, cakes. After graduation, Angélica entered City College of New York in Manhattan.

The first day at City College, Angélica met a professor of Spanish, Elizabeth Starcěvíc. Later on, Marshall Berman became another special person in her life. Professor Berman taught political science. Both professors became her mentors. "I called them 'Mama Starcěvíc' and 'Papa Berman,' " she says. They were her family at college. As expected, Angélica's major was political science. She was also privileged to assist in teaching with Professor Starcěvíc. "It was the most fascinating and happiest time of my life, besides my early childhood. One semester, I took Classical Greek, Women's Literature, Filmmaking, Hispanic America, and 18th Century Political Thought. I had the fortune to have people around me, like my mom, who understood my thirst and who offered me fellowships and other opportunities that added to my growth." Angélica pauses for a deep breath. "I also met Professor Haywood Burns, a noted civil rights lawyer. He originated the National Lawyers Guild for African American Lawyers. At City College, he introduced the Urban Legal Studies Program. He became my mentor in social justice issues." She stops to remember. "He became Daddy Haywood to me." After graduation, Angélica entered Queens College Law School. Professor Burns continued to monitor Angélica's career and encourage her work in civil rights and positions she took in her writing. Unfortunately, this learned and important scholar was killed in a car accident in Africa in the spring of 1996. The news devastated Angélica. In memory of her mentor, she vowed to work harder.

After law school, Angélica's first job was with the National Labor Relations Board, Region 2, investigating unfair labor practices. "There was a lot of racism within the office politics. It was very stressful. So I left and went to work in the Comptroller's Office in the unit of public policy. This was a very bad move. My immediate supervisor sexually harassed me. He made my life miserable. I reported him and filed a complaint. But it was his word against mine, so nothing happened. He grabbed my breasts and called me a whore and worse. At the end, they found no probable cause." The incident created an interest in Victims' Services, where Angélica did volunteer counseling. "I related to the abused women's experiences and feelings," she says with sadness in her voice.

Angélica voices her opinion about racism and equal rights at every opportunity. She tried to get work in the Dominican Republic but was thought
to be too radical with her liberal American views. Angélica used to write a
column in a Dominican newspaper about women's rights, pro-choice, and
sexual abuse. She was labeled a lesbian and Dominican feminist and was
taunted by some of her own people. Even her friends kept her at a distance.

Angélica considered running for public office and became a Democratic
candidate for the New York City Council for the 7th District in the 1997
primaries. However, the Establishment didn't feel she had enough support
to be a viable candidate, although she was part of a coalition seeking change.
Demonstrating her love and support, Nury's came to New York to be with
Angélica and face the challenge. Up to the point of running, Angélica was
coanchor and producer of *Latino Journal* on WBAI-FM, 99.5, member of
Pacifica Radio. She is also a regular contributor to *El Nacional*, a Dominican
daily, and a political editor for *Mia Magazine*, a monthly magazine aimed at
young Latinos and Latinas born and raised in the United States. She served
for a brief time as assistant editor for *El Diario/La Prensa*, where she left a
strong legacy of community involvement and participation. Angélica participated as a community resident and as an advocate for woman's rights for
President Clinton's "Initiative, at the Table." She is a frequent contributor
to *El Diario* and *Amsterdam News* and a cofounder of a newspaper on the
Internet.

Angélica is known in the Latino and African American community as an
advocate of battered women, youth, immigrants, and the underprivileged. "I
strongly believe I am an advocate and a leader for all, without distinction as
to race, class, gender, and sexual orientation." Recently, someone mentioned
to her that most civil rights leaders are dead. She responded, "If that's the
price I have to pay, so be it. I refuse to become paralyzed by fear. I gain
strength through setbacks, disappointments, and challenge. I'm a realist. I
have opened the door just a crack. But to be truly successful, I need to see
that door swing open freely." Angélica is beaming. "The sky is the limit,"
she concludes. "Our ancestors have paved the way."

Laura and Sahory

Some mother–daughter relationships continue to shape, stretch, and grow
even beyond the shores of different countries. Laura and Sahory, Dominican
Republic Americans, describe their relationship as one that changes and
grows stronger as it gains new and different dimensions.

Most mothers experience a sense of loss when their only daughter is about
to leave home for college. It is especially disconcerting when the daughter
has been the mother's best friend and confidante since the death of husband
and father five years earlier. Laura, the mother, believes that Sahory is ready

for separation. Their relationship has been built with trust, love, and mutual support.

Laura was destined to raise Sahory in the manner of her own upbringing in the islands. Fortunately, Laura realized early that the environment of New York City, with neighborhood violence, crime, drugs, and constant change of pace, called for a firm, realistic, and consistently supportive relationship with her daughter. Laura learned how to protect, rather than smother. She's flexible rather than rigid and is informed about an adolescent's needs. Together they developed a lifestyle agreeable to both.

"We chose Boston University, because it offers a strong program in accounting. My Mom is one, and her love of the field influenced me," Sahory explains, displaying poise and speech quite mature for a 16-year-old. She plans, on arriving at Boston University, just to roam around noting places and people. "I like to get my bearings before I meet new people," she says firmly. "I'll miss my mom a lot, but we will keep diaries and exchange them weekly, and there's e-mail, videos, and the telephone. We're very close, a family of two. My parents were separated before my father's death, so it's just been the two of us for a long time," Sahory says wistfully. Each year this young woman visits the Dominican Republic several times and enjoys being with her grandparents, aunts, uncles, cousins, and other kin. This is a wonderful time full of beach parties, barbecues, singing, and dancing. Her relationship with her grandparents is good but restrained, since they don't speak English. But since Sahory speaks English most of the time in the United States, her visits allow her to be bilingual and practice Spanish.

Sahory thinks that the best thing about the relationship with her mother is Laura's flexibility. "She has kept our cultural values but tempered them to meet the needs of a teenager growing up in New York." This includes permitting Sahory to enjoy sleepover pajama parties, go out with groups of girls without a chaperone, and enjoy activities with mixed groups. Like Laura, Sahory does not wear makeup or sexy or tight clothes or adapt exotic hairstyles. Jeans and tee shirts are their usual attire.

Laura finds herself in a paradoxical position. From her mother, she learned that virginity demonstrated respect for one's body and God. Laura would like Sahory to follow this tradition. Yet in the United States, teenage pregnancy does not incur shame or disaffiliation. Sahory is aware of the situation and has successfully avoided all potentially negative encounters. Her faith in God and her church attendance, sustained interest in a variety of positive activities, and good judgment have helped keep her focused, she thinks.

Laura is confident that Sahory will cope with her new environment and maintain her faith in traditional values. "She has to grow up and face the reality of society," Laura says with a sound of hope in her voice.

Mother and daughter volunteer at the Dominican Women's Caucus Information, which is a community-based agency that provides counseling and referral services to young women preparing for college. The focus is to help them gain skills and necessary tools for future leadership roles. This exposure has also helped Sahory prepare for her future.

"Although the Dominican Republic means family and roots, traditions have to be adjusted to life in the United States, which offers many opportunities for continuing growth and also potential for disaster." Sahory shows a quizzical look, as she seeks a comforting hug from her mother.

Laura had hoped to adopt the pattern of parenting that was practiced by her mother. By doing so, it would bind her closer to her mother and to the Dominican Republic and sustain that tie into still another generation of Dominicans. But she found herself being pushed and pulled between the traditional and the American culture of New York. Laura and Sahory appear to have combined the best of both worlds into a satisfying lifestyle.

REFERENCES

Azieri, M. "The Politics of Exiles: Trends and Dynamics of Political Change among Cuban Americans." *Cuban Studies* 11: 55–73, 1985.

Bach, R. L., Bach, J., and Triplett, T. "The Flotilla 'Entrants': Latest and Most Controversial." *Cuban Studies* 11: 29–48, 1981.

Bertot, L. "Images of Cuban Literature." Paper presented at the Distinguished Visiting Professors Series sponsored by Miami Dade Community College, Miami, 1990.

Boswell, T. D. "The Cuban American." In *Ethnicity in Contemporary America: A Geographical Appraisal*, ed. J. O. McKee. Dubuque, IA: Kendall/Hunt, 1985.

Fradd, S. "Cubans to Cuban Americans: Assimilation in the United States." *Migration Today* 11: 34–42, 1983.

Furino, A. *Health Policy and the Hispanic*. Boulder, CO: Westview, 1992.

Furino, A., and Munoz, E. "Health Status Among Hispanics: Major Themes and New Priorities." *JAMA* 265: 255–257, 1991.

Halbfinger, D. "Immigrants Continue to Reshape the City." *New York Times* (December 1, 1997: 4).

Hernandez, R., and Rivera-Batiz, F. "Dominican New Yorkers; A Socioeconomic Profile." Dominican Studies Institute, City College of New York, 1997.

Moss, M. *Immigration Is Transforming New York City*. New York: Taub Research Institute New York University, 1997.

Pedraza-Bailey, S. *Political and Economic Migrants in America: Cuban and Mexican*. Austin: University of Texas Press, 1985.

Perez, L. "Immigrant Economic Adjustment and Family Organization: The Cuban Success Story Reexamined." *International Migration Review* 20: 4–20, 1986.

Portes, A., Clark, J., and Lopez, M. "Six Years Later, the Process of Incorporation of Cuban Exiles in the United States, 1973–1979." *Cuban Studies* 11: 1–20, 1982.

Richmond, M. L. *Immigrant Adaptation and Family Structure among Cubans in Miami, Florida*. New York: Arno Press, 1980.

Sandoval, M. C. *Mariel and Cuban National Identity*. Miami, FL: Editorial SIBI, 1985.

Terris, M. "Public Health Policy for the 1990s." *Annual Review of Public Health* 1: 39–51, 1990.

Wilson, K. L., and Portes, A. "Immigrant Cubans in Miami." *American Journal of Sociology* 86: 295–319, 1980.

Zambana, R., Dorrington, C., and Hayes-Bautista, D. "Family and Child Health." In *Understanding Latino Families*, ed. R. Zambana. Thousand Oaks, CA: Sage, 1995.

11

Mexican Americans

The arrival of Cortés in Mexico in 1519 not only marked the start of the conquest of Native Americans but also resulted in the extension of Spanish domination through the Southwest. Some 300 years later (1821), Mexico gained its independence from Spain. However, when compared to the United States, Mexico was not strong militarily, and the American public was very supportive of expansion ideas. The philosophy of Manifest Destiny supplied the needed justification for America's expansionist ambitions and desires (Acuña, 1988).

Texas soon became the focal point of America's expansion plans. In 1821 Mexico granted Stephen F. Austin permission to establish a settlement in Texas. By the 1830s there were 20,000 settlers in Texas. Soon the Texans viewed the Mexicans as "intruders." The Texas revolt (1835) concluded with the defeat of the Mexicans at the Battle of San Jacinto (1836). Texas became a republic (1836–1845) and gained admission into the Union in 1845. The first Mexican Americans became part of the United States through annexation, rather than through immigration; the Mexicans were here when what is now Texas, New Mexico, Arizona, and California was incorporated into the Union after the Treaty of Guadalupe Hidalgo was signed, ending the war between Mexico and the United States. The treaty was ratified in the spring of 1848 and gave the United States the four previously mentioned states for $15 million. Mexico also recognized Texas as part of the United States. In addition, the citizens of Mexico living in the American Southwest were granted all of the rights of American citizenship (Moquin and Van

Doren, 1971). The result was granting of citizenship to 75,000 Mexicans in 1860. Quite distinct social patterns existed, however, among them.

Cattle ranching dominated the economy in Texas throughout the 19th century and, as land-ownership rather than cattle became the determining factor, the Mexicans became a depressed class, working the land and running cattle for the Anglos. An exception existed along the Rio Grande, where middle-class Mexican communities prospered in towns like Brownsville and Laredo. During the last decades of the century, cotton farming invaded the area, creating demand for cheap labor, and new Mexican immigrants joined the old Mexican settlers to fill the need. The suppression of Mexicans became complete, and stereotypes of Mexicans as ignorant, shiftless people solidified.

The situation in New Mexico was very different. There, where there were some 60,000 Mexican settlers by 1850, there were relatively few Anglos, and Spanish-speaking ranchers both dominated the economy and controlled the legislature. Intermarriage between Mexican and Anglo families occurred frequently, and the two groups lived in relative harmony. Gradually, depletion of the lands through overgrazing, the invasion of the railroads, and the diversion of lands into mining shifted the balance of power toward the Anglos, and much of the Mexican minority concentrated in towns, where they worked as laborers.

The few Spanish-speaking residents of what is now Arizona lived mostly in Tucson during the middle of the 19th century, where they clustered for protection against the Apache Indians. Soon, the railroads brought an Anglo invasion, and the land was opened for mining. Anglos owned and controlled the mines and encouraged immigration of Mexicans to work them. Discrimination, physical brutality, and cruelty became rampant.

Geographical isolation was instrumental in structuring the situation in California, where wealthy and powerful Mexican *rancheros* dominated the southern and central part of the state. The discovery of gold in the central region changed the situation drastically, bringing in hordes of Anglo miners and a massive migration of Mexicans. The elite and genteel culture of the native Castilians clashed with the crude and aggressive ways of the miners. The Anglo miners fought the Mexicans and made no distinctions in their hatred between lower-class Mexican miners and wealthy and cultured landowners. As mining withered and agriculture developed, Anglos simply settled on, and appropriated, large portions of the old Mexican land grants (Goode, 1971).

Statistics are available to assess legal immigration only. Although accurate estimates are not possible, some authorities believe that, in some years at least, three times as many Mexicans have entered the United States illegally as legally. From the early 20th century, agriculture and mining brought thousands; World War I brought the much-needed cheap labor, increasing both legal and illegal migrants. Even a special immigration regulation admitting "temporary" workers instituted in 1917 resulted in thousands staying on permanently. World War II drained manpower into the armed forces, causing the United States to change policies on immigration. Farm owners encouraged the illegal immigration of "wetbacks." Although their status was illegal, it was not illegal to hire them. The Immigration Service continued to expel illegal aliens in large numbers and promptly readmit them as *braceros*, Mexican laborers. Organized labor opposed the policy, which generated distrust and hatred of the authorities in Mexican American communities. The Immigration Act of 1965 limited the number of immigrants from the whole Western Hemisphere to 120,000, bringing some regularity in policies. However, the illegal immigrant remained a substantial problem in 1998.

In many cities, Mexican Americans live in segregated neighborhoods called *barrios*. These are comparable to other ethnic settlements of the Northeast and Midwest except that, in this case, the Mexicans were the original settlers, and the Anglos moved in around them. In other cities, Mexican Americans are not segregated and literally dominate the city. Laredo, Texas, may be the largest such city, but the pattern exists in many small towns in southern Texas and northern New Mexico. Despite rapid migration to the cities, many Mexican Americans still reside in rural areas. No other minority group has such highly varied living conditions (Goode, 1971).

First-, second-, and third-generation Mexican American experience may be compared to that of European immigrants. Most of the first generation, of course, have been unskilled laborers of low economic status. Incomes rise among the second generation but, probably as a result of discrimination, do not show significant increase again among the third generation. Third- and fourth-generation Mexican Americans generally are better educated, less likely to work at manual occupations, and more likely to intermarry with Anglos (Hayes-Bautista et al., 1992).

The origins of the Mexican American family can be traced to the Spanish conquest, when the Spanish infused their political system, their religion, and their military ambitions into Aztec society. From the beginning, the Catholic missionaries set out not only to convert the "heathens" but also to ensure that they would marry in the church and follow all Catholic religious teachings (Gonzales, 1964).

Following Mexico's independence from Spain, the Mexican government relieved the Catholic Church of much of its secular power, guaranteed freedom of religion, and allowed for divorce. Nonetheless, the family maintained many of the strong traditions acquired during the Spanish period.

As Mexican families settled in the larger cities of the Southwest, they were based on the extended family unit. This allowed the larger family grouping to share in child care and household expenses. This also meant that the adults could work longer hours and even remain away from home when needed, since other relatives were always available to tend to the children.

By the 1970s, Mexican Americans were predominantly urban. The urban environment not only encouraged the predominance of the nuclear family but also promoted smaller families as a necessity. Therefore, while Mexican American families have remained larger than the general population, and their fertility rate is still above average, their overall family size is in decline.

The role that women play in the family changed in the 1980s and 1990s. As with many other women, the Mexican American woman, or *chicana*, has been directly affected by the women's movement and the Civil Rights movement. The result is that today the Mexican American woman is no longer the subservient, submissive female of the mythical past (Baca-Zinn, 1975). While it is true that Mexican women have always played a central role in the family, today they have carried their role beyond the family. Today, *chicanas* are independent, are active in the labor force, and play a more significant role in the family. In part, the decline in fertility rates can be attributed to the ambitions of upwardly mobile women in the Mexican American family today (Gonzales, 1990).

CASE STUDIES

Gloria

There is tension in the air. Everyone is running around, making plans for a potential strike of thousands of county workers. Meetings of small and large groups are occurring simultaneously. As the clock ticks, the cliff-hanging situation grows foreboding. All appointments are canceled as preparations begin for around-the-clock negotiations. Piles of sandwiches, gallons of coffee, and baskets of fruit are on standby. The media lounge in the hallways with cameras, microphones, and lights. Suddenly, the doors swing open, and supervisors with smiling faces pour out of the immense meeting hall to loud cheers. The staff, laden with folders, memos, pads, contracts, and briefcases, rush for the elevators. The crisis has been averted, at least for one day.

Gloria Molina, supervisor of the First District of the Los Angeles County Board of Supervisors, is one of this group. In her office, she now relaxes for a moment behind a large oak desk in an immense, attractively decorated office. The tension has been replaced with a friendly smile. She begins, "I was born and raised in a suburb of Los Angeles. My parents were from Mexico, so I'm first-generation Mexican American. I'm the oldest of ten children. My parents, Leonardo and Concepcion, raised all of their children and are still living in Pico Rivera and enjoying good health. They have one grandchild. All the children are scattered around now."

The supervisor was raised in Montebello, the scene of her early schooling. When Gloria was in the fifth grade, her parents bought a home in another suburb, also in Los Angeles. They were the first Spanish-speaking family in the community, which is now about 90% populated by Hispanics.

As the eldest child, Gloria didn't need to be reminded of her responsibilities. First, her behavior would set an example. Second, Gloria had child-care and household tasks, which were done daily. "There was always a new baby in the house, and I became the second mom," she recalls.

Gloria belonged to several organizations and clubs when in high school. Social studies and current events were her special interests, but she didn't run for office or seek leadership roles. "I was shy and rather intimidated by those students who did. I was in awe of their bravado. It was a very exciting time. A lot was happening with Kennedy in the White House. Knowing and understanding United States history while observing and studying contemporary issues were exciting to me," she remembers. A favorite teacher at El Rancho High School was Mr. Walker, who taught a civics course in her sophomore year. He made the context challenging, and Gloria looked forward to his classes.

However, Gloria's role model was not found in school but in her family and elsewhere. Both of her grandmothers were strong women. "I used to read everything I found, like biographies of women leaders in history and in the 20th century. Their stories intrigued me. Later, contact with strong women influenced me, too."

As a teenager, Gloria didn't have too much time for socializing. Homework and responsibilities at home occupied her out-of-school hours. But she had friends, and, when possible, Gloria had fun with other adolescents. Her parents didn't permit dating. She remembers getting along with everyone in her small group of good friends.

Gloria's first "date" was at the senior prom at age 16. "It wasn't really a date, because his mother drove us and accompanied us the whole evening. My real first date occurred when I was 18," Gloria remembers with a chuckle.

Her first awareness of injustice to minorities came as a freshman at the Community College of East Los Angeles College. At the time, Cesar Chávez, who was becoming nationally known, was active and challenging the system for fair treatment and equal pay for farmworkers, especially the lettuce pickers. Before this period, Latinos were always aware of injustice and racial bias but appeared passive and not equipped to change the status quo. Even though people knew of the riots in Watts, there was still laxity on their part to get involved. "But," says Gloria, "Chávez helped to motivate people to action. I was 18 years old at that time. I was still intimidated but admired those who were speaking out against injustice. We met in small groups for discussions. In 1967–1968 there were school walkouts in Los Angeles and later the Chicano Moratorium, which motivated me to challenge the system and get involved to bring some change." According to Gloria, the situation was interesting because there were few women activists or advocates. The men had always looked at female groups as women who supported their efforts. But some men weren't willing to accept the new role of women. They wanted to continue viewing women as supporting men's advocacy pursuits. "We were expected to agree with the process but sit silently and watch them," Gloria remembers.

Community activity started early for Gloria. She joined the founding feminist groups like Chicano Feminists, seen by the community as a radical group. "We began working on reapportionment, which meant dividing seats on county councils and boards. At the time, I was working for an elected official. We feminists felt a woman was entitled to be elected to a seat also. Unfortunately, our choice was a congressional seat, but the men defeated our efforts by not supporting us, instead backing a stronger male candidate."

Gloria never envisioned herself as a candidate. "I thought of myself as someone's technical assistant to a fund-raiser. But in 1981, an assemblyman decided not to run. My friends thought I should campaign for the office. I agreed. It was a hard battle, because no Latina had ever been elected, although Anglo and black women had met with success." Many thought Gloria's candidacy was frivolous, not serious. Fund-raising was a tough issue. But the local group of feminists went statewide seeking financial and campaign support. In these meetings, the women agreed that it was essential that they run informed, with dignity and strong effort. Even if they were unsuccessful, their effort to challenge the status quo would be important. With this united effort, Gloria was elected in 1982 to the office of State Assembly for the 56th District.

Prior to being elected to public office, Gloria served in the Carter White House as deputy for presidential personnel. After leaving the White House, she served in San Francisco as deputy director for the Department of Health and Human Services.

With a reputation for candor and independence, Gloria is best known for her strong, issue-oriented style and her commitment to community empowerment. Noted for tenacious, effective leadership in the fight against putting a prison in East Los Angeles, Gloria has a legislative history of standing up for the average citizen against almost insurmountable odds.

In the State Assembly, she introduced bills aimed at protecting consumers from unfair bank charges, insurance redlining, and utility company rip-offs, as well as legislation that protected tuition-free community colleges and promoted the safety of children.

In addition, while on the City Council Gloria led the passage of sewage lifeline rates for senior citizens, introduced new laws to put "teeth" into the City's Historic Building Preservation Policy, and cast the critical swing vote to prevent oil drilling in the Pacific Palisades.

Active in local as well as national issues, Gloria serves on the boards of several prominent organizations, including the Metropolitan Transportation

Authority, the Robert F. Kennedy Memorial Board, the National Association of Latino Elected and Appointed Officials (NALEO), the Mexican-American Legal Defense and Educational Fund (MALDEF), the Southwest Voter Registration and Education Project, and the National Hispanic Leadership Agenda. Supervisor Molina was appointed by President Clinton to the Advisory Commission on Intergovernmental Affairs and appointed by the U.S. trade representative to the Intergovernmental Policy Advisory Committee.

In 1987 she was elected to the Los Angeles City Council, where she served as the councilwoman of the First District until 1991. In February 1991 she was elected to the Los Angeles County Board of Supervisors, representing the First Supervisorial District. Gloria is the first Latina to be elected to the California state legislature, the Los Angeles City Council, and the Los Angeles County Board of Supervisors.

Gloria was married in 1987 to Ron Martinez, a businessman. "At the time, I was in the legislature and preparing to run for a local council seat. It was going to be a tough fight. So we got married right in the middle of the campaign. The wedding was to be a small, intimate affair, but, with all of our relatives, it turned out to be a huge affair—but very nice," she reminisces.

Some traditions, like large families and the homebound wife, belong to a different era, according to the Martinez-Molina family. Ron realizes now that most women work, have careers, and limit their families. He is proud of Gloria's accomplishments and very supportive of her work. Gloria is also sensitive to, and aware of, traditions. She makes a special effort to have "private family time," to share day-to-day happenings when necessary, and to plan occasions when she is just a wife and mother, permitting Ron to be the head of the family.

In parenting, Ron is the caretaker when Gloria is not available. They both share in disciplining Valentina. Making decisions is a collaborative process with input from both. When Valentina was an infant, Gloria brought her to the office daily. "I was breast-feeding, so it made sense. Later when I worked at City Hall, there was a child-care facility, and she spent time there. Once Valentina began school, Ron provided her transportation, picking her up after school and taking her to all kinds of activities. His job provides that kind of flexibility."

Gloria remembers the happiness of her childhood. She duplicates everything her family did on holidays like Christmas and Easter and Mexican holidays. "I may make tamales, beans and rice, enchiladas with mole sauce, corn tortillas, chile en nagados, mole poblano con pollo, crepes camarones, roast pork, and white almond flan. A big holiday is the Cinco de Mayo, which celebrates the 1862 defeat of French forces in Pueblo by a ragtag army of defenders. We also celebrate Mexican Independence Day in September. Besides feasting, there are parades, festivals, carnivals, and mariachi bands." Gloria is teaching her daughter how to cook. Valentina is not very enthusiastic. She is learning that Mexican food is very fattening. "She carefully counts the calories," Gloria says with a soft laugh.

As to Mexican values, Gloria thinks that, for the most part, Mexican and other cultures have similar values when we are discussing families. "There are a lot of contemporary things we do that are not as traditional as in earlier days. But we attempt to duplicate as nearly as possible. For example, Valentina knows that it is important for her to be bilingual. We attempted to teach her the language but weren't successful." This summer, Valentina will have a tutor in Spanish. Her parents also expose their daughter to cultural activities to supplement the history she learns in school, so that Valentina knows how she fits into the history of Mexico.

On Saturdays especially, mother and daughter try cooking and shopping together, quilting and sewing, or go to tennis and ballet lessons. "Afterward, we go to lunch. These times together are very special, and we prize them." Valentina understands that Gloria's job is very important to her constituents and requires a lot of time.

Valentina would love to have a brother or sister. Both parents have discussed enlarging the family, but Ron feels that with their job demands, they cannot afford the added responsibility. Gloria has even suggested adoption, but the question of more children remains unsolved. "It seems so unnatural, because I came from a large family. My main concern is that Valentina doesn't feel that all of her blessings of a beautiful room, television, VCR, and plenty of pretty clothes are the norm and this is her baseline for future life." Gloria's frown reflects her worry. The Molinas have a close friend whose only daughter is about the same age as Valentina. "Lacking siblings, hopefully both children will be lifelong friends," Gloria adds.

Gloria discusses contemporary social problems with her daughter. "I try to impress upon her the need to be responsible for her thoughts and acts. She's seen homeless people with substance abuse problems. She knows about unfortunate poor families with hungry children. Valentina has her own checking account with mine (a joint account), pays bills, and is responsible for balancing the account. If she doesn't follow basic rules, her allowance is withheld, or television is denied. It is very hard to do this to a beautiful, happy child, but it is a must if we want her to develop into a responsible, capable adult." Both parents agree and share discipline, although it's difficult.

Incidents of racial bias occur regularly for Gloria. She recently was shown disrespect by an attendant on an airplane. When lobbying in Washington, it is only when someone takes note of her supervisory position that she is recognized. Her title and position give her credibility, but to many people, she's probably the cleaning lady. Gloria says this without rancor or disgust. She doesn't waste time fighting back on a personal level, because she knows change comes slowly. But she fights racism on a positive level, through civil rights lawsuits and by challenging people and organizations. "These issues will continue. Racism and gender bias will not go away. I try to prepare

Valentina for future confrontations, so that she can challenge them effectively and not just get angry. I doubt if things will change even in her lifetime," she concludes in a matter-of-fact tone.

Gloria grew up being a role model for her younger siblings. Her parents continually reminded her of the responsibility for setting an example. She remembers, "If I did misbehave, I was always punished more seriously than my siblings." After winning her first election, she was reminded that not only was she expected to succeed personally, but her success would influence a whole community of women who might be motivated to challenge the system. She was a role model for them. "I respect their faith in me and do the best that I can."

Gloria sees a real future for Latina women. More and more are coming forth to make changes, not only in politics but in other areas at every level. This motivates her to work even harder in helping them to open up more doors.

She has been listed by *Working Woman* magazine as "one of the ten women of power to watch in the 90's" and was identified as a member of a "Galaxy of Rising Stars" by *Time* magazine. *Hispanic Business* magazine has also recognized her as one of the most influential Hispanics in the nation.

"Success for me is what I'm doing every day in fulfilling my commitment. I feel good about the work I do and the role I play. It's a wonderful feeling knowing that you are doing well at what you're supposed to do." Gloria's future will perhaps be a leadership role in parent education. "I'm very satisfied with my life at present. But someday, I would like to direct an organization that empowers parents," she concludes with a broad smile.

Valentina

She is 10 years old but appears quite mature for her age. Her friendly smile, bright, dark eyes, and neatly trimmed, thick black hair add to the poise of this pretty young girl. Valentina, Gloria's daughter, is open and communicates easily with strangers. "I am in the fifth grade and like school a lot. Right now, I'm learning mathematics, how to read faster, English, and logic," Valentina says with a bright smile.

At home, she plays with her favorite doll, Libertad (which means "liberty" in Spanish). The doll has several outfits, which Valentina changes frequently; Libertad is a beauty in each one of them, Valentina believes. The doll also has long, wavy hair, which Valentina combs and arranges. Valentina's favorite television show is a weekly sitcom, *Friends*. "I also enjoyed Pocahontas and Cinderella on tapes," she adds.

About her mom's job, Valentina knows that it is a very important position. She is not too clear on the demands of the position or its description, but she is sure of one thing—"She is very helpful to a lot of people in the county."

Valentina hasn't really been involved in campaigning, although that might come later. She understands that her mom's job is a lot of hard work, but it's very important work. She enjoys the time she spends with her mom quilting, watching television, and cooking. She enjoyed reading "The Giver" and "Walk Two Moons." Just quietly talking to each other is also pleasurable.

She has good things to say about her dad, too. "My dad takes care of me. He takes me to school, picks me up, and takes me to my lessons. He's fun to be with." Valentina isn't quite ready to make a career decision. At the moment, it could be a teacher, nurse, or ballet dancer. But one thing she's sure of: "I would not like a job like mom's. It's too stressful!"

Being the only child can be lonely and boring. Valentina would love to have a sister. "I would name her Elizabeth, and we would talk and play together."

The nicest thing about her mom is that she's dependable. "She's always there to help me," Valentina says firmly. "She's a good mom." What does Valentina do to make her mother happy? "I cook dinner, clean the house, and do what she asks me to do!" she states with confidence.

REFERENCES

Acuña, R. *Occupied America: A History of Chicanos.* 3d ed. New York: Harper and Row, 1988.

Baca-Zinn, M. "Political Familism: Toward Sex Role Equality in Chicano Families in Chicago." *Aztlan* 6: 13–26, 1975.

Gonzales, J., Jr. *Racial and Ethnic Groups in America.* Dubuque, IA: Kendall/Hunt, 1990.

Gonzales, J., Jr. "The Origin of the Chicano Family in Mexico and the American Southwest." *The International Journal of Sociology of the Family* 16: 181–196, 1964.

Goode, W., Jr. *Contemporary American Families.* Chicago: Quadrangle Books, 1971.

Hayes-Bautista, D., Hurado, A., Valdez, R., and Hernandez, A.C.R. "No Longer a Minority: Latinos and Social Policy in Los Angeles, California." Chicano Research Center, University of California, Los Angeles, 1992.

Moquin, W., and Van Doren, C. *A Documentary History of the Mexican Americans.* New York: Bantam Books, 1971.

PERSONAL REFLECTIONS
by Gloria Holguín-Cuádraz

MEXICAN ETHNICITY

It has been 20 years since I left the comforts, the aromas, and the plentitude of home. In being asked to write about how I've returned home and the nature of my visits home, the phrase that immediately comes to mind is: change happens. Leaving my close-knit, "traditional," Mexican American family at the age of 20 to attend an undergraduate institution hundreds of miles from home represented a milestone for my siblings and parents—and a turning point for me. As my mother said to me on one occasion, "Had I known that pursuing your education meant you wouldn't come home again, I would have never let you go." As I've said to her, "In being able to pursue my passion for books and education, I have returned home in more ways than I ever could have, had I remained home to fulfill anyone's expectations but my own."

I would be the last person to say it has been easy. Going from the familiarity and comforts of home and the largely Mexican American *barrio* of my hometown to the predominantly Anglo, middle-class, privileged environments of two University of California campuses has been challenging, to say the least. In my courses today, when I address the various tenets of assimilation theory to my students, I make it a point to talk about how assimilation is not a linear process. It is not an apolitical process, nor is it noncontentious. The process of cultural fusion and integration is constantly in flux. Yet, change does not require losing or replacing one aspect of ourselves with another. Instead, it means being able to stretch our boundaries of knowledge and engage in the *claiming and reconstruction of ourselves and our communities*.

Today, as an assistant professor of American studies, to return home means packing my bags, books, papers to review, laptop computer, and a carload of gifts to visit my 76-year-old mother (who lives alone) and my seven sisters and one brother, all of whom have families and children and some even grandchildren of their own. Besides driving a four-hour stretch of desert, usually in a postsemester state of exhaustion, in the company of my dog, Tito, visiting home for me means having the opportunity to spiritually replenish. Not in the sense of having *rest*; on the contrary, my visits home have become very physically demanding, in terms of the sheer hours of work we put into making the tamales for our Christmas Eve celebration, for example, or the household and labor-intensive yard duties in need of attention. Rather, visiting home means having the moments to "just be," to sit around the table and listen to the chatter, slamming doors, children's cries, and children's laughter and smell a tortilla on the *comal* (grill) and *cumino* (spice) permeating the air. It means being surrounded by loved ones who aren't so concerned about whether or not I met my last deadline, as much as they are about "how I am"—about my well-being. That, in and of itself, is replenishing.

The ability to return home successfully in a manner *that honors who I am* has taken years to achieve. In the initial years following my departure from home, I recall returning home and feeling, while I was undergoing enormous changes (in identity, knowledge base, political consciousness about who I was as a Chicana, a woman, and the significance of class in the formation of my life and that of the Chicana/o community and other racial/ethnic communities), that life back home remained "still." Only in time did I come to appreciate that the lives of family members did not stand still. They were, in fact, building families and homes and doing all those things to establish and nurture their sense of community. In the meantime, as I advanced in my own graduate career, I experienced a disruption to my rootedness. I had lost the grounding of the relationships that had fortified me in the past and had chosen to rely on the academic community for support. Unfortunately, as a community it was limited in what it could actually provide.

As a result of the dislocation I experienced, I went through a process of reconciliation, asking myself, How can I reconcile my past and present in such a way that I honor all of what I am, all of my facets, interests, and multiple communities? How can I honor my race, my gender, my sexuality, and my changes in class location as I pursue relationships in my personal life and with my family of origin? Posing these questions to myself, while learning to make decisions that honored my ever-shifting, intersecting identities, allowed me the opportunity to "return home" and reclaim relationships—as I simultaneously carved new ones.

Today, by virtue of the changes that I've undergone in my own trajectory, I recognize that I, too, affect and shape the lives and thoughts of my family members, whether I am close or far away. As I strive to honor how my *past is in my present*, I embrace and choose to use this awareness to create new contexts for rituals and for building bonds between myself and *familia*.

This past holiday season, I returned to four generations of *familia* to celebrate and honor the Christmas season. Understanding I had little time to spend with the youngest members of the family, I decided to pursue the project of baking gingerbread houses with my nieces and great-nieces.

I baked one gingerbread house with my youngest sister's daughter, Sarina. Although she is barely 3½, but with a vocabulary and sentence enunciation of an 8-year-old, we proceeded to make the dough and to ice the tentatively built house. Imagine her joy as she placed the first red, sugary gumdrop on the roof. She was exuberant, and her brown eyes sparkled as she jumped with excitement at decorating her very first gingerbread house! Before we knew it, three hours had passed, but the essential goal had been achieved. We had shared in a *memory-making moment*, a moment that in the years to come had the possibility of becoming yet another family tradition. A new tradition that, hopefully, will be carried on with future generations.

It is memory-making moments that sustain me today.

12

Puerto Rican Americans

Puerto Rico is an island at the eastern end of the Caribbean Sea, 100 miles in length from east to west and 35 miles from north to south. It was discovered by Columbus during his second voyage, on November 19, 1493. In 1508 Ponce de Leon began the establishment of the Spanish colony on the island. He called it the Island of San Juan Bautista and gave the name Puerto Rico to the excellent harbor on the northern coast; by a strange transfer, the names became reversed. The island was strategically located at the eastern end of the Spanish colonial empire and was heavily fortified as a military outpost. For nearly 400 years, until 1898, it was to remain a Spanish colony.

When the Spanish discovered Puerto Rico, the island was inhabited by indigenous people called Tainos, who died out after the Spanish conquest. Most of them were killed or fell prey to European diseases brought by the Spanish colonists. Those few remaining were absorbed into the conquering population. Recent research on the Tainos in Puerto Rico has uncovered significant information about their society and culture. Beginning in 1511, black slaves were brought from Africa to replace the Tainos as laborers, and slavery remained a part of the economy until it was abolished in 1873.

The predominant features of Puerto Rico's people and culture remain those of the Spanish colonizers. Little of the Taino culture remains, although their physical features can still be seen on some Puerto Rican faces. The influence of blacks from Africa has been more substantial. Intermarriage and sexual union have resulted in a varied racial population ranging from completely Caucasoid to completely Negroid, with many variations in between. The language is Spanish; the common religion is Roman Catholicism; and social organization and culture have been Spanish colonial.

The island became a possession of the United States as a result of the Spanish-American War. It was formally ceded by the Treaty of Paris, December 10, 1898. After two years of military occupation, the Foraker Act established the first civil government in Puerto Rico under U.S. sovereignty in 1900. Under this act, the effective government of the island was vested in the president of the United States, who appointed a governor and an executive council, which acted as an upper house. This was a disappointment to the Puerto Rican people, who had expected a larger measure of autonomy from the nation that had boasted that it had come to bring the blessings of liberal institutions to a former Spanish colony.

Following the military conquest of Puerto Rico, the "American way" became the law of the land. The American governor of the island was "advised" by a two-chamber legislative body. All decisions of the legislature required the approval of the U.S. governor, and any action of these representatives could be nullified by the U.S. Congress. Clearly, Puerto Rico was a U.S. colony.

From the onset, English became the official language of government and commerce. With the idea that the children of the elite families of the island must be educated to accept the American way and aspire to American values, the U.S. government established the University of Puerto Rico by legislative act in March 1903. In response to a labor shortage in the United States, Puerto Ricans were granted American citizenship under the provisions of the Jones Act (1917). But this also made all Puerto Rican men eligible for the wartime draft.

Following years of local political turmoil and political conflict with the United States, Puerto Rico elected its first governor, Luis Muñoz Marin (1948–1964), and became a commonwealth in 1948. This new status, known as "Estado Libre Asociado" (associated free state), meant that while Puerto Ricans are U.S. citizens and can elect their own governor, they cannot vote in presidential elections and do not have a representative in Congress. They are subject to all federal laws, and their judicial system derives from the U.S. system of laws. Puerto Ricans pay local taxes but do not pay federal income taxes. Of course, all Puerto Ricans born on the mainland enjoy all of the rights and duties of citizenship of all U.S. citizens.

Puerto Rican migration can be viewed as having occurred in three distinct stages (Stevens-Arroyo and Diaz-Ramirez, 1982).

1. The pioneer migration (1900–1945) consisted primarily of landless peasants and unskilled laborers.

2. The great migration (1946–1964) was primarily based in New York City and concentrated in blue-collar jobs.

3. The revolving door migration (1965–present) is based on the movement of families between Puerto Rico and the mainland.

The first Puerto Rican migrants were drawn to the mainland by their search for new opportunities. While most were unskilled and poorly educated, they did find employment in the labor-intensive industrial sectors of New York City. Others found work as farm laborers and followed the crops from the heartland of New Jersey to the humid orchards of southern Florida (Maldonado-Denis, 1980).

The second flow of Puerto Ricans to the mainland exceeded all previous records following World War II. Between 1946 and 1964, a total of 615,000 migrants arrived on the mainland, for an annual average flow of 34,000. The high point in the migration was reached in 1953, when 74,600 arrived.

The revolving door migration was not affected by immigration reforms, since Puerto Ricans are U.S. citizens. However, it did have a dramatic influence on public opinion and the political climate of the day, as these reforms engendered a more liberal attitude toward all newcomers. Furthermore, this liberal political atmosphere allowed for the passage of the various civil rights acts during the 1960s, which fostered a renewed interest in the plight of the poor, in the frustration of the unemployed, and in the health and welfare of the needy (Gonzales, 1990).

This period of migration is often referred to as the "revolving door migration" because of the continuous movement of Puerto Ricans between the island and the mainland. For example, between 1965 and 1974, a total of 109,800 migrated to the mainland, for an annual average of almost 22,000. But during the same period, a total of 92,600 returned to Puerto Rico, for an annual average of 18,500. Therefore, the overall annual net increase in arrivals was 3,500 (*U.S. Civil Rights*, 1976).

The primary reason for the revolving door phenomenon was the evolution of the "transnational family." This simply means that the Puerto Rican community is divided between family members who now live permanently on the mainland and others who live permanently in Puerto Rico. Consequently, parents, children, and extended family members are constantly making trips to the island and then back to the mainland. This has resulted in the transnational family, as retired parents return to the homeland and younger Puerto Ricans set firm roots on the mainland (Gonzales, 1990).

Like the Mexican American family, the Puerto Rican family and culture were most profoundly affected by the Spanish conquest. Historically, five factors have contributed to the form and structure of the Puerto Rican family today:

1. The influence of the Tainos Indians
2. The infusion of the Spanish culture

3. The indoctrination to Catholicism
4. The impact of slave culture and society
5. The evolution of a "mestizo" Puerto Rican culture

To this day, little is known of family life among the Tainos, but it is known that they were a peaceful group of settlers who arrived in Borinquen (Puerto Rico) in 1270 from Venezuela.

With the arrival of the Spanish, Borinquen society was devastated, primarily as a result of disease and forced labor. As in Mexico, the Spanish priests destroyed all symbols of the indigenous religion and replaced their beliefs with Catholicism. They also organized the natives into productive villages, paired couples and insisted on early marriages, required baptism, and demanded unequivocal allegiance to the "crown."

The Spanish introduced slaves into Puerto Rico in the 1520s in an effort to replace the rapidly dwindling Indian population. Within the first generation, the Spanish sexually exploited Indian and slave women, which resulted in a very diverse racial mixture on the island. To this day, family members draw clear distinctions between their racial features and their social standing in the community. This genetic intrusion is often referred to as the great *mestizaje*, or racial blending of "Hispanio America" (Gonzales, 1990).

Following their migration to the mainland, the Puerto Rican family experienced some important modifications in terms of primary relationships and family structure. These changes occurred in response to the influence of American culture, the labor needs of an industrial-urban society, and the economic and social problems that have plagued the Puerto Rican community on the mainland. There are four family types:

1. *The nuclear family*, characterized by a two-generation structure of parents and their children. Families are confined to cramped apartments, to the demanding schedule of urban life, and to limited economic resources and employment opportunities.

2. *The extended family*, found among the long-term migrants in the central city. The extended family consists of three generations: the parents, their children, and their grandchildren. The extended family structure has traditionally provided social, emotional, and economic support to its members. As such, it evolved in response to the harsh and demanding conditions of life in the *barrio*.

3. *The attenuated nuclear family*, called the "blended family" by sociologists. This type of family is viewed as a new phenomenon among white, middle-class Americans; it has existed for years among the Puerto Ricans, particularly since their arrival in the "big city." It consists of two or more altered nuclear families who share a common household. Following divorce or separation, a man who has children from a previous marriage may marry a woman who also has children from a former marriage. This merging of nuclear families is further complicated by the introduction of stepchildren, that is, the children who are born to the husband and wife in the attenuated family.

4. *The female-headed family*, becoming more and more common in the Puerto Rican community. These families are supported by women who have experienced divorce, who have been abandoned by their husbands, who are widowed, or who have had children out of wedlock. Today, more than 45% of Puerto Rican families are headed by women, according to the U.S. Census 1994, and the number is climbing (Gonzales, 1990).

Although Latino families are clearly affected by some of the same dynamics faced by other families of color, they also have certain unique experiences. Latino families tend to be younger and have more children. In addition, as many are currently immigrant families, they must struggle to adjust to a foreign language and new culture. These struggles have been occurring in an era of fluctuating economic conditions, particularly in the 1980s and 1990s and in an era of declining economic opportunities for less-skilled workers. This, coupled with the federal government's increasing reluctance to provide economic security for American families in general, suggests that Latino families stand to suffer even worse material conditions in the future (Ortiz, 1995).

A study on how Puerto Ricans adjust to the mainland (Westfried, 1985) saw the task for members as finding meaning in their lives in a society that does not value their identity. Puerto Ricans face a challenging mission in searching for personal identity and must learn who they are, where they belong, and what their lives and actions mean.

CASE STUDIES

Dianna

It is late afternoon in a large metropolitan hospital. The steady ringing of the telephone can barely be heard over the multiple conversations of nurses, doctors, and technicians at the large, half-circle nurses' station. On the ninth ring, a nurse, busily writing her charts, picks up the receiver. "Seven Hudson South. This is Dianna Rodriguez. How may I help you?" she inquired. Dianna listened for a moment. "Discontinue tubal feedings and begin clear fluids by mouth," she repeated. "Thank you, Dr. Forest," Dianna said, replacing the receiver with her left hand as she quickly noted the new order on her assignment sheet. The large, round wall clock read 4:15 PM. Dianna scanned the assignment sheet: hang IV (intravenous) antibiotics for Mrs. Silver; catheterize urine specimen from Miss Garcia; change abdominal dressings on Mr. Reynolds; get Mr. Hernandez OOB (out of bed); do finger venous puncture testing on four diabetic patients; and prepare evening medication for six other patients. In addition, a new patient was waiting to be admitted to the unit. A low, soft sigh, almost inaudible, escaped from Dianna's pursed lips. A feeling of frustration was expressed by a puzzling frown, soon replaced by a broad grin as Dianna remembered Marie's earlier cautioning, "Mom, better wear your support hose today. It's Monday." Dianna was grateful for her daughter's suggestion.

The day began on a somber note. At precisely 7:40 AM, a patient, Mr. Stewart, suffered cardiac arrest (sudden cessation of the heartbeat). Dianna was taking his blood pressure at the time. She quickly alerted the staff, and emergency measures began immediately by bringing the red crash cart with emergency medicines and equipment to the bedside, placing a board under Mr. Stewart's back, setting up IV lines, readying suction equipment, and starting CPR (cardiopulmonary resuscitation). Within moments, the overhead page system operator's martial-like tones, heightened by newsroom typewriter rhythm, exclaimed, "Attention! Arrest! Repeat Arrest! Milstein Hudson South. Arrest! Arrest!" Twenty or more professionals came sprinting off elevators, escalators, and staircases, bounding down corridors to the unit. Flying white coats and pounding Nikes brushed aside stretchers, visitors, and staff in a desperate race to the patient. These specialists—doctors, nurses, technicians, and supervisors—literally drop or stop whatever they are doing in clinics, in labs, in the cafeteria, perhaps reading X-rays, suturing wounds in the Emergency Room, or completing rounds, to "go like the wind" to their mission. Today was no exception. Within minutes, the "flying squad" had IV lines of medication running into Mr. Stewart's veins, oxygen pumping through intubation tubes inserted down his trachea and heart rates and rhythm intermittently bleeping across the EKG (electrocardiogram) machine's printout. Tension remained high, until the bleeping machine's flat line became an irregular graph. Then sighs of relief echoed through the room, and the pace slowed a bit. After 35 minutes of intensive, organized, and precise treatment, Mr. Stewart's condition was declared to be stable enough to move him to ICCU (Intensive Cardiac Care Unit). Dianna accompanied the six-man transport team monitoring and observing the automatic chest compressor that provided external cardiac compression during the trip. In the unit, Dianna helped the ICCU staff get Mr. Stewart settled in his bed, and then she returned to the seventh floor. The tedious task of collecting the patient's property and tagging it for the Security Department was completed next. It was 9:00 AM, and Dianna's routines for the day had not begun. She took a few minutes to sit down and review her assignment sheet.

The rest of the morning, interrupted by two short meetings, passed quickly. But after she had a quick lunch, activity became intensified. Dianna was asked to assist in discharging two patients. Fortunately, she had cared for them a few days ago and was familiar with their needs. There were specific instructions to be given for home and follow-up care, doctor or clinic appointments to be checked, prescriptions to be reviewed, and referrals to be discussed for clarity and understanding. Dianna was completing this task when she received the call from Dr. Forest. It was 7:15 PM when Dianna sat down with her night relief nurse to review patients' conditions and treatments. Although her shift was officially over at 7:30, it was almost 8:00 when she called the ICCU. She was concerned about Mr. Stewart. The unit nurse reported that he was "stable and comfortable." Tired but with a great sense of personal satisfaction, Dianna walked slowly toward the elevator. Her stylish uniform, slightly wrinkled but still pristine white, contradicted the stressful trials of the past 12 hours. Her long day was almost at an end.

The bus ride home took Dianna through the "mean" streets of Washington Heights, one of the largest areas of illegal drug trafficking in New York City. Crack, or crack cocaine, is America's fastest growing drug epidemic of the last decade. It is cheap, plentiful, and intensely addictive—a drug whose potential for social disruption and individual tragedy is well documented. In 1995 its popularity had been challenged by the reappearance of another street drug—heroin. Police believe that drugs are the primary cause of increases in robberies and murders in the city. As the bus traveled along Broadway, police cars, some with sirens full-blast, sped by. The sounds made Dianna shiver and move away from the window. She forced herself to think of that happy day when she and her family would move from this war zone.

Manhattan Community District 12, which encompasses Washington Heights, is bordered on the south by West 155th Street, on the west by the Hudson River, and on the east and north by the Harlem River. The demographics of the area have changed dramatically over the past 25 years, from mainly a vibrant European Jewish and Irish working- and middle-class community, to a rapidly growing community of Dominican Republican immigrants. The majority of the residents are law-abiding families, but there is a small group of young men heavily involved in trafficking illegal drugs.

In fact, parts of Washington Heights would remind a veteran of Vietnam. There are police drug busts and rivalry shoot-outs between dealers, often injuring innocent victims caught in the crossfire. Increased police presence doesn't always guarantee safety for the residents. Drug dealing is increasingly obvious. Strangers roam the streets, and luxury and foreign cars with out-of-town license plates cruise the blocks with their drivers peering through tinted glass windows. On steps, in corners, and in doorways, the dealers lounge, waiting for round-the-clock sales. At night, low-flying helicopters aim brilliant lights toward rooftops, sending buyers and sellers scurrying down fire escapes like cockroaches faced with sudden light. Often the blazing illumination of the night sweeps, which the police make several times a month, lights up the apartment windows, frightening young children. Mothers rush to carry their screaming children to inner rooms to protect them from stray bullets.

When the bus neared her stop, Dianna elbowed her way toward the door. Making it through the two blocks to her home was always a challenge. She walked quickly, looking straight ahead, purse straps tightly wrapped around her arm and held close to her body. Dianna passed small groups of young men hanging out in front of record stores, bars, and communication centers that advertised discount telephone calls to South America for 75¢. Others sat with sullen faces in secondhand cars. Dianna's steps quickened when her building came into view, and her breathing became almost normal. But it was only when the elevator reached the sixth floor, and Dianna smelled the spicy roast pork coming from her apartment that the tenseness left her body. With keys in hand, she quickly opened the double locks. "I'm home, everybody!" she cried out with a sigh of relief. Dianna could relax now. She was safely home.

Compared with what many of today's youngsters face in growing up, Dianna had a comfortable, almost carefree early life in upper Manhattan. Born into a family with two other children, George and Jeannette Cowerly, Dianna was considered special. She was the "baby" and was cuddled and cherished by everyone. Dianna was her father's darling and could coax him into granting her every wish. Her father, an engineer, provided the family with all the necessities and a few luxuries as well. "My earliest memories include a favorite doll. She had lots of outfits, and I loved changing them." Another is playing doctor and nurse. "When I was 5 years old, I knew nursing was for me. I always played the doctor or nurse; my brother and sister and my dolls were the patients. I would bandage their legs and arms, peek into their throats and ears and stare at their stuck-out tongues." Dianna's expertise extended into the neighborhood, and she treated other children's simple cuts and bruises.

Halloween was a special day and night for children in Washington Heights, and one Halloween had a lasting effect when Dianna was about 10 years old. For days, she could think of nothing else. She would be a beautiful ballerina with shiny red, satin ballet slippers. Every day after school she stood patiently and quietly while her mother pinned and basted yards of white tulle to a tight fitting, white satin bodice. Bright red felt hearts fashioned in circles embellished the front and back of the bodice. Dianna knew that her outfit would be the prettiest on the block, making it possible for her to fill her large shopping bag quickly with "treats." Dianna's girlfriend, Maria, wanted to be a princess, like Sleeping Beauty. Maria's costume and tiara were made by a doting grandmother. The ankle-length, full-skirted dress of pale blue gauze was attached to an empire waist and hung loosely from wide blue and green embroidered straps. Under the dress, Maria wore a bright blue slip that matched the color of her Mary Jane shoes. Maria's tiara glittered with colored glass stones pasted onto an aluminum frame.

Their trick or treating began around 4:00 PM, just about dusk. Their mothers warned them not to leave the neighborhood, as it would soon be dark. The girls received many compliments from bodega, record store, and restaurant customers. In the beauty parlors, supermarkets, and bakeries, they did especially well, collecting cookies and cupcakes, fruit, candy, and small change. Their bags were filled, and they laughed happily as they turned to walk home. A tall, cleanly shaved, and well-dressed man approached them. He seemed friendly and asked questions about their pretty costumes, their school, and even what subjects they liked. As they neared a large apartment house, the man told them about all the goodies in his apartment. He offered to give them some small dolls. The girls were suspicious at first. Then he showed them a shiny police badge in the lining of his jacket. He explained that he was off-duty and not in uniform because he was also a security man for the apartment house. Maria refused to accompany him, but Dianna was captivated by his gentle manners, big smile, and offer of the dolls.

As the elevator ascended, he told Dianna that he had a daughter about her age. She could be Dianna's new friend. When the elevator stopped at the 12th floor, the policeman walked toward steps leading to the roof. Dianna wanted to know the location of his apartment. The policeman explained that the door to his apartment was on the roof because, as a security man, he had to look for robbers trying to break into apartments. When they reached the roof, Dianna became alarmed. The roof was dark and deserted. The policeman opened his belt and began to unzip his pants. Dianna turned toward the door, but he blocked her way. He grabbed her and began to pull up her skirt. At that moment, Dianna could think only of escaping. She quickly bent forward and bit his hand with all the strength she could muster. He screamed in pain, "You little bitch!" As he released his grip, tearing her skirt, Dianna slammed the door in his face. She believes that she ran down the 12 flights in less than one minute. Dianna never looked back. Maria was waiting in the lobby. When she saw the terror on Dianna's face and the torn skirt, she grabbed Dianna's hand and pulled her through the door. Together they ran for three blocks before stopping to get their breath back. They made a promise not to tell anyone about the incident.

Dianna explained the ripped skirt with, "It got caught on a shelf in a store." But for several years, she often had nightmares about the tall man on the roof. The incident also made her hesitate to talk to men in the neighborhood, even those she had known for years.

Between ages 9 and 11, Dianna was into "obituaries." She scanned the obituary pages daily, looking for diagnoses, and then searched through medical dictionaries for meanings. Some words, like "coma," "heart attack," "aneurysm," "cancer," "myeloma," "stroke," and "brain tumor," became part of her vocabulary. Her father interpreted phrases like "died in his sleep," "died after a long illness," or "succumbed to complications." For a while, her parents worried about Dianna's fascination with death. But by the age of 12, she collected baseball cards and competed with her older brother, George, which her parents found more realistic.

Like many preteenage girls, Dianna became increasingly concerned about her weight. She was not obese or very much overweight, but when she looked in the mirror, she saw a round-faced, short, fat girl. Often she left the dinner table after eating only half of the food on her plate. Dianna's

mother tried to reassure her daughter with talk about growing bodies needing adequate nutrition, but Dianna was disconsolate. "Fatness runs in our
families, but you'll grow out of it," her father told her. "Just wait and see."
But Dianna couldn't wait. Looking back, she realizes that she was bulimic.
She ate a big meal to satisfy her family and went to the bathroom and
regurgitated by sticking her fingers down her throat and gagging. Sometimes
Dianna would go on binges and secretly eat a quart of chocolate ice cream,
a bag of taco chips, and several bars of candy. Thinking that she had lost
control of her body, Dianna would force herself to vomit, believing that this
was the only way to regain control. Occasionally, she took laxatives like Ex-
lax to make food speed through her digestive system with little time to
release nutrients.

Growing up, Dianna was a model daughter and never caused her parents
any trouble. She was a perfectionist and a high achiever but worried about
being accepted by others and had a low self-image and minimum self-esteem.
Dianna envied tall, thin girls who could wear jeans that made them look
"sexy." In time, she lost weight, but she also lost her happy, charming personality. Dianna felt tired and irritable, was quick to take offense, and cried
easily. Her olive skin grew pale and contrasted sharply with her dark, curly
hair. Her menstrual periods were irregular or not at all. But Dianna was
attractive to many young men in the neighborhood. Her size 6 jeans were
shown appreciation by sharp, shrill whistles as she passed groups of them
hanging out on the corner. Dianna understands now how food disorders are
related to how one sees oneself and the ability to cope with the stresses of
everyday life. Some specialists believe that, in some cases, bulimia is related
to a fear of growing up, becoming independent. "This may have relevance.
I was the baby of the whole family and was catered to by everyone," she
recalls. The moment Robert entered her life, Dianna began to see herself
as beautiful, wanted, and needed and had no desire for binges, starvation, or
other dangerous eating habits.

Meeting Robert Rodriguez, when she was 13, brought a different and new
dimension into Dianna's life. The handsome 15-year-old lived just around
the corner. Within days, they were good friends in a loose, casual relationship. Dianna's happiness was short-lived when Robert and his family moved
to New Jersey a few months later. They promised to correspond every week.
Two years later, Robert's parents divorced, and Robert moved back to New
York City. Dianna was ecstatic. For a year, she had faced young drug dealers
alone. They dared, frightened, and threatened her by insisting that she try
marijuana. With Robert by her side, she could walk the streets without being
annoyed. Now 15 and 17 years old, with almost daily contact, their relationship became special, serious, and sexual. Although Dianna's parents liked
and approved of Robert, they were concerned about the obvious affection
the two young people displayed for each other and the potential for broken

hearts and dreams. This concern was shared by Dianna's grandparents, because in the Puerto Rican culture, the extended family is very important, and grandparents are included in all major family decisions.

Both the Rodriguez and the Cowerly families were Catholic and strongly supported abstinence before marriage. They also adhered to another tradition, early marriage for girls. Dianna's parents suspected that this would be the outcome of Dianna and Robert's love. But this was not Dianna's plan. "I loved Robert so much," she revealed. "I wanted something or someone that was ours only—like a baby. When I became pregnant, Robert was sort of ambivalent. He was happy, yet he was sad. We were still in high school, with few skills, no diploma and no money, and so no marriage!"

Having a child out of wedlock was not as widely accepted in 1977 as it is today. The young parents believed in each one's commitment to raise their child in the best way possible within their capabilities. In the presence of both sets of grandparents, Dianna and Robert made this sacred vow, while holding their parents' hands.

Over the last three decades, the age of first intercourse has declined (Hamburg, 1992). Higher percentages of adolescent women and men reported being sexually experienced at each age level between the ages of 15 and 20 in 1988 than in the early 1970s. In 1988, 27% of girls and 35% of boys had intercourse by their 15th birthday. So while it was unique for parents to be 15 and 17 years old in 1977, it is more common today.

For many minority male adolescents like Robert, there are few meaningful opportunities to participate directly in the adult world and in community life. Many, therefore, are uncertain how to be useful and earn the respect of their elders; they feel adult stress without experiencing the rewards of belonging in the value setting of adult life.

Dianna told her mother about the pregnancy at the beginning of her fourth month. Both families were disappointed and unhappy. When her mother took Dianna to a clinic for examination, the doctor suggested an abortion. "I was so upset and angry that I ran out of the building," recalls Dianna. Wearing bulky sweaters and oversized shirts, Dianna continued in school with one limitation. She was prohibited from taking physical education. Several of the sisters in her parochial school were understanding and cooperative. At home, her parents were energized with watching Dianna's diet, weight gain, and preparation for the coming baby. "They gave us 100 percent support," she recalls. In the evening, Dianna lay on the sofa, and Robert felt her bulging abdomen as the baby "kicked." Robert would put his ear down close to listen to the heartbeat. Frequently, he gently massaged her back when she was lying on her side, the only comfortable position for her. The rhythmic movements caused Dianna to doze for short periods, although Dianna could lay cradled in Robert's arms for hours.

On April 6, 1977, Dianna entered a program for teenage mothers at Misericordia Hospital in the Bronx. (She and Robert didn't marry until later.) Marie was born on April 16. Dianna returned to school May 1, 1977, and graduated with her class on June 23, 1977.

Dianna chose to work rather than stay home, care for her child, and accept welfare. Robert couldn't find a job with security or a big enough salary. This represented another break from the tradition of her culture. "Puerto Rican women should raise their children. That's their primary role. The male role of provider and sole wage earner was not available to Robert," Dianna says. But she had always worked through high school and in summers at Burger King or McDonald's, at baby-sitting, or other odd jobs. Dianna liked to be independent, and she was ambitious. Her mother willingly cared for Marie. "Robert often expressed anger or guilt, because he wasn't acting as a strong, virile man, according to his way of thinking," she remembers, but Dianna reassured him that things would get better and expressed faith in his commitment to his family.

That fall, Dianna entered Edna McConnell Clarke School of Nursing and began her studies leading to LPN (licensed practical nurse). Immediately upon graduation, she accepted employment at Presbyterian Hospital. Dianna was in charge during the evening shift (4:00 PM to 12:00 midnight) on an old-fashioned ward of 20–25 patients. She was bright-eyed, eager, and conscientious. Remembering those days, she states, "I marvel now at what I did. A new recruit handling a whole ward. I can't believe I did it at only 19 years old." She pauses in reflection. "I accepted responsibility without fear and tried hard to be a good nurse. It was a challenge. But it was also rewarding."

Puerto Ricans are family-oriented, and children are considered a blessing. Parents make great sacrifices to buy them presents, toys, and clothing. One major cultural barrier to education and skills training for women is the pressure to marry young and have large families. Women are expected to care for everyone's needs and even deny their own. Dianna, contrary to tradition, wanted to be educated and achieve success and personal fulfillment. "I always wanted to be a nurse—a professional. Even motherhood would not keep me from my goal." But Dianna's working and striving did affect Robert.

Depression is a common problem for millions of Americans. However, it's often ignored or untreated. This is what almost happened to Robert. Women are diagnosed as depressed more often simply because it is socially acceptable for women to be labeled "depressed." Men often are not diagnosed as depressed, but instead as "under pressure," "burned out," or "stressed" (Zambana, Dorrington, and Hayes-Bautista, 1995). For several months, Robert appeared withdrawn, felt a loss of pleasure, and experienced feelings of sadness and physical discomfort. For adolescents and young adults, social stress, struggles to obtain gainful employment, family responsibilities, and search for fulfillment can be causative agents. All of these played a part in Robert's illness, in addition to stress caused by interpersonal conflict arising out of his relationship with Dianna.

Dianna became aware of Robert's diminished appetite, insomnia, with-drawal from friends, and inability to find joy in pleasure-giving activities like baseball and basketball games. But his loss of sex drive worried Dianna most. Although Dianna was young, vibrant, and sensuous, Robert barely and rarely embraced or touched her. Dianna persuaded him to seek professional help.

Psychotherapy and drug treatment were recommended. Twice weekly ses-sions alone or with a group improved Robert's social and interpersonal func-tioning. Dianna stopped pressuring him to find work and spent more time with him. A vocational counselor helped Robert explore and evaluate the most appropriate areas for his interests and skills. Gradually, Robert re-sponded and was able to work part-time. Dianna feels this period was a test of the strengths and depth of their relationship. They grew closer in spite of the crisis situation.

At the beginning of 1980, Dianna and Robert saw the "light at the end of the tunnel." Robert was working, and they began to save for their own apartment. This was a significant step, but more importantly, it meant that they were now ready for marriage. Dianna and Robert planned a small, family wedding at City Hall. The date was August 12, 1980. It was a glorious, sunny day and everything went off as planned. The ceremony, though short, was sentimental. It was a big step in formalizing an already stable, loving relationship. Later, in their new apartment, festive with colorful balloons, bright crepe-paper streamers and flowers, family and friends danced wildly to salsa rhythms, cried, kissed, and hugged each other. The music was loud, and the singing off-key. A buffet of *arroz con gandules* (rice with pigeon peas) and pineapple flan was set up in one bedroom. A huge punch bowl held pineapple rum punch and provided an excuse for frequent toasts to the happy couple. Marie was dressed in a delicate creation of lace, ribbons, and or-gandy. Posing in front of her parents, she could be likened to a large, moving blob of fluffy pink cotton candy. She clutched a single pink rose in her hand, a vision captured by many cameras.

Over the next few years, Dianna combined motherhood and working. Two sons were born while she attended night school, prepared for an RN (registered nurse) license, and worked full-time. "It was difficult, but I kept my goal in sight. Robert was terrific, often caring for the children and doing household tasks while I worked or attended school. Often my mother pitched in with shopping, cooking, and also child care."

One Christmas, there was little money for toys. Although she was not very religious, Dianna prayed to St. Mary and asked for guidance in getting something for the children. Dianna and Robert were facing a joyless holiday. How could she tell the children that Santa was not coming to their house?

The next morning, Dianna and Robert went to a Salvation Army second-hand store. They bought a cash register, parts of a train set, a doll's crib, a small dollhouse, a wagon, a fire truck, a child's rocking chair, three dolls, a police car, and a wooden tricycle. The total cost was under $30.00. Dianna's parents felt bad, because Dianna would not accept money from them. Dianna and Robert were determined to use their own creativity and energy. They bought nontoxic paint and lacquer, remnants of colorful materials, ribbons, and lace. Yellow, black, and brown wool yarn was purchased for hair and black plastic for dolls' shoes. For the next two weeks, they worked late into the night, refurbishing the toys. Dianna designed dresses with matching panties, bonnets, and hats. The most difficult part was cutting and sewing plastic Mary Jane shoes and making hair from the yarn. Their exchanging of ideas and selecting colors made the project interesting and a demonstration of love and caring. Robert had well-developed mechanical skills, and Dianna became aware of an innate sense of color and an eye for design. Their sadness turned into warm companionship and pride in their accomplishment.

Christmas morning arrived with a prayer of thanks from Dianna and Robert and joyous squeals from excited children. The "new" toys were resplendent under the tinseled tree and appeared to be ready for a second life.

Dianna speaks openly about Robert's growing understanding of her desire and need to pursue a career—a need to find a way to express and demonstrate her talents. Today he is very proud of his wife's accomplishments and success. Dianna plans to earn a bachelor's degree in nursing. She continues on-the-job educational and skills training. As scientific and medical technology advance with new and different procedures, techniques, and treatments, nurses must continuously upgrade their knowledge and skills. Dianna is happy to be preparing for the 21st century.

Dianna's courage and strength have won the respect and admiration of colleagues. One is Luz, a Puerto Rican registered nurse with whom Dianna has worked. Luz says, "I have known Dianna for 12 years. It's amazing how she has managed to juggle work, family, and an education in such a rewarding manner. She has been able to strike a balance in her personal life, as an ambitious young woman, showing compassion for her patients and also enjoying motherhood. She loves her career, but her family is of equal importance. Dianna sets the best example for other Puerto Rican young women to follow. Her life proves that through sacrifice and with support, we can have it all."

Dianna hesitates to say that she may be considered successful. She feels that she has had success in her professional life. "I went from a nurse's aide, to a practical nurse, to a registered nurse with a college degree." At the moment, she feels that she is still climbing the ladder. Her ultimate goal is a home in the suburbs. "When I get my home, I'll be on the top step of the ladder and will be able to feel the real joy of accomplishment."

Marie

Marie is a typical American teenager. According to her mother, it seems that Marie spends hours on the telephone or in front of a mirror. Makeup, hairstyles, and clothes are of vital interest to this slim, attractive young woman who reads love stories and mysteries. She has a passion for real tear-jerkers and collects baseball cards as her mother did years ago. Her favorite kind of date is getting all dressed up and dining in an elegant restaurant that has soft music and dim lights. Marie is a romantic. But there is a serious side to her personality. She works in a public library and attends college full-time, enrolled in a prenursing degree course at New York Technological College in Brooklyn. Marie describes herself as friendly, reliable, and competitive. She is also concerned with social issues like poverty, homelessness, family abuse, and youth crime.

This daughter loves and admires her mother, especially for her great determination, helpfulness to others, and sincerity. "I think I inherited many of her qualities, but especially her determination. Like her, I've had some high and low points in my life, but I am still striving to reach my goals." Her maternal grandmother, Dianna's mother, provided much of the child care when Marie was growing up. Only when her grandmother moved out of the city did Marie assume some of the household chores. "I was a young teenager by then, and as the oldest child, I naturally assumed family responsibility." Marie's relationship with her parents has always been close and open. She explains, "They've never put me down; in fact, they always encourage me. When there are some major decisions to be made, they include me in the deliberations. If there is a difference of opinion, we talk it over and work it out satisfactorily."

Most young people have the greatest difficulty with peer pressure; usually, it is negative. But Marie is fortunate. "My friends are just like me—basically good kids! We all seem to be headed in the right direction. Most of my friends are in college. My boyfriend of 2½ years is also a college student." Did Dianna's love for higher education influence her? "I think in some ways. I always wanted to be a nurse. My mother's experiences have shown me just how difficult it is to work and raise a family and still be a student. So I'm going to complete my education before I start a family."

Marie enjoys singing but has never had any formal training. She did have dreams of being an actress and a dancer like lots of preteenagers. She used to perform in front of a mirror or for her brothers as an audience. Did she ever fantasize about Miss America? "No, not really," she says after a pause. There has never been a Puerto Rican winner or even a contestant, so far, although Puerto Ricans are the largest group of Hispanic people in the United States. Perhaps the almost mandatory college education requirement precludes some from aspiring to the crown. The tradition of early marriage for Puerto Rican women may also be a culprit. "Also," Marie adds, "many parents don't speak fluent English and have never attended college, families live in El Barrio, and girls don't get good guidance in schools and have few role models. These things limit fantasies. With more girls thinking about college and careers, there may be a Puerto Rican crowned by 2005," she concludes with a grin.

Two noted Hispanic women give their views on the status of Puerto Rican women. Bettina Flores, a Hispanic author, feels that Latina women have been held down by poverty, racism, and lack of education, but also by other forces created by their own culture, for example, machismo, the pressure to marry young and have large families, and the influence of the Catholic Church, which teaches obedience and servitude and preaches against artificial birth control.

Ana Fortana, former president of the National Conference of Puerto Rican Women, contends that it takes skills, energy, and "guts" to break cultural restraints. Education is the key to improving the situation of Latin women. Coming from a culture that places such emphasis on children and family, women are especially in conflict about leaving their children for the world of work and education. Lately, education is moving more in the direction of multiculturalism, thus alleviating the fear of "selling out" to Anglo culture. With bilingual education and substantial contributions of Hispanic culture being recognized, Latin women are able to keep a delicate balance in overcoming the old stereotypes.

Five years from now, Marie sees herself as a college graduate beginning her career as a registered nurse and making money. "Perhaps working with Dianna at Columbia-Presbyterian Medical Center—on the same floor would be great. We'd be the first Puerto Rican mother and daughter team there, or maybe anywhere!" Her dark eyes glisten with happiness as she forecasts. One important lesson Marie learned from Dianna is how to have a career, raise your children, and have a good relationship with your husband. "My Mom had some tough times, but she is still happily married to the first and only man in her life and has three children who adore her."

Gerald Leslie (1982: 539) writes,

There is some evidence from a wide resource of studies that maternal employment is positively correlated with the adjustment of adolescent children. Maternal employment appears to influence the self-concept of both sons and daughters, but in different ways. The daughters of working mothers appear likely to develop adequate self-concepts, to make minimal distinctions between household tasks deemed appropriate for men and women, and to anticipate employment themselves when they are older. An important variable is the mother's attitude toward her employment. When she is satisfied, the relationship between her and her children is likely to be close and rewarding.

Mary and Melissa

At times, mother and daughter are caught between two ideologies: "traditional mother" and "modern daughter." They want to enjoy both roles but often face frustration in attempting to reconcile their ideologies, especially when they may favor different values. So it is in the Puerto Rican family of Mary and Melissa.

It is ten o'clock and Melissa is having a breakfast of oatmeal from a Styrofoam cup. Between mouthfuls, she talks enthusiastically about attending a special satellite computer school. "There's lots of classroom work and few tests," she reveals. Besides music, Melissa is "into" sketching, videos, makeup, and horror movies. She feels that the best part of being an only child is not having to baby-sit or worry about siblings' birthday parties. "But it can be lonesome, too," she admits. Telephoning close friends several times a day and writing poetry offer some respite. Although she's only 13 years old, Melissa has had two poems published. She and her girlfriends take long walks, window-shop, enjoy movies, or just hang out gabbing about "girl talk."

When there is a problem, she seeks her mom's advice first and then gets some input from her friends. Her mom, Mary, is very observant and can usually sense when things are not quite right, Melissa believes. She considers Mary to be her best friend. "We spend lots of time together, and I introduce her to all of my friends."

Mary has earned an undergraduate degree and is seeking a master's degree in neuropsychopharmacology and hopes to continue on to a Ph.D. This field will prepare her to work with brain-injured trauma cases and patients with mental disorders.

Education is valued by Mary, but she appears to have some qualms about aiming too high. She may have to sacrifice the educational plans and goals of her daughter, and this would cause her pain. For one who holds traditional values, seeking such higher education is an enigma with which Mary is becoming comfortable. Melissa is inspired by Mary's hard work and multiple community involvements. Melissa plans a career that will enable her to work with animals, for example, a technician for a veterinarian. Animal rescue technology, which trains one to rescue animals caught in floods, fires, and other disasters, also is being considered. But at 13, so many things interest her, which is natural.

Mary holds values that represent Puerto Rican culture. She upholds virginity, family responsibility, education, Christian moral behavior, and postponement of dating. On the other hand, she admires Melissa's desire to be a free spirit and make her own choices about chastity, career, and motherhood. At 13, her daughter is physically mature and attractive. "We talk about AIDS, STDs [sexually transmitted diseases], and pregnancy. She knows the facts, but will she have the maturity and sophistication to make the right choices?" she ponders. Mary is concerned about statistics that report more than 13,000 HIV positive adolescents in Puerto Rico. "Melissa knows that she alone has the responsibility for her own body, mind, and soul," Mary concludes in a voice expressing confidence.

Mary and Melissa are constantly aware of the old and the new lifestyles.

Melissa has traveled to Oregon, California, and Puerto Rico to visit relatives, young and old. Being a single parent forces Mary to have a career that will support the family and pay for the education needed for her and Melissa's careers. Melissa's hopes revolve around technology, independence, and the need to express her sense of creativity in poetry, makeup, and designer clothes. Between them differences appear to have been resolved in a manner that pleases both. Mary advises that every mother develop a relationship with her daughter, because girls are sensitive to everything in their environment, and Mary respects them for expressing themselves in whatever form they choose.

REFERENCES

Gonzales, J. Jr. *Racial and Ethnic Groups in America*. Dubuque, IA: Kendall/Hunt, 1990.

Hamburg, D. A. *Today's Children: Creating a Future for a Generation in Crisis*. New York: New York Times Books, 1992.

Leslie, G. *The Family in Social Context*. 5th ed. New York: Oxford University Press, 1982.

Maldonado-Denis, M. *The Emigration Dialect: Puerto Rico and the United States of America*. New York: International, 1980.

Ortiz, V. "The Diversity of Latino Families." In *Understanding Latino Families*, ed. Ruth Zambrano. Thousand Oaks, CA: Sage, 1995.

Stevens-Arroyo, A. M., and Diaz-Ramirez, A. M. "Puerto Ricans in the States: A Struggle for Identity." In *The Minority Report*, ed. S. G. Dworkin and R. J. Dworkin. Austin, TX: Holt, Rinehart, and Winston, 1982.

U.S. Government Printing Office. *U.S. Civil Rights. Puerto-Ricans in the Continental United States: An Uncertain Future*. Washington, DC: U.S. Government Printing Office, 1976.

Westfried, R. *Three Puerto Rican Families*. Salem, WI: Sheffield, 1965.

Zambana, R. E., Dorrington, C., and Hayes-Bautista, D. "Family and Child Health." In *Understanding Latino Families*. Thousand Oaks, CA.: Sage, 1995.

PERSONAL REFLECTIONS
by Natalie Gomez-Velez

CONSIDERING THE ROLE OF RACE, ETHNICITY, AND GENDER IN EDUCATIONAL EXPERIENCE

When approached to write this chapter, I was delighted to have the opportunity to discuss issues of race, ethnicity, and gender from the point of view of a lawyer and law teacher. I also was a little apprehensive—there is a lot to say. As I began to think about the topic, I considered discussing in the abstract the development and current state of the law in areas of particular importance, such as education, to serve as a backdrop to the stories told by women of color about their successes and those of their daughters. Given my sense of the expectations of those who would read the book, I thought I might briefly discuss some of the major historical developments and then focus on the current debates around education in the context of broader concerns such as affirmative action, immigration, and welfare reform, high-lighting past struggles, victories, and defeats, noting current battles.

However, every time I began to write, I found myself drawn to a narrative about my family's and my own experience placed in the context of broader legal and political responses to issues of race, ethnicity, gender, and class as related to a host of issues, including education. I attributed this impulse to my understanding of the focus of the book on successful women of color and their daughters, combined with a natural desire to tell my mother's story and to explore its relationship to my own in this context. At first, I recoiled from the urge to incorporate a personal narrative into a broader discussion of race, ethnicity, and gender, believing that such an account would be dismissed as somehow unauthentic, illegitimate, and not important in the context of a discussion about the law. However, in thinking about the problem, I realized that this impetus to place a discussion of race, ethnicity, gender, and law within a narrative about the journey of my particular Puerto Rican family springs from the recognition that there really is no abstract way in which to discuss these issues.

Indeed, the very notion of abstract, "neutral" legal principles may be viewed as one of the most effective tools supporting the perpetuation of racial, ethnic, and gender inequity in American society.[1] Much of law and legal study is about extrapolating abstract principles from lived experience (most often the lived experience of those most privileged in society), treating those principles as "universal" (as though they exist apart from particular narratives coming from particular kinds of experiences and particular points of view), and then learning to apply those abstract principles to predict and shape outcomes in various categories of lived experience. Our "law" is made up of federal and state constitutions that set forth the broad principles of governance and are subject to interpretation; of statutes that are the product of legislative debate and compromise; and of case law that consists of judicial opinions and jury verdicts arrived at in response to particular disputes. All of the sources of law involve interpretations of fact, law, and policy. All of the foundations of law incorporate experiences and points of view, and only by continually placing the assumptions found in law against our own experience can we see our way to making needed improvements. A good amount of legal scholarship in the areas of critical legal studies,[2] critical race theory,[3] and critical race feminism[4] has been devoted to getting behind the notion of "neutral principles" often put forth in the study and practice of law to unmask the unstated assumptions behind the principles and precepts that support the law's development and treatment of various classes of issues and classes of people.

The absence of "neutrality" in the development of the law is particularly apparent in current legal and political discussions representing shifts in the law and in public perception that are of particular concern to women of color. Discussions and legal developments addressing educational opportunity, affirmative action, welfare reform, immigration, and discrimination recently have taken on a tone that exposes the fact that they are anything but neutral.

My focus here is on education and the degree to which the current debates surrounding public education, such as privatizing aspects of education and gender segregation to help develop self-esteem, can and should be informed by the experiences of women of color for whom public education has been the key to overcoming many of the restrictions imposed by both overt and subtle discrimination. I know that for my mother and myself access to educational opportunity has made all of the difference, not only as a path to professional careers but also as part of our development as complete persons. Both my mother and I were lucky in that we were afforded wonderful opportunities through public education and were in the position to take advantage of those opportunities. Perhaps a brief sketch of my mother's story can provide some context.

My mother arrived in the United States from Puerto Rico at the age of 10. Her mother had been a teacher in Puerto Rico, and her father had owned a small fabric business. Unfortunate economic circumstances forced my grandfather to come to the States to work in a factory. My grandmother followed shortly thereafter with my mother, her sisters, and brother to join him. When my mother went to public school, she was placed in one of the "C" classes designed for the children of the immigrants arriving as a result of World War II. The "C" classes combined English immersion with instruction in English as a second language.

Because my mother was literate in Spanish, had a good grasp of grammar, and was well read, she learned English quickly and did well in school. However, she was quickly made aware that, bright or not, she was not welcome by many in her new classes, including some of her teachers. She recalls direct statements from teachers demanding, "Why don't you go back where you came from?" and admonishing her not to speak "that garbage" when she was caught speaking Spanish. She learned not to speak Spanish except at home. She remembers that many of her teachers expressed disbelief that she had any knowledge about art and literature and that some took offense if she shared that knowledge. She learned to be careful about what she said when she thought it might offend her teachers or classmates. But even as she learned to navigate the minefields that seemed always present at school, she did not get discouraged. She persisted in her studies at school (although often the work was less than challenging). Her mother continued to take an active interest in her education, exposing her to the works of various artistic and literary masters, attending class trips, and organizing plays and readings with neighborhood children.

In high school, she again did very well. However, just prior to the beginning of her senior year, she discovered that she had been steered away from the courses needed for an academic diploma. Because she was "not supposed to go to college," her guidance counselor had substituted vocational courses for several of the academic courses that were prerequisites to earning a Regents diploma and college admission, this notwithstanding her high grades and excellent overall school performance. As a result, she was forced to take a full load of academic courses in her senior year and to pass five Regents exams that summer to get into college. Thankfully, she managed and was accepted at Brooklyn College, a public college of the City University of New York.

At the time, Brooklyn College was tuition-free and very competitive. When she got there, my mother found that it was much more challenging than high school had been and that her relatively poor study habits (which had not hindered her in high school) made the transition difficult. To compound the difficulty, she found that she was given very little information and no guidance about course selection, study assistance, career planning, or anything else. Moreover, even after she had adjusted and had more than met the demands of college-level work, she soon discovered that she did not have an "A-face," as one professor explicitly put it, when approached about why she had gotten a B when a student she had tutored got an A.[5] Although the discrimination she experienced in college was not always blatant, it was ever-present in the words and actions of some of her professors and fellow students, and it required her to scale unnecessary obstacles to make it through.

Life also intervened to complicate matters. My mother was forced to leave college when her mother fell seriously ill. She stayed at home to care for my grandmother until her death. When my grandmother died, my mother was 19, and her world had collapsed. Unable to return to school, she worked full-time. At 21, she married my father. Four years later she gave birth to my brother, then to me. She stayed at home with my brother and me for three years, then finished college, earned two master's degrees, and became an early childhood and bilingual teacher, a bilingual education coordinator, and, for a time, an adjunct professor at Brooklyn College. Throughout her career, she encountered the sting of racism, both directly and through more subtle slights and snubs. Yet her persistence, hard work, belief in herself, and a little luck got her through, as did the opportunities afforded by the public education system and the strides made by the Civil Rights and women's movements of the 1960s and 1970s.

When I talk to her now about her experiences, she expresses no bitterness. Rather, she sees the bundle of experiences related to her education and career, both positive and negative, as having provided her with the ability to see the world through various sets of eyes. This multidimensional worldview was as much a means of survival as a point of interest.

As I sketch my mother's story, I sense that it might sound a little hokey, a bit too much like Horatio Alger. Yet stories like hers are currently being obscured by a focus on narratives about "unworthy" and "inferior" classes of people undeserving of opportunity. As the political tide has turned, much of the current debate surrounding public education seems to ignore past successes like my mother's and instead remains focused on the aspects of the system that have been underfunded and left in disarray. For example, crumbling school buildings, large class sizes, underprepared teachers, and falling test scores are held up as evidence that public education does not work, rather than as evidence that a greater commitment to education is needed. Worse yet, the blame for the shortcomings of public education is more often being placed on the students whom it has failed in terms that echo the false justifications for discrimination in the past. From Charles Murray's attempts to assert the intellectual inferiority of certain races, to New York City mayor Rudolph Giuliani's assault on transitional programs at the city's public community colleges, those shortchanged by the educational system increasingly are being blamed for failures wrought by inequality of opportunity and lack of commitment to education. The arguments increasingly are being made in terms that invoke negative stereotypes based on race, sex, and national origin.

In hearing many of the arguments in the current debates about educational opportunity, I cannot help but relate those arguments to my mother's and my own journey as Puerto Rican women living in a society whose social constructs often seem disconnected from our lived experience and how that dissonance caused us to have multiple identities and to experience the world refracted through our various "selves"—as American citizens, as Puerto Ricans, as girls, as women, as poor, as privileged, as powerless, as powerful.[6] Though difficult, this process is not necessarily negative and can enable us to view the world from various perspectives and to adapt to myriad circumstances in a way that can strengthen our resilience. Of course, this is true only so long as no damage is done to the core of our identity in the process. Thinking through legal constructs affecting race, ethnicity, gender, and class from a perspective that includes all of the different parts of ourselves, particularly those parts that we have most often had to keep in hiding in order to achieve success, provides a mechanism by which to expose some of the harmful subtexts supporting existing legal principles.

Viewing events from a perspective that includes the parts of ourselves most often rejected by mainstream society helps to expose the underlying assumptions of a system that has done much to eradicate overt discrimination but has done precious little to address root causes of inequality and discrimination. As a result, long-recognized injustices are perpetuated, notwithstanding professed commitments to equality.

Of course, I do not mean or intend to discount the advances achieved through the Civil Rights movement and the development of legislation and jurisprudence aimed at achieving equality of opportunity and equal justice—they are truly monumental. But in the current political climate, we are at risk of moving backward because the continuing effects of racism, bigotry, and sexism are at risk of coming to the foreground just as lawmakers roll up and pack away many of the safety nets that have permitted achievement for people who otherwise would have been without opportunity. This is not to say that I am without hope. To the contrary, I remain optimistic. My experience has shown that there are many people of goodwill who support equality and who celebrate the American experiment in bringing together people of various races, ethnicities, and cultures. I have also discovered that many members of traditionally disfranchised communities have begun to find their voices and document their experiences in ways that can only help to foster change for the better. This is not an easy process. Like others who are doing fairly well yet feeling fairly overwhelmed, I often find myself at risk of adopting uncritically structures, assumptions, and thought processes that have contributed to (or at least have not hindered) my own success.

Stepping into my own past and considering the various roles and experiences of all of my created selves put me in a place where I can begin to see and to address not only the obvious denials of full citizenship and impediments to success expressed in the law but also the more hidden, underlying assumptions about my various selves and the lack of recognition of my whole self in the law's structure, even as parts of who I am are accorded value and provided opportunities. Stepping back in this way causes me to see that the law really has no paradigm for me, as a Puerto Rican woman, in its dichotomous structure. The law can deal with me only as either male or female, white or nonwhite, privileged or oppressed, worthy or unworthy. If female, I am presumed white. If nonwhite, I am presumed male. If female and nonwhite, I have to pick one, and whatever I pick is other than the norm articulated in American law and carries the threat of my being characterized as unworthy or, at best, "unusual," "special," an aberration.[7] As for privilege or oppression, every step I take risks placing me in one category or the other.

Perhaps I can clarify what I mean by looking more closely at some of the debates surrounding public education. Most people would agree that quality education is important not only to our development as informed and complete citizens but also as a key to meaningful work, economic self-sufficiency, and professional success. In the United States there has long been a stated commitment to public education as essential to the development and maintenance of a free, democratic society. I know that access to quality public education was at the center of my mother's and my own success. Yet on all levels, public education is under attack. At the elementary and high school levels, we see the continuation of separate and unequal systems more than 40 years after the U.S. Supreme Court's decision in

Brown v. Board of Education[8] declared such inequality unconstitutional. Our public schools maintain separate and unequal systems divided by race and ethnicity and, most starkly, by class distinctions. We read daily reports about failing schools in terms of both educational preparation and physical plant.[9] At the college level, we see attacks on public institutions and on affirmative action initiatives as well as prohibitive tuition costs that deny access to all but the privileged and those lucky enough to scale the mounting obstacles.

This is not to say that there is no public debate about the state of education or that efforts to improve the quality of education do not exist. They do. What is troubling is that the subtext of these efforts is that education is a privilege for the few rather than a basic right accessible to all. There is an unspoken view that some children are deserving of the best of everything, while others are not quite entitled to even basic educational opportunity. That view is somewhat reflected in the law's treatment of discrimination in educational opportunity and in the structure of a constitutional scheme that is based on negative, rather than positive, rights. "The 'education right' was conceived and is presently comprehended as a negative right in the sense that, rather than imposing any affirmative obligation upon government to provide education, it simply forbids government from impeding individuals in their quest for education and enlightenment."[10] A constitutional system that bases its notion of rights on what the government cannot do without stating any requirements regarding what government must minimally provide to its citizens can be said to start from the premise that "Them that's got shall get, and them that's not shall lose." In other words, there is a basic, underlying assumption that government is not required to provide any positive benefits and, consequently, that such benefits shall accrue to those deserving of them, and everyone else can expect only noninterference from the government with respect to those benefits it decides voluntarily to provide. This, of course, is an oversimplification. The layers of laws addressing educational opportunity on the federal, state, and local level require the government to do more than refrain from intentional discrimination in education.[11] However, the fact that the entire system is based on a constitutional framework of negative rights leaves standing a basic notion that government need do no more.[12]

Underlying this notion are some basic assumptions that are rarely stated aloud but that I believe are part of the reason that public education is permitted to remain in decline for many, if not most, children of color. The idea that public education was to help create informed and enlightened citizenry[13] came about at a time when the notion of "citizenship" excluded African Americans, Latino/as, women, and people of various racial and ethnic backgrounds that differed from those of the so-called Founding Fathers.[14] Thus, the commitment to public education was designed for a citizenry that looked different from the one we have today and to erase, rather than celebrate, difference. This, I believe, has developed into an unspoken assumption that only those who can make themselves look like the worthy citizens for whom the system was designed are entitled to reap its benefits (notwithstanding the stated egalitarian goals of public education). When I say that to be "worthy" one must "look like" a particular kind of "citizen," I refer not just to physical appearance; I am also talking about behavioral "norms"—ways of speaking, ways of thinking, ways of being. To be deemed "worthy" of the benefits of public education, one must fit within a certain norm.[15] The problem is that despite much progress, the "norm" often remains white and male and leaves little room for the incorporation of alternative ways of looking, speaking, thinking. Lani Guinier phrased it well in the law school context: "becoming gentlemen."[16] Compounding the problem is the broad sense that those outside this norm are expected to be inferior and somehow incapable of meeting even basic challenges, never mind achieving excellence.

Looking back on my own educational experience, I distinctly recall moments when I was treated as something of an anomaly in circumstances that for me were perfectly normal. In the second grade I remember being introduced to a new teacher who was stunned that I could read the word "tremendous." At my high school graduation, I was greeted with shocked surprise and told, "You don't look smart," upon receiving several academic awards. In college, my presence in the honors program similarly was viewed with surprise, and I was characterized as "different" from most Puerto Ricans that my fellow students knew. I, of course, was not different at all from most Puerto Ricans *I* know and was taken aback when I realized the way in which I had been categorized by people whom I had viewed as not that different from myself.

All of this is a long way of saying that underlying the debate about public education is a dangerous notion that "certain" children are not really worthy of a quality education. This notion stems, in part, from historical development, from a constitutional framework that may be characterized as bestowing "negative," rather than "positive," rights in this area, and from a social narrative about ability, ambition, and worthiness that often excludes or, at best, marginalizes children of color. The most striking recent example of the negative effects of this narrative of unworthiness is the simultaneous release of studies about the importance of the preschool years in cognitive development and the proposals by some politicians that Head Start programs for disadvantaged children be cut back. Those promoting the cuts are all but stating explicitly that they want certain classes of American children to fail. The lack of access to quality education goes hand in hand with the notion that these same children are incapable of excellence, and for too many children this notion develops into a self-fulfilling prophecy.

Ironically, many of the proposals to save public education go about it piecemeal in a way that can serve to reinforce barriers for some children, even as they open the door to success for others. For example, there is a lot of attention given to magnet schools, to vouchers to help pay for private schools, and to "theme" schools like the Young Women's Leadership School in New York City's East Harlem.[17] The Young Women's Leadership School promises to take a small number of adolescent girls from East Harlem ("El Barrio") and provide them a challenging, quality educational experience in a sex-segregated environment where they also will learn leadership skills and what I call the "art of social climbing," including how to have tea like proper young ladies.

As someone who benefited from "special programs" within public education and who went to an all-girl parochial high school, I am torn about proposals that certainly help to save some children but that weaken the chances for the children left behind. The argument that at least some children will get a chance at success is compelling. But the unspoken assumption about those who won't be drawn to the magnet schools is that they are unworthy of attention. I know that my parents would have taken advantage of something like the Young Women's Leadership School and that I, too, would avail my daughter of such a school, were there no better options. As much as I hated my all-girl, practically all-white Catholic high school, I was aware of the space it gave me to focus on my studies, to learn from committed teachers, to have my voice heard, and to be free from the distraction fostered by adolescent hormones in a coeducational environment. I am aware of studies about differences in learning styles and moral reasoning between girls and boys, women and men and of the arguments in favor of sex segregation in schools.[18] As someone who has worked as a staff attorney with the American Civil Liberties Union and who has struggled with sex discrimination and inequality, I am also well aware of the arguments that sex segregation often results in inequality of opportunity to the detriment of girls and women who have less power in the society.[19] With all of this in mind, I look at the Young Women's Leadership School and cannot decide whether it is something I support or whether I should join the protests against it.

On one hand, when I can see myself in the small number of young women enrolled in the school being given a chance at success, I think, Why deny them that chance? On the other hand, when I can see a brother, sister, cousin, friend excluded from such a program and left in an environment where lowered expectations, violence, ignorance, and invisibility crush the natural creativity, curiosity, and potential that are the most valuable and joyful characteristics of youth, I wonder whether saving the few admitted to the Leadership School or its various counterparts is worth the risk of allowing the system to give up on those left behind. Should I even be thinking in these terms? Are the prospects for achieving both excellence and equity in public education that grim? I continue to believe that they are not. But I also believe that it will take a tremendous force of will and a change in our ways of seeing and thinking to achieve the full promise of public education. It will require that we throw off, or at least look behind, many of the narratives about expected "norms," about "otherness," about what is valued and what is overlooked, that have become deeply ingrained in our collective culture and psyche.

I had a flash of this need to change ways of seeing as I read an article entitled "Thurgood Marshall's Image of the Blue-Eyed Child in *Brown*."[20] The article talks about *Brown v. Board of Education* and how Marshall constructed a narrative in that case in which a fair-skinned, blue-eyed child is subjected to a separate and substandard school for "colored" children because she has African American blood. Marshall saw that only by presenting this image of a white child subjected to a senseless racism that had fostered the inequality of educational opportunity and resultant psychological scarring, could many people truly see the inequity. A white-skinned, blue-eyed child carried with her an unspoken "value" that privileged her to deserve to be treated fairly and with dignity. So accepted was that sense of value that it blinded many people to the degree to which black children were devalued and rendered virtually invisible. The differences in valuation based on race, ethnicity, and gender continue. Though much has been done to minimize their effects, these ideas about relative worth persist and ring through the current debates about public education, affirmative action, welfare reform, and so on—but not just these. They exist as well in our narratives about money and business, wealth and power.

As women of color who **have** successfully challenged and countered these negative narratives, we **must** continue to work to have our voices heard and to contribute to the efforts needed for greater inclusion. To do this, we must do more than "fit in" to structures that are loath to incorporate us. We must also do the work that is needed to make those structures more welcoming and inclusive. Most difficult of all, perhaps, we must reconsider some of the strategies that we used to achieve success and work to construct a model that will do more to help remove obstacles for those who continue to suffer the worst consequences of having been deemed "unworthy." At the same time, though, I do not believe we should abandon any and every opportunity that is presented as a possible means for achieving success. This society has a long way to go before its playing fields are leveled—that is why we must continue to work, to challenge, and to have our voices heard at every level.

NOTES

1. See, for example, Patricia J. Williams, "The Brass Ring and the Deep Blue Sea" in *The Alchemy of Race and Rights* (1991), 8–9. As Williams aptly notes:

"Theoretical legal understanding" is characterized, in Anglo-American jurisprudence, by at least three features of thought and rhetoric:

  1. The hypostatization of exclusive categories and definitional polarities, the drawing of bright lines and clear taxonomies that purport to make life simpler in the face of life's complication: rights/needs, moral/immoral, public/private, white/black.

2. The existence of transcendent, acontextual, universal legal truths or pure procedures. . . .

3. The existence of objective, "unmediated" voices by which those transcendent, universal truths find their expression.

2. See, generally, Richard Delgado, "Critical Legal Studies and the Realities of Race—Does the Fundamental Contradiction Have a Corollary?" *Harvard Civil Rights—Civil Liberties Law Review* 23:407, 1988.

3. Ibid.

4. See, for example, Patricia J. Williams, *Crimes without Passion*, in *The Alchemy of Race and Rights*, 92–93.

5. Some of my negative experiences in school mirror those that my mother faced a generation earlier. For example, I remember having to challenge a college writing teacher who insisted on giving me a grade of B+ + even when she could find nothing in my papers that required improvement. In fact, she regularly asked me to read my papers aloud as examples to the rest of the class. I became concerned about the grades because I knew that the "pluses" would not carry to my final grade; I wanted an A, and I was given no guidance on how I might improve. When I challenged the B+ + practice, the professor glibly told me, "I know an A paper when I see it." This statement echoed in my mind as a sad reincarnation of a professor's comment to my mother years earlier that she did not have an "A-face."

6. Professor Margaret Montoya tells a similar story about the creation and use of masks and methods of presenting oneself as a necessary strategy for navigating the different worlds represented by her private and public selves. See Margaret E. Montoya, "Mascaras, Trenzas, y Grenas: Un/masking the Self While Un/braiding Latina Stories and Legal Discourse," in *Critical Race Feminism*, ed. Adrienne Katherine Wing. New York and London: New York University Press (1997).

7. This sense of otherness is keenly felt and powerfully addressed by a number of women of color in the legal academy, many of whom note a heightened sense of "otherness," a feeling of being "outside" or of feeling "illegal," as a good friend of mine aptly puts it. See, for example, Lani Guinier, "Of Gentlemen and Role Models"; Linda S. Greene, "Tokens, Role Models, and Pedagogical Politics: Lamentations of an African American Female Law Professor;" Rachel Moral, "Full Circle," in *Critical Race Feminism*.

8. 347 U.S. 483 (1954). In *Brown*, the U.S. Supreme Court held that separate educational facilities are inherently unequal and that segregation that is the result of intentional governmental acts of discrimination is unconstitutional. While *Brown* represented a tremendous victory against segregation and extreme discrimination in educational opportunity, it is important to note that there are limits to the protection provided by *Brown* that are based on constitutional principles driven by the notion of "negative" rather than "positive" rights; that is, the Constitution does not require equal or even equivalent access to education; it only prohibits intentional, government-sanctioned discrimination.

9. See Rene Sanchez, "Urban Students Not Making the Mark: Majority in U.S. Fail to Score Even 'Basic' Level of Achievement," *Washington Post* (January 8, 1998), A18; see also, Susan Bitensky, "Legal Theory: Theoretical Foundations for a Right to Education under the U.S. Constitution: A Beginning to the End of the National Education Crisis," *Northwestern University Law Review* 86: 550, 551–552, 1992.

10. Bitensky, 552, 564.

11. Indeed, education law in this country is built on such a complex framework of federal, state, and local law that I do not pretend to begin to claim expertise in the area. All I am saying is that, taken together, the laws may be said to withhold as much as they give.

12. It should be noted that some state constitutions provide greater and more positive rights to education (including the right to an adequate education) and have served as a means by which to further equality of educational opportunity. See, for example, *McDuffy v. Secretary of the Executive Office of Educ.*, 615 N.E.2d 516 (Mass. 1993). Also, many scholars and commentators have argued for a constitutional interpretation that recognizes a positive right to education under the U.S. Constitution. See for example, Bitensky, 552–554.

13. See, generally, Bitensky, 550.

14. See, for example, Kevin Brown, "Do African Americans Need Immersion Schools?: The Paradoxes Created by Legal Conceptualization of Race and Public Education," *Iowa Law Review* 78: 813, 834–835, 1993. Brown describes the history of traditional (assimilationist) education as a "tool to promote Anglo-American cultural values."

15. How many times have those of us who have achieved what society calls "success" been told that we were somehow "different" from others in our racial or ethnic group?

16. See Lani Guinier et al., "Becoming Gentlemen: Women's Experiences at One Ivy League Law School," *University of Pennsylvania Law Review* 143: 1, 1994.

17. See Maria Alvarez, "City's All-Girls School Set for No-Frills Battle," *New York Post* (March 15, 1998), 14; Connie Leslie with Claudia Kalb, "Separate and Unequal?" *Newsweek* (March 23, 1998), 55.

18. See, for example, Carol Gilligan, *In a Different Voice: Psychological Theory and Women's Development*, Cambridge, MA: Harvard University Press, 1993; Deborah Tannen, *You Just Don't Understand: Women and Men in Conversation* New York: William Morrow and Company, Inc., 1990.

19. See, generally, Mackenzie Carpenter, "Engendering Debate; Report Claims Separating Students by Sex Offers No Answer to Gender Inequity," *Pittsburgh Post-Gazette* (March 12, 1998), A-1.

20. Anthony Amsterdam, "Thurgood Marshall's Image of the Blue-eyed Child in *Brown*," *New York University Law Review* 68: 226, 236, 1993. "It is interesting to watch the transformation of Thurgood's image of the innocent blue-eyed child in all of this. S/he first emerges as an ostensible example of irrational classification—a homey and familiar illustration of a meaningless class distinction utterly unrelated to race. Then s/he becomes the blue-eyed, white-skinned African American child, indistinguishable from her white playmate even in appearance, but consigned to segregated schools by the mere accident of her ancestry. Finally, s/he reappears in Thurgood's coda, following the scene of the children playing together. Against the background of that company of innocents, it is no longer possible to tell or care from what race the blue-eyed child has sprung. And that, of course, is no small part of Thurgood's point—or of his legacy" (236).

PART IV

NATIVE AMERICANS

Determining the region of the world from which American Indians originated is intriguing and has had lasting romantic appeal. Probing the origins
of anything is a legitimate concern of humanists; laypersons or scientific
persons in all categories have long puzzled over the original home of Indians
in the Americas. Surprisingly, each of the major theories advanced to explain
the derivation and spread of Indians involves something that is lost to modern times. Similarly, the Lost Tribes of Israel, the lost continents of Atlantis
and Lemurin(m), and the sunken land bridge across the Bering Strait show
the common characteristic that supporting data must be indirect because
fully conclusive evidence remains elusive.

However, scientists have made several discoveries in New Mexico, Texas,
and New Jersey of ancient flint points, bison bones, abalone shells, and skulls
but are unable to date these archaeologic remains as proof of early human
occupation of America. The majority of archaeologists, however, do accept
the results of a symposium organized by Richard Shuter, devoted to the
presence of early humans in North America, that recognized a growing body
of evidence that people have been in the New World for at least 35,000
years.

In all likelihood, the first people to arrive in the New World entered over
a land bridge in the Bering Strait area. They probably lingered in Alaska for
a considerable length of time and eventually followed western mountains
southward into Canada, ventured on into the western United States and
Mexico, and finally continued southward into South America. The economic
lives of the earliest migrants must have been based on hunting methods

adapted to subarctic conditions. The Bering Strait entryway appears to have
served as a cultural filter through which only hunters could pass. Their way
of life must have been unelaborate, and most of the later complexities in
their cultures must have developed in the Americas. In much later times, but
long before the arrival of Columbus, new groups of peoples from the Old
World continued to enter the Americas along the Bering Strait route and
possibly via a number of other passages.

In the 16th century, as ever-increasing numbers of European maritime
explorers ventured to the Americas, there was no difficulty in establishing
who was an Indian. The racial, linguistic, and cultural differences separating
Europeans and Indians were apparent to all observers. Indians belonged to
the Mongoloid racial stock, in obvious contrast with the Caucasian racial
background of the intruders. Indians spoke languages that differed widely
from one tribe to another, but none could be understood by the explorers.
Indians dressed in an unaccustomed manner, and their bodily adornments
were unusual, if not bizarre, to a traveler from England, France, or Spain.
Then, too, the main crops that Indians raise, maize and beans, were not
cultivated in Europe (Oswald, 1978).

In the history of U.S. Indian law, there has not been a uniform definition
of an Indian. In general, however, if a person is considered an Indian by
other individuals in the community, he or she is legally an Indian. The
problem of classifying a person as an Indian became more complex with the
arrival of European adventurers, fishermen, missionaries, settlers, traders,
and trappers. Three conditions resulting from these contacts were important.
First, white men mated with Indian women to produce persons of mixed
blood; second, Indians sometimes captured whites and made them "Indians";
and third, some Indians lost their identity by assimilation into white society.

The real need for defining an Indian is with reference to a piece of legislation at a particular time. A person who is on the roll of a tribe and lives
on a reservation clearly is an Indian; if that person moves from a reservation
but remains on the roll, he or she continues to be an Indian. If he or she
receives a clear title to allotted reservation land, he or she may or may not
subsequently remain an Indian, depending on the circumstances. Indian
status also is lost by voluntary disassociation from other Indians and by identifying with some other social segment of society.

No matter where Europeans settled in North America, it soon became
apparent that Indians had arrived at an earlier time and that a great deal of
diversity existed among them. In physical appearance, the members of some
groups differed from those found elsewhere, and even within a community
there might be considerable variation. Then, too, some Indians were primarily fishermen, others farmed, and still others hunted. They spoke highly
diverse languages and organized themselves in ways ranging from small, mobile, autonomous communities to large, stable confederations (Oswald,
1978).

Any reasonably systematic account of the lives of a people is called an ethnography. Their manufactures, language, social and political organization, art, knowledge, and myths are all ethnographic dimensions. The first comprehensive ethnography of an Indian tribe—or of any aboriginal people, for that matter—that made a significant impact on anthropology was written in 1851. The author was Lewis H. Morgan, and his study was of the Iroquois Indians in New York state. Most ethnographies written by anthropologists about American Indians are reconstructions made long after the first historic contacts of the groups studied. The time factor often could not be held constant for the early historic period, and as a result many descriptions were actually composites of customs at various times.

Different groups of Indians are usually called "tribes," yet no general agreement for the criteria of a tribe accommodates all North American Indians. The difficulties in deriving a concept that encompasses the diversity of social norms and cultural forms may be illustrated by a typical definition. A true tribe has a name, a dialect, and a territory (Kroeber, 1925). Yet among the nearly 50 major Indian groups in California, only the Yokutus and the San Joaquin had all those characteristics. Later, Kroeber (1955) reports that generally denominated tribes really describe small nationalities possessing uniform speech and customs. One should be aware that a tribe is not consistently a "tribe" (Helm, 1968).

Of approximately 300 aboriginal languages spoken during the early historical period, about half are now extinct. It is estimated (Chafe, 1967) that about half of surviving languages are not spoken by children of the tribe involved, and it seems unlikely that these languages will endure beyond the present century. Those that seem likely to last longer are Cree, Eskimo, and Navajo; Chafe is doubtful that even these will be spoken 150 years from now.

Linguists first established relationships among tribes on a sound base by identifying families of related languages. By 1896 Otis T. Mason had formulated a means of grouping ethnographic information based on environments or culture areas. The idea of describing Indians in terms of geographic clusters was relatively well accepted at the time, but Mason was the first to detail the characteristics of each area. A cultural area is a geographical sector of the world whose occupants exhibit more similarities with each other than with people in other such areas (Mason, 1896).

The concept was applied to American Indians most systematically by Clark Wissler (1942), and it has served as the organizational basis for most continent-wide discussions of Indians. The system has the advantage of fitting all tribes into a relatively small number of groups. Its major disadvantages are that it refers to a single time and tends to stress material culture. No two classifiers agree on the same number of areas and their borders, a disagreement that partially reflects the impressionistic basis for evaluation.

In 1824 the Bureau of Indian Affairs (BIA) was established by Congress to administer and supervise all activities of Native Americans and to ensure their welfare and eventual integration into American society. But in reality, the BIA was part of the government's plan not only to delay their progress but to ensure their removal to an area where they would not cause difficulties (Cahn, 1969). The first Indian reservation was established in Oklahoma, where from 1830 to 1880 Native Americans were forcibly removed from the Mississippi Valley and eastern settlement areas. To add insult to injury, the BIA sought desolate, barren, and unsuitable farming areas, far off the beaten path to isolate the Native Americans.

This treatment denied them the right to earn a living by the only skills they had. It also denied them the opportunity to practice their cultural activities. As a result, many native peoples, stripped of their dignity, became powerless and dependent on the government for total physical, financial, and emotional support. This system of "population management" is the best example of "internal colonization," as the Indians had been stripped of their land, culture, and political rights and of their means of survival (Gonzales, 1990).

The 1860 census was the first to obtain a complete census of American Indians throughout the country. In the first half of the 20th century, the American Indian population grew slowly, in contrast to the period from 1950 to 1990, which was one of rapid growth. Projections show growth of the population reaching 4.6 million by 2050. Nearly one-half of the American Indian population lived in the West in 1990, 29 percent in the South, 17% in the Midwest, and 6% in the Northeast. Between 1980 and 1990 the proportion of American Indians increased noticeably only in the South, from 26% to 29%.

The 500 American Indian tribes vary greatly in size. In 1990 the only tribes with more than 100,000 persons were the Cherokee, Navajo, Chippewa, and Sioux. Approximately 16% of all Indians reported themselves as Cherokee, 12% as Navajo, and 6% each as Chippewa and Sioux. The 1990 census showed that 14 tribes had a population between 10,000 and 21,000 persons.

In 1990 more than half of the American Indian population lived in just six states: Oklahoma, California, Arizona, New Mexico, Alaska, and Washington. Oklahoma was the state with the largest American Indian population in 1990, climbing from second position in 1980. Between 1980 and 1990 California dropped from first to second place, and Arizona and New Mexico stayed at third and fourth place, respectively.

REFERENCES

Cahn, E., ed. *Our Brother's Keeper: The Indian in White America*. New York: New Community Press, 1969.

Chafe, M. "A Challenge for Linguistics Today." In *The Philadelphia Anthropological Society*, ed. J. W. Gruber. New York: The Philadelphia Anthropological Society, 1967.

Gonzales, J., Jr. *Racial and Ethnic Groups in America*. Dubuque, IA: Kendall/Hunt, 1990.

Helm, J. "Essays on the Problem of Tribes." *American Ethnological Society*. Seattle, WA: American Ethnological Society, 1968.

Kroeber, A. "Nature of the Land-Holding Group." *Ethnohistory* 2: 305–314, 1955.

Kroeber, A. "Handbook of the Indians of California." *Bureau of American Ethnology*, Bulletin 78, 1925.

Mason, O. "Influence of Environment upon Human Industries or Arts." In *Annual Report of the Board of Regents of the Smithsonian Institute*. Washington, DC, 1896, unpublished.

Oswald, H. *This Land Was Theirs: A Study of North American Indians*. New York: John Wiley and Sons, 1978.

"Reviewing Native Economies." *Dollars & Sense* (9): 18–20, October 1991.

Wissler, C. "The American Indian and the American Philosophical Society." *Proceedings of the American Philosophical Society* 86, 1942.

13

Native Americans

Among the country's 442,000 American Indian families in 1990, six in ten were married-couple families, compared with about eight in ten of the country's 64.5 million families. Consistent with the national trend, the proportion of American Indian families maintained by a female householder without a husband present increased during the last decade and reached 27% in 1990. This proportion was considerably larger than the national figure of 17% American Indian families were slightly larger than other families—3.6 persons per family versus 3.2 persons per family. In 1990 American Indian married-couple families (54%) were less likely to have children under 18 years old compared with all married-couple families (70%) (U.S. Census, 1993).

The most impressive strides have been in the field of Native American education. Almost overnight, 26 Indian-controlled tribal colleges have sprung up. Before the 1969 Senate Subcommittee Report on Indian Education, there were fewer than five predominantly Native American postsecondary institutions. Title V of the Indian Education Act has opened the door for Native Americans to be involved in the teaching of their children and to integrate native language, history, and culture into the school curriculum.

Although the Native American high school dropout rate exceeds the national average by 7% it is gradually decreasing, and over 103,000 Native Americans attend two- and four-year postsecondary institutions, an increase of 36% over 1976 (O'Brien, 1992). Of all the states with large numbers of Native Americans, Minnesota has done the most to improve the level of

Native Americans' education from preschool through postsecondary, and the Minnesota compact between the states and Indian communities serves as a viable model to follow.

In 1990 the median family income of American Indians (including Eskimos and Aleuts) was $21,750, compared with $35,225 for the total population. Stated another way, for every $100 U.S. families received, American Indian families received $62. The median income of American Indian married-couple families was $28,287, or 71% of the $39,584 median for all married-couple families. Twenty-seven percent of all American Indian families were maintained by a female householder with no husband present in 1990. The median income for these families was $10,742, about 62% of the $17,414 median for all families maintained by women without husbands.

The proportion of American Indian (including Eskimo and Aleut) persons and families living below the official government poverty level in 1989 was considerably higher than that of the total population. In 1989 about 603,000, or 31% of American Indians were living below the poverty level. The national poverty rate was about 13% (31.7 million persons). Twenty-seven percent, or 125,000 American Indian families, were in poverty in 1989 compared with 10% of all families (6.5 million). Fifty percent of American Indian families maintained by females with no husband present were in poverty, compared with 31% of all families maintained by women without husbands (U.S. Department of Commerce, 1993).

When one reviews Native American health figures, it appears that the statistics are from an underdeveloped country in Asia or Africa. The infant mortality rate among Native Americans is 27.5% per 1,000 births, almost double the U.S. rate ("Reviewing Native Economies," 1991). Death from alcoholism among all Native Americans is 27%, over five times the average U.S. rate. Indian suicides ran 15 per thousand in 1988, four percentage points higher than in the United States as a whole. However, suicide among Native American males 18–44 years of age exceeds the national average by almost 100%.

Almost two-thirds of all 1.9 million Native Americans live off-reservation in cities, towns, and rural areas. This exodus from the reservation began after World War II and was accelerated by federal government policies of "termination" and "relocation." This fact, perhaps, presents the single greatest challenge to Native Americans in the years ahead. Historically, the reservation has been the center of Indian life and culture for over 150 years. Indianness and cultural identity of Native Americans are intimately bound up with language, culture, lifestyle, family, and community (tribe).

Few of these support systems exist in the off-reservation settings to the degree they do on reservation. Moreover, off-reservation Native Americans do not necessarily receive the legal, educational, and medical services and entitlement that their tribal counterparts do. Despite the attempts of urban Indians to organize in support of their entitlement as "enrolled Indians" or legally recognized Native Americans (one-quarter Indian blood quantum), both the lack of federal funding and reluctance to extend federal services to off-reservation Indians have greatly hampered the extension of services and federal protection to a majority of Native Americans (Wells, 1994).

Most important, a new generation of Indian leadership, on and off the reservation, has emerged: better educated, assertive, entrepreneurial, and schooled in dealing with the larger white society. It is increasingly determined to find Indian solutions to Indian problems. The emergence of 26 Indian-controlled colleges provides the nucleus of an indigenous higher education system run by Native Americans. Whether the cloud of dependency will be lifted in the near future is dependent on federal recognition of Indian self-determination and the ability of Native American communities to come forward with creative solutions to problems that have plagued Indian people for a century and a half. Without doubt, that renaissance is under way in "Indian country," and it has taken many forms.

CASE STUDIES

Asiba

Asiba is one of the Native Americans who, more than 300 years ago, called most of Long Island home. She favors the term "indigenous people" because it preceded all notions or inventions known as "Native Americans," which were used by the U.S. Bureau of the Census and other federal offices.

Asiba is a woman of the Matinecoc Nation. Her mother is also a member of the Matinecoc Nation; it is an Algonkian group, which is matrilineal. "My maternal grandmother was Matinecoc also, and her husband was Cherokee." Asiba's vibrant voice conveys pride and solemnity. Asiba has dual ancestry, because her father is Caribbean American of African descent. The 45-year-old single mother is very proud of her ancestry and very clear about the treatment of her nation by government authorities and corporate and community officials.

"We are an Algonkian people, in other words, the indigenous groups of the Northeast; we have many different groupings and share a common linguistic stock and a common cultural base, while there are some variations." Asiba elaborates. "Some nations have different accents, but because they are Algonkian, one can understand them. The Algonkians, while different, are called by the names of the land they inhabit. Shinnecock means 'flat land,' and they are farther to the east, but they are our relatives. Words like 'Indian tribes' and other terminology used bureaucratized us, so we tend to think of each other as separate and apart entities."

Asiba gives one example. "At Shinnecock powwows, some elder relatives might say, 'Let's go look at the Indians.' But they are revealing their own psychological detachment from our indigenous nationhood. They are really talking about their cousins!" Most senior relatives of the nation will have their celebrations, picnics, or barbecues at each other's homes. Although some elder members continue to participate in the powwows, others do not. These members regard the powwow as a family reunion, and they enjoy themselves away from the eyes of tourists.

Asiba grew up in Nassau County. When she was young, her mother worked as a domestic, while her father was employed by the local government. Asiba attended parochial elementary school for a few years. At the age of 5, her parents divorced. "After that, there was a lot of moving around," she remembers. Early on, Asiba felt the way to get along was not to be visible, so she internalized everything that she experienced in her environment.

Asiba attended a public high school. She loved cooking and wanted to take home economics. But her mother remembered the era when that subject was suggested for women of color as being best for their talents. Asiba's teachers had a more elaborate career in mind—restaurant management. "Of course, I would have to drop my social studies, literature, and foreign language for the change—all the courses that I needed for college. I could imagine my mother's reaction, since she was determined that I attend college. After 30 years, in some areas people of color continued to be denied equal opportunity," Asiba says in a voice tinged with anger and disgust. "I wanted to go to college, but when I sought help from the guidance counselor, he left me confused and disillusioned. "You would be wasting your mother's money. You are not college material," she was told. Asiba was disappointed, because her goal was C. W. Post College. This led to another unhappy experience. On her own, Asiba submitted an application and portfolio to C. W. Post College. Every week, she inquired about the status of the application from her counselor. Weeks passed without any news. Ultimately, she acquired information about colleges from a neighbor who happened to be a Shinnecock. Asiba asked her counselor about having a recruiter from Howard University visit the high school. The counselor was not enthusiastic but did invite one. It was a history-making event—a black recruiter from a black college visiting Mineola High School. Asiba was ecstatic just remembering his name—Mr. Blackburn. Her mother encouraged Asiba to apply to Howard; she did and was accepted. "I found my college years to be fruitful and fulfilling. Later I discovered that I had been accepted at C. W. Post, but my counselor never told me. But I'm not bitter." Mr. Blackburn is dead, but there is a Blackburn Center in his honor at Howard. "It was a proud moment when I stood with my children outside the building admiring his bronze features on the wall," Asiba says softly.

After graduation, Asiba taught in public school. "I told my students about studying and growing up at Howard. I recommended the college as a place of intellectual excellence and spiritual growth."

After teaching in, and experiencing, the large public school system, Asiba chose home schooling for her children as an option. "I think that I am knowledgeable about testing and learning. I discovered that part of my difficulty with public schools was the result of my being placed in a 'slow track' by the administration. I will not let my children be hurt or denied that way!" Asiba's words reflect her deep concern for her children's education.

About marriage and family, Asiba reveals her thoughts. She had not planned on marriage or family. But after confirming that she was pregnant, and since marriage was not in the foreseeable future, Asiba decided to have her baby on her own. She was 27 years old.

All of her life, she heard rumors about a destroyed burial ground where Northern Boulevard is now located. The story related by elders tells of officials recognizing the sacred ground and digging up a small part of it. The remains were removed to a mass grave, and a plaque erected in the 1930s in Douglaston behind the Douglaston Episcopal Zion Church on Northern Boulevard. Over the years, vandals razed the area. But what remains is a large boulder-type stone on which is engraved, "Here Rest the Last of the Matinecoc Indians." Elders repeat the story of how relatives, Matinecoc Nation survivors, surrounded the grave site, silently standing by ceremoniously while the farce was carried out. There appeared to be some pressure for compliance to make white officials happy. The event caused a lot of pain in families, because not everyone was pleased about it, nor were they willing to dress up and pose for photographs. Some seemed to feel that going to this event was a way of paying respect to the memory of loved ones who were unearthed from their original graves in a Matinecoc burial ground that stood in the way of the widening of Northern Boulevard.

Asiba believes that it was important to declare the last of Matinecocs all at the same time rather than as individual demises. The compliance, the silence, the righteousness of the Daughters of the American Revolution (DAR) types, the clergy, and the Boy Scouts led Asiba to examine and explore issues of victimized people who stay voiceless in the midst of being violated and the pathology of those who feed off violating others.

Does Asiba feel cheated? She replies, "I think, as any Jewish person feels cheated of moneys hidden in Swiss banks during the Nazi siege, I feel cheated due to the very morbid condition that permits the continued disregard of all indigenous peoples, while others are compensated, vindicated, assured and make a profit from our losses." Finding the site, Asiba reread the plaque several times and declared, "No way. This is not the last of the Matinecocs. I'm not getting married and may never marry. This may be my only chance." So standing at that grave, she said, "Here comes another one." There was no way she would terminate the pregnancy.

Asiba speaks lovingly of her children. "They are just wonderful. I used to think when I was alone I knew everything. But I learn something new every day because of them. As a single parent, working, writing, speaking, I just plan one day at a time." Her hope is that both children grow to be people who understand that they are entitled to the unlimited boundaries of this universe. "They know that they have talent. My kids love to learn. Fortunately, they are not subject to the bureaucracy of institutionalized education." She adds, "They study all year 'round. My son has to be reminded that it is past midnight; he is an avid reader of everything. Suntama is fluent in Japanese and corresponds with friends using their language."

As a traditional people, Matinecocs regard every season with spiritual significance. "Spring marks the new year. It's the time for the first plantings and what some call "June Meeting." In summer, the year is in its youth, and the corn is green. Some have what is called "Green Corn Festivals," but the youth of the season is in keeping with all the summer travels and summer socializing. The fall is the time for harvest when the year is maturing. It's the time for thanksgiving. When the year is in old age, the time of wisdom, we have midwinter ceremonies, or what some call "Spirit Feasts" or "Ghost Suppers," when the ancestors are honored. Storytelling is a vital part of interaction, too. It instills discipline within the young and is a means of passing on history and tradition. One of the significant features of the culture is developing a sense of responsibility and caring in the youth so that they wait on the aged, sick, and the children. Every person born Matinecoc isn't traditional. Some are defined by the concept of Christianity and couldn't care less about the seasons, except for a Christmas tree and summer vacations."

The word "successful" means "just functioning" to Asiba. "To me it means having the ability to assess your past behavior and gain insight for future behavior." Asiba, an energetic, articulate, focused woman, has spent the last 17 years investigating the emotional, psychological, and behavioral dynamics of the impact of "extinction" and documenting the presence of her people. She says that there are many parallels to being systematically raped and systematically extinguished. She has written and recorded tapes about the subject. Asiba edits and publishes *The Spirit of January Reflection*, a periodical that features stories of oppression, racism, conspiracy, violence, and other indignities against the human spirit. Asiba has energy and drive that fuel her passionate zeal as an advocate. Most of us would call her successful.

Suntama

"My name is Suntama, and I was born February 2, 1982." The attractive face is smiling, and the voice is full of cheer. "Actually, I was born in Mineola," she adds. Suntama was named after a great Matinecoc sachem who was a heroine for the Algonkian nation. "She was one of the activists for our people, fighting against oppression," Suntama explains. "Native Americans do not like the label of 'tribes' and prefer being called 'nations,' " Suntama goes on, explaining that most things are not written in words like in other cultures, but characters are used instead. Most indigenous languages are not written. English is not important as long as the sounds are phonetically clear.

Suntama has home schooling. "My level is comparable to the ninth grade in public school. I progress at my own rate. Subjects like mathematics and science are interrelated. Think of a tree with branches. I can select what I need as I progress. The Internet provides a lot of information." This young woman is excited by challenge. When Suntama studies biochemistry, she researches the source of the chemicals and herbs in the library. She discovers how they interact within the body. Often Suntama uses the Internet for direct contact with specialists who are familiar with the particular subject. Her eyes sparkle as she excitedly describes her self-designed program. Suntama finds the whole process motivating. "It's sort of like a stew. It has a little bit of everything in it, and it tastes good." She giggles.

An avid reader and a poet, Suntama is now reviewing movies. After carefully screening a film, she writes a detailed report, including her reactions. *Willie Wonka and the Chocolate Factory*, made in 1971, was her latest.

Suntama has made friends on the Internet. Some are Japanese teenagers. "I learned the language and now enjoy corresponding with them, writing in their language." Most of her peers are "pen pals" or "computer pals." They learn about each other's cultures and values. "It's fun to discover how we are alike and how we differ, but can interact with each other."

She holds a deep appreciation for people who share and those who are considerate of others. "I believe in being neutral—not trapping yourself in a certain mind-set. You keep your mind open and learn," Suntama says. This young woman wouldn't use the word "loyal" because it sounds so threatening. " 'Loyal' sounds like you own the person, but you don't really own anybody. I like 'reliable' better!" She is emphatic.

As for housekeeping, Suntama prefers to use words like "helping out the family" rather than "chores." She does the laundry and some cooking and cleans up the bathrooms. Cooking soups and making pastries are her specialties. "I make 'fried bread,' which Native Americans like. It can be stuffed with rice or fruit."

For leisure, Suntama and her mother draw and paint. "My mom's very talented and used to teach an art class. We go to Eisenhower Park and draw trees, too." Mother and daughter relationships have been mutually agreeable. "I've never had a big problem yet to discuss with her. We get along fine," says Suntama, smiling. Another adult in Suntama's life is Aunt Frances, who is very knowledgeable about herbal healing. *Kitsi* is a word from one native language that means "aunt." Aunt Frances is of Cherokee and African American descent. The word "family" has a special meaning for Native Americans. You do not have to be blood-related to someone in order to call him or her "cousin." If you are a Native American, you automatically become cousin to all others.

Suntama and her brother participated in ceremonies that are essential to young people reaching the age of puberty. The young man's coming-of-age is celebrated after his "Fire Light Vigil," where he is taken and left alone to spend the night with the creatures, his soul, and all others who gather with him. Some people call this *Keesaquan*. When the boy is successful, his people celebrate. For Suntama, her arrival at adolescence is marked by her first menstrual period. Her vigil is kept all night long by the women in her life. She's no longer a little girl and hereafter is accepted into the fold. She is told everything she wants to know. She's now expected to assume responsibilities as a powerful woman who menstruates. She has to respect such things as not preparing food for others, especially for ceremonies, and staying out of prayer circles. Because Algonkian peoples are matrilineal, the identity follows the mother. A girl's crossing is an extremely important event for the nation. Suntama feels these ceremonies are important, but she has strong feelings. "I really feel that sharing your first menstrual period with adults is really an invasion of privacy. If you spent the night with girls your own age, it would be more meaningful."

In the summer, Suntama swims and picks strawberries near the Shinnecock Reservation. During the winter, she cooks soups and stews.

"I like my mother, particularly the way she conducts herself and talks to people. I think maybe I inherited some of that trait. I'm not as strong as she is, but I think I can hold my own." Suntama is articulate. She wears some of her beadwork and earrings and rings that are her designs. "My plan is to learn how to type and become a typist when I'm 17. I'll also earn money with my beadwork." She wants to consider all options before getting serious about the future. One possibility is medicine. Suntama feels that she has built-in self-discipline. When facing a problem, she looks at the bigger picture and does what's practical for the bigger problem. If that works, it will work in the small situation, too.

Suntama gets along with her brother very well, she assumes. He's in her corner when Suntama needs him. Home schooling is the best thing that ever happened to her, she says with a serious look. "Public school was frustrating and monotonous, and those routines would never have provoked me to try to excel. I like home schooling perhaps because I have some control and need control to direct all of my energies into things that interest me."

Asiba and Suntama

In midadolescence, there are a catching up of understanding and a push of the self away from childhood. The self wants new boundaries and seeks confirmation of these new boundaries from the mother. The adolescent girl sees her mother as willing to listen and willing to see. Suntama is moving away from dependence on Asiba as a sole model of knowledge. When studying biochemistry, Suntama uses the Internet for direct contact with specialists. She is screening and reviewing films. Asiba recognizes and praises Suntama's talents and desire to grow. Her hope is that Suntama will understand that she's entitled to the unlimited boundaries of the universe.

Mother and daughter seek challenge and outlets for their talents. Some are shared; others are individual pursuits. There are highly exacting needs of the adolescent girl who wants her mother to watch and appreciate but not misunderstand, to watch and see and understand, but not to intrude, to allow individuality, to be enthusiastic and confident about growth and maturity, yet not to let go, not to forget, and, above all, not to abandon. This highly positive mother–daughter relationship holds promise for continuing in some form as long as the mother and daughter can look at one another and acknowledge whom they see (Apter, 1990).

REFERENCES

Apter, T. *Altered Loves* New York: St. Martin's Press, 1990.

Bolton, R. P. *New York City in Indian Possessions*. Vol. 2, no. 7 of *Indian Notes and Monographs*. 2d ed. Museum of the American Indian, Heye Foundation, 1975.

O'Brien, E. "American Indians in Higher Education." *Research Brief.* Washington, DC: American Council on Education, 3(3): 1, 1992.

"Reviewing Native Economies." *Dollars and Sense* 1(9): 18–20, October, 1991.

U.S. Department of Commerce, Bureau of the Census. "We the First Americans," 1993.

Wells, R. M. *Native American Resurgence and Renewal*. Metuchen, NJ: Scarecrow Press, 1994.

PERSONAL REFLECTIONS
by Janine Pease-Pretty on Top

IN HER HANDS

In the Crow Indian tradition, the eldest daughter is called "little mother." In my family, I have that role among my siblings and first cousins. Now, with my daughter's generation, my daughter has the role of "little mother" for all her years ahead. This is a complex responsibility that unfolds over the course of childhood and young and older adulthood. The Crow Indian culture is both matrilineal and matriarchal, two integral characteristics of our culture that invest even greater leadership and central focus on the daughters of the family. The matrilineal qualities of our Crow Indian culture are apparent in the determination of clan membership; each person is a member of the mother's clan. For the Crow Indian persons, there are three mothers: Mother Earth, biological mothers, and clan mothers. The "little mothers" in our families are assistants and substitutes until they become actual mothers.

My daughter Roses holds full membership in our family, clan, and district societies. At 21, she has acquired a rich and meaningful role, the role of a Crow Indian woman, a mother. She has come to this role through many years of assuming the "little mother" duties and experiences. Today, I have indelible faith in her capacities, abilities, and creativity. Today I have first-hand knowledge of her commitments to our family, clan, and society. My daughter has achieved this membership over the course of her lifetime in ways that engendered our treasured ways of life to her, as a student of these ways and a participant in these ways. The Crow way of life has brought her a name and a name giver that set life-giving patterns for her (explained later), has allowed her to partner in the design and implementation of ceremonial and family events and encampments that furnish and arrange her thinking, feeling, and worship, and has made her lifelong relations among her family and clan elders that model honor and respect in life's blessings.

The Naming and Name Giver

Part of being a Crow Indian person is the honor of receiving a name of your very own. In the Crow Indian tradition, parents and grandparents convene a meeting to discuss the need for a name and possible "name givers." The parents will observe persons in their family and clan whose lives exemplify highly treasured traits, like family devotion, religious commitments, community standing, and special achievements. Sometimes the search for just the right "name giver" is an arduous one. In a meeting of the extended family, the parents consult about the potential choices of name giver, and a consensus is built through discussion. With the choice made, the family appoints a liaison to the "name giver" and designates a time for the naming to take place.

The family liaison approaches the "name giver" with respect, basic gifts, and the request. The "name giver" usually accepts, for the request is considered in itself a blessing. But this request is not easy to satisfy. Many "name givers" seek appropriate names for months. They seek the name through dreams, prayer, participation in the sweat lodge, fasting, and introspection. The name must typify a theme or remarkable achievement in the name giver's lifetime. The name must be of a quality to be meaningful for the recipient's lifetime. Having given five names myself, I know what a deliberation with myself, my family, and the Creator this search for a name can be. The "name giver" usually designs three or four names befitting the child.

At the appointed time, the extended family holds a naming feast. The name giver presents the name options to the parents and grandparents. They, in turn, debate among themselves about these names. Sometimes they discuss the virtues of each for even an hour. The choice made, the name giver is informed which one is chosen. Then the name giver tells the story of the name, when it was conceptualized, and the background to the name story.

My daughter was named by my father's eldest sister. Roses and her brother received names at the same naming feast, when Roses was only 5 years old. My daughter received the name "Leads the Parade Three Times." In the context of Crow Indian culture, the parade is an event that marks the moving to a new place or a new season or the marking of extraordinary achievements. The procession is single file and on horseback. Riders dress in full, traditional regalia on horseback, the horses in full regalia with fully beaded trappings. Leading the procession is a virtuous woman, chosen by her people for her good works. With this name, the name giver chose to wish for Roses that she would acquire a position among the people to "Lead the Parade Three Times." We were truly blessed by the magnitude of this name and knew that we had lots of work to do to live up to its potential as a path for my daughter's life.

From the naming ceremony, a special relationship was made between Roses and "Gramma Jo." Roses was apprenticed by her name giver, spending many afternoons and evenings listening to her advice, stories, and challenges. For my daughter, the life experiences of Gramma Jo had become a classroom full of information, experiences, admonishment, humor, talents, abilities, and prayer.

When Roses became 17 years old, we were notified that she had been chosen "Valley of the Chiefs Princess." The district known as the "Valley of the Chiefs" had selected her to represent them during ceremonial events throughout the year. In this role, my daughter was a participant in the planning of the whole year of events both social and ceremonial in nature. During her year of responsibility, she helped plan the five-day encampment we have in July, led six grand entries into the arbor arena for the dancers, led the parade on horseback three times, spoke to the people at the evening powwows three times, led the clan honoring ceremony, and had a giveaway dance honoring her clan relatives. By the age of 17, Roses had doubly achieved her name—more than most women achieve in an entire lifetime. The district committee chose Roses because of her lifetime of training, her family devotion to the Crow way of life, and the path she had taken as a "little mother."

Her experience with the "Valley of the Chiefs Princess" office brought her into firsthand experience with the district leaders and designated speakers. She acquired a sense of protocol for the grand entry ceremonies, the parades and their internal order, and for clan ceremonies and her own clan members. Roses took the whole winter to assemble her various regalia. In the course of design, she consulted with her paternal auntie Henrietta about the construction, design, and tailoring of an elk's-tooth dress and shawls. As a team, our whole family took assignments in the course of completing the heavy, wool, cloth dress, applying beaded triangles with star symbols and the 500 (imitation) elk teeth on the dress. Our horses were being trained for parading, and Roses was practicing her horsemanship—not an easy task. To prepare, plan, and perform the duties of this office, my daughter acquired numerous traditional skills, knowledge of relationships among the people, protocols of honor and respect, and the spiritual practices in the ceremonies.

The Giveaway Ceremony

As eldest daughter in my family, I have organized many giveaways to honor those whose prayers have helped our family survive through the years. My brother, my two sons, my husband, my sisters, and I have sponsored "giveaways" to thank our clan relatives for their prayers, advice, and help. Throughout my daughter's life, she has been the official assistant for my responsibility as giveaway organizer. On its face, it looks like a pile of blankets and fabrics, given to nice people for acquaintance reasons. However, this ceremony is one of great complexity. The "giveaway" is a time for the sponsor to give back a small symbol of gratefulness to the clan parents or relatives who have taken a major role in the sponsor's upbringing and livelihood. The gift is no trinket, either. The gift has specific parts to it, usually including a Pendleton blanket, quilts or comforters, shirts, fabrics for dresses, fringed shawls, tobacco, and sweet grass or sage. The gift components have symbolic significance: the blanket is part of the lodge or home, the clothing is shelter for the person, the shawls are for dancing or expression of joy, and the tobacco or sweet grass is for prayers and relationship with the Creator. The choice of gift recipient has to do with clan membership. Those chosen to receive gifts have been involved daily and weekly in the life of the giveaway sponsor. The honor dance is not just a "popular powwow song" but the individual song made or composed to mark the remarkable achievement of a prominent family member of the giveaway sponsor. Roses danced to the song the Drum Keeper composed for me some years ago, when I completed my doctorate and received the MacArthur Fellowship. The song invests special blessings, as the music is a gift from the Creator. With each gift that is given in the district assembly, the clan relative makes a pledge to pray for the sponsor every time he or she prays and gives best wishes for the future of the sponsor.

To Study Is to Know

Roses is a bookworm. She became a reader at the age of 3 (so did my son). As a teacher and college administrator, I have been a writer and reader with a fever. As a single mom, I took my kids to work with me frequently. They both spent after-school afternoons in the library, at the computer, or sleeping under the table during my meetings. We went to graduate school together as a trio. From earliest memory I have of my parents, they were reading and studying, then sharing their reflections at the dinner table. I replicated that pattern and shared what I could of my reading, writing, and business with my kids. My daughter has taken up the business of self-education, going far beyond the normal "what's required" in a class, even to studying and self-directed learning. In preparation for childbirth last year, she read three books on pregnancy. When she had to write a ten-resource research paper in Composition II at Little Big Horn College (where she is a sophomore in computer science), she got a fever for pursuing "Crow Indian Women's Roles" and had nearly 30 references. In the course of my speech preparation on Chief Plenty Coups and education, we galloped through at least five books and as many journals to encompass what Chief Plenty Coups had said about education for the Crow people. We wrote the speech on our way up to the Monument Park some eight miles away. I gave the speech, and she critiqued the speech. To know is to imagine, to realize, and to put into action. In my lifetime, I have harked to the words of the Crow Indian Chief Plenty Coups: "Education is your most powerful weapon: with it you are an equal; without it you are a slave." To me, education is freedom. My daughter has truly caught that fever for freedom.

The Prayer Place

Elders pray in the morning and evening with the smudge of cedar, sage, or sweet grass. Each material brings to mind the many places our Crow Indian people live: the cedar from the mountaintops, the sage from the prairies, and the sweet grass from the river and creek bottoms or wetlands. So every day, at least twice, we take a smudge throughout the house and pray to the Creator. Although it is a routine time of prayer that I usually perform, my daughter and son are often asked to stand in for us, especially if they are up later than my husband and I. My daughter is always glad to fulfill this duty. Nearly each week, we take up prayer in the sweat lodge. For the Crows, the men and women sweat separately, for cleansing and a prayer service. The sweat bath is a half spherical, woven, willow frame covered with carpets and blankets. Inside, 12 of our women relatives fit, side by side. Just to the side of the door, a pit is carved in Mother Earth, where 30 to 40 fire-reddened rocks are placed. The elder auntie convenes the sweat ceremony and begins with smudges of cedar, sage, or sweet grass and other smudges for good living. Then come dipperfuls of water poured gently over the sizzling rocks. My daughter takes up the topics of her visiting aunties and sisters and, as the temperature and steam intensify, the prayers that reflect the worries and hopes of their families. These same ten sisters and aunties come there even in the subzero weather of the Montana winters. In yet another way, we have a place at the mountaintops where we bring our most ardent prayers, in a small mountain range near our home. In this place, quite alone, my daughter and I have prayed for our loved ones, our own heartaches, our hopes and dreams.

The Sun Dance encampment and lodge are another place of prayer wherein my daughter has brought her challenges and hopes. Every summer our family camps in the hills or mountains with 50 other families for nearly two weeks. Our camp is the first to be built, since we have the Chief Lodge for the encampment. My husband is the Sun Dance Chief. My daughter, my nieces, and I have lots of lodge builders to welcome and feed. As the dancers arrive, many come to visit with the Sun Dance Chief. The dancers go into the lodge; over 100 fast together in the July weather of cool nights and hot, dusty days. The fasting dancers pursue their prayers and sacrifice the comforts of life for three long days, never leaving the lodge. Meanwhile, outside in the encampment, the families of the dancers attend to the singers and their families' needs, to the fire makers and their all-night vigil to keep the fire burning, and to the announcers whose doorway leadership moves the ceremony through its course. Together we feed up to 30 people a meal, sometimes coffee and biscuits in the middle of the night. Although the actual cooking has not become her duty, my daughter knows the importance of all of these people, the singers, fire keepers, and announcers. She pursues the healing inside the lodge at the center pole, having been taken there as a little girl by her name giver.

We are American Baptists, since before the turn of the century. In the postsettlement history of the Crow people, the American Baptists were prominent in all of the districts of our reservation in southeastern Montana. The missionaries who came in 1904 and stayed for 50 years were influential in who our family has become. They were essential to the primary interest all of our family members have and have had in higher education. My father and his sister were among the first five tribal members to achieve a bachelor's degree. My mother, who is English and German from Butte, Montana, is also the first in her family to achieve a degree and is also American Baptist. The church was the only legal place for families to assemble up until the 1940s. Our family had the Baptist Church for coming together, for teaching themselves sewing and food preservation, and for the school the Baptists ran. The school was a day school, so that children could acquire an education and go home to their families after school. This Baptist presence made the Crow language and culture far stronger over the years, for the tearing disruption of the boarding school experience was not a part of the injury Crows had to experience in the early reservation years. Together, Roses and I have worshiped and held membership in this church, along with mostly our female relatives. My brother is the vice moderator there. But to note the full circle of this piece of our story, my daughter helped plan this year's "Honored People's Feast." During the feast, people bring their church memories and, in memory of loved ones passed on to the "other side camp," donations to the "Jesus Plate," and Roses determined to introduce her five-month-old baby girl (a new little mother), Tillie, to the feast throng. She said to them that she was happy to recognize Tillie Baby as the sixth generation in the First Crow Indian Baptist Church. The crowd applauded, and she gave $50 to the "Jesus Plate."

In Her Hands

The culture of the Crow people is in the women's hands. This is what we say about our way of life. Recently, we gathered as an extended family in my parents' home. As we were deeply involved in a debate over tribal affairs with my sisters and brothers, Roses' grandpa was overheard to say to his brother (both in their 70s), "Don't worry about Roses; I would put my life in her hands." This remark was not showstopping; there was not a pause that made us all forget what we were saying. It was a part of the living we have that is our way of life, and we know that "in her hands" our way of life will move forward into the future terrain of the Crow way of life.

PART V

VALUES

14

Family and Education

In this study, the mother–daughter relationships in 13 cultures were examined. All cultures listed the *family* as the most important ethnic value. This value has been honored and revered down through generations. Some of the mothers, particularly the Asians, voiced concern about the possibility of their daughters' marrying outside their ethnic group. Doing so would cause pain, disappointment, and shame to family members. Although each family engaged in practices that tend to strengthen ethnicity—for example, visits to the country of origin such as China, Japan, Korea, Puerto Rico, the Philippines, and the Dominican Republic; learning and speaking the mother tongue; studying the country's history; and providing occasions for interacting with kin—the potential for exogamy exists.

One daughter in the group is happily married to a Caucasian and has two children. In two cases, both products of intermarriage, daughters are dating Caucasian young men. Another mother sadly revealed that within six months, her daughter is expected to marry outside her ethnic group.

All mothers realized that as their children are exposed to diversity within schools, colleges, and the community, intimacy with other ethnic groups will occur. "We raised them to be self-directing and capable of making decisions. And it turns out to be a mixed blessing," they argued.

This is how *family* was described by each group in the study:

Ethnic Group	Description
Chinese	Without family, life is like a ship without a rudder.
Korean	Of all values, family ranks highest in importance.

Cuban	Family plays a vital role in reunification of refugees.
East Asian	Family is the source of East Asian ethnicity.
Native American	Strong kinship is vital in maintaining a tightly knit family.
Vietnamese	The family acts as a buffer against life's hardships, providing solace in time of need.
Puerto Rican	The family gives substance and hope to the lives of its members.
Filipina	The family is the beacon of light that guides its members through the stormy waters of life.
Mexican	The family gives credence to all of the cultural values of our ethnicity.
Dominican Republic	When all else fails, the family sustains its members.
Japanese	From one generation to the next generation, family values continue to represent ethnicity.
African American	For African Americans, the family follows God in importance, providing faith and hope to nuclear and extended families.
Haitian	Family is an expansion of the human spirit.

An extremely important function of the family is to preserve the lineage and the ethnic identity of the group through the raising and socialization of the young. Anyone foreign to the traditions, roles, and viewpoints governing behavior would disrupt the norms and prevailing ways. Therefore, the decision of selecting mates was an extremely important family concern and not left to young people. Personal attraction and compatibility between husband and wife were not the primary considerations in the decision making; it was the continuity of family and stability of society.

Betty Sung (1990) offers this explanation:

Parents see in their offspring the immortality of themselves. They want continuity of their flesh and spirit in an unending chain. Someone different in race and nationality coming into the family breaks this chain and blood will be altered for future generations. Invariably, ties to the extended group are loosened. Parents sense the act of intermarriage as a rejection of themselves and a refutation of their upbringing. Family bonds may be shattered if the alien member does not speak the same language and communication lines are blocked. (75)

Education as a value is perceived as being almost equal to *family* values by all women of color. Education facilitates the pursuit of significant goals, especially for minority populations. It can:

1. prepare positive role models needed for youth
2. provide symbols of achievement for families as well as the ethnic group
3. supply knowledge and incentives for resisting and combating racism
4. offer means for succeeding generations to surpass the ones before
5. fulfill the dream of immigration—a better life
6. serve as self-enhancement as well as group advancement

Thus, *family* and *education* values endure as mainstays for sustaining and enriching the lives and cultures of people of color.

REFERENCE

Sung, B. *Chinese American Intermarriage*. New York: Center for Migration Studies, 1990.

15

East and West

EAST (JAPANESE) VALUES

As many scientists have observed and noted, there are many areas of values congruent between white, Anglo-Saxon, Protestant civilization and Japan that have made successful adaptation possible (see Table 15.1).

Kendis (1989) described the "model minority" who succeeded in American society in the years following World War II like this:

Within the space of two generations and without violence and confrontation tactics of other minority groups, the nisei and their children, the sansei, made remarkable strides in socio-economic advancement and that advancement, in turn, is positively related to assimilation. In a study done by Schmid and Noble, based on the 1960 census, it was shown that the Japanese population in America had a greater percentage of college graduates than the white population (18.4% Japanese vs. 10.3% white). They had a greater percentage of their people in white collar occupations (56% Japanese vs. 42.1% white). They were second only to white males in terms of median income. (The median income for Japanese males was 99.3% of the median income of white males.) This ethnic group had done so well that people both within and outside the ethnic community felt that the third generation was, in everything except appearance, white. (21)

A significant difference in cultures is reflected by the low rate of assimilation noted by a 1978 group of Vietnamese comparing Eastern with Western values (see Table 15.2).

Montero (1980) studied changing patterns of ethnic affiliation over three generations, focusing upon four basic indicators of assimilation for the Jap-

Table 15.1
Japanese American Values

Name	Source	Year	Value
Mamoris Iga	"Do Most Japanese-Americans Living in the United States Still Retain Traditional Japanese Personality?" Kashu Mainichi, *Los Angeles Daily News*, June 21, 1967	1966	Self-needs have lower priority than group needs; loyalty to family; obligation to family; loyalty to specific groups; conformity; paternalistic loyalty; hard work; aspirations; competitiveness; compromise
Gene Levine; Colbert Rhodes	*The Japanese-American Community: A Three-Generation Study*. Westport, CT: Praeger, 1981, Ch. 6, 67–75	1981	High sense of family obligation; conformity; loyalty; careful work habits; good citizenship; achievement; group orientation; keeping a low profile; high educational achievement
Harry H. L. Kitano	"Cultural Sensitivity and Values" (work in progress)	1991	Duty and obligation to family; ethnocentrism; trust in parental authority; independence of family authority; alienation from community authority; social acceptance; competitiveness; personal excellence

anese American community: (1) visiting patterns with relatives; (2) ethnicity of favorite organizations; (3) ethnicity of closest friends; and (4) rate of intermarriage. The theoretical implications of Montero's findings indicated that as the Japanese Americans continue to move up the socioeconomic ladder, the very mortar that serves to cement together the ethnic community may begin to crumble. Family visiting patterns have profound implications for the maintenance of the Japanese American community. In other words, the higher the occupational and educational status the nisei have attained, the less likely that they will visit their relatives. This elevated status was accompanied by a trend away from Japanese affiliation, the choice of best friend being non-Japanese and possible intermarriage. Montero's findings lead to the probability, theoretically, that the ethnic community may have hastened its own demise by that very support that it has provided in order to enable its members to advance socioeconomically.

Table 15.2
An Asian View of Cultural Differences

In 1978 a group of Vietnamese, after suffering cultural shock in the United States, drafted a list of cultural differences. The list, with additions, is an excellent summary of cultural differences from an Asian perspective.

East	West
We live in time.	We live in space.
We are always at rest.	We are always on the move.
We are passive.	We are aggressive.
We accept the world as it is.	We try to change it according to our blueprint.
We like to contemplate.	We like to act.
We live in peace with nature.	We try to impose our will on nature.
Religion is our first love.	Technology is our passion.
We delight to think about the meaning of life.	We delight in physics.
We believe in freedom of silence.	We believe in freedom of speech.
We lapse in meditation.	We strive for articulation.
We marry first, then love.	We love first, then marry.
Our marriage is the beginning of a love affair.	Our marriage is the happy end of a romance.
Love is an indissoluble bond.	Love is a contract.
Our love is mute.	Our love is vocal.
We try to conceal it from the world.	We delight in showing it to others.
Self-denial is a secret to our survival.	Self-assertiveness is the key to our success.
We are taught from the cradle to want less and less.	We are urged every day to want more and more.
We glorify austerity and renunciation.	We emphasize gracious living and enjoyment.
Poverty is to us a badge of spiritual elevation.	Poverty is to us a sign of degradation.
In the sunset years of life we renounce the world and prepare for the hereafter.	We retire to enjoy the fruits of our labor.

Source: M. Furuto, R. Biswas, M. Chung, K. Murase, and F. Ross-Sheriff, eds., *Social Work Practice with Asian Americans*, p. 35, copyright © 1992. Reprinted by Permission of Sage Publications, Inc.

Fond and Yung (1995) found that Japanese and Chinese were the first to immigrate to the United States and were among the first Asian minorities to outmarry, usually to whites, suggesting that the decision to outmarry is influenced not only by proximity to whites but also by a wide array of factors that include upward mobility and similarity of values and traditions.

Montero, in an earlier study (1975) investigating generational changes in ethnic affiliation, forecast the importance of increasing rates of exogamy between the two generations. He wrote that the increasing outmarriage rate will have the greatest impact on the form of the Japanese American community. He found that the exogamous are moving away from Japanese culture (linguistic influence, religion, institutions, Japanese American organizations) and affiliations to a much greater extent than their endogamous peers. He predicted that if the present dating patterns of the youngest subgeneration of sansei serve as still another indicator, the prognosis for maintenance of community is not good. His findings indicate that over five in ten are engaged to, or dating, a non-Japanese.

Tinker (1982) indicated in his review of research on Japanese American intermarriage that the rate ranges up to 50% of all Japanese marriages in the continental United States and that the rate is much higher for the second generation of Japanese born in the United States than for the children of Japanese immigrants. This provides evidence of the thorough assimilation of Japanese Americans into the dominant culture.

Kitano's (1993) predictions are more ominous:

The present trend away from the Japanese culture in terms of norms, values, and personality means that in the near future there will be almost complete acculturation. For example, although Japanese and Americans have differed in the past in their collective and individualist orientations, the collectivity orientation has diminished among *sansei* and at present is similar to that of Caucasian samples. Egotistic behavior and the importance of self over others have developed to such an extent that it appears some *sansei* hold more individualistic positions than non-Japanese Americans. Similarly, standards of discipline, paternalism, status distinctions, and other parameters of the American value system show that the *sansei* are for all practical purposes completely acculturated. (201–202)

Mass (1992) examined psychological adjustment and ethnic identity development in interracial Japanese Americans as a result of increasing interracial marriages in Japanese American communities, finding that interracial Japanese Americans do not necessarily lose their sense of ethnic identity and that they may become more aware of their Japanese heritage because they have to struggle to affirm and come to terms with their dual racial backgrounds. The study also indicates that not all offspring of Japanese interracial marriages show social or psychological damage from their experience of being interracial.

As their values become more congruent with those of the larger American society, Japanese Americans will most likely begin to mirror the achievement patterns of American society in general.

WEST (AMERICAN) VALUES

What are American values? Defining them is comparable to answering a question asked by a foreigner, "What is a typical American meal?" The most nearly correct answer would be that an American meal is really whatever you wish: Cajun, Thai, French, Ethiopian, Mexican, Moroccan, Japanese, Creole, or Chinese. Values and cultures are dramatic conversations about things that matter to their participants, and American culture is no exception. From its early days, some Americans have seen the purpose and goal of the nation as the effort to realize the ancient biblical hope of a just and compassionate society. Others have struggled to shape the spirit of their lives and the laws of the nation in accordance with the ideals of republican citizenship and participation. Yet others have promoted dreams of manifest and national glory. Always there have been the proponents, often passionate, of the notion that liberty means the spirit of enterprise and the right to amass wealth and power for oneself. The themes of success, freedom, and justice are found in all three of the central strands of our culture—biblical, republican, and modern individualist—but they take on different meanings in each context. American culture remains alive so long as the conversation continues and the argument is intense (Bellah, 1985). See Table 15.3.

One of the first to speak of the specifically American character was J. Hector St. John de Crevecoeur, a French settler who published his *Letters from an American Farmer* in 1782. He set the tone for many future discussions when he observed that Americans tended to act with far greater personal initiative and self-reliance than Europeans and that they tended to be unimpressed by social rank or long usage of American values (Bellah, 1985).

Alexis de Tocqueville, another Frenchman who visited the United States in the 1820s, felt that the optimism of the Enlightenment had been tempered by the experience of the French Revolution and its aftermath and that the prophecies of the early political economists were finding an alarming negative fulfillment in the industrial infernos of English mill towns. Tocqueville came to the United States as a sympathetic observer, eager to determine what lessons the first 50 years of the first true nation might have to teach prudent and uncertain Europeans. He added to Crevecoeur's earlier sketch a more penetrating and complex understanding of the new society, informed by republican convictions and a deep sensitivity to the place of religion in human life.

Tocqueville spoke of mores, defining them variously as "habits of the heart," notions, opinions, and ideas that "shape mental habits," the sum of moral and intellectual dispositions of people in society. He gave currency to

Table 15.3
Brief Historical Review of Some American Values

Name	Source	Year	Values
Governor John Winthrop 1588–1649	*A Model of Christian Charity: Puritan Political Ideas, 1558–1794,* ed. Edmond S. Morgan. Indianapolis: Bobbs-Merrill, 1965, 92.	1630	Moral freedom; substantive morality; kinship; religious commitment
Benjamin Franklin 1706–1790	Poor Richard's Almanack. *The Political Thoughts of Benjamin Franklin,* ed. R. Ketcham. Indianapolis: Bobbs-Merrill, 1965, 341.	1732	Individual self-improvement; utilitarian individualism
Thomas Jefferson 1743–1826	Declaration of Independence. *Inventing America: Jefferson's Declaration of Independence,* Gary Willis. Garden City, NY: Doubleday, 1978, Chapters 15, 22.	1776	Religious freedom; freedom of expression; expressive individualism
J. Hector St. John de Crevecoeur	*Letters from an American Farmer.* New York: Penguin Books, 1981, 83.	1792	Personal initiative, self-reliance, self-interest
Alexis de Tocqueville	*Democracy in America,* ed. G. Lawrence and J. P. Mayer. New York: Doubleday Anchor Books, 1960, 279.	1835, 1840	"Habits of the heart": religious tradition; participation in local politics; investment in common concerns; self-improvement; acquisition; utilitarian individualism

Robert E. Lynd and Helen Lynd	*Middletown: A Study of Contemporary American Culture*, 1929 and *Middletown in Transition*, 1937. New York: Harcourt and Brace.	1929, 1937	Decline of independent citizen; rise of utilitarian individualism
David Riesman	*The Lonely Crowd: A Study of the Changing American Character*. New Haven, CT: Yale University Press, 1950	1950	Expressive individualism; autonomous character
Herve Varenne	*Americans Together: Structured Diversity in a Midwestern Town*. New York: Teachers College Press, 1977.	1977	Utilitarian and expressive individualism as mores of culture and character interaction
David Yankelovich	*New Rules: Searching for Self-Fulfillment in a World Turned Upside Down*. New York: Random House, 1981, 252–298.	1981	Self-actualization; commitment to others; sense of relationship to the past, future, and natural environment
James Oliver Robertson	*American Myth, American Reality*. New York: Hill and Wang, 1981, 223.	1981	Independence; being self-educated and self-reliant; volunteering to serve others for the greater good of the community; friendliness and neighborliness; a homogeneous group of like-thinking and like-acting people
Fermin Diez	"The Popularity of Sports in America: An Analysis of Sports and the Role of the Media." In *Researching American Culture*, ed. Conrad Phillip Kottay. Ann Arbor: University of Michigan Press, 1982, 259–265.	1982	Sports TV (media hype); physical prowess; hard work; identification of fans with team image; importance of winning; athletes as heroes; identification with the losers

Table 15.3 (*continued*)

Name	Source	Year	Values
Robert Bellah Richard Madison William Sullivan Ann Swidler Steven Tipton	*Habits of the Heart: Individualism and Commitment in American Life.* Berkeley: University of California Press, 1985, 1114–1116.	1985	Family; extended kinship; religious commitment; civic friendship; sense of community
Rupert Wilkerson	*The Pursuit of American Character.* New York: Harper and Row, 1988, 36–41.	1988	Self-fulfillment; charitable and volunteer activities; self-actualization
Mary C. Waters	*Ethnic Options: Choosing Identities in America.* Berkeley: University of California Press, 1990, Chapters 1–4.	1990	High value placed on family; high value placed on education; loyalty to God and country
Eight Propositions on Family and Child Rearing	Publication No. W.P. 21, New York: Institute for American Values.	1992	Family values: responsibility, honesty, cooperation, sharing, personal autonomy, self-actualization, commitment to others, tolerance, privacy

a new word, "individualism," as a calm and considered feeling that disposes citizens to isolate themselves from the mass of their fellows and withdraw into the circle of family and friends, a little society formed to their taste (Bellah, 1985). Tocqueville mainly observed the utilitarian individualism associated with Franklin, the self-made man.

Robert and Helen Lynd in *Middletown* (1929) and *Middletown in Transition* (1937) offered the most extensive sociological study hitherto undertaken of a single American community (Muncie, Indiana). The Lynds sought to show what was happening to America under the impact of industrialization and the social changes accompanying it. The Lynds brought a rich harvest of sociological detail to document what was by then an old theme among social critics, namely, the decline of the culture of the independent citizen, with its strong biblical and republican elements, in the face of the rise of the business (managerial) class and its dominant ethos of utilitarian individualism (Bellah, 1985).

David Riesman's *The Lonely Crowd* (1950) heralds the increasing importance of the expressive, individualistic style in postwar America. The autonomous character is what he admires. His concept is clearly related to some of the ideas of Erich Fromm and seems to be close to what has been called the expressive, individualist type, especially in its relatively pure, therapeutic form (Bellah, 1985).

Herve Varenne's *Americans Together* (1977) is a classic study of a small town in southern Wisconsin in the subtlest depiction to date of how American culture and character interacted in recent times. Varenne clearly sees the dominance of utilitarian and expressive individualism as modes of character and cultural interaction, especially the delicate balance between them and their mutual dependence. The drive toward independence and mastery makes sense only where the individual can also find a context to express love and happiness that are his or her deepest feelings and desires.

Today we see a number of surviving forms of the old ideal of the independent citizen, the civic volunteer, and the movement activist. None of these present-day representatives of the ideal of the independent citizen can avoid being influenced by utilitarian and expressive individualism, the pervasive world of the manager and the therapist. But they give evidence that the old cultural argument is not over and that all strands of our tradition are still alive and still speak to our present need (Bellah, 1985).

Wilkerson, writing in *The Pursuit of American Character* (1988:3), states, "Modern American character consists of those attitudes and traits that Americans *tend* to have *more* than other people have, or than they themselves used to have."

James Oliver Robertson (1981) describes Americans and their values as follows:

The Americans who live in real communities are independent individuals (sturdy yeomen) who work hard to sustain themselves and their families (on their own land,

in their own homes), who are self-educated and self-reliant, who volunteer to serve
others for the greater good of the community, a homogeneous group of like-acting
people. That is the logic of community. Americans are to be found today seeking to
live in, create, improve, build and preserve such communities, whether they are in
great cities or in the countryside, in Paris or New York or Vietnam or Alaska, whatever their variety of American—Black, Puerto Rican, Chicano or WASP, Jewish or
Presbyterian, Catholic or Muslim. The predominant symbol, metaphor and model
for the logic of real community in America remains the rural agrarian small town.
(223)

When asked for contemporary definitions of American core values, several
academicians responded as follows:

It means different things to different people. It's sort of like defining pornography:
"I don't know what it is, but I know it when I see it." It's difficult to describe and
there's nothing concrete. Family and community are basic. Extending one's self into
the educational, religious and specific welfare communities is vital. (Professor Sharon
Saffler, Sociology Department, Hunter College, New York City)

It is a complicated process to define, which calls for difficult distinctions to be drawn.
American values reflect a nostalgia for the past—a small town philosophy or idealism.
There is a traditional Anglo-Saxon Protestant work ethic. Individuals transcend whatever categories to which they belong to adopt a collective identity. Americans tend
to want it all, but there are group rights which are significant. You could say American values are just about whatever the Silent Majority may be against, e.g., affirmative action, racial issues and abortion. The fundamental question is to what extent
do the children of foreign-born parents adopt the dominant ways of society—one
way or another? They adopt them, not all at once, but adopt them more than they
change the society of which they become a part. That's essential, else the country
would fall apart. (Professor David Apter, Chairman, Sociology Department, Yale
University, New Haven, Connecticut)

It is impossible to answer simply, but in broad terms, I would say: (1) high value is
put on family; (2) self sufficiency; (3) strong work ethic; and (4) sense of community
and respect for others. (Professor Paul DiMaggio, Chairman, Sociology Department,
Princeton University, Princeton, New Jersey)

God, country and family—all understood in a modern kind of way. God is some
kind of all judging, all commanding God, but a God of love and affection. Family is
very important, as is the work ethic. Modern families respect individuals. People at
times need to be helped out, but at the same time, importance is placed upon independence. There is less commitment to the greater society than in earlier times.
(Professor Alan Wolfe, Sociology Department, Boston University; author of *One
Nation After All* New York: Viking Press, 1998)

There are a few values, but they might be quite general. There is a shared notion
of distributing justice. For example, in places like Thailand and India, people are

quite comfortable in thinking people should receive more or less by the very nature of what category human being they happened to be, i.e., caste. In the United States, we do that in practice, but we're not comfortable with it. There is this general ideal of fairness. (Professor Randall Stokes, Chairman, Sociology Department, University of Massachusetts at Amherst)

It seems to me that core values would be what the group regards as most sacred and most essential for group and personal existence. (Professor Eileen Leonard, Chairman, Sociology Department, Vassar College, Poughkeepsie, New York)

Historically, immigrants from other countries have resisted their children's assimilating into other cultures. Perhaps trying to find reasons why children assimilate is the real parental concern. Historically, this has been true of other groups too. When Jews arrived in America, they worried about their children marrying non-Jews. The Irish were concerned that their children not marry Protestants too. I think it is a typical reaction of parents who have come from a different country. I feel wanting children to marry within their ethnic group is most important. (Professor Allan Horwitz, Chairman, Sociology Department, Rutgers University, New Brunswick, New Jersey)

Core values include tremendous respect for the individual and tremendous respect for economic endeavors and mobility. Great value is placed on the nuclear family and on the local level, preservation of the neighborhood and community where one participates civically and politically. (Professor Nazli Kibria, Sociology Department, Boston University; author of *Family Tightrope: The Changing Lives of Vietnamese Americans* Princeton, NJ: University Press of Princeton, 1993)

In general, core values in the United States revolve around the notion of liberalism, individual freedom and individual identity. (Professor John Campbell, Chairman of Sociology, Dartmouth College, Hanover, New Hampshire)

By and large, it appears that core values are those variables that positively affect people, their lives, and their environment.

Intergenerational Perception of Ethnic Values

Immigrant parents and their offspring are likely to receive different opportunities for exposure to the host culture, and the nature of exposure may differ appreciably. Research suggests that the younger generation acculturates more rapidly than their parents (Boman and Edwards, 1984; Born, 1970; Matsuoka, 1990; Rosenthal, 1984). Children and adolescents, by establishing peer networks that include members of the dominant and other cultures and by having less entrenched traditional values relative to those of the older generation (Phinney, 1990), are more likely than their parents to abandon traditional behaviors and values and adopt those that are seen to be adaptive in the host culture. This generational discrepancy in behaviors and values, it has been suggested, is likely to lead to parent–adolescent conflict (e.g., Nguyen and Williams, 1988) and a widening of the popularly termed "generation gap."

Rosenthal (1984) found more conflict between parents and adolescents among immigrant than among nonimmigrant families. This finding may suggest that value discrepancies due to acculturation underlie this conflict. In this survey, when compared with the seven nonimmigrant participating mothers, this appeared to be true. However, two of the daughters were pre-adolescents. On the other hand, the greatest levels of conflict were observed among the most assimilated adolescents, suggesting, although inconclusively, that value discrepancy plays a role in determining conflict levels (Rosenthal and Efklides, 1989). Similarly, in the present sample, the older daughters, also more assimilated, appeared to experience the most conflict personally.

Another study (Rosenthal, Ranierti, and Klimidis, 1996) examined relationships between perception of self and parental values, intergenerational conflict, and gender satisfaction. Their study confirmed that adolescents perceived that they had fewer traditional values than their parents. This pattern was stronger for girls than for boys. Girls valued Vietnamese traditions less than did their male peers, regarded their parents as being less accepting of independence, and were more dissatisfied with their gender role than boys. For girls but not for boys, discrepancy between adolescent and parental values was associated with more conflict and greater gender dissatisfaction. The study suggests that girls have more difficulty than boys in dealing simultaneously with the expectations of two cultures.

In this book, the group of 17 mothers included 10 who were born outside the United States. All of their children expressed mixed feelings regarding the traditional values of their parents. All accepted wholeheartedly loyalty and obligation to family, competitiveness, high educational achievement, hard work, and priority of group needs. Other values, however, for example, religion, paternalistic loyalty, and conformity, were often seen as outdated and not relevant to contemporary life. In two cases, daughters were so distanced from traditional living that they were searching for a "category" with which to identify.

Although Japanese values have been described here in detail, similar value systems and structures are found in all Asian cultures, including Chinese, Korean, Filipino, Vietnamese, and Asian Indian.

REFERENCES

Bellah, R., Madison, R., Sullivan, W., Swidler, A., and Tipton, S. *Habits of the Heart.* Berkeley: CA: University of California Press, 1985, 35–39, 48–51, 127–129.

Boman, B., and Edwards, M. "The Indochinese Refugee: An Overview." *Australian and New Zealand Journal of Psychiatry* 18: 40–52, 1984.

Born, D. D. "Psychological Adaptation and Development under Acculturative Stress: Toward a General Model." *Social Science and Medicine* 3: 529–547, 1984.

Fond, C., and Yung, J. "In Search of the Right Spouse: Interracial Marriage among Chinese and Japanese Americans." *Amerasia Journal* 21: 77–97, 1995.

Kendis, K. O. *A Matter of Comfort: Ethnic Maintenance and Ethnic Style among Third Generation Japanese Americans*. New York: A. M. Press, 1989.

Kitano, H. *Generations and Identity: The Japanese American*. New York: Ginn Press, 1993.

Mass, A. I. *Interracial Japanese Americans: The Best of Both Worlds or the End of Japanese American Community?* Newbury Park, CA: Sage, 1992.

Matsuoka, J. K. "Differential Acculturation among Vietnamese Refugees." *Social Work* 35: 341–345, 1990.

Montero, D. *Japanese Americans: Changing Patterns of Ethnic Affiliation over Three Generations*. Boulder, CO: Westview Press, 1980.

Montero, D. "*The Japanese Community: A Study of Generational Change in Ethnic Affiliation*." Diss., University of California at Los Angeles, 1975.

Nguyen, N. A., and Williams, H. L. "Transition from East to West: Vietnamese Adolescents and Their Parents." *Journal of the American Academy of Child and Adolescent Psychiatry* 28: 505–515, 1988.

Phinney, J. S. "Ethnic Identity in Adolescents and Adults: A Review of Research." *Psychological Bulletin* 108: 499–514, 1990.

Robertson, J. O. *American Myths—American Reality*. New York: Hill and Wang, 1981, 223.

Rosenthal, D. A. "Intergenerational Conflict and Culture: A Study of Immigrant and Non-Immigrant Adolescents and Their Parents." *Genetic Psychology Monographs* 109: 53–75, 1984.

Rosenthal, D. A., and Efklides, A. "A Cross-National Study of the Influence of Culture on Conflict between Parents and Adolescents." *International Journal of Behavioral Development* 12: 207–219, 1989.

Rosenthal, D. A., Ranierti, N., and Klimidis, S. "Vietnamese Adolescents in Australia: Relationships between Perceptions of Self and Parental Values, Intergenerational Conflict, and Gender Dissatisfaction." *International Journal of Psychology* 31(2): 81–91, 1996.

Tinker, J. N. "Interracial Marriage and Assimilation in a Plural Society: Japanese-Americans in the United States." *Marriage and Family Review* 5: 61–74, 1982.

Wilkerson, R. *The Pursuit of American Character*. New York: Harper and Row, 1988, 40–41.

PART VI

EVALUATION

16

Findings

Education is today's frontier, today's civil rights struggle—the critical door of opportunity. Early recognition of talent is essential for women of color if they are to be successful in life.

EARLY RECOGNITION OF TALENT

Of the 19 daughters in the book, 7 were Asian Americans. Excluding the younger 6 in grades lower than 9, 13 were enrolled in gifted programs and honors courses, made the dean's list, and graduated cum laude. As for other talents, 7 were accomplished players of the piano, cello, violin, and flute. One was a noted mezzo-soprano, and 2 were members of a school or professional orchestra. Others earned awards in poetry, art, foreign languages, and oratory and engaged in a variety of sports and extracurricular activities. Table 16.1 shows this distribution. Likewise, the 17 mothers demonstrated excellence in talent (music and poetry) early in elementary school. Their education level ranged from graduation from a community college to earning a Ph.D. degree. Five graduated from professional schools of medicine, nursing, pharmacology, law, and music. Table 16.2 shows mothers' academic achievement.

PERSONALITY TRAITS OF MOTHERS

During interviews with mothers and daughters, many personality traits of mothers were elicited. Some were perceived as being "passed" on to their

Table 16.1
Academic and Extracurricular Activities of Daughters (Ages 9–34)

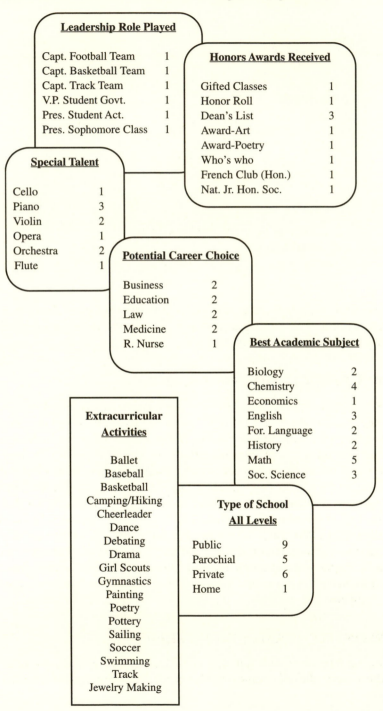

Leadership Role Played

Capt. Football Team	1
Capt. Basketball Team	1
Capt. Track Team	1
V.P. Student Govt.	1
Pres. Student Act.	1
Pres. Sophomore Class	1

Honors Awards Received

Gifted Classes	1
Honor Roll	1
Dean's List	3
Award-Art	1
Award-Poetry	1
Who's who	1
French Club (Hon.)	1
Nat. Jr. Hon. Soc.	1

Special Talent

Cello	1
Piano	3
Violin	2
Opera	1
Orchestra	2
Flute	1

Potential Career Choice

Business	2
Education	2
Law	2
Medicine	2
R. Nurse	1

Best Academic Subject

Biology	2
Chemistry	4
Economics	1
English	3
For. Language	2
History	2
Math	5
Soc. Science	3

Extracurricular Activities

Ballet
Baseball
Basketball
Camping/Hiking
Cheerleader
Dance
Debating
Drama
Girl Scouts
Gymnastics
Painting
Poetry
Pottery
Sailing
Soccer
Swimming
Track
Jewelry Making

Type of School All Levels

Public	9
Parochial	5
Private	6
Home	1

Table 16.2
Mothers' Academic Achievement

No. of Mothers	Years of School Completed		Vocations
1	Less than 4 yrs. of High School		Academic Dean
1	Community College		Consumer Affairs Dir.
1	Two Years of College		County Supervisor
			Criminal Court Judge
6	Bachelors Degree		Dir. Health/Welfare/
2	Masters Degree+		Social Programs
1	Doctorate		Editor/Publisher
			Hotel/Housekeeper
No. of Mothers	**Graduate of Pro-fessional Schools**		Journalist
			Medicine
1	School of Nursing		Pianist/Teacher/
1	School of Medicine		Director
			Pharmacist
1	School of Law		Real Estate Broker
1	Academy of Music		Registered Nurse
1	School of Pharmacy		Registrar's Office Clerk
			Senior Program Officer
			Supervisor of Education
			U.S. Congresswoman

daughters: generosity, independence, commitment, strength, advocacy, and creativity. For example:

Generosity in donating time and energy to helping others in the family and community was common among all mothers. They were active in registration for voting drives, alien registration, church organizations, community health drives, rallies, ethnic groups, and professional organizations.

Independence in thought and performance was shown in mothers as being nonconformists, self-reliant, bearers of responsibility for work, child care, and household simultaneously with a minimum of support, and solvers of problems without help.

Commitment to an idea, obligation, or goal was noted by all mothers who established a school or a young people's orchestra, completed medical school or higher education, or cared for an ill parent while holding down an important job.

Strength was demonstrated in handling hardships, unemployment, disappointments, divorce, rejection within the family and in the workplace, and completion of a rehabilitation program.

Advocacy was manifested by mothers who were "champions" of the poor, homeless, abused, misguided inner-city youth, and the elderly. They strove to make a difference through federal and municipal legislation and use of the media to create an awareness and worked with programs for new immigrants.

Creativity in the form of accomplishment both within and outside the school context across a broad spectrum of talent domains, including visual, performing arts, and music, was found in almost all of the mothers and daughters. They were poets, musicians, noted composers, acclaimed painters, published authors, journalists, and creators and publishers of periodicals.

MOTHER–DAUGHTER RELATIONSHIPS

There are different kinds of separations at different stages of life. Most of the daughters in this book received enough support from their mothers to emerge from the stage of complete symbiosis in early infancy. Becoming a mother in her own right is also considered to be a time of growth and separation from one's own mother, and this is often the case. But if a daughter merely assumes her mother's role, she does not achieve a real sense of herself as an individual who can support her own daughter's separation into selfhood. This confusion of roles occurred in one of the daughters who tried to imitate her mother's role. She suffered guilt and insecurity. As a working mother, the daughter tried to be a "supermom," just like her mother. But she soon discovered that "doing her own thing" was more realistic and, more importantly, gave her a sense of self.

In a 1997 survey by Columbia Broadcasting System (CBS), one question asked of survey participants was, "If you had a daughter growing up today, what one lesson that you've learned would you like to teach her to help her as a woman growing up in today's society?" The lessons most frequently named were "have strong morals/family values" and "be self-sufficient/independent." These choices were similar to those of this book's mothers. Table 16.3 shows how participants responded to the question.

Some researchers feel that three generations are involved in the feelings and behavior of a mother toward a daughter. They are closely connected with the kind of relationship the mother had with her own female parent. Toni Morrison's fiction, examined by Schneiderman (1995), is useful for studying an important dimension of the mother–daughter relationship as modified by the author's imagination and informed by her insights. This dimension refers to the mother's role in furthering or empowering the

Table 16.3
Parental Experiences Provide Values Lessons

	Men (%)	Women (%)	Average (%)	Women By Age			
				18–20	30–44	45–64	65+
Have strong morals/family values	24	16	20	16	10	17	39
Get a good education	16	21	19	18	26	23	7
Be self-sufficient/independent	11	18	15	27	22	20	11
Can do/be anything	12	13	13	11	18	10	1
Be true to yourself	9	9	9	11	7	9	12
Don't rush into marriage	2	3	3	2	2	5	3
Children/being a mother	2	3	2	1	1	1	6
No drugs/smoking	2	2	2	0	1	1	4
Don't have sex too soon	2	2	2	3	1	0	3
Don't need a man	2	2	2	1	1	4	5
Be treated with respect	1	1	1	1	2	1	1
Others	3	3	2	2	3	2	1
DK/NA	14	7	10	7	6	7	7

If you had a daughter growing up today, what one lesson that you've learned would you like
to teach her to help her as a woman growing up in today's society?

daughter's individuation process. In addition, Morrison explores the significance of intergenerational continuity as between grandmothers, mothers, and daughters. In the case of at least five of the book's mothers (African American, Japanese American, Chinese American, Cuban American, and Puerto Rican), grandmothers played a major role. They helped mothers internalize a strong mother figure, shaped survival strategies, promoted attachment strategies, and reinforced ethnic values passed from one generation to another.

INFLUENCE OF SOCIAL SUPPORT AND STRESS

Other researchers studied the intrusion of parental work patterns into family life and their effects on family relationships, social activities, and child raising (Bronfenbrenner and Crouter, 1982). By locating families in clearly defined communities and sampling those with similar social backgrounds but different work patterns (Cotterell, 1986), it has been demonstrated that factors outside the home exert influences on the child raising of families with young children. More direct paths of influence were found for work and community features with respect to observable behavior and practices of mothers than with respect to their attitudes about child raising, suggesting the existence of environmental dependencies in the relation between outside factors and child raising practices. The mothers in the study sought homes in communities that offered schools with extracurricular programs, as well as strong academic courses, libraries, museums, art galleries, and ethnic organizations that supported and enhanced their child raising practices and values. Mothers even sought employment that provided child care. Teenage daughters also found volunteer opportunities available.

In the previously mentioned, September 1997 CBS telephone poll among a nationwide random sample of 1,051 adults (580 women were interviewed), the purpose was to identify major changes in women's status over the past 25 years. Findings include: (1) the greatest impact on women's status has been the job opportunities that have opened up for women and the fact that so many women are working outside the home (37% mentioned they were), and (2) by the largest margin since the question was first asked in 1974, women say they would prefer having a job outside the home to staying home and taking care of a house and family. Half now say this, compared with 36% who preferred working outside the home in 1974. Younger women are sure of this.

Working women are also more likely than they were a decade ago to say their work is a career and not just a job. In 1985, 41% of working women described their work as a career. That figure is now 59%.

FAMILIES

All mothers considered the family as having the most significant personal value. The family is sacred, and all members honor and respect its power.

For spouses of the mothers, some aspects of the rigid traditional patriarchal role was seen in those born outside the United States in that they were considered to be the "head" of the family and made all major decisions concerning its members. When one mother won an award (money), it was quickly turned over to her spouse. But the majority of the spouses in the survey appeared to be more egalitarian—sharing child care, household tasks, and decision making. For African American families, the stereotypical matriarchal structure did not exist. There was role flexibility in sharing of roles between husband and wife. Mack (1978) studied African American families and found that patterns of dominance varied by geographical region, age, and the context of the situation. Willie's studies (1976, 1978) similarly have shown that patterns of power relationships between both middle and working-class black spouses were predominantly egalitarian.

Research on decision making among spouses in intergenerationally linked Puerto Rican families in the United States showed significant differences in assimilation between the parent and child generations. The sociocultural norms of the parent generation, born and raised in Puerto Rico, reflect those of a modified patriarchal society, while the sociocultural norms of the child generation, born and raised in the United States, reflect those of a transitional egalitarian society (Cooney et al., 1982).

All of the mothers made significant use of extended family members to provide child care, escort service, after-school supervision, household tasks, shopping, and vacations. An examination of upwardly mobile patterns in black families and other families of color indicates that the education and achievement of middle-class individuals often are impossible without the support of extended family. This was clearly the case of the family of our Korean mother, whose father sponsored and supported all nieces and nephews in college. Upward mobility, the result of professional training, leading to high-paying jobs, appears to require intensive effort by family members, and without perseverance, there is a tendency for status to decline. The employment of both parents is required for initiation and maintenance of upward mobility, but maternal employment appears to lessen if the husband is able to support the family adequately on his salary. Families with only one parent are at a distinct disadvantage and find it difficult to maintain their hard-earned status (McAdoo, 1997).

Latinos, regardless of their national origins (e.g., Mexican American, Central American, Cuban American, Puerto Rican, Dominican Republic), have reported a strong commitment to family.

Certain dimensions of family are stronger than others with each successive generation in the United States. For example, regardless of acculturation levels, Latinos perceive a high level of family support and desire geographical closeness to their families (Keefe and Padilla, 1987). Other dimensions of family decrease with increasing levels of acculturation, for example, using family members as role models exclusively and needing to be the only source of material and emotional support to members of their extended family

(Cooney and Rogler, 1982). However, even among the most acculturated individuals, Latinos' attitudes and behaviors are still more family-oriented than those of Anglos (Hurtado, 1995).

Dorenbusch et al. (1985) studied mother-only households and found that these females are associated with particular patterns of family decision making and adolescence deviance, even when family income and parental education were controlled. To the contrary, the survey mothers praised their adolescent daughters for effective decision-making ability, excellent surrogate mother skills, reliable and competent judgment, and cooperation. Mothers perceived that such activities promoted the daughters' maturity and self-assurance. As to families with one child, these daughters exhibited similar positive characteristics. The daughters complained of loneliness in growing up without siblings. They felt the need for sibling companionship, interaction, and love.

PARENTING

Parents develop their own parenting theory based on their culture and reference group socialization, in addition to individual and family experiences, personality styles, and characteristics of their children (Brooks, 1991). African Americans, Hispanics, and Asian Americans constitute the three major ethnic groups in the United States. Ethnic groups share the same aspirations as the majority culture but often lack the means to attain these goals. Also common to these groups is their use of adaptive strategies, including extended families, role flexibility, biculturism, and collectivism versus individualism, including loyalty to the group (Harrison et al., 1990).

Gender equality in the future depends partly on how women and men combine employment and family responsibilities in the present. The decisions that mother and father make about work and family, especially about how they care for their children, help shape children's cognitive maps, social behavior, and personal expectations. Brayfield (1995) explored the impact of employment schedules on fathers' caring for children. His findings reinforce the idea that time, as a finite, scarce, and valuable resource, is an instrumental facet of the parent role. Particular employment schedules may allow men to commit more time to nurturing activities with their children, thereby enhancing the men's experience of the father role. Paternal involvement in child raising may reduce the role stress/overload or the feelings of inequity of many mothers. The spouse of one of the survey mothers provides sole supervision of his young daughter's activities after school and into the evening, if her mother is still working.

In a related area, other researchers studied the effect of fathers' time spent with their children and the children's academic achievement. Although time spent with children had marginal effects on grades, regardless of the activity that father and child shared, time shared was well spent. The importance of building a trusting relationship and providing a positive role model is stressed as vital. Fathers spending time with children may not improve achievement or intelligence scores, but, according to a recent study, breast-feeding may. Harwood and Fergusson's study (1998) suggests that young-sters who were breast-fed as babies do better in school and score higher in standardized tests of math and reading skills. The authors involved more than 1,000 New Zealand children through age 18 and bolstered evidence that breast-feeding helps make smarter kids. They subscribe to the theory that fatty acids that are present in breast milk, but not in formulas, promoted lasting brain development, which increases the longer the breast-feeding continues. Fourteen of the survey breast-fed their children or child. Three were unable to, due to pregnancy complications, the demands of their job, or war conditions. They increased nurturing, cuddling, singing, and talk-ing to their babies to substitute for the breast-feeding. Of the mothers themselves, 15 remembered being told by their mothers that they were breast-fed.

SOCIAL MOBILITY ACROSS GENERATIONS

The transmission of values, status, and behaviors from one generation to the next has been a central concern to family sociologists over the past half century, in part because it sheds light on the family's role in reproducing or modifying the social structure through the socialization of children (Biblarz, Bengston, and Bucur, 1996). One dimension of the debate over "American family decline" (Popenoe, 1993) is how social changes in the 20th century have affected transmission of socioeconomic and cultural resources.

Bengston (1975) tracked members of subsequent generations down family lineages and compared the level of transmission of values among the three generations. He found considerable value similarity between parents and children in both intergenerational dyads. Generation membership did not seem to condition the impact that parents' values had on children's values. Biblarz, Bengston, and Bucur (1996) studied differences in patterns of social mobility experienced by three generations. Grandmothers, mothers, and daughters were subjected to very similar experiences of occupational segre-gation. The sample studied consisted of predominantly white families who, in 1971, had been in the United States for at least three generations. Among this group, researchers found both change and stability in the patterns of mobility across generations. Findings are consistent with the conclusion that gender-based occupational discrimination has made it equally difficult for three successive generations of daughters to choose occupations that go against type. One hypothesis, which predicted that each generation would achieve overall higher occupational positions than those of the parent's gen-eration, was supported.

In the area of occupational choices, this book's parental choices of nursing, education, law, music, medicine, and journalism are the potential choices of the daughters whose mothers are enjoying these occupations. Careers in science are still difficult for women to enter, as are positions in the corporate structure. Barriers still remain at the highest levels of teaching in medical schools and hospitals.

Twelve of the survey mothers were still actively involved with their own mothers and are maintaining a positive, warm relationship with them. These 12 grandmothers recognize transmission of artistic, musical, and communication talents and leadership skills in their granddaughters, which were also characteristic of their mothers.

In this survey, mothers hope their own education and experience will serve as an excellent model for their daughters. In turn, the daughters' own expanding education and experiences will assist them in raising their children as independent and self-actualizing girls and boys. As barriers to achievement drop, perceptions change and grow, and daughters continue to evolve over the next decade with an effective sense of self and increasing assertiveness and coping strategies, they will follow individual paths to achievement. Their mothers' contributions to their daughters and granddaughters will branch out and affect the lives of many future generations of girls—an incomparable gift to society.

REFERENCES

Bengston, V. L. "Generations and Family Effects in Values, Socialization." *American Sociological Review* 40, 1975.

Biblarz, T. J., Bengston, V., and Bucur, A. "Social Mobility across Three Generations." *Journal of Marriage and the Family*, 1996.

Brayfield, A. "Juggling Jobs and Kids; The Impact of Employment Schedules in Fathers' Caring for Children." *Journal of Marriage and Family* 57, May 1995.

Bronfenbrenner, W., and Crouter, A. C. "Work and Family through Time and Space." In *Families That Work: Children in a Changing World*, ed. S. B. Kamernan and C. D. Hayes. Washington, DC: National Academy, 1982, 39–83.

Brooks, J. B. *The Process of Parenting*, Toronto: Mayfield, 1991.

Columbia Broadcasting System (CBS) News Poll. "Major Changes in Women's Status over the Past 25 Years." 1997.

Cooney, R. S., Rogler, J., Hurrel, R., and Ortiz, V., "Decision Making in Intergenerational Puerto Rican Families." *Journal of Marriage and the Family*, 44(3), August 1982.

Cotterell, J. "Work and Community Influences on the Quality of Child Rearing." *Child Development* 57: 362–374, 1986.

Dorenbusch, S., Caresmith, J. Bushwall, S., Ritter, P., Leiderman, H., Hastorf, A., and Gross, R. "Single Parents, Extended Households and the Control of Adolescents." *Child Development* 56: 326–341, 1985.

Garbarino, J., and Sherman, D. "High-Risk Neighborhoods and High-Risk Families: The Human Ecology of Child Maltreatment." *Child Development* 51: 188–198, 1980.

Harrison, A. O., Wilson, M. N., Pine, C. J, Chan, S. Q., and Buriel, B. "Family Ecologies of Ethnic Minority Children." *Child Development* 61: 347–362, 1990.

Harwood, L. J., and Ferguson, D. M. "Breastfeeding and Later Cognitive Academic Outcomes." *Pediatrics* 101(1): 70, January 1998.

Hurtado, A. "Variations, Combinations and Evolutions: Latino Families in the United States." In *Understanding Latino Families*, ed. R. Zambana. Thousand Oaks, CA: Sage, 1995.

Keefe, S., and Padilla, D. *Chicago Ethnicity*. Albuquerque, NM: University of New Mexico, 1987.

Mack, D. "The Power Relationship in Black Families and White Families." In *The Black Family: Essays and Studies*, ed. R. Staples. Belmont, CA: Wadsworth, 1978, 144–149.

McAdoo, H. P. "Upward Mobility across Generations in African-American Families." In *Black Families*, ed. H. McAdoo. Thousand Oaks, CA: Sage, 1997.

Popenoe, D. "American Family Decline, 1960–1990: A Reason and Appraisal." *Journal of Marriage and Family*, 55, 1993.

Schneiderman, L. *"Toni Morrison: Mothers and Daughters": Imagination, Cognition and Personality*. Amityville, NY: Baywood. 14 (4), 1994–1995.

Waters, M. *Ethnic Options: Choosing Ethnic Identities in America*. Berkeley, CA: University of California, 1990, Ch. 1–4.

Willie, C. *A New Look at Black Families*. Bayside, NY: General Hall, 1976.

Willie, C., and Greenblatt, S. "Four Classic Studies of Power Relationships in Black Families: A Review and Look to the Future." *Journal of Marriage and Family*, November 1978.

17

Summary and Conclusions

As we enter the 21st century, the United States has once again become a nation of immigrants. This population transition is occurring in a historical context that includes the restructuring of the U.S. economy and the advent of a conservative political climate. Many changes in American life, including a great influx of people from around the world, have created a nation of diversity. How many of these new American women will have the opportunity for self-actualization? Only time will tell.

The women's case studies reveal how they learned to set effective limits, set high standards without feeling guilty, and occasionally reevaluate their goals in terms of expending energy, time, and effort.

They believed their dreams were possible. Their biggest challenge was achieving a balance among work, family, and home responsibilities and relationships. Many studies substantiate this difficulty.

Several of the women were expected to adopt the male model of achievement and success, which embodies public acclaim and affirmation, peer approval, and financial rewards. Attempting to identify with the male model of success can be destructive to one's physical and mental health. But, like the others, these women chose to pursue their goals with subtle differences and be content with inner rewards over public recognition.

Many circumstances in the lives of the women appeared to be overwhelming; they were capable of looking into the depths of themselves and facing inequities in spite of the potential lowering of self-respect and self-esteem. Quite often, women who challenge the status quo and the autonomy of men jeopardize their social status, economic security, future goals, and well-being. These women chanced this situation. Some, at times, received derision, criticism, and estrangement from family and kin. They heard the familiar, "How many degrees do you want?," "Your children need you," or "What about your husband?" Yet they felt strong and confident about their choices and persevered—taking the risk of going against tradition and culture.

Environmental factors were significant within the family and within the community. Seventy-five percent of mothers came from stable, middle-class families; most had at least one parent who had attended or graduated from college; 50% had siblings who were professionals; and 75% had either parents or aunts and uncles who were recipients of higher education. Twenty-five percent of the mothers were products of stable, working-class backgrounds. The community at large offered many opportunities for continuing education, career exploration, artistic and literary enrichment, and personal growth and development.

Some coping strategies used were neither profound nor dynamic but could be homilies that would be useful to anyone, for example: accept racism as being alive and thriving in the United States, but don't let it blind you; persevere despite disappointment and failure; seek out and use available resources; consider alternatives; create new pathways to solutions; and discover support, strength, and solace from a "higher power"—pray. Mothers' strategies also included seduction, diplomacy, invitations to other important parts of their lives, and innocent intrigue. But most importantly, their belief that family is the most sacred value helped to convince spouses and kin that an informed mother is one who is better able to help her children grow and develop into mature, self-supporting adults.

Although earlier research completed by Terman (1916) emphasized the hereditary aspects of recognized genius, Leta Hollingworth (1926) stressed the essential environmental components: education and opportunity. She acknowledged that what a person is capable of doing might depend on heredity, but what he or she actually does accomplish most likely depends on the environment. These women of color had both. For this group, "success" was, for the most part, due more to their socioeconomic status than to their membership in a particular ethnic group.

The futures of immigrant children appear bright. Reuben G. Rumbaut, a sociologist at Michigan State University, and his colleague at Princeton University recently reported findings of a multiyear survey that is the largest ever of the children of immigrants (Dugger, 1998). These children now account for almost one in five American children, overwhelmingly prefer English to their parents' native tongues, and have higher grades and lower school dropout rates than other American children. The research team first interviewed 5,200 youngsters in southern California and south Florida in 1992, when the youths were in the eighth or ninth grades, and tracked down 82% of them for a second interview in 1996, when most were high school seniors.

The most striking findings of the bicoastal survey from San Diego and Miami, Dade, and Broward Counties in south Florida have to do with the contentious issue of language. While nine out of ten of the youths surveyed spoke a language other than English at home, almost the same proportion, 85% preferred English by the end of high school.

The study presents a generally upbeat portrayal of the children of immigrants as ambitious, hopeful, and resilient in the face of discrimination. In San Diego, the children of immigrants had better grades than their American peers in every grade. The gap narrowed over time, largely because poorly performing children of immigrants were more likely to stay in school than their peers who were not children of immigrants, the researchers believe. The team also found when studying national origin that levels of scholastic success diverged sharply. Generally, the children whose immigrant parents had better education and jobs and who came from stable, two-parent families were predictably more successful, with a few startling exceptions. But the question of how these children will do in college and the job market is still open. The study investigators said the survey brought into sharp relief the extraordinary diversity of the children of immigrants, not only by national origin but also by social class (Rumbaut and Portes, 1998).

Seventeen mothers representing 13 different ethnic groups and 19 of their daughters participated in this microethnographic survey of successful women of color and their daughters. They were deemed to be "successful" by personnel of social, health, and community agencies and educational institutions. They were also perceived to be talented and gifted by their nominees. In this survey, "talented" and "gifted" are terms used to describe outstanding, demonstrated, or potential intellect, expressive and practical ability in a domain compared with others of the same ethnic group and opportunity. In this sense, giftedness includes cognitive, verbal, artistic, spatial, interpersonal, and healing arts. Survey questions dealt with ability to achieve despite traditional and ethnic barriers, mother–daughter relationships, achievement, role of working mother, daughters' self-perception, coping mechanisms, and personal definition of success.

REFERENCES

Dugger, C. "Among Young of Immigrants, Outlook Rises," *New York Times*, March 21, 1998.

Hollingworth, L. *Adolescence: That Difficult Age*. Chicago, IL: University of Chicago, 1931.

Rumbaut, R., and Portes, A. *Children of Immigrants: Longitudinal Study*. New York: Russell Sage Foundation, 1989– .

Terman, L. *Measuring Intelligence: An Exploration Guide*. Boston: Houghton Mifflin, 1916.

Index

Page numbers in *italics* refer to tables or figures.

About the Contributors

ESSIE E. LEE is professor Emerita of Urban Public Health Program at Hunter College of CUNY, where she was Coordinator of Field Experiences for graduate and undergraduate students and taught group dynamics to graduate students. Her most recent books include *A Matter of Life and Technology* (1987) and *Breaking the Connection* (1988).

REV. THELMA B. BURGONIO-WATSON is the mother of Anastasia, 10. In 1984 she became the first Filipina to be ordained in the Ministry of the Word in the Presbyterian Church (USA). As a program specialist at the Center for the Prevention of Sexual and Domestic Violence, she coordinates the Asian Pacific Islander Program, edits the news journal *Working Together*, and participates in the overall educational and training program of Domestic Violence and Child Abuse Prevention. She is a 1994 recipient of the Very Impressive Pinay (VIP) Award from the Seattle Chapter of National Filipino American Historical Society. She is one of the three recipients of the Woman of Faith Award from the Presbyterian Church (USA) for her work addressing violence against women and children and racism.

CAROLLE CHARLES is Associate Professor of Sociology at Baruch College, CUNY. Born in Haiti, she has lived in the United States for more than 25 years and is the mother of a 12-year-old girl. Her work centers around the areas of gender studies and immigrant identities, about which she has written extensively. "Haitian Life in New York City" appeared in the *Immigrant Left* (1996).

HIROSHI FUKURAI taught at Texas A&M University for two years before serving as a senior policy adviser at a Japanese branch campus of Texas A&M University in Koriyama, Japan. He is Associate Professor of Sociology and Legal Studies at the University of California, Santa Cruz.

NATALIE GOMEZ-VELEZ is a native of Brooklyn, New York. While at NYU Law, she was awarded an Arthur Garfield Hays Civil Rights/Civil Liberties Fellowship and was a member of the Moot Court Board. Following law school, she embarked on a varied and exciting legal career that has included private practice as a litigation associate, government work as general counsel to a New York City agency, and public interest litigation addressing reproductive freedom. She taught lawyering at NYU Law School and is now in the Division of Public Advocacy of the Attorney General's Office.

GLORIA HOLGUÍN-CUÁDRAZ is Assistant Professor of American Studies at Arizona State University West. She is completing her book, *A Major Fluke of History: Chicana/o Intellectuals in the Age of Affirmative Action*. She is also a member of the Latina Comparative Feminist Research Group, a nationally based, intergenerational Pan-Latina group of intellectuals collectively writing an anthology of articles, essays, prose, and poetry, tentatively titled *Latina Feminist Testimonios: Papelitos Guardados* (*Latin Feminist Testimonies: Memos Saved*). In 1997 she was one of seven featured faculty members in the PBS video *Shattering the Silences: Minorities Break into the Ivory Tower*.

REGINA JENNINGS is Assistant Professor of English at Franklin and Marshall College in Lancaster, Pennsylvania. She has published numerous articles, some of which appear in the following: *Pennsylvania English* (Fall 1999), *Africana History, Culture, and Public Policy* (1999), *The Black Panther Party Reconsidered* (1998), and *Journal of Black Studies* (Fall 1998). She is the author of *Midnight Morning Musings: Poems of an American African* (1998), *From g/Guinea to African-American: The Transformed Image of Africa and the X-Factor Influence*, and *The Black Panther Party and Poetry: Ogun's Offspring and Offerings*.

PYONG GAP MIN is Professor of Sociology at Queens College and the Graduate School of the City University of New York. He has taught courses on race and ethnic relations, marriage and the family, and Asian Americans. He has done research mainly on Asian immigrants, especially Korean immigrants, with a focus on immigrant entrepreneurship, intergroup conflicts, ethnic solidarity, and gender roles. Recently, he has started research on second-generation Asian Americans and gender relations in South Korea and Japan. He is the author of *Changes and Conflicts: Korean Immigrant Families in New York* (1998). He has been influential in the New York Korean community partly through many of his articles published in Korean ethnic dailies and partly through his involvement in various ethnic organizations.

THANH-THUY NGUYEN, at 8 years old, escaped Vietnam by boat with her father and brothers. She eventually came to the United States as a refugee. Even though she had to learn English, she graduated from high school at the age of 16 and college at age 20. She is presently a Human Resource Manager at SDA International, Inc. She is also very involved in advocacy and community service in the Asian Pacific American community. She enjoys writing, public speaking, reading Asian and women's literature, and playing volleyball.

JANINE PEASE-PRETTY ON TOP (formerly Windy Boy) was the first woman of Crow descent to earn a doctorate. In the 1970s she was a counselor for Navajo Community College and director of the first adult education program on the Crow reservation, the precursor to Little Big Horn College. She was also the director of Indian Career Services at Eastern Montana College from 1981 to 1982 but returned to the Crow reservation to begin the process of accreditation for Little Big Horn College. During the course of her career, she has been active in many areas related to the welfare and education of Native Americans. She was named Indian Educator of the Year by the National Indian Education Association in 1990.

ISBN 0-275-96033-1

HARDCOVER BAR CODE